PRIMAL MYTHS

Creating the World

BARBARA C. SPROUL

Published in San Francisco by
HARPER & ROW, PUBLISHERS
New York, Hagerstown, San Francisco, London

For Herb

Library of Congress Cataloging in Publication Data

Sproul, Barbara C.
  Primal myths.

  Bibliography
  Includes index.
  1. Creation—Comparative studies.   I. Title
BL325.C7S68 1979   291.2   78-4429
ISBN 0-06-067501-2

79 80 81 82 83   10 9 8 7 6 5 4 3 2 1

CONTENTS

PREFACE

In many cultures, creation myths form only the first part of an extended mythological tradition which recounts social and cultural as well as natural foundations of present reality. Such cultures make no firm distinctions between creation myths and socio-cultural ones insofar as they understand no gross separation between themselves and the rest of nature. Therefore many of the myths included in this anthology are somewhat arbitrarily truncated—cut off from the more historical myths which follow them—so that in subject matter they might match more closely those explicitly cosmological myths which deal directly with the creation of being, the gods, the universe, and people.

In each case, I have sought the most authentic translation—the version which, even though it might not be as smooth or as easily available to Western readers as another, most authentically evokes its cultural and religious source. For the most part, diacritical marks and footnotes have been omitted as unnecessary for the general reader, but each myth has been introduced with basic information concerning its setting, date, authorship, and main symbols.

To maintain consistency, only book titles have been italicized; the titles of individual myths have not. Partly for the same reason, but also to be clear, the terms "God," "Being—Itself," "Not-Being-Itself," and the "Holy" have been capitalized when they refer to absolute reality. Generic terms for divinities and principles which seem to symbolize only a partial aspect of that reality appear in lower case.

This is only a partial collection of the creation myths of the world: given the limits of one volume, I have tried to choose the most powerful myths, offering examples from each religious tradition and yet avoiding duplication of themes or attitudes. I hope that, by its range, this collection still provides an introduction to the cosmological and theological thinking of the world's religions.

Among those to whom I am particularly grateful are teachers whose passion for their own subjects has inspired me in pursuit of my own. Isabel Stevens, David Bailey, Joseph Campbell, Ada Bozeman, Maurice Friedman, Roy Finch, Rudolf Arnheim, Tom Driver, and Theodor Gaster have each taught me a great deal—not so much by virtue of the answers they gave but by the questions they asked—and I am in their debt.

Barbara C. Sproul
New York City
February 1979

INTRODUCTION

T HE MOST PROFOUND human questions are the ones that give rise to creation myths: Who are we? Why are we here? What is the purpose of our lives and our deaths? How should we understand our place in the world, in time and space? These are central questions of value and meaning, and, while they are influenced by issues of fact, they are not in themselves factual questions; rather, they involve attitudes toward facts and reality. As such, the issues that they raise are addressed most directly by myths.

Myths proclaim such attitudes toward reality. They organize the way we perceive facts and understand ourselves and the world. Whether we adhere to them consciously or not, they remain pervasively influential. Think of the power of the first myth of Genesis (1–2:3) in the Old Testament. While the scientific claims it incorporates, so obviously at odds with modern ones, may be rejected, what about the myth itself? Most Westerners, whether or not they are practicing Jews or Christians, still show themselves to be the heirs of this tradition by holding to the view that people are sacred, the creatures of God. Declared unbelievers often dispense with the frankly religious language of this assertion by renouncing God, yet even they still cherish the *consequence* of the myth's claim and affirm that people have inalienable rights *(as if* they were created by God). And, further, consider the beliefs that human beings are superior to all other creatures and are properly set above the rest of the physical world by intelligence and spirit with the obligation to govern it—these beliefs are still current and very powerful. Even the notion that time is properly organized into seven-day weeks, with one day for rest, remains widely accepted. These attitudes toward reality are all part of the first myth of Genesis. And whether people go to temple or church, whether they consider themselves religious, to the extent they reflect these attitudes in their daily behavior, they are still deeply Judeo-Christian.

But the power of a specific myth is not as important to realize as the power of myth itself. Indeed, each of the claims made by the first Genesis myth has been attacked from some quarter. What is essential to understand is that they have been challenged not by new facts but by new attitudes toward facts; they have been challenged by new myths.

There is no escaping our dependence on myth. Without it, we cannot determine what things are, what to do with them, or how to be in relation to them. The fundamental structures of understanding that myths provide, even though in part dictated by matter and instinct, are nevertheless essentially arbitrary because they describe not just the "real" world of "fact" but our perception and experience of that world.

This is true even when we try to understand our "selves." How do we approach the most basic question of personal identity? Who is the "I" who is perceiving and experiencing the world? Initially, we presume identity is a physiological reality evident in a body's ability to distinguish between "me" (affirmed and protected by my body's defenses) and "not-me" (denied, attacked, and rejected, as happens in transplant operations). But, even though it rests on so firm a physical foundation and is so settled in instinct, the "fact" of identity is still variously determined by people. With growing intelligence and the progressive freedom that results from it, people construct other than purely reactive, physical ways of responding to and interacting with their environments. "I" is no longer synonymous with body. Indeed, the question is instantly complicated as time enters into consciousness with memory and imagination and you ask *which* body you identify with. Today's? Yesterday's? The body you will have a month from now if you go on a diet? The body you had as a child? And, as people add more factors to the structural grid of understanding, identity grows to include other matters. Gender, race, profession, nationality, age, position, and the like all become relevant as the "I" in all those bodies comes to think of itself as something constant and essentially connected to larger social realities. In many cases, such identifications are so powerful that they overcome the initial one of "'I' equals 'body.'" People begin to make distinctions between various aspects of a complex "I"; they value some as "higher selves" and others as "lower," and they make choices emphasizing one at the expense of another. This is what happens in wartime when people who have come to identify themselves not only physically but also nationally willingly sacrifice their "body selves" to their "citizen selves."

Where does identity *really* lie? How should we understand the simple world of "fact" in this situation? Is the "real fact" the physical autonomy of the individual? The autonomy of the state of which individuals are only a temporary part? The autonomy of the universe in which both states and their generations of members are only temporary constituents? Or, moving from macrocosm to microcosm, is "reality" the autonomy of the atom or quark, of which the individual, state, and universe are only temporary configurations? Even in this matter, we need myths to determine and then evaluate the various facts presented to us. We need myths to answer the questions, "Who am I? How do I fit into the worlds of society and nature? How should I live?"

While all cultures have specific myths through which they respond to these kinds of questions, it is in their creation myths that the most basic answers are to be found. Not only are creation myths the most comprehensive of mythic statements, addressing themselves to the widest range of questions of meaning, but they are also the most profound. They deal with first causes, the essences of what their cultures perceive reality to be. In them people set forth their primary understanding of man and the world, time and space. And in them cultures express most directly, before they become involved in the fine points of sophisticated dogma, their understanding of and awe before the absolute reality, the most basic fact of *being*.

It is no accident that cultures think their creation myths the most sacred, for these myths are the ground on which all later myths stand. In them members of the group (and now outsiders) can perceive the main elements of entire structures of value and meaning. Usually, we learn only covertly and piecemeal of the attitudes these myths announce openly and wholly. Watch any parent with a small child, and you will see such attitudes being transmitted and received almost unconsciously. Values derived from the myths are virtually integral to speech itself. "What's that?" asks the child. "And this? How does that smell? How does it feel? How does this taste?" "Be gentle, that's a daisy," her mother answers. "And that's a puddle. Watch out, that's a piece of glass; and look, there's a shiny new penny." And, along with her mother's words, the little girl hears her tone and acquires from both the basic blocks for a whole structure of value and meaning. Only when she understands how to place and esteem each of the things can she make her own decisions about them. Only then can she know which is good to sniff, which to jump and splash in, and which to put away in a treasure box. And, while many of these attitudes toward reality are conveyed by parents, others come from the culture at large, from education, laws, entertainment, and ritual. In a society as diverse and rapidly changing as ours, attitudes from different and occasionally conflicting myths are promulgated simultaneously. Even so, they are often accepted without question, by adults as well as by children, as "the way things are," as "facts."

Thus, because of the way in which domestic myths are transmitted, people often never learn that they *are* myths; people become submerged in their viewpoints, prisoners of their own traditions. They readily confuse attitudes toward reality (proclamations of value) with reality itself (statements of fact). Failing to see their own myths as myths, they consider all other myths false. They do not understand that the truth of all myths is existential and not necessarily theoretical. That is, they forget that myths are true to the extent they are effective. (In a sense, myths are self-fulfilling prophecies: they create facts out of the values they propound. Thinking we are superior to other creatures, for instance, we set ourselves up as such and use them ruthlessly. Peoples that think of themselves as brothers to the beasts live with them in harmony and respect.)

As circumstances change and perceptions alter (often, as is the case with our feelings about the ecosystem, because an old myth has been so successful that it produces a new reality and thereby engenders a new attitude toward it), cultures constantly revise their myths. This practice is evident in several of the myths in this collection as well as in our own modern culture. Such revision is accomplished with remarkable ease if only the meaning of specific myths, not the words themselves, is altered. Our belief that "all men are created equal," for example, is still firm, even though we have come to include black men and all women in an originally more restrictive claim. Although much changed, the "fact" of equality is still considered to be unchallenged. When words as well as meanings are altered, people respond with more hesitation. Sometimes they live for a while with two different attitudes toward the same reality. Conflicting views of the proper attitude toward women, for example, can be seen side by side not only in any newspaper but also in the first book of the Old Testament. The myth of Adam and Eve (Genesis 2:4–23, c. 900 B.C.) speaks of the first woman as dependent on (and derivative of) the first man, while the myth of creation in six days (Genesis 1–2:3, c. 400 B.C.) describes the genders as of equal origin.

Holding literally to the claims of any particular myth then, is a great error in that it mistakes myth's values for science's facts and results in the worst sort of religiosity. Such literalism requires a faith that splits rather than unifies our consciousness. Thinking particular myths to be valuable in themselves undermines the genuine power of all myth to reveal value in the world; it transforms myths into obstacles to meaning rather than conveyers of it. Frozen in time, myth's doctrines come to describe a world removed from and irrelevant to our timely one; its followers, consequently, become strangers to modernity and its real progress. Those of such blind faith are forced to sacrifice intellect, emotion, and the honesty of both to the safety of their creeds. And this kind of literalism is revealed as fundamentally idolatrous, the opposite of genuine faith.

Looking at many myths inhibits this sort of religious provincialism and its attendant dangers of dogmatism and false faith. Indeed, one of the benefits of considering myths is that we come to understand them (and by analogy our own) *as myths*. We become conscious of the power of myth itself to generate attitudes toward reality and, along with ritual, to win acceptance for these attitudes. The faithful literalists fear that, by admitting their myths *are* myths and by comparing them to others, they will implicitly be describing their myths as untrue, mere projections of the mythmakers' relative and particular situations into imagined absolute and universal realms. And the literalist unfaithful—those who mistakenly disparage all myths as false—agree (happily) with this presumption. Both groups are convinced that when the claims of various myths are known and compared their disagreements will cause all myths to be thought untrue. After all, how can all myths be true if each claims different things? If one culture envisions a good god forming a world out of a watery chaos, a second depicts a host of deities fighting for divine control of a world they have fashioned piece by piece, and a third describes the universe as the outgrowth of a cosmic duel between principles of good and evil, how are we to distinguish between them and find truth in any of their imaginings? And if we find that each myth reflects the social, historical, and political situation of its adherents, they argue, that further demonstrates the nature of myths as false.

But both groups are wrong. Not only do they confuse theoretical and existential truth but also each forgets that, while languages may differ, the meaning expressed in them may be the same. This collection of creation myths does not show any essential disparity in understanding; rather, it reveals a similarity of views from a rich variety of viewpoints. To be sure, comparisons among the myths demonstrate that the way things are seen is dependent on the seers, their cultures and circumstances. In that sense, this collection provides a useful argument against dogmatism and idolatry. But, as the Buddhist parable counsels, one must not mistake the finger pointing at the moon for the moon itself. In discovering that myths are human products, we are freed equally of blind faith and blind disbelief. We can understand that creation myths are not merely projections into a vacuum. Rather, they are responses to a real world that seek, in their various conditioned ways, to reveal to their adherents an unconditioned reality. Recognizing this, we can reach beyond the variety of languages to their common meanings, beyond the disparity of religions to their common revelations. We can shift our sight from the pointing fingers to the moon itself.

O NE OF THE drawbacks of our piecemeal introductions to mythic ideas is that each one—from the most particular attitude toward pennies or puddles to the most general considerations of the proper role of women in society or humanity in nature—is taught and even debated out of context. Although we often treat such issues apart from their mythic sources, it is really only within the myths that we can properly understand them. For myths do not just reflect random attitudes toward reality. Rather, they begin with a perception of reality as a whole and in its light construct an integrated system for understanding all its parts.

Myth is an integral part of religion. As such, it proclaims a central reality and then builds a structure of valuation around and in relation to it. We commonly understand a similar, although secular, manner of organizing attitudes when we say that someone has made a "religion" out of, say, tennis. What we mean is that the person thinks the game is all important and as a result makes all his choices on the basis of playing it: when considering new friends, he inquires about their game; when deciding whether to go to a party, he considers the shape he will be in the next morning when he could be out on the courts. Anything that brings him closer to the game is judged good; anything that takes him away is bad. When asked about himself, our athletic friend tells of his history in terms of tennis; when he learned to play, how he developed his backhand—these become the significant factors. He has created a myth, an attitude toward reality that makes his past sensible, present meaningful, and future possible. Around its central value, he constructs his life.

The problem with all of this, of course, is that the game of tennis is not an *absolute* reality. It is highly dependent on fitness, ability, equipment, and so on, and as a viable center of religion it is severely limited. The meaning it offers for one's life is equally circumscribed. While it provides a certain amount of satisfaction in terms of bodily health and sporting fellowship, it does not really address itself to more far-reaching concerns. The tennis devotee, then, is reduced in our estimation to a "jock," and we consider him somewhat limited in his understanding of himself as "tennis player" only, and not more broadly and deeply as "human."

Regardless of what we think of the athlete's "religion" of tennis, to the extent we understand how he constructs his life and determines his values around what is for him the supreme reality of the game, we can comprehend the basic structure of all religion. All religion posits such a supreme reality and subsequently builds an entire system of valuation around it. The difference between pseudo-religions like the athlete's and real ones is that *genuine religions proclaim an absolute reality as the centerpoint of their structure.* That is, religion insists that what is essentially real and important to you subjectively must also be that which is essentially real and important in the objective world of fact.

This is what distinguishes the religious point of view from all others. It proclaims an *absolute reality* that is both transcendent (true for all times and places) and immanent (true in the here and now). This reality is not relative; it is not dependent on changing factors of time and space. It is a reality of absolute value in relation to which all other values can be established.

To be absolute, this reality cannot be a thing or a being, because all things and beings are dependent on others for their existence. They all have beginnings and ends, temporal or spatial limits, and they are all subject to change. Limited in these ways, things have a relative, but not absolute reality. To be absolute, the reality that religion proclaims through its myths must be eternal (not temporal), independent (not dependent), active (not reactive), and unchanging (constant). Specific religions characterize this reality in different ways and call it by different names, but they all agree on its absoluteness.

While all myths assume this absolute reality and proffer a structure of value relative to it, creation myths do so more frankly and obviously than others. Only creation myths have as their primary task the proclamation of this absolute reality and description of its relation to all other, relative realities. Only creation myths establish the basic structure of *all* valuation based on the supreme value of the primary reality. Creation myths are required to do this by both the range and depth of their questions. Although these myths are of varying degrees of profundity, at their best they consider the essential structure of the *whole* of reality: matter, spirit, nature, society, and culture. They consider the origin and nature of *being*, the very fact of existence. Thus the Rig-Veda (c. 1200 B.C.) begins:

> Then neither Being nor Not-Being was
> Nor atmosphere, nor firmament, nor what is beyond.
> What did it encompass? Where? In whose protection?
> What was water, the deep, unfathomable?
> Neither death nor immortality was there then,
> No sign of night or day.

Not all creation myths are this wide-ranging in their questioning. Some ask only how a specific instance of being came to be—how this universe was formed, how the earth and sky were made, or how the land or the people or the society was fashioned. The second myth in Genesis (c. 900 B.C.), for instance, displays little interest in the origin of the universe and begins:

> (2:4) In the day that the Lord God made the earth and the heavens, (5) when no plant of the field was yet in the earth and no herb of the field had yet sprung up—for the Lord God had not caused it to rain upon the earth, and there was no

man to till the ground; (6) but a mist went up from the earth and watered the whole face of the ground—(7) then the Lord God formed man of dust from the ground, and breathed into his nostrils the breath of life; and man became a living being.

But even in myths such as this, which are limited in the *range* of their considerations, the same profound *depth* of questioning is apparent. They are still concerned with creation, with the relations of death to life, nonexistence to existence, not-being to being. Whether the myth addresses the issue of creation in its broadest sense as the origin of all being, or in its narrowest sense as the origin of a particular being, the same mystery is central: the nature of reality itself.

In this respect, creation myths do not merely deal with the known or even seek to make determinations about the unknown. Rather, their real concern is with the relation of the known to the *unknowable*. They push at the limits of all thinking, reaching to the very edge of the world of matter and ideas. The creation of the universe, for instance, represents the limit of being in time and space. Beyond it, or at its edge, begins the unknowable. This is true regardless of the size of the universe being described: the relation of the finite to the infinite is mysterious whatever the relative size of the finite. Before the creation, there was nothing, and even "nothing" is too definite a term. You can still seem to be saying something by it. (In *Alice in Wonderland,* the Red King asks Alice, "What do you see?" "Nothing," answers Alice, and the Red King comments with a certain degree of admiration, "My, what good eyes you have.") But religions go beyond this: they think about a "nothing-that-was-not" and focus on this *unknowable* because they believe it the key to determining and valuing everything that flows from it, the known and the unknown.

Creation myths reveal this religious concern most clearly. They ask, essentially, what was before anything was, what is the source, the *ground* of being? The word *ground* is a useful here because it helps to demonstrate the unknowable nature of the source of being; it points to the fact that we have no independent position from which to scrutinize and know that source. Imagine trying to see the underside of the ground you are standing on. If you dig it up and turn it over, you will have exposed the ground you *were* standing on, but not that which supports you while you are digging—*that* ground is unknowable; there is no perspective from which you can study it. This is the kind of problem religion faces when it attempts to describe the ground of being.

This point is well demonstrated in the Book of Job in the Old Testament. Barely surviving a plague of misfortunes, Job calls upon God to justify his suffering. He thus challenges God; he asks God to account for his actions. But when God finally speaks he does not reply to Job's charges. Rather, he questions Job's power and right to make them. Appearing in all his majesty as the source of being, God demands to know how Job could have defined himself sufficiently independent of the creator to make such a challenge in the first place. "Who is this that darkeneth counsel by words without knowledge? Gird up now thy loins like a man; for I will demand of thee, and answer thou me. Where wast thou when I laid the foundations of the earth? Declare, if thou hast understanding." And God shows in the following speech how Job is a dependent creature that requires God merely in order to *be*. In himself Job has no solidity, no place to stand which is not God's, so his challenge is hollow. It is as if your own words were to speak back to your tongue: what voice of their own would they have? Finally understanding this, Job repents in dust and ashes.

In creation myths, the ground of being is not only physical but also metaphysical. The ground they speak of is the source of mind as well as of matter. The Indian Kena Upanishad (800–400 B.C.) tries to make this clear when it asks:

> Who sends the mind to wander afar? Who first drives life to start on its journey? Who impels us to utter these words? Who is the Spirit behind the eye and the ear? . . .
> We know not, we cannot understand, how he can be explained: He is above the known, and he is above the unknown.

And then it proceeds to describe this "unknowable" as "what cannot be spoken with words, but [is] that whereby words are spoken . . . what cannot be thought with the mind, but [is] that whereby the mind can think . . . what cannot be seen with the eye, but [is] that whereby the eye can see." This *unknowable*, this ground of being, this spatial and temporal limit of reality is what religions consider to be the *absolute* reality or, for want of a better term for the moment, what they call "God." Forget all of your own religious conceptions of the word "God" for a little while, and think about this ground of being. It is purely definitional: you will inevitably come to it if you think enough about the limit of any finite thing. Where did you come from? Your parents gave birth to you. And your parents? From their parents; and so on down through the animals to micro-organisms and chemicals and elements and matter and energy to what? To the moment of creation and the "creator," if it is possible to name such a force. And that is the same place that religions end up in their speculation. Everything *within* the created universe of matter and mind is derived from something else and therefore has existence that is dependent or relative. (You are dependent on your parents for your being; your "reality" in physical terms is relative to theirs.) Only what stands as the *source* of all existence, the ground of all being, is self-derived and independent; only *that* reality is absolute.

Now, religions have a great deal of trouble describing this absolute reality because they have no absolute perspective. They cannot stand outside the universe with the Holy and encompass the world of time and space; they are inevitably within that world. Like fish in water, they have no way to stand aside and describe the sea objectively. Since the absolute reality that religions strive to understand is the ground of all thinking, it cannot be known. Since it is beyond any subject–object distinction, being by definition the ground of both, it cannot be objectified.

Part of this problem is that our whole way of understanding operates with the use of polar oppositions. We categorize things by how much they are like any one part of such a pair of opposites, how unlike the other they are. It is as if we imagine a multidimensional grid in which each of the oppositions has a line: tall–

short, here–there, high–low, old–young, hard–soft, red–green, good–bad, matter–mind, life–death, existence–nonexistence, and a million others. We understand things when we have decided where to place them on each of these lines in the grid; finally we see how they fit into the whole. Now the most basic of such pairings is being and not-being, the positive and negative alternatives expressed in terms of existence. And, as with all polar oppositions, the parts of this primary one require each other. What "is" derives from what "is not"; what "is not" comes from what "is." Which came first, being or not being? Which came first, the chicken or the egg?

1. In the beginning, my dear, this world was just Being, one only, without a second. To be sure, some people say: "In the beginning this world was just Not-Being, one only, without a second; that from Not-Being Being was produced."

2. But verily, my dear, whence could this be? said he. How from Not-Being could Being be produced? On the contrary, in the beginning this world was just Being, one only, without a second.

This is how the Chandogya Upanishad (c. 700 B.C.) tried to resolve the problem. But of course the solution must finally be more profound than this. To pick any part of the opposition is to remain within it. "The egg came first!" announces the child when he first hears the question. "But who laid the egg?" And back he plunges into the ultimate riddle.

The only solution lies in asking about the ground of the polar opposition itself. What should we call that which produces both being and not-being? What is prior to both the positive and the negative? Thus the language of creation myths reaches beyond itself to absoluteness.

Some religions characterize the holy ground of all in seemingly positive terms. They call it *Being-Itself* and rush to qualify the statement by saying that Being-Itself incorporates both being and not-being. "The Lord giveth and the Lord taketh away; praise be the Lord!" Both life and death, existence and nonexistence, are controlled by such a power. And, as the Rig-Veda says, "Neither Being nor Not-Being was there then . . . . Only the One breathed, windless, by its own energy."

Other religions, however, favor the negative side of the polarity and proclaim in effect that *Not-Being-Itself* is the source of all being and not-being. The Maori of New Zealand chant:

From nothing the begetting
From nothing the increase
From nothing the abundance
The power of increasing
The living breath . . . .

Because both of these solutions are obviously open to misunderstanding, many religions try to transcend both positive and negative characterizations by describing the original reality as divine Chaos. In this primordial stew, all distinctions are blurred but still potentially present; such Chaos is the potentiality and not the actuality of being. It should not be confused with the sort of chaos that is merely negative, the destroyer of order. Rather, this is the happy sort of Chaos out of which both order and dis-order can be made. It is like raw clay before some clay has been made into pots and the rest has been discarded as unnecessary. In one sense, the Chaos is ultimately positive: it is all, everything, the totality of Being, in that there is nothing else besides it. In the other and equally valid sense, it is ultimately negative: it is Nothing (*no-thing*), in that it has no internal distinctions. Solid and liquid, spirit and matter, good and evil, light and dark—all the oppositions through which reality exists are not yet delineated.

The creation occurs when part, if not all, of this Chaos coalesces and forms internal divisions, like the internal mass of a cell dividing itself into nucleus and matter. The part that is formed and thereby distinguished from the rest of the unformed mass then acts upon it to produce further distinctions and thereby create the world. Which is the absolute reality here? The Chaos itself? Or the child of Chaos that acts on it? *Both*. They are one. At some point, the myths step back from the mystery and affirm the essential and unbreakable unity of the creator and creation. Ultimately they insist on the interdependence of being and not-being, and it is the inexplicable transcendent unity of these two that they recognize in wonder and awe as absolute and call *Holy*.

All creation myths that consider the nature of being and not-being at this most profound level reach this conclusion. Others less ambitious in their theorizing, however, avoid the issue by merely beginning with one or the other side of this polar opposition. "Being was first," they say, and they never ask where it came from; or, with equal force, they say "Not-Being was first," and they fail to consider whence Not-Being evolved. In some versions of the Myth of Ptah from Memphis (c. 1400 B.C.), for instance, the gods (powers of being) are born from the waters of chaos (fertile not-being). Do they mean that not-being is prior to being? No, for other versions of the same myth describe the gods giving birth to those waters. Sometimes you start with the chicken and sometimes with the egg. In most cases, both are already present and distinguished. Throughout the world, creation myths express and dramatize this primary religious proclamation of the absolute reality in its dual form of being and not-being. Eternal gods of every kind reach out over the equally eternal chaos of not-being and distinguish within it all the forces and realities of the world: light is separated from darkness, heaven from earth, water from land, good from bad, masculine from feminine, matter from spirit, life from death, being from not-being. And thus the world of "reality," our world of oppositions, change, and development is established.

Not all religions describe this essential nature of reality by setting this issue in time and speaking consequently of a beginning, a moment of creation. Jinasena (c. 900 A.D.), a great Jain teacher, rejects this whole model and asserts there never was a creation:

> Some foolish men declare that a Creator made the world.
> The doctrine that the world was created is ill-advised and should be rejected.
> If God created the world, where was he before creation? . . .
> How could God have made the world without any raw material? If you say he

made this first, and then the world, you are faced with an endless regression. . . .
Know that the world is uncreated, as time itself is, without beginning and end.
And it is based on the principles, life and the rest.
Uncreated and indestructible, it endures under the compulsion of its own nature.

And Buddhism, like some current cosmological theories in science, insists that the universe expands and contracts, dissolves into non-being and re-evolves into being in an eternal rhythm.

Although it might seem that such a rejection of the idea of creation would set the myths of Jainism and Buddhism radically apart from those of other religions, in fact it does not. To be sure, most myths temporalize their claims and speak of the *absolute* reality as the *first* one, but such a connection is not necessary. Creation myths are not just interested in the "unknowable" because it is *first*; they are interested in it because it is *always*.

This sounds particularly complicated but is in fact rather simple and commonplace. Think about how, when you are becoming close friends with someone, you tell each other about your pasts. You tell all about your parents, your childhoods, where you grew up, who your best freinds were, how you succeeded and failed, what you liked to do, and what you were afraid of. Why do you say all of this? To provide historical facts? No, it is not the past but the present that is interesting. The point of these stories is to reveal who you really are now, to show how deeply (in the story, how "long ago") you feel about stewed tomatoes or dogs or Harry or heights. It is the same with myths about the past of the world. Such creation myths are really revelations of essences, of realities that were not just true once and *then* but are equally true now and *always*. The Jains and the Buddhists manage to reveal these essences without speaking of a temporal limit for creation, without locating the primary reality at the beginning of time. What is timeless, what is eternal, is always real.

Whether they locate it at the "beginning" or not, creation myths proclaim an absolute reality that is both transcendent and immanent—true eternally and true in the moment. Certainly when the myths are describing what was before anything was, they are specifically talking about the transcendent side of that absolute, that "Holy." They go even further than this: they invent gods. That is, they speak about the unknowable in terms of the known.

In order to communicate their apprehension of the Holy, the unlimited reality that is the ground of all being and not-being and that is, by definition, absolute, religions use the only words we have—relative words. Those who emphasize the positive or manifest aspect of the Holy call it *God* and claim it is eternal (absolute), self-created (independent), creative (active and not reactive), omnipresent (without limit in the physical world), omniscient (without limit in the mental world), and omnipotent (without limit in terms of energy and force). What is most important to notice here is that such gods are thought of, as much as is possible, within the limits of such relative terms, as *prior* to most polar oppositions; they *are* without qualification. "I AM WHO I AM," such a god says to Moses. But as these kinds of descriptions gradually evolve, God takes on other and more limiting attributes. The ground of being eventually is depicted as human—it is anthropomorphized—to dramatize properly its various relations to the created world: it is shown as male (our "father") or female (our "mother"), as seems appropriate; it is very, very old (an expression of its eternality) or very young (an expression of its vitality and potency); and it is very wise (an echo of omniscience), big (omnipotent), high (superior), and so on.

Such a god can also be one or two or many (and these distinctions can be internal to the god, as in Christianity's trinity, or they can be external, as in polytheistic religions), depending on which aspects of the absolute reality the myth wants to proclaim. The Dinka in Africa worship innumerable deities and yet still affirm that "divinity is one." What they mean is simply that there is one divine power, one absolute reality, perceived in many different aspects; like light refracted in many colors, it is all a matter of perception. We express a similar paradox when we speak of the power of the law under which democracy operates: there is one power, yet it is expressed variously and in different amounts by the president, governors, mayors, and citizens. When such an understanding is expressed religiously, the gods are thought to have only *dependent* reality; they "exist" only as people recognize them to be symbols of the absolute reality. That Holy itself, however, exists by definition and not only as an idea or symbol, but as the only absolute reality.

People commonly misunderstand this essential point and take literally all of these relative descriptions of the absolute reality. They think of "God," for instance, as male, old, and fierce, and thereby limit what is unlimitable and forget its absoluteness. Because of this tendency to idolatry, some religions eschew all relative characterizations of the Holy and emphasize its negative and unmanifest aspect. They refuse anthropomorphism and deny any association of the Holy with a being or thing. "Not this, not that" claim the myths of these religions. As Lao Tzu (c. 600 B.C.?) writes:

> There is a thing confusedly formed
> Born before heaven and earth
> Silent and void
> It stands alone and does not change,
> Goes round and does not weary.
> It is capable of being the mother of the world.
> I know not its name
> So I style it "the way."
>
> The way that can be told
> Is not the constant way
> The name that can be named
> Is not the constant name . . . .

And myths around the world echo his perception. The Incas' hidden face of God; the Hebrews' unspeakable name of God; the idea everywhere expressed that God is unseeable, a "spirit"—even religions that *do* characterize the Holy in relative terms keep trying to point out the fundamental inappropriateness, the misleading limitations of their descriptions.

Whether they do it positively or negatively, creation myths proclaim more frankly than any other kind of myth the absolute reality that religions recognize. But speculation about the Holy is not their sole intent. They not only consider the ground of being but go on to describe the relation of that absolute reality to all relative realities, the relation of the infinite and unknowable to the finite and known. They announce that the absolute permeates every instance of being, every thing. "You can't kill time without wounding eternity," as Thoreau declared. Religions realize that the infinite is not only the ground of the *condition* of finitude but through it the ground of everything finite. Thus the Holy is here as well as everywhere; it is now as well as always; it is the basis of this and that, of you and me, as well as of being itself. *The Holy is immanent as well as transcendent.* This is one of the central messages of creation myths.

Religions argue through their myths that all things that are—all things that exist and have being—partake of the Holy, just as all things beautiful partake of beauty. The myths show how such an eternal and absolute reality is connected to us in our very relative, changing world and affirm that there is a way in which each person and thing can be considered absolute, possessing dignity (absolute, nonexchangable value) and not merely worth (relative, exchangable value).

We are so used to thinking of ourselves "relatively"—in relation to others and to the societies in which we live—that this idea may seem a bit foreign at first. Commonly we characterize ourselves by function—parent, child, student, teacher, and so on—and each of these functions *is* real in a relative way; that is, each of these descriptions is true insofar as certain criteria are met. In order for you to be a parent, you must have a child; to be a child, you must have a parent. Teachers similarly require students, and vice versa. Other relative characterizations are equally dependent and temporal. There must be shorter people for you to be "tall," black people for you to be "white," males for you to be "female," rich people for you to be "poor," foreigners for you to be a "national." For any of these terms to have meaning, their counterparts must also exist. In themselves, in isolation, these terms are meaningless; they have no *absolute* validity. And people who define themselves only in such relative ways are left with ascribing to themselves only relative and dependent worth. They can even put a price on it and frequently do by taking out insurance policies: if a parent dies, $100,000 will pay for a substitute.

But through myth and ritual, religion makes the claim that this is not the entire case. It argues that in all these relative ways and aspects of being an *absolute* aspect, a dimension that is unique, independent, and of eternal validity is revealed. That is what religions mean when they affirm that people are "sacred," that they have dignity as well as worth. Religions see that people are not only *relatively* valuable as parents and children but that they are *absolutely* valuable as themselves; your parents could have had another child, but never another you.

This absolute dimension of the self is often named and called *soul* (or *jiva*, or *ka*, or some other term). Problems arise only when we forget its formal nature and come to think of it as material, as a thing, something we have in addition to our other physical organs. Having misunderstood soul in this fashion (just as we often misunderstand God), we become disappointed when we cannot find it and dismiss it as an illusion, another fraud perpetrated by religion. But soul is not a thing; it is a dimension of depth in a thing. Like justness in a judge's decision or beauty in a painting, soul is a quality of absoluteness revealed in something relative. And myths argue that, understood profoundly, people are connected to the holiness of the world in such a way that they reveal a dimension of holiness in themselves, a dimension of depth that is absolute.

W E HAVE SEEN how myths have to speak of the transcendent and immanent aspects of the unknowable in terms of the known in order to speak of them at all, but we have not really seen how far they go in doing this. Myths are not merely static pronouncements; they are not just pictures or images that might be meaningful to the already convinced but that would be meaningless to the unenlightened. Rather, they are whole stories, dramas placed in the familiar world of time and space that attempt to reveal, through their common details and particulars, truths that are uncommon and universal.

What is most evident when you read them is that *myths use symbols to express their truths.* This is not so peculiar in itself: all language uses symbols. When you say the word *friend* and apply it to the person closest to you, you are using a symbol. The sound *friend* and the letters you form when writing it out are all symbols; they are not your friend himself but are representative of him. The successful use of such symbols requires a certain kind of consent by other people. They have to know what you are talking about; they have to understand both the *fact* of the person you are referring to and the *value* you ascribe to him, or else the symbol is meaningless. At the simplest level, *friend* means nothing to people who do not understand English; more profoundly, it means nothing to people incapable of loving, of sharing with you the experience of valuing a person in that way.

But symbols are not always this easy to understand. They may be related to their referents in very complex ways. Based on common experience and shared history, we build up a wide range of conceptual associations and use these to enrich language and suggest more involved relations between things. Eventually we perceive underlying similarities in the structures of such relations and create metaphors to express them. Justice, for instance, is "blind" because, like a person who cannot see, it is unimpressed with superficial factors of wealth and class; it determines its findings on the sole basis of the weight of the arguments brought before it. Metaphors like this also require a certain amount of consent from their hearers. Without it, they are taken literally and misunderstood. Heard wrongly, even such a common metaphor as "justice is blind" leads us to believe the speaker thinks justice is a living creature with eyes that cannot see.

Such misunderstandings seem obvious and silly when you understand the metaphor, yet it is precisely because people so often do not understand that there is so much confusion about myths. Because in reading them you deal mostly with material from other cultures and other times, material belonging to people with whom you share no common history or outlook, it is easy to mistake the metaphors of the myths for literal statements. This is particularly true if you adopt a parochial mentality and define the relative sophistication of all cultures by criteria recognized only by your own. People who consider technology the only indicator of a society's wisdom, for instance, often think that those with it are "advanced" (intelligent, rational, and sophisticated) while those without it are "primitive" (stupid, irrational, and innocent). It rarely occurs to them that this standard of judgment may not be universal and that other, nontechnological cultures may worry more about the ends of life than about the means to them. It is wrong to conclude that some people ("sophisticates" like us) can use metaphors creatively while others ("primitives" like them) cannot.

In a discussion between Marcel Griaule, a French ethnologist who recorded the Dogon myth included in this collection, and Ogotemmeli, the Dogon wise man who related it, Griaule became curious about just this point. How sophisticalled *was* Ogotemmeli in his use of language and metaphor? How literally did he intend his myth? Not sure, Griaule inquired about the number of animals crowded onto the steps of a celestial granary that Ogotemmeli claimed descended from heaven. Griaule had calculated that, given the overall dimensions of the granary, each step was less than a cubit deep, hardly big enough to accommodate several large animals. "How could all these animals find room on a step one cubit wide and one cubit deep?" he asked. And Ogotemmeli carefully explained, "All of this has to be said in words, but everything on the step is a symbol, symbolic antelopes, symbolic vultures, symbolic hyenas . . . . Any number of symbols could find room on a one-cubit step." And, as Griaule reports, "For the word 'symbol' he used a composite expression, the literal meaning of which is 'word of this lower world.' "

This is not to say that in all cultures all people understand the sophisticated use of symbols as Ogotemmeli did. There are various levels of understanding even in our own culture. Those who put religious statuettes on the dashboards of their cars to protect themselves against accident are missing the point. And those who presume a physical place called "heaven," pearly gates intact, floating around somewhere in the sky have misunderstood a metaphoric rendering of the absolute as surely as any literalist from another culture. But there is no reason to define ideas by their misunderstanding simply because they can be and often are misunderstood. To really comprehend myths, you have to grant other cultures in other times the same freedom with language we grant ourselves. And to grasp their meaning, you must see what kinds of associations are being made and used by the myth in its metaphors.

In a myth such as the Assyrians' "Another Version of the Creation of Man" (c. 800 B.C.), for instance, the initial scene, in which Anu, Enlil, Shamash, Ea, and Anunnak—all great gods—are sitting in their heaven discussing the progress of creation, makes little sense unless you recognize its symbolic meaning. If you understand what these deities represented to the Assyrians, if you realize that Anu symbolized the power of the sky, Enlil that of the earth, Shamash the sun or fire, Ea the water, and the Anunnaki destiny, you begin to see that the

Assyrians understood creation as a process in which air, earth, water, fire, and time all evolved together. Reading further, you will see that people are to be made out of the blood (the essence, the life force) of slain gods (great concentrations of power) to serve their creators with festivals and to maintain and increase the fertility of the earth. That is the Assyrian faith—a celebration of the wondrous natural forces that created the world, a recognition of a particular mission for people, and a perception of their essential relation to the forces that created them. Understanding the symbols—seeing what they meant to their authors—eliminates confusion from our reading of them and permits what were intended as timeless truths to be freed of their limited and temporal expressions. Or, to be more precise, by such "translation," we come to understand these truths in expressions more fitting our own equally but differently limited perception.

Sometimes this sort of reinterpretation involves the perception of facts. Since cultures use facts, as they understand them, to build their metaphors and express their values, occasionally you must allow for real differences in levels of science available to mythmakers. You have to think about what the "facts" meant to the people who used them and find equivalent modern "facts" to substitute for them. The first Genesis myth, for instance, declares that God made the universe in six days and rested on the seventh. It is difficult to know if the Hebrew authors of this text intended this claim literally and actually thought of a six-day creation as "factual" or whether they hoped merely to use it symbolically to represent a completed amount of time, a sacred week that matched and therefore sanctified their own work week. (Myths usually use factual statements in this way; rarely do they attempt to be scientifically comprehensive in their descriptions of what was created.) But if they did mean the claim literally in this case, then to be comprehended today it must be revised, translated into our current (and still changing) scientific understanding of cosmology in the same way we translate the words themselves from one language to another to make them relevant to new listeners. To be sure, when we do this and speak of a creation taking billions of years rather than six days, we have to sacrifice the structural similarity between the time of God's divine work and that of our ordinary labors. But the main point of the myth is not lost. On the contrary, it becomes more available to us in our situation. To think that myth is tied to such "facts" and to defend their literal interpretation is to confuse myth with science and to miss the point. Myth seeks to proclaim values and to declare meaning. To the extent that it requires facts to do this, it is aided by science. Pitting the two against one another reveals a profound misunderstanding of the intentions of both.

Nowhere is the need for such translation more apparent than in the myths' descriptions of *how* the absolute reality is related to the relative. The moment of creation itself is almost always highly metaphoric. "God created the world" is the general claim—but what do the myths mean by this? How do they envision such a creation? And what do they understand to be the subsequent relation of creation to creator?

Rarely are myths as straightforward as the Hopi Indian one that begins with Taiowa and endless space (being and not-being) existing together:

The first world was Tokpela [Endless Space].

But first, they say, there was only the Creator, Taiowa. All else was endless space. There was no beginning and no end, no time, no shape, no life. Just an immeasurable void that had its beginning and end, time, shape, and life in the mind of Taiowa the Creator.

Then he, the infinite, conceived the finite. First he created Sotuknang to make it manifest, saying to him, "I have created you, the first power and instrument as a person, to carry out my plan for life in endless space. I am your Uncle. You are my Nephew. Go now and lay out these universes in proper order so they make work harmoniously with one another according to my plan."

Sotuknang did as he was commanded. From endless space he gathered that which was to be manifest as solid substance, molded it into forms.

The point that the infinite conceived the finite is made in most of the myths, but they depict this wondrous event in different ways. Those metaphors easily understood speak of the unknowable in terms of the most commonly known: they speak of the creation in terms of procreation. In this scheme, a sky father god and an earth mother goddess—(active, masculine, "being" and passive, feminine, "nonbeing")—lie close together and, with rain as the divine fertilizing agent, produce as children all the natural forces and creatures.

The usefulness of this metaphor for describing the origin of the many from the two is demonstrated by the fact that it is used even when only one god is envisioned. In these instances, the polar oppositions (reduced here to a male–female duality) are just internalized in the one. Thus, when the power of being is characterized overtly as feminine, an earth mother goddess gives birth spontaneously and independently, without need of a mate. If the sole deity is seen as male, either he externalizes the duality—imagines a mate into being and produces the creatures with her—or he keeps the duality inside and uses aspects of himself as the feminine "other." These myths maintain exactly the same principle of distinguishing a directing agent (manifest being) and the raw material of creation (unmanifest not-being) as more abstract myths do in speaking of the original Chaos as self-dividing. Only here, personalized as they are, the myths are more dramatic and involving. Some tell how the god sacrifices a part of himself, cutting off a piece of his "body" and fashioning it into the world. Others describe him vomiting or excreting the world or giving birth to it in some other related manner. In the Aranda myth from Australia, for example, the great totemic ancestor gives birth to people through his armpit.

Some myths hold to the procreative metaphor more closely and describe instances of divine masturbation. The "Egyptian History of the Creation of the World" affirms that the god Neb-er-tcher contains all duality—manifest and unmanifest, masculine and feminine, physical and mental—within himself. These aspects interact with each other as the god has union with his clenched hand, pours the semen into his mouth and, having fertilized it in that womb of words and ideas, spits it forth as creation. What seems to us initially only a story of masturbation, strange to use as a model of behavior, becomes sacred and revealing about the nature of reality if only we understand what was meant by it.

All the myths that use procreation as a way of understanding creation stress the extraordinary fertility, the overabundance of the power of being, that qualifies gods as symbols of the absolute ground of being. This is what the myths celebrate when they talk about an endlessly productive earth mother goddess or, more graphically, as in the Aborigine myth of the Djanggawul gods, about deities with enormous genitalia. They are also showing how the relation of the creation to the creator, so ambiguous and difficult to pin down precisely, can be understood if put in terms of the relation of a child to its parent. How much more powerful it is to use this kind of metaphoric illustration than to define abstractly the complex relation of constant structure and changing form.

Myths also use other metaphors to describe the creation. Sometimes they conceive the primary duality of being and not-being in terms of an order-chaos opposition and envision god as a kind of great administrator. Often identified as good, this sort of god takes on chaos (evil) as a challenge and, like any of us trying to get our houses in shape, begins by establishing basic principles. Light over here, dark there; solids in this place, liquids in that; and thus day and night, earth and water, come into being. Occasionally in such myths a part of chaos—not the fruitful whole that is *pre*-order but the negative part that is *dis*-order, which threatens to overcome the order—is symbolized as a terrible monster, and the dragon or snake, like the bull in the china shop, has to be slain or at least sufficiently controlled. All over the world, in the Babylonians' Enuma Elish and in the earliest creed of the Celts, in the books of Job and Psalms from the Old Testament, in the myths of the Hottentots of Africa and those of the Mandan and of the Huron Indians of North America, valiant defenders of the principles of being and order do fierce battle with the forces of not-being and chaos and finally subdue them so that order and life can be established.

In yet another kind of metaphor, myths represent creation as a mental activity. Just as our environments result from our relative dreams and plans, so the world here is understood as the product of an absolute imagination and intelligence: it is dreamed, thought, or spoken. The Mayan Popol Vuh (c. 1600 A.D.) describes creation in these terms:

> There was only immobility and silence in the darkness, in the night. Only the Creator, the Maker, Tepeu, Gucumatz, the Forefathers, were in the water surrounded with light .... By nature they were great sages or thinkers. In this manner the sky existed and also the Heart of Heaven, which is the name of God, and thus He is called.
>
> Then came the word. Tepeu and Gucumatz came together in the darkness, in the night, and Tepeu and Gucumatz talked together. They talked then, discussing and deliberating; they agreed, they united their words and thoughts.
>
> Then, while they meditated, it became clear to them that when dawn would break, man must appear. Then they planned the creation, and the growth of trees and the thickets and the birth of life and the creation of man. Thus it was arranged in the darkness and the night by the Heart of Heaven.

Myths like this argue that gods are endlessly powerful: they only have to command something and it is accomplished; what they think or say becomes a physical reality. In this sense, their potency is both mental and physical. (As the Koran says of Allah: "It is He who giveth life and death; and when he decreeth a thing, He only saith, 'Be,' and it is.")

How words establish realities becomes clear if you remember the child learning the names of things, and it becomes clearer still if you consider how we change people's names when they marry or join religious orders or how we make up new names for countries when we declare their independence. We create new identities, new things, by giving them new names. Gods too create by naming—*man, woman, tree, animal*—these terms announce values, functions, and identities as well as establishing facts of being. And even if they have not used the naming metaphor to describe the creation of the whole world of being, most myths still apply it to the creation of specific parts of being. They still insist that names must be assigned very carefully. Some underscore the creative function of naming by showing the relation of the powers of speech and procreation; both are thought so sacred that only the god can teach people how to use them. In the Hopi myth, for example, a lesser goddess (Spider Woman) makes people with all abilities except these two; only the manifest god (Sotuknang) can complete them:

> "As you commanded me, I have created these First People. They are fully and firmly formed; they are properly colored; they have life; they have movement. But they cannot talk. That is the proper thing that they lack. So I want you to give them speech. Also the wisdom and the power to reproduce, so that they may enjoy their life and give thanks to the Creator."
>
> So Sotuknang gave them speech, a different language to each color, with respect for each other's difference. He gave them the wisdom and power to reproduce and multiply.

In procreating and speaking, we act like the gods—we create worlds of being and meaning—and therefore have to learn how to do so properly by keeping the absolute principles of creation in mind.

Many myths use a more direct metaphor and describe creation in terms of forming. Here the emphasis is on the physical side of the mind-matter duality, and the god is portrayed as an artist or craftsman: taking some unmanifest raw material, he fashions it into a specific shape, animates it, and instructs it in the appropriate way of being. In many Eskimo and North American Indian myths, the creators bring up a little mud from the bottom of the chaotic waters and stretch it out into the earth, and gods all over the world use clay or dust to make people and animals. Myths that speak of the creation in this way usually think of the world as an expression of the creator. What is made still shows the traces of its maker; the known reveals the unknowable or, as the Old Testament puts it, "The Heavens declare the glory of God and the firmament sheweth his handiwork."

One of the most profound metaphors myths use to describe creation involves divine sacrifice. Here the absolute, symbolized as a great loving God, dies to become the relative world. The Chinese myth of P'an Ku is typical:

> The world was never finished until P'an Ku died. Only his death could perfect the universe: From his skull was shaped the dome of the sky, and from his flesh

was formed the soil of the fields; from his bones came the rocks, from his blood the rivers and the seas; from his hair came all vegatation. His breath was the wind, his voice made thunder; his right eye became the moon, his left eye the sun. From his saliva or sweat came rain. And from the vermin which covered his body came forth mankind.

In such myths the polar opposites of being and not-being are connected by a single act. When he becomes manifest and dynamic, as the world, P'an Ku dies to his unmanifest and static state of perfection as God.

Sacrifice is a rich and subtle metaphor because it not only expresses this fact but so much of the ambivalence we feel in understanding the creation and facing the life that springs from it. On the one hand, the metaphor celebrates the glory of the gift of being. The world, after all, and all life within it is sanctified by this act, *sacrifice: sacer*—holy, *facere*—to make. On the other hand, myths that speak of such sacrifice recognize the enormous cost of this gift. "God" has died to the world; the static perfection of the absolute is lost to the dynamic change and flow of temporal reality. The ground of being and not-being, that holy and mysterious unity, has dissolved into flux. Now, in the created world we experience that unity only through its duality in the polar oppositions of being and not-being, life and death, and so on.

All creation myths express this ambiguity in some way. Usually they stress the difference between the creator and the creation, between the absolute that is the ground of being and the relative beings (people, things, forces) that are dependent on it. Now, most myths, as we have seen, emphasize the fact that the absolute is still perceivable in the relative. They show how the world can be experienced as holy if it is understood properly. Other myths, however, stress the loss of perfection resulting from creation. They envision that timeless, unchanging, and absolute reality as sullied by time, change, and relativity. They concentrate on the difficulties involved in recognizing the absolute through the relative and encourage their followers to reject everything that is temporal.

It is a bit like the difference between the optimist and the pessimist: the first delights that his glass is half full, while the second complains that his is half empty. Most religious sytems contain some of this pessimism, but few are so starkly despairing as Gnosticism, which thinks of creation almost entirely in terms of the loss of (absolute) reality and perfection. Hope, in Gnostic myths, takes the form of a messenger from the absolute who reveals how all being is under the limitation of not-being, how all life leads to death, and who instructs his listeners to renounce the manifest world and escape back into the unmanifest purity. You have to read through a great deal of symbolism to get the point, but few scenes of loss and despair are so powerful as that in the creation myth of Mani (215–275 A.D.) in which Adam (mankind) suddenly realizes how he has become trapped in relativity, how his eternal soul has become ensnared by the temporal matter of his body. Longing to return to the perfection of the ground of being and not-being, to the unmanifest absolute, he "cried and lamented; terribly he smote his breast and spoke: 'Woe, Woe unto the shaper of my body, unto those who fettered my soul, and unto the rebels that enslaved me!' "

A T THIS POINT we can begin to see how myths constitute structures of value. First, they consider the nature of reality so profoundly that they pierce its limits. When they describe these limits physically (and thus spatially and temporally), they speak of a "creation," and when the limits are defined metaphysically, the myths proclaim the relativity of our reality. They understand that each thing that has life and being and the totality of all such things are limited and conditioned by their opposites, death, nonexistence, and not-being. As the myths that use the physical model come to understand a "creator" as the source of creation, myths that speak metaphysically claim the absolute as the ground of being and not-being. Being-Itself (or Not-Being-Itself), the Holy, the Unknowable—these are the terms that myths employ to describe this indescribable and absolute ground.

Recognizing how difficult all of this is to understand abstractly, myths use symbols and metaphors to make their point concretely. They temporalize and personalize and dramatize the argument so people will comprehend it. They talk about our relative world as dependent on the absolute as a child is dependent for being on his parent or a word is dependent on its speaker for reality. Through these dramatizations, it becomes clear that myths are also making value judgments. Immediately you can see that they stand in awe and wonder before the Holy. If the reason for this is still not clear, if these essentially religious responses are difficult to comprehend *because* of their religiosity, forget religion and put yourself in the place of the mythmakers who invented it. Just think about the universe and about the fact of existence. It is difficult, because to do this you have to think beyond and through all the relative values you ascribe to things. But think grandly, consider yourself and the land you live on; the continent and the earth (imagine *that* reality just being in space!); and then the solar system and the galaxy and the universe. All that reality! All that matter and energy and mind! The very fact that it *is* is wondrous. And religions go beyond the universe of change to consider the changeless structures basic to it. They describe a cosmic dance between being and not-being: matter coalescing and disintegrating; suns being born or blowing up; waters solidifying gradually into land or land dissolving into water; new trees growing out of the rotting wood of their own kind; generations of people bearing and giving way to the next; and societies, like clusters of cells, growing and dying to others.

Religions stand before the fact of all this reality and think it wondrous. They find it awesome that it *is*. And, keeping that in mind, they find each part of reality wondrous in that *it* is, that it becomes and ceases to be in the same way as the whole. That star is dying, this tree is coming into being, that baby is being formed. Imagine that! (Here again the difference between myth as an expression of religion and cosmology as an expression of science is evident. While they often speak of the same subjects, the focus of myths is on value and meaning; that of science is on facts. Both religion and science speak of moments of universal and particular creation; only religion declares them wondrous and sacred.)

In all of this, myths assert that the Holy is absolutely real and that the world, perceived *un*grounded, is only relatively so. But, they argue, if you just understand how the world *is* grounded in the absolute, how the eternal flow of being and not-being reflects the internal dynamic of the Holy itself, then you will be able to see the absolute dimension of all relative realities. You will be able to understand, too, in what way all relativities have absolute value, are eternal and true and sacred. And this applies to your own being and your own situation, here and now.

It is clear in many of the metaphors myths use to express the essential nature of reality that they recognize no terrible division between spirit and matter, mind and body. The "creation" involves the whole of reality, mental as well as physical, and its absolute dimension is not limited to only one part. The myths' claim that you have such an absolute dimension, then, is not restricted to your mind or some "spirit" confused with mind. There is no presumption here that mind is "good" and body "evil." To be sure, when myths try to dramatize the relativity of aspects of reality, they often talk about the temporality of material things. Bodies change, they say, how can you think of them as absolutely real and eternal? How can you take what you know to be only a relative reality so seriously? Look to what is deeper than that, look to something constant that you can really count on. But this "thing" that you can really count on is not antiphysical or antimaterial; it is primal energy, raw, unmanifest stuff, the eternal potentiality of specific beings and material things. Each individual thing—a tree, for instance—comes forth from such stuff and eventually decomposes back into it before being formed into another.

Have you ever seen a tree down in the forest, so old and rotted that it is like an illusion? From one angle you can still discern that it is a tree, while from another, it is indistinguishable from the earth around it. You are seeing the moment when being slides back into non-being, and if you look closer, you will probably also find in that rich and rotting stuff the beginnings of a new tree, a sprout so tiny and fragile, so dependent still on its seed and soil that it can barely be recognized as a sprout. This birth of being from not-being cannot really be perceived without a microscope, but if you look to larger realities—days, for instance, or storms, or even buildings—you can watch the process with a naked eye. When is it no longer night? Where does the day start? When is a building not just a pile of bricks? What is the moment when being is established over not-being?

Stepping back from relativity much further, creation myths ask the same question of the whole of reality, not just days but light itself, not just storms but weather, not just buildings but the universe. And they proclaim the creation of it all just as wondrous as the creation of any part of it.

If we persist in needing to think of mind separately, ask how ideas are born in consciousness as ideas. What is the moment when they rise from unconsciousness and deeper still from instinct and reflex and body itself to become ideas and grow into theories and attitudes that eventually, in turn, shape other matter? When does consciousness arise from unconsciousness? The myths ask this question, too, and find the source of both, consciousness and unconsciousness, along with that of matter, in the absolute of the Holy, the "mind of God." The Maori people of New Zealand chant:

From the conception the increase,
From the increase the thought,
From the thought the remembrance,
From the remembrance the consciousness,
From the consciousness the desire.

And from the desire the object of desire: the idea and the reality of the world.

But myths do not find this distinction essential; they do not think of mind ungrounded in matter or body left unknowing and stupid, cut off from spirit. Rather they proclaim first the unity of both in being and second their joint sacrality as a part of the being–not-being duality contained in the larger unity of the Holy. Christianity, for example, tries to make this point when it speaks of the resurrection of the body as well as the spirit. The absolute is a dimension of the *whole* of reality, not just a part. The merely *worldly* is disparaged in all religions, rejected for its relativity. But what they mean is only that you should not forget the dependence of our reality and pretend against all evidence of change that it is constant and eternal. Praise of the *world,* rightly understood as a reflection of the absolute, is just as central to religion.

Myths clarify this distinction between the worldly and the world. Demonstrating how the temporal realm of change and flux reveals the structure and the way of the timeless, myths try to show how everything considered merely profane and ordinary in itself is really sacred and extraordinary. Essentially, they point out structural similarities between the relative and absolute and argue that things in each realm are grounded in the same pattern of relations. This temporal reality (a) stands to that one (b) in the same relation as this eternal reality (A) stands to that (B). A child (a) is to her parent (b) as all reality, all matter (A) is to Chaos or the Holy (B). A husband (a) is in the same relation to his wife (b) as the sky (A) is to the earth (B). This is not to say that myths intend to confuse relative realities with absolute ones. The parent is not the Holy nor is the husband the sky; "a" is not "A." Such confusion is idolatrous, anathema to genuine religion.

What the myths do is to assert that the structure of the absolute pervades the relative: the Holy is the *ground* of being. And further they argue that the ways of the absolute are appropriate models for the relative: they are eternal, abundantly powerful and vital, endlessly productive of being, existence, and life. Not only are these ways the ground of all being, definitions of what we essentially *are,* but they should also be understood as the *goal* of being, indications of what we should become. Live as the world lives, the myths advise; be as God is.

This proclamation of the Holy as the goal of being presumes that we have lost touch with it as the ground. After all, if the Holy is the ground of being, we already are absolute. Why do we need all this direction? Because we have forgotten it, we have become confused and overwhelmed by relative and dependent realities, we have become mistakenly attached to the temporal and created world in its worldly aspects. In short, and in religious language, we have "fallen." Most religions talk about this "fall" in some way or other. Some consider it less central to the human condition than others and do not mention it in their creation myths, waiting until later myths of conquest or adventure to describe it. What is interesting, however, is how many cultures think of the fall as so defining of people that they discuss it right along with the creation.

In the West, we are quite familiar with the fall as dramatized in the myth of Adam and Eve. There it seems a matter of acquiring false knowledge of opposites as real. The duality of good and evil, their polar opposition, becomes the central focus and any notion of the unifying sacrality of Being-Itself is lost. Similar explanations for the fall are given in other traditions. African myths, which, more than any others, stress this loss of absoluteness, speak of the fall as the result of man's distinguishing himself from the rest of nature. He rises above the animals and out of the harmony of the natural world to impose his own temporal and essentially evil order on it. Doing so, he forgets the harmony of the divine order and, as the myths put it symbolically, drives God away from the earth.

Some myths temporalize the fall from absoluteness and speak of various ages of man, descending in power and virtue until they devolve into the present lot. Hesiod's Five Ages of Man, the Hopi Indians' myth of four worlds, and the Laws of Manu from India are only three examples of this universal theme. Other myths imagine a sort of spatial hierarchy with the relative below on earth and the absolute above in heaven (a wonderfully appropriate symbol in that the sky is both transcendent and immanent, and is also the domain of the sun, moon, and stars, whose regular movements so impress people). In this case, the two are connected by an *axis mundi,* a huge pole, rope or pillar that stretches from one realm to the other. After the fall, this *axis mundi* is destroyed, and the traffic between the worlds comes to a halt. Now all attempts to reach the absolute realm, like the Old Testament's Tower of Babel or, in the Eskimo creation myth, Raven's feeble efforts to fly upward, are thwarted.

What happens as a result of this fall is crushing: people perceive themselves as only relative, dependent, and conditioned—as beings under the constant threat of not-being and consequent meaninglessness. They are cut off from any recognition of themselves as participants in the Holy, which transcends the created opposition of being and not-being. And the world is understood similarly. Uprooted from its absolute ground, the world waits for its destruction as societies wait for revolution and individuals for death. Everything is meaningless and vacuous and essentially unreal. "God," as the current expression goes, "is dead."

The myths attempt to correct this misperception. They serve as a response to the "fall" and urge their followers to stand again on firmer ground, on the absolute which was and is always present, which they have temporarily forgotten. And it is not only individuals that the myths seek to sanctify but the whole of reality—physical, social, and cultural. The point is made clearly by another myth that speaks of creation in terms of sacrifice. In this hymn from the Rig-Veda (c. 1200 B.C.), one quarter of the holy Chaos dies to static not-being and is born as the dynamic and manifest world of being:

> From this sacrifice completely offered
> Were born the Rig- and Sama-Vedas;
> From this were born the metres,

From this was the Yajur-Veda born. . . .
    The Brahman was his mouth,
The arms were made the Prince,
His thighs the common people,
And from his feet the serf was born.
    From his mind the moon was born,
And from his eye the sun,
From his mouth Indra and the fire,
And from his breath the wind was born.
    From his navel arose the atmosphere,
From his head the sky evolved,
From his feet the earth, and from his ear
The cardinal points of the compass:
So did they fashion forth these worlds . . .
    With sacrifice the gods
Made sacrifice to sacrifice.

All the social classes (Brahman priests, warrior princes, common people, and serfs); all the forces and powers of nature, some of which are deified; and all of culture and religion, symbolized by the sacred books of the Vedas—the world in all its aspects is born from this great sacrifice. All its parts are essentially holy, and all exhibit the same structure as the absolute itself.

In the Babylonian Temple Program the connection between the temporal reign of the king and the absolute one of the god Marduk is equally clear. Standing in the same relation to his kingdom as Marduk does to nature, the king reaffirms his understanding of himself in this context and proclaims anew that his realm of the state will be ruled on the absolute principles evident in nature. Similarly, in another Babylonian myth ("When Anu Had Created the Heavens"), the structural resemblance of the temple to the universe is underscored. Here the gods of sky and water fashion the earth and man and then make all the lesser deities of carpentry, smithing, engraving, and the like, *just as* people building the temple construct it and use equivalent, temporal craftsmen. Myths all over the world reformulate this perception as gods and heroes of all sorts descend into time and space to instruct people in the way of proper, absolute being: "Walk this way! Speak this way! Multiply in this manner! Organize yourselves in this way! Be like this!" From Babylonian to Chuckchi Eskimo myths, the gods reveal that the appropriate ways of personal and social being are the same as nature's. Just as various aspects of nature relate to each other harmoniously and fruitfully, so should aspects of society and aspects of the self. As Lao Tzu announces in the Tao Te Ching (c. 600 B.C.?):

Man models himself on earth,
Earth on heaven,
Heaven on the way,
And the way on that which is naturally so.

If the myths in themselves do not make clear this proclamation of an absolute pattern present in all aspects of relativity, it is often obvious in their use in rituals. Ritual is the other half of the mythic statement: when myths speak only of the absolute reality, rituals ground it in the relative. The Bushman myth of Cagn, for instance, describes the many adventures of that ambiguous character: it tells how he ordered the world, slew the monsters of chaos, died and was miraculously reborn. So far all that is revealed is the Bushmen's understanding of that great force of being that brought order out of chaos and thereby created the world. To understand how such a philosophical viewpoint is relevant to ordinary people living in an ordinary world, it becomes very important to recognize that this myth was told during the initiation rites of young men. A living existential metaphor, a metaphor of the flesh was established by this use of the myth. The young men hearing it came to perceive themselves in the same way as they did Cagn: they, too, were to die to their youths and be reborn as responsible members of the seemingly eternal group; they, too, were to slay monsters of chaos wherever they encountered them and to establish a meaningful order.

Or consider the ritual use of the "Outbursters," the creation myth of the Yami, an Indonesian people living on the island of Batel-Tobago off the coast of Formosa. The myth describes the creation of islands and men, and tells how the first people learned to make sturdy canoes and become great fishermen. Every year at the time of the Flying Fish Festival, the Yami call the fish as their divine ancestors did, repeating their song:

> From Ipaptok, the place of the outbursting of man,
> The first one descended to the plain of the sea.
> He performed the fish-calling rite;
> The torch was lighted: and the fish
> Were dazzled by the flames.

In repeating the creation myth at this time, in lighting their torches and calling the fish, and in singing the song of their culture heroes, the Yami are not just trying to influence the gods magically and to win favor. Rather, they do these things so that they can act as heroes themselves. They do them so that they will be conscious of themselves as formally connected (through the repetition of similar acts and the assumption of similar roles) and materially connected (through history, through the generations) with their primal heroes. They perform the ritual and tell the myth so they can remind themselves of their own eternality realized within the moment, always and now on this night when the fish are dazzled by the flames.

The purpose of such ritual myths is sometimes misperceived as an attempt to escape the moment, to refuse history and pretend that temporal existence is as timeless as the static dimension of the absolute, the "realm of the gods." How pleasant to dream of heavens and deities when the "real" world of politics and economics is so painfully imperfect and changing! And to be sure, some people in all cultures misuse religion as such an escape. But this is not *religion's* purpose; this is not what the myths intend. On the contrary, people such as the Yami or Bushmen (or the Jews when they repeat the Passover story, or the Christians when they tell the Easter story) are not trying to escape the temporal but are taking it seriously, trying to understand it in its depths as an expression of eternality. They are trying to ground the momentary in time itself and to understand how the immanence of *now* expresses the transcendent reality of *always.*

In comparing a great number and wide variety of creation myths, it becomes clear that the origins of which they speak are important not for their historical and *prototypical* value alone but for their religious and *archetypical* value as well. The difference is subtle but crucial. Prototypes are acts or events that happen in time and are effective through history. They are so formative that they change people's lives and continue to influence subsequent generations. When the acts involved in them are repeated, it is because they were effective once and people hope they will be so again. And when their anniversaries are celebrated, it is because, in nostalgia, people remember and honor that which changed their condition. Prototypes are relevant only for the direct inheritors of the world that they effected. Archetypes, on the other hand, have universal application. And, whether or not they took place in time, it is not their historicity but their timelessness that people value. Archetypes reveal and define form, showing how a truth of the moment has the same structure and meaning as an absolute and eternal one. Prototypes were true once and may still be so; archetypes are true always.

This distinction is essential for religion. As we have seen in considering the creation itself, myths often speak of archetypes in terms of prototypes. They describe the absolute nature of reality as the first and original one. But to understand their point you have to realize that by "first" they mean "always." Adam is relevant to us because he represents the essential man (an archetype), not just the first man (prototype). His "original sin" is thus ours; it is inherent in the human condition. We do not inherit such sin just through time, genetically, like some sort of proclivity for contracting a disease or for playing the piano. Rather, we inherit it to the extent we inherit our humanity; we inherit it through the form. Similarly, the Jews celebrate Passover not just because it describes the prototypical act of deliverance whose benefit they inherit historically as free men; religiously, they celebrate Passover because it symbolizes the archetypical deliverance of all men (now as well as then; always) from enslavement (to Egyptians, or to an oppressor in any form).

While creation myths often speak of events as prototypical, then, their real interest lies in recognizing them as archetypical. This is as true of the "origin" of the state or the individual as it was of the "creation" of the world. Myths talk about temporal limits because they are a simple, if roundabout, way of determining definitions. Limits are merely definitions put negatively. To say that you were born and will die is one way of defining the temporality and dependence of the life that stretches between. This somewhat misleading way of defining by limits is used even by the "historical" religions of the West; even they are interested in historical events primarily for their timeless truths. Jesus, the Christians claim, rises from the tomb and transcends his relativity *always,* now as well as on the first Easter. And Allah, for Islam, wondrously creates the light every day, not only on the first day of creation.

The archetypical beginnings described in creation myths are absolute and essential. Their truths are always valid. We are so accustomed to thinking historically and linearly, placing the past "back there," that this notion is somewhat difficult for us to grasp right away. But it is not inscrutable if you think of time cyclically, repeating itself like the seasons, rather than progressively, marching along some imaginary line. It is also easier to understand if you envision the past as "deep within," at the core, like the first age ring of a tree's growth.

The attempt of creation myths to reflect and express our recognition of such essences sometimes seems to make for faulty history, later rewrites of what "actually" was. The Declaration of Independence, to use a current myth, argues that we were endowed by our creator with certain inalienable rights, presumably at the beginning. But when did that happen? Did the first human beings understand the absoluteness of their "rights" on the sixth day? Later on, in Old Testament times? Were they recognized in the Middle Ages or even in the Europe from which the Declaration's authors fled? Of course not, but the proclamation of these rights is couched in such historical terms only to make the mythic statement powerful. The "factual" nature of such mythical history is not at issue. What has happened is that a positive judgment concerning the human condition of personal freedom, perceived as essential and absolute, has been expressed mythologically as being established at the beginning, in timelessness. A value judgment made in the eighteenth century is understood as absolutely true; transferred into a temporal structure, it is expressed as *always* true—therefore, true from the beginning.

Such mythological revolutions are fairly common. The Assiniboine Indians, for instance, claim that horses were created along with men by the wolf-god Inktonmi in the beginning. The fact that these people of the American plains only acquired horses in real numbers in the eighteenth century and that their association with them is therefore relatively recent may render this claim bad "history" but it is still good myth: it appropriately reflects the self-understanding of the Assiniboine as riders; it affirms their essential identity now as horsemen. The fault is not in the myth but in our own attempt to read it as history.

It is particularly important to remember the dangers of this confusion of myth with history when you read myths of transition, myths which describe overtly how old attitudes toward reality were discarded for new ones. Such myths use historical events to make their point, but they are not "historical" themselves. The creation myth of the Chiricahua Apache, for instance, sadly reflects their conquest by the white men and the Christian religion they imposed; more importantly, it expresses their understanding of such a conquest as essential to their being as Indians:

> There were many people on earth. They did not know God. They prayed to Gaye [mountain-dwelling gods], Lightning, and Wind. They did not know about the living God. So the ocean began to rise and covered the earth. These people of ancient times were drowned. Just a few were saved. . . .
> After the water had gone down, a bow and arrow and a gun were put before two men. The man who had the first choice took the gun and he became the white man. The other had to take the bow and he became the Indian. If the second man had got the gun, he would have been the white man, they say.

Some myths reflect such historical changes covertly. When one group of people conquers another, their creation myth often reveals their new perception of the absolute in the conquest itself. It shows how that conquest reveals an absolute pattern by describing similar triumphs in the divine realm. Frozen at the moment of transition, these myths tell of great battles between the old, degenerate gods of the conquered people and the young, energetic deities of the conquerors. The great Babylonian epic, the Enuma Elish, for instance, describes warfare between primarily Sumerian gods (Anu, the power of the sky; Enlil, that of the earth; Apsu, that of the ocean, and so on) and the triumphant young local deity of Babylonia, Marduk, and his followers. And as Marduk slays the monsters of chaos and establishes a great and meaningful order, an order that pervades nature and culture, so did the Babylonians who honored him. Similar myths appear all over the world: Hesiod's Theogony and the Olympian Creation Myth reveal the victory of the masculine sky gods of the invading Aryans over the fertile and feminine earth goddesses of the Pelasgians and Cretans; the Earliest Creed of the Celts and the Maori Cosmologies both tell of the successful rebellion of divine sons against their primordial parents and reflect the triumph of new cultures over indigenous ones; and the Melanesian myth of Qat from the Banks Islands presumably echoes similar social upheavals in its portrayal of the successful creator (god of the conquerors) and his witless brother (god of the conquered). That these myths of transition also have validity in understanding our own personal growth (each child's eventual victory over his parents, each generation's progressive conquest over the prior one) further contributes to their usefulness as a way of perceiving the world. But what is important is that, whether the context is social or personal, an absolute dimension of relative reality is revealed. The myths change because people's perception of that absolute changes.

From the outside, such myths may look like projections, attempts on the part of believers to justify their current situation by announcing its sanction by the gods. But if you consider the myths more profoundly, you will find that they are not projections but revelations. As religious expressions, they begin with the absolute reality of the Holy and show how it pervades all relative realities—this society, the one which it supplanted, *and* the one which will eventually overthrow it—the status quos and the revolutions. Having focused on one particular manifestation of the Holy, they do not mean to say it is the *only* one. That again is idolatrous, a confusion of a symbol of the Holy and the Holy itself.

C REATION MYTHS attempt to reveal the absolute dimension of the relative world. They proclaim the Holy as the ground of being and, taking into account the human experience of alienation from this ground, proclaim it also as the goal of all being. They encourage people to understand themselves, physically, mentally, and spiritually, in the context of the cyclic flow of being and not-being and ultimately in the absolute union of these two.

In a time when old myths are being rejected and "faith" is under attack, these myths rise above the dogmatism and institutionalism which plague all established religions to serve as a testament of their common concern. While showing the provinciality of each religion, they demonstrate the universality of the religious. And they vividly express the fundamental religious point that, while the worldly is meaningless, the world is full of meaning: people, their cultures, and nature itself are all revelations of the Holy, occasions in which the transcendent absolute is immanently manifest. The myths are still valid, because they show how life is a symbol to be lived.

ONE

AFRICAN MYTHS

BUSHMAN

Cagn Orders the World

The Bushmen of Southern Africa are related to the Pygmies and Hottentots in their short stature, complex languages, and rich mythology. As nomadic hunters, their social groupings were necessarily small, rendering them vulnerable to the Bantu and white settlers who moved into their territory south of the Zambezi River. Those who survived with their culture intact moved to the more remote desert regions of Namibia, South Africa, and southern Angola.

The Bushmen believe not only in a good creator god (Kaang, Khu, or Thora, depending on the specific tribe) but also in an evil deity (Gauna or Gawa, god of the dead and of wicked spirits), the source of all trouble in the world. Some scholars have argued, however, that these high gods reflect Bantu influence. All agree that the main feature of the Bushmen's religion is belief in animal spirits, the most prominent of which (Cagn) is the hero of this myth.

Sometimes confused with Kaang, as he is here, Cagn is a perfunctory creator at best. His real interest lies on earth, where he reigns as the great magician and organizer. Ordering the world, enjoying endless adventures, and even slaying monsters, Cagn himself finally dies and is reborn—a sacred event whose story is repeated during the initiation of young men so that they may die to their youth and be reconstituted in a similar manner.

CAGN was the first being; he gave orders and caused all things to appear, and to be made, the sun, the moon, stars, wind, mountains, and animals. His wife's name was Coti. He had two sons, and the eldest was chief, and his name was Cogaz; the name of the second was Gewi. . . . He was at that time making all animals and things, and making them fit for the use of men, and making snares and weapons. He made then the partridge and the striped mouse, and he made the wind in order that game should smell up the wind—so they run up the wind still. . . .

A daughter of Cagn became cross because her father had scolded her and she ran away to destroy herself by throwing herself among the snakes (qabu). The snakes were also men, and their chief married her and they ate snake's meat, but they gave her eland's meat to eat, because the child of Cagn must eat no evil thing. Cagn used to know things that were far off, and he sent his son Cogaz to bring her back, so Cogaz went with his young men, and Cagn lent him his tooth to make him strong. When the snakes saw Cogaz approaching with his party, they became angry and began to hide their heads, but their chief said, "You must not get angry, they are coming to their child," so the snakes went away to hunt, and his sister gave him meat, and they told her to tell her husband they were come to fetch her and she prepared food for the road and they went with her next morning, and they prepared themselves by binding rushes round their limbs and bodies, and three snakes followed them. These tried to bite them, but they only bit the rushes; they tried to beat them with reins, but they only beat rushes, and they tried throwing sand at them to cause wind to drive them into the water, not knowing he had the tooth of Cagn, and they failed. The children at home, the young men with the chief of the snakes, knew that when those snakes came back they would fill the country with water. So they commenced to build a high stage with willow poles, and the female snakes took their husbands on their return and threw them into the water, and it rose about the mountains, but the chief and his young men were saved on the high stage; and Cagn sent Cogaz for them to come and turn from being snakes, and he told them to lie down, and he struck them with his stick, and as he struck each the body of a person came out, and the skin of a snake was left on the ground, and he sprinkled the skins with canna, and the snakes turned from being snakes, and they became his people. . . .

Cagn sent Cogaz to cut sticks to make bows. When Cogaz came to the bush, the baboons (cogn) caught him. They called all the other baboons together to hear him, and they asked him who sent him there. He said his father sent him to cut sticks to make bows. So they said—"Your father thinks himself more clever than we are, he wants those bows to kill us, so we'll kill you," and they killed Cogaz, and tied him up in the top of a tree, and they danced around the tree singing (an untranscribable baboon song), with a chorus saying, "Cagn thinks he is clever." Cagn was asleep when Cogaz was killed, but when he awoke he told Coti to give him his charms, and he put some on his nose, and said the baboons have hung Cogaz. So he went to where the baboons were, and when they saw him coming close by, they changed their song so as to omit the words about Cagn, but a little baboon girl said, "Don't sing that way; sing the way you were singing before." And Cagn said, "Sing as the little girl wishes," and they sang and danced away as before. And Cagn said, "That is the song I heard, that is what I wanted, go on dancing till I return"; and he went and fetched a bag full of pegs, and he went behind each of them as they were dancing and making a great dust, and he drove a peg into each one's back, and gave it a crack, and sent them off to the mountains to live on roots, beetles and scorpions, as a punishment. Before that baboons were men, but since that they have tails, and their tails hang crooked.

Then Cagn took Cogaz down, and gave him canna and made him alive again.

Cagn found an eagle getting honey from a precipice, and said, "My friend, give me some too," and it said, "Wait a bit," and it took a comb and put it down, and went back and took more, and told Cagn to take the rest, and he climbed up and licked only what remained on the rock, and when he tried to come down he found he could not. Presently he thought of his charms, and took some from his belt, and caused them to go to Cogaz to ask advice; and Cogaz sent word back by means of the charms that he was to make water to run down the rock, and he would find himself able to come down; and he did so, and when he got down, he descended into the ground and came up again, and he did this three times, and the third time he came up near the eagle, in the form of a huge bull eland; and the eagle said, "What a big eland," and went to kill it, and it threw an assegai, which passed it on the right side, and then another, which missed it, to the left, and a third, which passed between its legs, and the eagle trampled on it, and immediately hail fell and stunned the eagle, and Cagn killed it, and took some of the honey home to Cogaz, and told him he had killed the eagle which had acted treacherously to him, and Cogaz said, "You will get harm some day by these fightings." And Cagn found a woman named Cgorioinsi, who eats men, and she had made a big fire and was dancing round it, and she used to seize men and throw them into the fire, and Cagn began to roast roots at the fire, and at last she came and pitched him in, but he slipped through at the other side, and went on roasting and eating his roots, and she pitched him in again and again, and he only said "Wait a bit until I have finished my roots and I'll show you what I am." And when he had done he threw her into the fire as a punishment for killing people. Then Cagn went back to the mountain, where he had left some of the honey he took from the eagle, and he left his sticks there, and went down to the river, and there was a person in the river named Quuisi, who had been standing there a long time, something having caught him by the foot, and held him there since the winter, and he called to Cagn to come and help him, and Cagn went to help him, and put his hand down into the water to loosen his leg, and the thing let go the man's leg, and seized Cagn's arm. And the man ran stumbling out of the water, for his leg was stiffened by his being so long held fast, and he called out, "Now you will be held there till the winter," and he went to the honey, and threw Cagn's sticks away; and Cagn began to bethink him of his charms, and he sent to ask Cogaz for advice through his charms, and Cogaz sent word and told him to let down a piece of his garment into the water alongside his hand, and he did so, and the thing let go his hand and seized his garment, and he cut off the end of his garment, and ran and collected his sticks, and pursued the man and killed him, and took the honey to Cogaz.

The thorns (dobbletjes) were people—they are called Cagn-cagn—they were dwarfs, and Cagn found them fighting together, and he went to separate them, and they all turned upon him and killed him, and the biting ants helped them, and they ate Cagn up; but after a time they and the dwarfs collected his bones, and put them together and tied his head on, and these went stumbling home, and Cogaz cured him and made him all right again, and asked what had happened to him, and he told him; and Cogaz gave him advice and power, telling him how to fight them, that he was to make feints and strike as if at their legs, and then hit them on the head, and he went and killed many, and drove the rest into the mountains.

—J. M. Orpen. "A Glimpse into the Mythology of the Maluti Bushmen." *The Cape Monthly Magazine,* 1874. —Reprinted in *Folklore,* 1919, pp. 143–152.

HOTTENTOT

The Supreme Being
The Hottentots were the first native people to encounter the Dutch settlers who emigrated to their land c. 1650. Dispossessed of their territory on the coast of the Cape of Good Hope, enslaved, and killed, the Hottentots were all but destroyed. Remnants of the people now live mainly in Namibia and in the northwestern part of South Africa.

Like the Bushmen, Hottentots speak a Khoisan dialect of the "click" languages: the "clicks," implosive sounds analagous to consonants, are marked by double vertical lines in this text. Similar to the Bushmen in religion as well, the Hottentots posit a dualistic order in which Tsui||goab ("wounded knee") finally triumphs over the evil ||Gaunab, lord of the "dark heaven" and of the dead. Given the relation of ||Gaunab to the supreme god of the neighboring Damara people, his presence here may reflect a long history of tribal warfare as much as an essentially dualistic world view.

Although generally credited with creation, Tsui||goab is thoroughly anthropomorphized and very much of the world. In fact, he is portrayed here as the first ancestor, miraculous in his regenerative power, but still vulnerable and evolving more in the way of a creature than a creator.

TSUI-||GOAB was a great powerful chief of the Khoikhoi; in fact, he was the first Khoikhoib, from whom all the Khoikhoi tribes took their origin. But Tsui||goab was not his original name. This Tsui||goab went to war with another chief, ||Gaunab, because the latter always killed great numbers of Tsui||goab's people. In this fight, however, Tsui||goab was repeatedly overpowered by ||Gaunab, but in every battle the former grew stronger; and at last he was so strong and big that he easily destroyed ||Gaunab, by giving him one blow behind the ear. While ||Gaunab was expiring he gave his enemy a blow on the knee. Since that day the conqueror of ||Gaunab received the name Tsui-||goab, "sore knee," or "wounded knee." Henceforth he could not walk properly, because he was lame. He could do wonderful things, which no other man could do, because he was very wise. He could tell what would happen in future times. He died several times, and several times he rose again. And whenever he came back to us, there were great feastings and rejoicings. Milk was brought from every kraal, and fat cows and fat ewes were slaughtered. Tsui||goab gave every man plenty of cattle and sheep, because he was very rich. He gives rain, he makes the clouds, he lives in the clouds, and he makes our cows and sheep fruitful.

Tsui‖goab lives in a beautiful heaven, and ‖Gaunab lives in a dark heaven, quite separated from the heaven of Tsui‖goab.

—Theodore Hahn. *Tsui‖Goab, the Supreme Being of the Khoi-Khoi.* London: (no publisher) 1881, p. 61.

BAROTSE

God Retreats to the Sky
While the Old Testament and other ancient Near Eastern texts describe the separation of God and man in terms of man's expulsion from paradise, African myths often express the same point in terms of God's abandonment of the world. Presumably climatic and geographical differences account for the metaphoric ones.

The Barotse (or Lozi) people of Zambia tell of a harmonious and sacred beginning when the creator Nyambi lived on earth with his wife and made all things. Because of man's transgression—he murdered other creatures—Nyambi first banished him from his sacred realm; later he forgave his errant creature and presented him with land to till, but Kamonu reverted to his old ways. Finally, in despair, Nyambi retreated from the world.

Aside from asserting the appropriateness of farming as an occupation in harmony with the sacred way of the world and describing the disruption of that harmony caused by hunting, the myth clearly depicts human nature as ambitious and aggressive, at odds with the will of God. Kamonu is more intelligent but less sensible than others, as is evidenced by his final attempt to restore his connection to Nyambi. Having caused the breach, he attempts to repair it by building a great tower to heaven (an *axis mundi* similar to the Tower of Babel), but his failure shows the irrevocable nature of the split. Cut off from his creator, he can only greet him now as the sun.

First visited by David Livingstone in 1851, Barotseland became part of a British protectorate forty years later and a province of Northern Rhodesia when it was formed in 1911. In 1964, the country—now called Zambia—won its inpendence.

I N THE BEGINNING Nyambi made all things. He made animals, fishes, birds. At that time he lived on earth with his wife, Nasilele. One of Nyambi's creatures was different from all the others. His name was Kamonu. Kamonu imitated Nyambi in everything Nyambi did. When Nyambi worked in wood, Kamonu worked in wood; when Nyambi forged iron Kamonu forged iron.

After a while Nyambi began to fear Kamonu.

Then one day Kamonu forged a spear and killed a male antelope, and he went on killing. Nyambi grew very angry at this.

"Man, you are acting badly," he said to Kamonu. "These are your brothers. Do not kill them."

Nyambi drove Kamonu out into another land. But after a while Kamonu returned. Nyambi allowed him to stay and gave him a garden to cultivate.

It happened that at night buffaloes wandered into Kamonu's garden and he speared them; after that, some elands, and he killed one. After some time Kamonu's dog died; then his pot broke; then his child died. When Kamonu went to

Nyambi to tell him what had happened he found his dog and his pot and his child at Nyambi's.

Then Kamonu said to Nyambi, "Give me medicine so that I may keep my things." But Nyambi refused to give him medicine. After this, Nyambi met with his two counselors and said, "How shall we live since Kamonu knows too well the road hither?"

Nyambi tried various means to flee Kamonu. He removed himself and his court to an island across the river. But Kamonu made a raft of reeds and crossed over to Nyambi's island. Then Nyambi piled up a huge mountain and went to live on its peak. Still Nyambi could not get away from man. Kamonu found his way to him. In the meantime men were multiplying and spreading all over the earth.

Finally Nyambi sent birds to go look for a place for Litoma, god's town. But the birds failed to find a place. Nyambi sought council from a diviner. The diviner said, "Your life depends on Spider." And Spider went and found an abode for Nyambi and his court in the sky. Then Spider spun a thread from earth to the sky and Nyambi climbed up on the thread. Then the diviner advised Nyambi to put out Spider's eyes so that he could never see the way to heaven again and Nyambi did so.

After Nyambi disappeared into the sky Kamonu gathered some men around him and said, "Let us build a high tower and climb up to Nyambi." They cut down trees and put log on log, higher and higher toward the sky. But the weight was too great and the tower collapsed. So that Kamonu never found his way to Nyambi's home.

But every morning when the sun appeared, Kamonu greeted it, saying, "Here is our king. He has come." And all the other people greeted him shouting and clapping. At the time of the new moon men call on Nasilele, Nyambi's wife.

—Susan Feldman (ed.). *African Myths and Tales.* New York: Dell Publishing, 1963, pp. 36–37. — Adapted from E. W. Smith. *African Ideas of God.* London: Edinburgh House Press, 1950.

YAO

The Chameleon Finds
The Yao live on the shores of Lake Nyasa in northern Mozambique. Unlike many other Bantu tribes who envision a heavenly origin for people, the Yao assert their emergence from the earth (born from a hole in the ground) or, as is the case here, from the water. The Yao agree, however, with other Africans in their estimation of human character. Peoples' "progress" in controlling their environment, their ability to hunt successfully and to make fires, is seen from the perspective of the rest of nature and its creator as destructive and cruel. Having violated the sacred harmony of the world, people force God to retreat to the sky.

AT FIRST there were no people. Only Mulungu and the decent peaceful beasts were in the world.

One day Chameleon sat weaving a fish-trap, and when he had finished he set it in the river. In the morning he pulled the trap and it was full of fish, which he took home and ate.

He set the trap again. In the morning he pulled it out and it was empty: no fish.

"Bad luck," he said, and set the trap again.

The next morning when he pulled the trap he found a little man and woman in it. He had never seen any creatures like this.

"What can they be?" he said. "Today I behold the unknown." And he picked up the fish-trap and took the two creatures to Mulungu.

"Father," said Chameleon, "see what I have brought."

Mulungu looked. "Take them out of the trap," he said. "Put them down on the earth and they will grow."

Chameleon did this. And the man and woman grew. They grew until they became as tall as men and women are today.

All the animals watched to see what the people would do. They made fire. They rubbed two sticks together in a special way and thus made fire. The fire caught in the bush and roared through the forest and the animals had to run to escape the flames.

The people caught a buffalo and killed it and roasted it in the fire and ate it. Then next day they did the same thing. Every day they set fires and killed some animal and ate it.

"They are burning up everything!" said Mulungu. "They are killing my people!"

All the beasts ran into the forest as far away from mankind as they could get. Chameleon went into the high trees.

"I'm leaving!" said Mulungu.

He called to Spider. "How do you climb on high?" he said.

"Very nicely," said Spider. And Spider spun a rope for Mulungu and Mulungu climbed the rope and went to live in the sky.

Thus the gods were driven off the face of the earth by the cruelty of man.

—Maria Leach. *The Beginning.* New York: Funk and Wagnalls, 1956, pp. 143–144. —Retold from material in Duff Macdonald. *Africana: The Heart of Heathen Africa.* Vol. 1. London: (no publisher) 1882, pp. 295ff.

SWAHILI

Making the World and Man
Islam entered East Africa from the Red Sea and Indian Ocean and gained converts among the Hamitic nomads on a tribal basis. Inland south of Somali, however, it did not begin to spread until c. 1850 and then did so on a much slower, more individual basis. While it did not affect most Bantu peoples, Islam did attract many Swahili-speaking groups along the coast of Kenya and Tanzania. A Swahili culture based on Islamic teachings sprang up and eventually incorporated Shirazi (inhabitants of Zanzibar and Pemba Islands), Afro-Arabs, descendants of slaves (brought to Islam through the Arab slave trade), and detribalized laborers from the interior.

These Swahili creation myths are thoroughly Islamic. The first describes the creation of holy things (Mohammed's soul, heaven and hell, angels, God's laws and his apocalyptic trumpet, and so on). Although God was present before time, there seems to be some notion of not-being also "existing" here. It was from this "nothingness" that God molded his creations.

The second myth portrays God ordering the universe, separating opposite elements (light and dark, land and sea) and causing them to bear creatures. The last myth describes God's creation of man: although the angels were apprehensive, God made Adam a mix of light and darkness, spirit and matter, to be his servant and to rule over the created world.

I Before the beginning of time there was God. He was never born nor will He ever die. If He wishes a thing, He merely says to it: "Be!" and it exists.

So God said: "There be light!" And there was light. God took a fistful of this light and it shone in His hand. Then He said: "I am pleased with you, my light, I will make out of you my prophet, I will mould you into the soul of Mohammed."

When he had created the soul of the prophet Mohammed (May God pray for him and give him peace), He loved it so much that He decided to create mankind so that He might send Mohammed to it as His messenger to bring His word to Earth. His word would teach the peoples of the earth the distinction between Good and Evil, and in the end God would judge all the souls and reward those who had chosen to follow the Good Messenger, and reject the others.

With his infinite knowledge God foresaw all the events that would happen in the centuries to follow until the last day. With His unlimited power God began to create all the things He would need for some purpose which He alone knew.

First He created the Throne and the Carpet for Himself to sit on at the Last Judgement. The Throne has four legs supported by four strong beasts. The Carpet that covers it has all the lovely colours of the rainbow and stretches out along the skies as far as the borders of space. Under the Throne there is the most delightful place in the Universe: the souls who are allowed to dwell in the shadow of the Carpet will rejoice for ever. The brilliant light of the Divine Presence is softly filtered by the many-coloured veils of which the Carpet is composed.

The third thing God created was the Well-preserved Tablet. It is a board so large that it can contain a complete and detailed description of all the events that ever take place anywhere in past and future. The Tablet has a soul of her own and is one of God's most faithful servants. She carries all His wisdom and all His commandments for ever and ever. She is called the Mother of Books, because all the Sacred Books of Mankind in which God has revealed some of His Truth contain only fragments of her contents. The secrets of the Universe, in so far as they were ever represented by symbols, are inscribed on her surface, in characters which only He can read.

With the Tablet He created the Pen to write His commandments. The Pen is as long as the distance between Heaven and Earth. It has a thinking head and a personality, and as soon as it had come into existence, God ordered it: "Write!" The Pen asked: "What shall I write, my Lord?" God said: "Destiny." Since that moment the Pen has been busy writing on the Tablet all the deeds of men.

Of course, if it pleases God to change His mind, He does so. If He projects a different future than was foreseen in previous plans, the writing will disappear from the Tablet and the Pen will record new facts.

The fifth thing God created was the Trumpet, and with it the archangel Serafili [Asrafel]. The angel holds the Trumpet to his mouth, waiting patiently in the same position, century after century, until it pleases God to terminate history. Then He will give the signal, and Serafili will blow his first blast. The Trumpet has such a powerful voice that at its first sound the mountains will collapse, the stars will come plummeting down and Doomsday will begin.

The sixth thing which God created was the Garden of Delights which was destined for the good souls. There they would sojourn for ever and ever, forgetting the sufferings of their lives on earth. In it there are streams of limpid water, rivers of milk and honey, fragrant flowers and trees whose branches bend down heavy with fruits. The fruits are soft and sweet and juicy and as soon as one falls off, a new one grows on the same branch in no time. Who would not give everything he possessed to be there? Who would not endure a short span of life on earth to dwell in that garden for all eternity?

The seventh thing which God created, foreseeing in His wisdom that many souls would not follow the good Messenger, was the Fire. Crackling, it sprang up from the deepest bottom of shadows, in the remotest pit of space. Evil smell and smoke is its essence, roaring thunder its voice. "My Lord," cried the Fire, "where are the souls of sinners, I want to see them suffer!" Who would not pray night and day that his soul may avoid this eternal torture.

God went on and on creating, taking things out of not-being, for God requires no rest; neither sleep nor slumber seize Him.

God now created the angels, a myriad voices who proclaim His praise. Out of pure light He created them; their minds are lucid as the light itself, their hearts are pure as morning air. The thought of sin never occurs to them, they never hatch evil plans in their bosoms. They are as honest as the light that is their element and always shines through their bodies. This is why they are devoted servants of their Lord, and the idea of disobedience cannot arise in their hearts. Their wings are shining white and soft; they tremble with the fear of God.

The first of the archangels is Jiburili [Gabriel] whose task it is to carry God's Word to His prophets. Therefore Jiburili is also called the Trustworthy Spirit.

The tradition says that Mohammed, during his life on earth, asked Jiburili: "Show me your true shape." Jiburili warned him that this would be dangerous, but Mohammed insisted. Then Jiburili showed himself, and lo! he filled the whole horizon, and his many wings rustled through the skies from east to west. The prophet fainted with fear, and fell. Jiburili lifted him up and said: "Do not fear, I am your brother Jiburili."

When God had doomed the cities of Lot, He sent Jiburili to destroy them. To this end, Jiburili unfolded two special black wings that spell perdition whenever they appear. With these wings he tore the two cities out of the earth like poisonous toadstools, raised them so high that the inhabitants of heaven could hear their cocks crowing, and then flung them down into the Fire.

Mikaili [Michael] is the second archangel. He is in charge of the sustenance of all the creatures of the earth. Thousands of angels serve under his command and are busy day and night. They provide all living beings with all the things they need, according to God's decree. Some will receive plenty, others may starve, and He alone knows the reason. No mortal being need fear that he will not receive his due. What God has destined for him will come to him: air to breathe, water to drink, food to eat, partners to procreate with. We do not have to look for these things; they will be brought to us. We are all like beggars sitting at the Lord's door, and praying that He may throw us a few coins daily.

Serafili [Asrafel], the angel of the Trumpet, has already been mentioned. His task is simply to wait for the signal of the end.

Zeraili [Azrael] is the angel of death, the taker of souls, who brings each creature the last message. He obeys God alone, he commands kings and caliphs, jinns and giants, and they all follow him humbly into the unknown.

Maliki is the guardian of the Fire in which the sinful souls, the hypocrites and heathens, are punished. His face is terrible to see; he is created out of the glowing clouds of God's wrath.

Ridhuani is the custodian of Paradise. He opens its seven gates whenever God thus orders him, so that a thousand pleasant smells are spread out over the earth.

Many other angels live in heaven, more than we can know. There is an angel with a thousand heads: each head has a thousand mouths and every mouth proclaims God's glory in a different language.

There is an angel whose left half is fire, and his right half snow; the snow does not extinguish the fire, nor the fire melt the snow, because God wills it so. At His order two opposing elements can exist side by side; and He can make enemies meet.

There is also a cock in heaven: its feet are on the lowest level of Paradise but its head is above the seventh level. Its function is to crow at the precise moment God has destined for the *salat-asububi*, the prayer of dawn. Every morning before sunrise it crows jubilantly, flapping its wings, and all the angels of heaven immediately assemble for the morning prayer. Its joyful *Kuku-likuu* can be heard on earth by all the cocks, on the farms as well as in the bush, and they all repeat it, encouraging each other. This is a sign for men to rise from their couches and prepare themselves for the first prayer of the day.

II When God's moment had come, He began creating the world of matter. He rolled out the day-sky and night-sky like an immense tent, or like carpets full of mysterious signs and symbols. In the night-sky He placed the fixed stars like lamps with motionless flames. Others move along the sky, each following a path which only He knows. The moon too travels along the night-sky, changing its shape as He wishes. In the radiant blue day-sky He placed the glowing sun and ordered her to rise in the East, travel along the sky and set in the West. He created clouds, and painted them in different colours, to sail like ships along the day-sky; towards evening He makes them glow red. Some are dark and heavy with rain which He will shower over the lands He wishes to bear fruit.

He constructed the Universe in seven heavens, the seventh being the lowest level of Paradise. Each heaven has its own planet, the lowest being the moon. The second heaven is ruled by Mercury, the third by Venus, the fourth by Mars, the fifth by Jupiter, the sixth by Saturn and the seventh by the Sun. The guardians of these heavens are the souls of eight prophets of God. They are Adam in the first heaven, Isa [Jesus] and his cousin Yahya [John the Baptist], together in the second, Yusufu [Joseph] in the third, Idirisi [Enoch] in the fourth, Haruni [Aaron] in the fifth and Musa [Moses] in the sixth. Abraham is the guardian of the seventh heaven; his station is near the wall of the Celestial Mosque where 70,000 angels come to pray every day—and they are never the same ones.

Opposite the high heavens, there are the deep hells, seven layers of them, each one more terrible than the one above it, each one destined for a particular type of sinner. In the deepest Hell, farthest away from their Maker, will dwell the unbelievers, who will be tortured there eternally.

Then God spread out the earth, like a carpet for men to sit on during their meal. For the Earth is full of food for all the creatures of the Lord. And He caused some parts to be barren sands, but wherever He wished made grass sprout for the hooved animals, and trees for the monkeys, and fruit-bearing vegetation with colourful products, a pleasure for the tongue.

He divided the land from the sea, creating the immeasurable ocean on one side, and the high walls of the continents on the other. He heaped up the rocks to be menacing mountains, then told the streams to rush down them in crystal torrents.

He sowed the islands, to be colourful bouquets growing out of the ocean, and a pleasure for the sailing skippers. He commanded quiet pools to reflect the blue skies and the mighty rivers to spread out over the marshes.

He gave a voice to the wind, so that it can whisper as well as roar while it travels over the countries. It pushes the clouds in all directions and it carries the birds on its powerful back. It blows the ships to their destination and it whips up the waves into frenzy.

Then He told the Earth to teem with insects, and lo, a hundred thousand kinds crawled through the sand, and flew up into the air on diaphanous wings. The butterflies flutter and the beetles creep; they all have the symbols of their Maker written on their backs. Then He released swarms of birds who flew joyfully into the air. Some sat down on branches to praise their Maker with songs in unknown languages. Others built their nests, and He alone was their Teacher.

Then He told the ocean to be full of fishes of different forms, and so it happened. Only He knows how many there are—and they all have different colours. Then He told the lizards to exist and they obeyed, basking in His sunshine, and the croaking frogs who praise the Lord in their own language. Only He knows how many there are and how many eggs they must lay.

Then the Merciful Maker called to the heavy animals to come into existence and they did, praising Him by lowing and bleating. He created the flesh-eating beasts with claws, and the howling ones which eat carrion. He designed the quiet giraffe and the irascible buffalo, herds of antelope and striped donkeys, the river-dwelling hippopotamus and the gigantic elephant.

Only He knows how many species there are; He knows the colour of every feather, the sharpness of every tooth. He created the herds of docile cows, their bulging udders full of milk, and the strong-legged camels who travel without thirst. He decided the life-time of the butterfly, and He lit the glowing light of the fire-fly. He decided the law of His creation: that the small fishes will be eaten by the big ones, and they in their turn swallowed by yet bigger fishes. The vultures will descend from the sky to pick the bones of those that die. He makes green leaves for the goats; He makes the dove unaware of the swift swoop of the hawk. He gives the dead bodies to the worms and maggots; then He gives the worms to the chickens and the unsuspecting chicken to the bateleur eagle, who flies up with it into the pillarless sky.

He caused all his creatures to grow and multiply. Fresh green grass stalks sprout after every bush fire; smooth reddish mangoes bulge every year between the dark green leaves of the mother tree.

In every rainy season the white ants swarm out, rustling in their myriads like the first heavy showers. The black ants march along their own roads, hatching their young in their mounds. Which animal is there that does not have children? The baboon-babies cling to their mothers' breasts, the long-legged giraffe sucks his mother. What is there that He has forgotten? Are all these miracles not signs to you of His infinite wisdom, of His immense power?

III God made the night cover the day, and so their alternation marks the progress of time.

One day, He called together His angels. They all appeared before His Throne, performing the ritual prayer of morning-time. Then the Lord spoke: It has pleased Me to decide that I will create a being—with brains like you, but his substance will be clay. I will mould him out of earth, and on earth he will live. He will rear cattle and till the fields. He will learn to sail the perilous ocean and catch My silver fishes in nets. He will take possession of all My creatures on earth and rule them, following My laws. He will be My servant; his children will spread out over the face of the earth, as numerous as ants, and they will work and worship Me.

The angels are permitted to express their feelings, and the strongest one is apprehension. With their lucid minds they foresee what will happen. They themselves are made out of the substance of pure light. Their transparence makes them honest: they have no solid faces behind which evil can be hid. They are pure, and without sin. Their high intelligence makes them perceive the sufferings of other creatures, and the wishes of their Master. And so they are devoted to worship and service, to helping and relieving others. Their purity also gives them altruism: Their diaphanous brains breed no egoism, they cannot think of anything to wish for; no desire swells up in their sinless souls.

But what will man be like? His body will be lumpy and full of lust like that of dogs and pigs; like them, he will want to procreate and multiply, to fight and to kill. He will not be transparent like sunrays in the morning, he will be foggy like dark rainclouds. Apart from greed and cruelty, there will be stupidity and dishonesty in him. Brains of clay will be tardy and turgid. His thinking will be sensual rather than sensible, reluctant to accept the necessary, slow to service, prone to pride. He will hide his hate and lust behind a stony skull. Worst of all, he will satisfy his senses rather than sing hymns to praise his Maker.

His involved thinking will not solve problems, but will lead to complications which his lack of honesty will seek to conceal rather than simplify: direct thinking is the fruit of honesty. His greed will cause him to steal fruits and females from his neighbour's garden, and jealousy will inflame his mind. He will seek glory by conquering portions of God's earth, and he will take pleasure in killing, like a martin. The intelligent angels could already see black clouds of smoke hanging over the earth: the fierce fire of war.

But their Lord reassured them: do not fear, I will what I will, I know what I know. I have a purpose which I will fulfill after thousands of years. Then you will see the reason for the creation of man.

The angels said no more but intoned hymns to praise His wisdom.

Then God took some fat clay, grey and solid, and kneaded it in the shape of a man. Adam ["earth"] was ready; he lacked only one thing: Life. God pronounced the word, and it came to Adam. Life spread through his body, entering through his mouth. Life throbbed through Adam's veins, adding colour to his skin. Blood travelled to his hands and feet and made them ready for movement. Warmth rippled through his muscles and the first sparks of thought lit up in his dark brain. Adam shuddered; his eyelids trembled and then opened, like the lid on a coffer full of jewels. The angels held their breath as they saw this handsome lad open his crystal eyes to admit the sunlight. Adam opened his mouth, drew breath, his tongue moved, and his voice rang out, proclaiming the greatness of his Maker: "Al-Hamdu Lillahi r-Rahmani r-Rahim!"

The angels were greatly astonished to see this clay creature speak intelligently and devoutly. They admired this beautiful new creation, and all obeyed their Lord when He commanded them to prostrate themselves before Adam and worship him. Except one.

—Jan Knappert. *Myths and Legends of the Swahili.* Nairobi: Heinemann Educational Press, 1970, pp. 14–24.

BUSHONGO

Bumba Vomits the World

The Bushongo or Bakuba, a Bantu people of the Congo River region in Zaire, describe creation in generative terms. Along in the dark and watery chaos, without a mate, Bumba vomited forth the powers of the world. The structural similarities between this and more common birth metaphors (mouth–womb; vomit–baby; pain of delivery in both cases) are clear and serve to underscore Bumba's extraordinary fertility.

Bumba first vomited the sun, whose heat caused the primordial waters to recede and land to form. Next he vomited forth nine prototypical creatures each of which made others of his own kind. Only lightning proved obstreperous and had to be banished from earth. Lastly, Bumba created men, one of which was white like himself (signifying light or purity? the influence of Christianity and European domination?) and in the role of culture hero taught them to make fire.

Awe before the power and beauty of nature, often obscured in the pessimistic overtones of African myths more concerned with man's sins, is stated here simply in Bumba's benediction: "Behold these wonders. They belong to you."

The Bushongo kingdom was the oldest and most advanced of the Bantu realms in the Congo area. Its oral tradition traces some 120 rulers since its founding in the fifth century A.D.

IN THE BEGINNING, in the dark, there was nothing but water. And Bumba was alone.

One day Bumba was in terrible pain. He retched and strained and vomited up the sun. After that light spread over everything. The heat of the sun dried up the water until the black edges of the world began to show. Black sandbanks and reefs could be seen. But there were no living things.

Bumba vomited up the moon and then the stars, and after that the night had its own light also.

Still Bumba was in pain. He strained again and nine living creatures came forth: the leopard named Koy Bumba, and Pongo Bumba the crested eagle, the crocodile, Ganda Bumba, and one little fish named Yo; next, old Kono Bumba, the tortoise, and Tsetse, the lightning, swift, deadly, beautiful like the leopard, then the white heron, Nyanyi Bumba, also one beetle, and the goat named Budi.

Last of all came forth men. There were many men, but only one was white like Bumba. His name was Loko Yima.

The creatures themselves then created all the creatures. The heron created all the birds of the air except the kite. He did not make the kite. The crocodile made serpents and the iguana. The goat produced every beast with horns. Yo, the small fish, brought forth all the fish of all the seas and waters. The beetle created insects.

Then the serpents in their turn made grasshoppers, and the iguana made the creatures without horns.

Then the three sons of Bumba said they would finish the world. The first, Nyonye Ngana, made the white ants; but he was not equal to the task, and died of it. The ants, however, thankful for life and being, went searching for black earth in the depths of the world and covered the barren sands to bury and honor their creator.

Chonganda, the second son, brought forth a marvelous living plant from which all the trees and grasses and flowers and plants in the world have sprung. The third son, Chedi Bumba, wanted something different, but for all his trying made only the bird called the kite.

Of all the creatures, Tsetse, lightning, was the only troublemaker. She stirred up so much trouble that Bumba chased her into the sky. Then mankind was without fire until Bumba showed the people how to draw fire out of trees. "There is fire in every tree," he told them, and showed them how to make the firedrill and liberate it. Sometimes today Tsetse still leaps down and strikes the earth and causes damage.

When at last the work of creation was finished, Bumba walked through the peaceful villages and said to the people, "Behold these wonders. They belong to you." Thus from Bumba, the Creator, the First Ancestor, came forth all the wonders that we see and hold and use, and all the brotherhood of beasts and man.

—Maria Leach. *The Beginning*. New York: Funk and Wagnalls, 1956, pp. 145–147. —Translated and adapted from material in E. Torday and T. A. Joyce. *Les Boshongo, Annales du Musée de Congo Belge, Ethnographie Anthropologie*, Serie 4, t. 2. Brussels, 1910, pp. 20ff.

BULU

How Zambe Created Man, the Chimpanzee, and the Gorilla

The effects of oppression and colonialism are evident in this myth from the Bulu people of the Cameroons. Given a good god, the only explanation for such suffering as they experienced was human error. Therefore, when Zambe, the son the supreme god Mebe'e ("the One who bears the world"), made men, chimpanzees and gorillas, all but the white man denied his sacred gifts and were punished accordingly. In another version told by the Fan people, the black man catches the white's malaria and in the end lies dying on the coast of Africa, longing for his former relation to God.

When this myth was collected in 1912, the Cameroons were under German control. Occupied by the French and British during World War I, they eventually became mandates and trust territories. By 1961, moves for independence were completed when the British region was joined to the French to become the Federal Republic of Cameroons.

S OME PEOPLE have believed that Zambe, the son of Mebe'e, created the man Zambe, the chimpanzee Zambe, the gorilla Zambe, and the elephant Zambe. One man was black, the other one white. He gave unto them, moreover, fire and cutlasses and hoes and axes and water. After this they stirred up the fire; and when the white man came and sat by the fire, when he looked into the fire, the smoke came into his eyes, so that the tears came. Therefore he arose and went away from the fire. The only thing which the white man treasured was the book which he held in his hand.

The chimpanzee saw a cluster of mvut-fruit ripening on a tree standing in the unplanted border of a clearing; so he threw away all he had, and went and ate the fruit of the mvut-tree. He and the gorilla Zambe did in this manner.

The black man stirred up the fire around the standing stump of an adum-tree, but he neglected the book.

The elephant also had enough things, but he did not remember one of them.

When Zambe, the son of Mebe'e, came, he called them together and asked them, "All the things which I left in your possession, where are they?" The Chimpanzee made answer, and said, "My things I left where I ate the fruit of the mvut-tree." So he said to him, "Go and fetch them!" When, however, the chimpanzee came to the place where he had left them, he found not a single one of them there. Therefore Zambe, the son of Mebe'e, became angry with him, and said to him, "You are a fool." And he dipped his hands into a pool of water, and sprinkled hair all over the body of the chimpanzee; he gave him also large teeth in his mouth, and said to him, moreover, "You will always live in the forests." The same he said to the gorilla: "You and the chimpanzee will be alike."

After this he also asked the black man, "Where is your book?" and he replied, "I threw it away." Zambe therefore said to him, "You will be left without knowledge, because you threw away the book." Moreover, Zambe, the son of Mebe'e, said to him, "You will go to a man and ask of him a wife in return for goods, you will also work for him." He also said again to the black man, "You will be always tending the fire, for it is the one thing you especially looked after." Thereupon said Zambe to the white man. "In all the days to come you will never put away the book, because you did look after the book which I gave you; therefore you will be a man of understanding, because you cared for a real thing." He said to him also, "You will always live without fire, for you cared but little for the fire."

Thus it is that the chimpanzees and gorillas and elephants went to the forest to live; and they alway cry and howl, because Zambe, the son of Mebe'e, gave them a curse because they did not keep the things he had given them to keep.

Therefore we now perceive that the white men are men of understanding, but the black people are ignorant; moreover, also the black men go and serve them; the black people also warm themselves at the fire.

—Adolf N. Krug. "Bulu Tales from Kamerun, West Africa." *Journal of American Folklore*, 25, 1912–1913, pp. 111–112. (New York: G. E. Stechert, for the American Folklore Society.)

NGOMBE

The Quarrelsomeness of Man and

How the Earth was Peopled
Living in the dense forests of Zaire, the Ngombe worship Akongo, "the Unexplainable," "the One who causes all things to be." In this first Ngombe myth fragment, the sacred harmony of the beginning is destroyed by man's quarrelsomeness. The "creation" as such thus represents a devolution.

Similarly, the second myth depicts a heavenly origin for all, but in this case a woman is at fault. Cast out of paradise, she descends to earth with her children and encourages them in incest. Another woman, her daughter, then falls prey to the witchcraft of Ebenga, the evil power of the earth world, and the ambiguous nature of life is established. Much like the Garden of Eden myth in the Old Testament, this Ngombe story of the fall fails to account for the origin of evil. If Akongo is both good and powerful, where did Ebenga come from?

I Akongo was not always as he is now. In the beginning the creator lived among men; but men were quarrelsome. One day they had a big quarrel and Akongo left them to themselves. He went and hid in the forest and nobody has seen him since. People today can't tell what he is like.

II In the beginning there were no men on earth. The people lived in the sky with Akongo and they were happy. But there was a woman named Mbokomu who bothered everybody.

One day Akongo put the woman in a basket with her son and her daughter, some cassava, maize, and sugarcane and lowered the basket down to the earth.

The family planted a garden on earth and the garden flourished through their care.

One day the mother said to her son: "When we die there will be no one left to tend the garden."

"That can't be helped," the son replied.

"You must have children," the mother said.

"How?" asked the son. "We are the only people here. Where shall I find a wife?"

"Your sister is a woman," his mother replied. "Take her and have children by her." But the son recoiled from his mother's suggestion. The mother insisted, however. "That, or die childless, with nobody to continue our work. You can only get children by your sister so go and take her."

In the end the son gave in and went to his sister. The sister yielded to him quite willingly and became pregnant.

One day the sister met a creature who looked like a man except that he was completely covered by hair. She was afraid but the creature spoke so kindly to her that after a while they became friends. One day the sister took her husband's razor and went out to look for the hairy man. When she found him she made him lie down and shaved him. Now he looked like a man. His name was Ebenga, meaning the beginner.

Ebenga betwitched the woman, so that when her child was born it brought witchcraft into the world. The child grew up under the spell of Ebenga. He practiced witchcraft and brought evil and sorrow to men.

In the course of time the brother and sister had other children. So the earth was peopled. But evil and witchcraft continued to the present.

The sky is supported by two creatures, Libanja and Songo. Libanja holds up the sky in the east by an enormous pole, and Songo in the west. When they grow tired the sky will fall down and men will turn into lizards.

—Susan Feldman (ed.). *African Myths and Tales.* New York: Dell Publishing, 1963, pp. 37–39. — Adapted from material in E. W. Smith. *African Ideas of God.* London: Edinburgh House Press, 1950.

NANDI

When God Came to Earth Like other Nilotic cultures, the Nandi have a stratified mythology that reflects the merger of Hamitic and Paleo-Negritic peoples. The Nandi found Dorobo hunters when they entered Kenya; they thought the Dorobo so primordial that in some myths they portrayed them as the progenitors of the human race. (One of these myths tells how the first Dorobo gave birth to children through his knees.)

This tale also asserts Dorobo primacy. Along with the elephant and thunder, the Dorobo already inhabited the earth when God (the sun, Asista) came to prepare the order of things. And as in many other African myths, the "progress" of the first men is disparaged here. When people set themselves against the other creatures, the original harmony of nature is destroyed and evil enters the world.

W HEN GOD came to the earth to prepare the present order of things, he found three beings there, the thunder, an elephant, and a Dorobo, all living together.

One day the thunder remarked: "What sort of a creature is this man? If he wishes to turn over from one side to the other when he is asleep, he is able to do so. If I wish to turn over, I have first of all to get up."

The elephant said: "It is the same with me; before I can turn over from one side to the other, I have to stand up."

The thunder declared that he was afraid of the man and said he would run away and go to the heavens. At this the elephant laughed and inquired why he was running away, for the man after all was only a small creature. "But he is bad," the thunder replied, "he can turn over when asleep"; and with that he fled and went to the heavens, where he has remained ever since.

The man seeing the thunder go away was pleased, and said: "The person I was afraid of has fled. I do not mind the elephant." He then went to the woods and made some poison into which he dipped an arrow, and having cut a bow, he returned to the kraal, and shot the elephant.

The elephant wept and lifted his trunk to the heavens, crying out to the thunder to take him up.

The thunder refused, however, and said: "I shall not take you, for when I warned you that the man was bad, you laughed and said he was small."

The elephant cried out again and begged to be taken to heaven, as he was on the point of death.

But the thunder only replied: "Die by yourself."

And the elephant died, and the man became great in all the countries.

—A. C. Hollis. *The Nandi, Their Language and Folklore.* Oxford, England: Clarendon Press, 1909, pp. 111–114.

DOGON

The First Words
An agricultural people of Mali and Upper Volta, the Dogon were thought even by their neighbors to be so primitive as to have virtually no sophisticated religious beliefs. It was with considerable surprise, then, that Marcel Griaule, a French ethnologist who had worked among the Dogon for years, finally heard their amazingly complex and profound cosmology from the wise man Ogotemmeli who had been delegated to reveal it.

While only a short part of the whole myth is recounted here, it serves to demonstrate the rich system of correspondences between the natural order, the social realm, and personal life. Structural similarities abound to the extent that the individual, while still only a part of the whole on one plane, is representative of it on another. In his actions, he thus affects the same cosmic order which he displays, making his life sacred on several levels at once.

The Dogon envisage creation in several stages, each culminating in a sacred "word" or revelation. The first is nature, a simple but eloquent language expressed in the sounds of grasses covering the nakedness of the earth. The second, an attempt to redeem mankind, concerns the social order and is symbolized by weaving. This word caused men to leave their caves and live with each other in community. The third revelation includes two things: (1) the sacred granary, paradigmatic not only of earthly granaries but also of the world order of creation on the cosmic plane and the digestive system of individuals on the personal level; and (2) the drum, a primary method of communication and symbolic of verbal language and culture.

These sacred words are the products of various stages of sacred development: the creation of the earth by the god Amma; his frustrated attempt to mate with her and her subsequent defilement by incestuous rape; the perfect birth of the Nummo twins, divine creatures of water and light who purify earth and order the creation of the eight ancestors; the expulsion of the ancestors from heaven and the ordering of the natural and social realms of earth. Throughout, the principle of polar opposition is maintained and cherished. Only by clarifying such oppositions does interrelation and further creation result.

Of particular interest in this regard is the notion of double-sexed souls. All children are both male and female until one sexual orientation is encouraged by the physical removal of the other through circumcision or excision rites. The recessive sex remains as a shadow image, a perception not unlike Jung's of the anima and animus. Only after such rites is the young man or woman sexually and psychologically ready for a fruitful union.

OGOTEMMELI, seating himself on his threshold, scraped his stiff leather snuff-box, and put a pinch of yellow powder on his tongue. "Tobacco," he said, "makes for right thinking."

So saying, he set to work to analyse the world system, for it was essential to begin with the dawn of all things. He rejected as a detail of no interest, the popular account of how the fourteen solar systems were formed from flat circular slabs of earth one on top of the other. He was only prepared to speak of the serviceable solar system; he agreed to consider the stars, though they only played a secondary part.

"It is quite true," he said, "that in course of time women took down the stars to give them to their children. The children put spindles through them and made them spin like fiery tops to show themselves how the world turned. But that was only a game."

The stars came from pellets of earth flung out into space by the God Amma, the one God. He had created the sun and the moon by a more complicated process, which was not the first known to man but is the first attested invention of God: the art of pottery. The sun is, in a sense, a pot raised once for all to white heat and surrounded by a spiral of red copper with eight turns. The moon is the same shape, but its copper is white. It was heated only one quarter at a time. Ogotemmeli said he would explain later the movements of these bodies. For the moment he was concerned only to indicate the main lines of the design, and from that to pass to its actors.

He was anxious, however, to give an idea of the size of the sun.

"Some," he said, "think it is as large as this encampment, which would mean thirty cubits. But it is really bigger. Its surface area is bigger than the whole of Sanga Canton."

And after some hesitation he added:

"It is perhaps even bigger than that."

He refused to linger over the dimensions of the moon, nor did he ever say anything about them. The moon's function was not important, and he would speak of it later. He said however that, while Africans were creatures of light emanating from the fullness of the sun, Europeans were creatures of the moonlight: hence their immature appearance.

He spat out his tobacco as he spoke. Ogotemmeli had nothing against Europeans. He was not even sorry for them. He left them to their destiny in the lands of the north.

The God Amma, it appeared, took a lump of clay, squeezed it in his hand and flung it from him, as he had done with the stars. The clay spread and fell on the north, which is the top, and from there stretched out to the south, which is the bottom, of the world, although the whole movement was horizontal. The earth lies flat, but the north is at the top. It extends east and west with separate members like a foetus in the womb. It is a body, that is to say, a thing with members branching out from a central mass. This body, lying flat, face upwards, in a line from north to south, is feminine. Its sexual organ is an anthill, and its clitoris a termite hill. Amma, being lonely and desirous of intercourse with this creature, approached it. That was the occasion of the first breach of the order of the universe.

Ogotemmeli ceased speaking. His hands crossed above his head, he sought to distinguish the different sounds coming from the courtyards and roofs. He had reached the point of the origin of troubles and of the primordial blunder of God.

"If they overheard me, I should be fined an ox!"

At God's approach the termite hill rose up, barring the passage and displaying its masculinity. It was as strong as the organ of the stranger, and intercourse could not take place. But God is all-powerful. He cut down the termite hill, and had intercourse with the excised earth. But the original incident was destined to affect the course of things for ever; from this defective union there was born, instead of the intended twins, a single being, the *Thos aureus* or jackal, symbol of the difficulties of God. Ogotemmeli's voice sank lower and lower. It was no longer a question of women's ears listening to what he was saying; other, nonmaterial, ear-drums might vibrate to his important discourse. The European and his African assistant, Sergeant Koguem, were leaning towards the old man as if hatching plots of the most alarming nature.

But, when he came to the beneficent acts of God, Ogotemmeli's voice again assumed its normal tone.

God had further intercourse with his earth-wife, and this time without mishaps of any kind, the excision of the offending member having removed the cause of the former disorder. Water, which is the divine seed, was thus able to enter the womb of the earth and the normal reproductive cycle resulted in the birth of twins. Two beings were thus formed. God created them like water. They were green in colour, half human beings and half serpents. From the head to the loins they were human: below that they were serpents. Their red eyes were wide open like human eyes, and their tongues were forked like the tongues of reptiles. Their arms were flexible and without joints. Their bodies were green and sleek all over, shining like the surface of water, and covered with short green hairs, a presage of vegetation and germination.

These spirits, called Nummo, were thus two homogeneous products of God, of divine essence like himself, conceived without untoward incidents and developed normally in the womb of the earth. Their destiny took them to Heaven, where they received the instructions of their father. Not that God had to teach them speech, that indispensable necessity of all beings, as it is of the world-system; the Pair were born perfect and complete; they had eight members, and their number was eight, which is the symbol of speech.

They were also of the essence of God, since they were made of his seed, which is at once the ground, the form, and the substance of the life-force of the world, from which derives the motion and the persistence of created being. This force is water, and the Pair are present in all water: they *are* water, the water of the seas, of coasts, of torrents, of storms, and of the spoonfuls we drink.

Ogotemmeli used the terms "Water" and "Nummo" indiscriminately.

"Without Nummo," he said, "it was not even possible to create the earth, for the earth was moulded clay and it is from water (that is, from Nummo) that its life is derived."

"What life is there in the earth?" asked the European.

"The life-force of the earth is water. God moulded the earth with water. Blood too he made out of water. Even in a stone there is this force, for there is moisture in everything.

"But if Nummo is water, it also produces copper. When the sky is overcast, the sun's rays may be seen materializing on the misty horizon. These rays, excreted by the spirits, are of copper and are light. They are water too, because they uphold the earth's moisture as it rises. The Pair excrete light, because they are also light."

While he was speaking, Ogotemmeli had been searching for something in the dust. He finally collected a number of small stones. With a rapid movement he flung them into the courtyard over the heads of his two interlocutors, who had no time to bend down. The stones fell just where the Hogon's cock had been crowing a few seconds before.

"That cock is a squalling nuisance. He makes all conversation impossible."

The bird began to crow again on the other side of the wall, so Ogotemmeli sent Koguem to throw a bit of wood at him. When Koguem came back, he asked whether the cock was now outside the limits of the Tabda quarter.

"He is in the Hogon's field," said Koguem. "I have set four children to watch him."

"Good!" said Ogotemmeli with a little laugh. "Let him make the most of what remains to him of life! They tell me he is to be eaten at the next Feast of Twins."

He returned to the subject of the Nummo spirits, or (as he more usually put it, in the singular) of Nummo, for this pair of twins, he explained, represented the perfect, the ideal unit.

The Nummo, looking down from Heaven, saw their mother, the earth, naked and speechless, as a consequence no doubt of the original incident in her relations with the God Amma. It was necessary to put an end to this state of disorder. The Nummo accordingly came down to earth, bringing with them fibres pulled from plants already created in the heavenly regions. They took ten bunches of these fibres, corresponding to the number of their ten fingers, and made two strands of them, one for the front and one for behind. To this day masked men still wear these appendages hanging down to their feet in thick tendrils.

But the purpose of this garment was not merely modesty. It manifested on earth the first act in the ordering of the universe and the revelation of the helicoid sign in the form of an undulating broken line.

For the fibres fell in coils, symbol of tornadoes, of the windings of torrents, of eddies and whirlwinds, of the undulating movement of reptiles. They recall also the eight-fold spirals of the sun, which sucks up moisture. They were themselves a channel of moisture, impregnated as they were with the freshness of the celestial plants. They were full of the essence of Nummo: they *were* Nummo in motion, as shown in the undulating line, which can be prolonged to infinity.

When Nummo speaks, what comes from his mouth is a warm vapour which conveys, and itself constitutes, speech. This vapour, like all water, has sound, dies away in a helicoid line. The coiled fringes of the skirt were therefore the chosen vehicle for the words which the Spirit desired to reveal to the earth. He endued his hands with magic power by raising them to his lips while he plaited the skirt, so that the moisture of his words was imparted to the damp plaits, and the spiritual revelation was embodied in the technical instruction.

In these fibres full of water and words, placed over his mother's genitalia, Nummo is thus always present.

Thus clothed, the earth had a language, the first language of this world and the most primitive of all time. Its syntax was elementary, its verbs few, and its vocabulary without elegance. The words were breathed sounds scarcely differentiated from one another, but nevertheless vehicles. Such as it was, this ill-defined speech sufficed for the great works of the beginning of all things.

In the middle of a word Ogotemmeli gave a loud cry in answer to the hunter's halloo which the discreet Akundyo, priest of women dying in childbirth and of stillborn children, had called through the gap in the wall.

Akundyo first spat to one side, his eye riveted on the group of men. He was wearing a red Phrygian cap which covered his ears, with a raised point like a uraeus on the bridge of the nose in the fashion known as "the wind blows." His cheek-bones were prominent, and his teeth shone. He uttered a formal salutation to which the old man at once replied and the exchange of courtesies became more and more fulsome.

"God's curse," exclaimed Ogotemmeli, "on any in Lower Ogol who love you not!"

With growing emotion Akundyo made shift to out-do the vigour of the imprecation.

"May God's curse rest on me," said the blind man at last, "if I love you not!"

The four men breathed again. They exchanged humorous comments on the meagerness of the game in the I valley. Eventually Akundyo took his leave of them, asserting in the slangy French of a native soldier that he was going to "look for porcupine," an animal much esteemed by these people.

The conversation reverted to the subject of speech. Its function was organization, and therefore it was good; nevertheless from the start it let loose disorder.

This was because the jackal, the deluded and deceitful son of God, desired to possess speech, and laid hands on the fibres in which language was embodied, that is to say, on his mother's skirt. His mother, the earth, resisted this incestuous action. She buried herself in her own womb, that is to say, in the anthill, disguised as an ant. But the jackal followed her. There was, it should be explained, no other woman in the world whom he could desire. The hole which the earth made in the anthill was never deep enough, and in the end she had to admit defeat. This prefigured the even-handed struggles between men and women, which, however, always end in the victory of the male.

The incestuous act was of great consequence. In the first place it endowed the jackal with the gift of speech so that ever afterwards he was able to reveal to diviners the designs of God.

It was also the cause of the flow of menstrual blood, which stained the fibres. The resulting defilement of the earth was incompatible with the reign of God. God rejected that spouse, and decided to create living beings directly. Modelling a womb in damp clay, he placed it on the earth and covered it with a pellet flung out into space from heaven. He made a male organ in the same way and having put it on the ground, he flung out a sphere which stuck to it.

The two lumps forthwith took organic shape; their life began to develop. Members separated from the central core, bodies appeared, and a human pair arose out of the lumps of earth.

At this point the Nummo Pair appeared on the scene for the purpose of further action. The Nummo foresaw that the original rule of twin births was bound to disappear, and that errors might result comparable to those of the jackal, whose birth was single. For it was because of his solitary state that the first son of God acted as he did.

"The jackal was alone from birth," said Ogotemmeli, "and because of this he did more things than can be told."

The Spirit drew two outlines on the ground, one on top of the other, one male and the other female. The man stretched himself out on these two shadows of himself, and took both of them for his own. The same thing was done for the woman. Thus it came about that each human being from the first was endowed with two souls of different sex, or rather with two principles corresponding to two distinct persons. In the man the female soul was located in the prepuce; in the woman the male soul was in the clitoris.

But the foreknowledge of the Nummo no doubt revealed to him the disadvantages of this makeshift. Man's life was not capable of supporting both beings: each person would have to merge himself in the sex for which he appeared to be best fitted.

The Nummo accordingly circumcised the man, thus removing from him all the femininity of his prepuce. The prepuce, however, changed itself into an animal which is "neither a serpent nor an insect, but is classed with serpents." This animal is called a *nay*. It is said to be a sort of lizard, black and white like the pall which covers the dead. Its name also means 'four,' the female number, the 'Sun,' which is a female being. The *nay* symbolized the pain of circumcision and the need for the man to suffer in his sex as the woman does.

The man then had intercourse with the woman, who later bore the first two children of a series of eight, who were to become the ancestors of the Dogon people. In the moment of birth the pain of parturition was concentrated in the woman's clitoris, which was excised by an invisible hand, detached itself and left her, and was changed into the form of a scorpion. The pouch and the sting symbolized the organ: the venom was the water and the blood of the pain.

The European, returning through the millet field, found himself wondering about the significance of all these actions and counteractions, all these sudden jerks in the thought of the myth.

Here, he reflected, is a Creator God spoiling his first creation; restoration is effected by the excision of the earth, and then by the birth of a pair of spirits, inventive beings who construct the world and bring to it the first spoken words; an incestuous act destroys the created order, and jeopardizes the principle of twin-births. Order is restored by the creation of a pair of human beings, and twin-births are replaced by dual souls. (But why, he asked himself, twin-births at all?)

The dual soul is a danger; a man should be male, and a woman female. Circumcision and excision are once again the remedy. (But why the *nay?* Why the scorpion?)

The answers to these questions were to come later, and to take their place in the massive structure of doctrine, which the blind old man was causing to emerge bit by bit from the mists of time.

Over the heads of the European and Koguem the dark millet clusters stood out against the leaden sky. They were passing through a field of heavy ears, stiffly erect and motionless in the breeze. When the crop is backward and thin, the ears are light and move with the slightest breath of wind. Thin crops are therefore full of sound. An abundant crop, on the other hand, is weighed down by the wind and bows itself in silence.

ANYONE entering the courtyard upset its arrangements. It was so cramped that the kites, most cunning of all the acrobats of the air, could not get at the poultry. In a hollow stone there were the remains, or rather, the dregs of some millet-beer, which the poultry, cock, hen and chickens, were glad to drink. So was a yellow and white striped dog with tail erect like an Ethiopian sabre. When the door banged, all these creatures dispersed, leaving the courtyard to the humans.

Ogotemmeli, ensconced in his doorway, proceeded to enumerate the eight original ancestors born of the couple created by God. The four eldest were males: the four others were females. But by a special dispensation, permitted only to them, they were able to fertilize themselves, being dual and bisexual. From them are descended the eight Dogon families.

For humanity was organizing itself in this makeshift condition. The permanent calamity of single births was slightly mitigated by the grant of the dual soul, which the Nummo traced on the ground beside women in childbirth. Dual souls were implanted in the new-born child by holding it by the thighs above the place of the drawings with its hands and feet touching the ground. Later the superfluous soul was eliminated by circumcision, and humanity limped towards its obscure destiny.

But the divine thirst for perfection was not extinguished, and the Nummo Pair, who were gradually taking the place of God their father, had in mind projects of redemption. But, in order to improve human conditions, reforms and instruction had to be carried out on the human level. The Nummo were afraid of the terrifying effect of contact between creatures of flesh and blood on the one hand and purely spiritual beings on the other. There had to be actions that could be understood, taking place within the ambit of the beneficiaries and in their own environment. Men after regeneration must be drawn towards the ideal as a peasant is drawn to rich farmland.

The Nummo accordingly came down to earth, and entered the anthill, that is to say, the sexual part of which they were themselves the issue. Thus, they were able, among other tasks, to defend their mother against possible attempts by their elder, the incestuous jackal. At the same time, by their moist, luminous, and articulate presence, they were purging that body which was for ever defiled in the sight of God, but was nevertheless capable of acquiring in some degree the purity required for the activities of life.

In the anthill the male Nummo took the place of the masculine element, which had been eliminated by the excision of the termite-hill clitoris, while the female Nummo took the place of the female element, and her womb became part of the womb of the earth.

The Pair could then proceed to the work of regeneration, which they intended to carry out in agreement with God and in God's stead.

"Nummo in Amma's place," said Ogotemmeli, "was working the work of Amma."

In those obscure beginnings of the evolution of the world, men had no knowledge of death, and the eight ancestors, offspring of the first human couple, lived on indefinitely. They had eight separate lines of descendants, each of them being self-propagating since each was both male and female. The four males and the four females were couples in consequence of their lower, i.e. of their sexual, parts. The four males were man and woman, and the four females were woman and man. In the case of the males it was the man, and in the case of the females it was the woman, who played the dominant role. They coupled and became pregnant each in him or herself, and so produced their offspring.

But in the fullness of time an obscure instinct led the eldest of them towards the anthill which had been occupied by the Nummo. He wore on his head as head-dress and to protect him from the sun, the wooden bowl he used for his food. He put his two feet into the opening of the anthill, that is of the earth's womb, and sank in slowly as if for a parturition *a tergo*.

The whole of him thus entered into the earth, and his head itself disappeared. But he left on the ground, as evidence of his passage into that world, the bowl which had caught on the edges of the opening. All that remained on the anthill was the round wooden bowl, still bearing traces of the food and the fingerprints of its vanished owner, symbol of his body and of his human nature, as, in the animal world, is the skin which a reptile has shed.

Liberated form his earthly condition, the ancestor was taken in charge by the regenerating Pair. The male Nummo led him into the depths of the earth, where, in the waters of the womb of his partner he curled himself up like a foetus and shrank to germinal form, and acquired the quality of water, the seed of god and the essence of the two Spirits.

And all this process was the work of the Word. The male with his voice accompanied the female Nummo who was speaking to herself and to her own sex. The spoken Word entered into her and wound itself round her womb in a spiral of eight turns. Just as the helical band of coper round the sun gives to it its daily movement, so the spiral of the Word gave to the womb its regenerative movement.

Thus perfected by water and words, the new Spirit was expelled and went up to Heaven.

All the eight ancestors in succession had to undergo this process of transformation; but, when the turn of the seventh ancestor came, the change was the occasion of a notable occurrence.

The seventh in a series, it must be remembered, represents perfection. Though equal in quality with the others, he is the sum of the feminine element, which is four, and the masculine element, which is three. He is thus the completion of the perfect series, symbol of the total union of male and female, that is to say of unity.

And to this homogeneous whole belongs especially the mastery of words, this is, of language; and the appearance on earth of such a one was bound to be the prelude to revolutionary developments of a beneficent character.

In the earth's womb he became, like the others, water and spirit, and his development, like theirs, followed the rhythm of the words uttered by the two transforming Nummo.

"The words which the female Nummo spoke to herself," Ogotemmeli explained, "turned into a spiral and entered into her sexual part. The male Nummo helped her. These are the words which the seventh ancestor learnt inside the womb."

The others equally possessed the knowledge of these words in virtue of their experiences in the same place; but they had not attained the mastery of them nor was it given to them to develop their use. What the seventh ancestor had received, therefore, was the perfect knowledge of a Word—the second Word to be heard on earth, clearer than the first and not, like the first, reserved for particular recipeints, but destined for all mankind. Thus he was able to achieve progress for the world. In particular, he enabled mankind to take precedence over God's wicked son, the jackal. The latter, it is true, still possessed knowledge of the first Word, and could still therefore reveal to diviners certain heavenly purposes; but in the future order of things he was to be merely a laggard in the process of revelation.

The potent second Word developed the powers of its new possessor. Gradually he came to regard his regeneration in the womb of the earth as equivalent to the capture and occupation of that womb, and little by little he took possession of the whole organism, making such use of it as suited him for the purpose of his activities. His lips began to merge with the edges of the anthill, which widened and became a mouth. Pointed teeth made their appearance, seven for each lip, then ten, the number of the fingers, later forty, and finally eighty, that is to say, ten for each ancestor.

These numbers indicated the future rates of increase of the families; the appearance of the teeth was a sign that the time for new instruction was drawing near.

But here again the scruples of the Spirits made themselves felt. It was not directly to men, but to the ant, avatar of the earth and native to the locality, that the seventh ancestor imparted instruction.

At sunrise on the appointed day the seventh ancestor Spirit spat out eighty threads of cotton; these he distributed between his upper teeth which acted as the teeth of a weaver's reed. In this way he made the uneven threads of a warp. He did the same with the lower teeth to make the even threads. By opening and shutting his jaws the Spirit caused the threads of the warp to make the movements required in weaving. His whole face took part in the work, his nose studs serving as the block, while the stud in his lower lip was the shuttle.

As the threads crossed and uncrossed, the two tips of the Spirit's forked tongue pushed the thread of the weft to and fro, and the web took shape from his mouth in the breath of the second revealed Word.

For the Spirit was speaking while the work proceeded. As did the Nummo in the first revelation, he imparted his Word by means of a technical process, so that all men could understand. By so doing he showed the identity of material actions and spiritual forces, or rather the need for their co-operation.

The words that the Spirit uttered filled all the interstices of the stuff: they were woven in the threads, and formed part and parcel of the cloth. They were the cloth, and the cloth was the Word. That is why woven material is called *soy*, which means "It is the spoken word." *Soy* also means "seven," for the Spirit who spoke as he wove was seventh in the series of ancestors.

While the work was going on, the ant came and went on the edge of the opening in the breath of the Spirit, hearing and remembering his words. The new instruction, which she thus received, she passed on to the men who lived in those regions, and who had already followed the transformation of the sex of the earth.

Up to the time of the ancestors' descent into the anthill, men had lived in holes dug in the level soil like the lairs of animals. When their attention was drawn to the bowls which the ancestors had left behind them, they began to notice the shape of the anthill, which they thought much better than their holes.

They copied the shape of the anthill accordingly, making passages and rooms as shelters from the rain, and began to store the produce of the crops for food.

They were thus advancing towards a less primitve way of life; and, when they noticed the growth of teeth round the opening, they imitated these too as a means of protection against wild beasts. They moulded great teeth of clay, dried them and set them up round the entrances to their dwellings.

At the moment of the second instruction, therefore, men were living in dens which were already, in some sort, a prefiguration of the place of revelation and of the womb into which each of them in due course would descend to be regenerated. And, moreover, the human anthill, with its occupants and its store-chambers for grain, was a rudimentary image of the system which, much later, was to come down to them from Heaven in the form of a marvellous granary.

These dim outlines of things to come predisposed men to take advice from the ant. The latter, after what it had seen the Spirit do, had laid in a store of cotton-fibres. These it had made into threads and, in the sight of men, drew them between the teeth of the anthill entrance as the Spirit had done. As the warp emerged, the men passed the thread of the weft, throwing it right and left in time to the opening and shutting movements of the jaws, and the resulting web was rolled round a piece of wood, fore-runner of the beam.

The ant at the same time revealed the words it had heard and the man repeated them. Thus there was recreated by human lips the concept of life in motion, of the transposition of forces, of the efficacy of the breath of the Spirit, which the seventh ancestor had created; and thus the interlacing of warp and weft enclosed the same words, the new instruction which became the heritage of mankind and was handed on from generation to generation of weavers to the accompaniment of the clapping of the shuttle and the creaking of the block, which they call the "creaking of the Word."

All these operations took place by daylight, for spinning and weaving are work for the daytime. Working at night would mean weaving webs of silence and darkness.

OGOTEMMELI had no very clear idea of what happened in Heaven after the transformation of the eight ancestors into Nummo. It is true that the eight, after leaving the earth, having completed their labours, came to the celestial region where the eldest Pair, who had transformed them, reigned. It is true also that these elders had precedence of the others, and did not fail to impose on them at once a form of organization and rules of life.

But it was never quite clear why this celestial world was disturbed to the point of disintegration, or why these disorders led to a reorganization of the terrestrial world, which had nothing to do with the celestial disputes. What is certain is that in the end the eight came down to earth again in a vast apparatus of symbols, in which was included a third and definitive Word necessary for the working of the modern world.

All that could be gathered from Ogotemmeli, by dint of patient attention to his words, was the evasive answer:

"Spirits do not fall from Heaven except in anger or because they are expelled."

It was obvious that he was conscious of the infinite complexity of the idea of God or the Spirits who took his place, and was reluctant to explain it. However an outline, slight but nevertheless adequate, of this obscure period was eventually obtained.

The Nummo Pair had received the transformed eight in Heaven. But though they were all of the same essence, the Pair had the rights of the elder generation in relation to the newcomers, on whom they imposed an organization with a network of rules, of which the most onerous was the one which separated them from one another and forbade them to visit one another.

The fact was that, like human societies in which numbers are a source of trouble, the celestial society would have been heading for disorder, if all its members had gathered together.

Though this rule was their security, the new generation of Nummo, however, proceeded to break it and thereby overthrew their destiny; and this was how it came about.

God had given the eight a collection of eight different grains intended for their food, and for these the first ancestor was responsible. Of the eight, the last was the *Digitaria,* which had been publicly rejected by the first ancestor when it was given to him, on the pretext that it was so small and so difficult to prepare. He even went so far as to swear he would never eat it.

There came, however, a critical period when all the grains were nearly exhausted except the last. The first and second ancestors, who incidentally had already broken the rule about separation, met together to eat this last food. Their action was the crowning breach of order, confirming as it did their first offence by a breach of faith. The two ancestors thereby became unclean—that is to say, of an essence incompatible with life in the celestial world. They resolved to quit that region, where they felt themselves to be strangers, and the six other ancestors threw in their lot with them and made the same decision. Moreover, they proposed to take with them when they left anything that might be of use to the men they were going to rejoin. It was then that the first ancestor, no doubt with the approval and perhaps with the help of God, began to make preparations for his own departure.

He took a woven basket with a circular opening and a square base in which to carry the earth and puddled clay required for the construction of a world-system, of which he was to be one of the counsellors. This basket served as a model for a basket-work structure of considerable size which he built upside down, as it were, with the opening, twenty cubits in diameter, on the ground, the square base, with sides eight cubits long, formed a flat roof, and the height was ten cubits. This framework he covered with puddled clay made of the earth from heaven, and in the thickness of the clay, starting from the centre of each side of the square, he made stairways of ten steps each facing towards one of the cardinal points. At the sixth step of the north staircase he put a door giving access to the interior in which were eight chambers arranged on two floors.

The symbolic significance of this structure was as follows:

The circular base represented the sun.

The square roof represented the sky.

A circle in the centre of the roof represented the moon.

The tread of each step being female and the rise of each step male, the four stairways of ten steps together prefigured the eight tens of families, off-spring of the eight ancestors.

Each stairway held one kind of creature, and was associated with a constellation, as follows:

The north stairway, associated with the Pleiades, was for men and fishes;

The south stairway, associated with Orion's Belt, was for domestic animals.

The east stairway, associated with Venus, was for birds.

The west stairway, associated with the so-called "Long-Tailed Star," was for wild animals, vegetables, and insects.

In fact, the picture of the system was not easily or immediately grasped from Ogotemmeli's account of it.

"When the ancestor came down from Heaven," he said at first, "he was standing on a square piece of Heaven, not a very big piece, about the size of a sleeping-mat, or perhaps a bit bigger."

"How could he stand on this piece of Heaven?"

"It was a piece of celestial earth."

"A thick piece?"

"Yes! As thick as a house. It was ten cubits high with stairs on each side facing the four cardinal points."

The blind man had raised his head, which was almost always bent towards the ground. How was he to explain these geometrical forms, these steps, these exact measurements? The European had begun by thinking that what was meant was a tall prism flanked by four stairways forming a cross. He kept returning to this conception in order to get it quite clear, while the other, patiently groping in the darkness which enveloped him, sought for fresh details.

At last his ravaged face broke into a kind of smile: he had found what he wanted. Reaching into the inside of his house and lying almost flat on his back, he searched among a number of objects which grated or sounded hollow as they scraped the earth under his hand. Only his thin knees and his feet were still visible in the embrasure of the doorway; the rest disappeared in the shadows within. The front of the house looked like a great face with the mouth closed on two skinny shin-bones.

After much tugging, an object emerged from the depths and appeared framed in the doorway. It was a woven basket, black with dust and soot of the interior, with a round opening and a square base, crushed and broken, a wretched spectacle.

The thing was placed before the door, losing several strands in the pro-

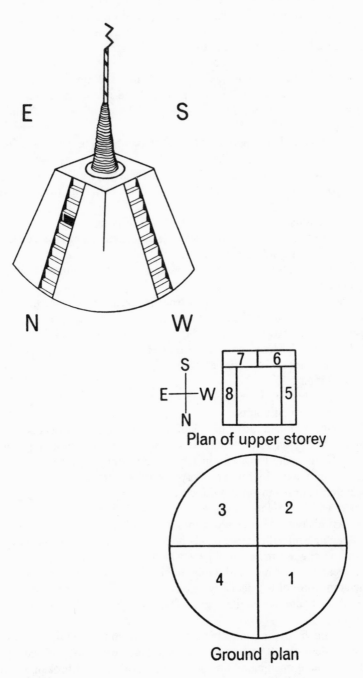

Plan of upper storey

Ground plan

World-system: plan

cess, while the whole of the blind man's body reappeared, his hand still firmly grasping the basket.

"Its only use now is to put chicken in," he said.

He passed his hands slowly over its battered remains, and proceeded to explain the world-system.

THE BASKET had been put away, with some embarrassment; returned to the place of mystery behind Ogotemmeli's back, no one ever alluded to it again. The exposure of this ruin to the light of day had been, as it were, a defiance of worldly vanity; but it had served its purpose. All was now clear and the divine geometry was defined. It was possible to make a beginning with the detailed enumeration of the beings posted at the four cardinal points of the structure.

The west stairway was occupied by wild animals. From the top stair to the bottom stair it was given up to antelopes, hyenas, cats (two stairs for these), reptiles and saurians, apes, gazelles, marmots, the lion, and the elephant.

After the sixth step came the trees from the baobab to the *Lannea acida,* and on each of them were the insects commonly found there today.

On the south stairway were the domestic animals, beginning with fowls, then sheep, goats, cattle, horses, dogs and cats.

On the eighth and ninth steps were the chelonians, the giant tortoises, which today in each family take the place of the family heads, while these are absent, and the small tortoises, which are slowly done to death in the regional purification sacrifices.

On the tenth step were mice and rats (house and field).

The east stairway was occupied by birds. On the first step were the larger birds of prey and the hornbills; on the second were ostriches and storks; on the third, the small bustards and lapwings; on the fourth, vultures. Then came the smaller birds of prey, and then the herons. On the seventh step were the pigeons; on the eighth, turtle-doves; on the ninth, ducks; and last of all, the great bustards, white and black.

The north stairway was that of men and fish.

This clearly presented complications, for Ogotemmeli had to go through it more than once before he could give a satisfactory account of it.

He certainly thought the men were Bozo, the original inhabitants of the Niger and still regarded by all the peoples of the Niger Bend as the only true fishermen. But their several positions on the different steps embarrassed Ogotemmeli, and it was not until his second reference to the subject at the end of the day that he arrived at a final version, probably after consultation with another elder.

On each of the first two steps stood a male Bozo with a fish attached to his navel and hanging between his legs. This attachment to the navel had a significance for Ogotemmeli which the European could not grasp. The man's navel was nipped between the fins of the fish: that is to say, the fish was quite clear of the man's belly. On the other hand, the name that the Dogon gave to the Bozo was thought by Ogotemmeli to indicate that the fish was in process of passing into the body of the man.

This name *sologonon* or *sorogonon,* from which is derived *Sorko,* another name for the Bozo, does in fact mean "which has not completely passed." It would apply therefore primarily to the fish, but ultimately to the Bozo himself, the two (i.e., the man and the fish) being twin brothers, as indicated by the umbilical connection.

On each of the next two steps was a Bozo woman, also attached to a fish. On the fifth step was a Bozo woman standing alone.

The five last steps were empty.

A question occurred to the European: "Only some of the animals and vegetables were on the building; where were the rest?"

"Each of those mentioned was as it were a file-leader. All the others of his kind were behind him. The antelope on the first step of the west stairway is the *walbanu,* the red antelope. After him come the white, the black and the *ka* antelopes. So too on the first step of the south stairway, where the poultry stand, the guinea-fowl, the partridge and the rock-fowl behind."

"How could all these beasts find room on a step one cubit deep and one cubit high?"

The European had calculated that, according to the slope of the walls, the tread of each step must be six-tenths of a cubit deep. But he made no mention of the fact out of politeness, so as not to seem to be examining heavenly matters too closely.

"All this had to be said in words," said Ogotemmeli, "but everything on the steps is a symbol, symbolic antelopes, symbolic vultures, symbolic hyenas." He paused for a moment, and added: "Any number of symbols could find room on a one-cubit step."

For the word "symbol" he used a composite expression, the literal meaning of which is "word of this (lower) world."

Ogotemmeli, having described the structure as a granary, now proceeded to explain its design.

"The whole thing," he said, "with its stairways is called the 'Granary of the Master of Pure Earth.' It is divided into eight compartments, four below and four above. The door opens to the north on the sixth stair. It is as it were the mouth, and the granary is the belly, that is the interior, of the world."

The structure having set the pattern for present-day granaries, the European wished to get a closer view of the arrangement of the system, and whispered to his assistant Koguem that he ought to see one of these constructions.

In point of fact nearly half the circumference of the courtyard was surrounded by granaries, some half a dozen of them in number. But to poke one's head into a granary is to invade the privacy of the family, to pry into its secrets. To scrutinize the foodstuffs, the seeds and ears of grain lying steeped in the darkness, is to measure up present resources and intrude into the provision for future needs.

Koguem put the point to the old man, suggesting a visit to an empty house he had noticed in Dyamini-Kuradondo, a village belonging to another family: but perhaps, he said, they could find a specimen nearer at hand.

Ogotemmeli reflected. Obviously he was considering, in his blindness, possible ruined granaries in the locality. At the end of his list appeared no doubt his own granaries, for he pointed to two of these in the backyard.

The farthest of these was a ruin; it was there that Kõguem used to throw stones a dozen times a day at the children who came to listen with ears alert to catch the secrets that were being talked about. The other granary was in good condition, empty but closed. A pair of hoes were needed to open it, for the door was fastened as if in the jaws of a vice. Ogotemmeli waited on his threshold, his hands crossed as always above his head. From time to time Koguem reported on the progress of the work. When the door at length gave way, the European took up a position in the embrasure, from which came the smell of old grain.

The four lower compartments in a Dogon granary are separated by two intersecting partitions, the junction of which forms a cup-like depression in the earth big enough to hold a round jar. This jar, containing grain or valuable objects, is the centre of the whole building. The door opens above these compartments, and is only just wide enough to admit the passage of a man's body.

Above the door is the upper storey comprising four other compartments, two of them in a line along the back wall and the other two along the side walls. They form a sort of ledge round the three sides, leaving the space at the entry free so that if a man crouched on the top of the lower compartments his shoulders would be level with the balcony.

In the celestial granary these compartments had a numbered order. The first was to the right of the entry on the lower floor; the second was the one on the right at the back, and so on round the building. The fifth was on the upper floor on the right, and so on to the eighth, which was to the left on the upper floor.

Each of these compartments contained one of the eight seeds given by God to the eight ancestors in the following order: little millet, white millet, dark millet, female millet, beans, sorrel, rice and *Digitaria*. With each of these seeds were all the varieties of the same species.

But the eight compartments were not merely receptacles for the seeds which were to be introduced to human use. They also represented the eight principal organs of the Spirit of water, which are comparable to the organs of men with the addition of the gizzard, for the Spirit has the speed of birds.

These organs were disposed in the following order: stomach, gizzard, heart, small liver, spleen, intestines, great liver, gallbladder.

A round jar in the centre symbolized the womb; a second smaller jar closed the first; it contained oil of *Lannea acida,* and represented the foetus. On top of it again was a still smaller jar containing perfume, and on the top of this last was a double cup.

All the eight organs were held in place by the outer walls and the inner partitions which symbolized the skeleton. The four uprights ending in the corners of the square roof were the arms and legs. Thus the granary was like a woman, lying on her back (representing the sun) with her arms and legs raised and supporting the roof (representing the sky). The two legs were on the north side, and the door at the sixth step marked the sexual parts.

The granary and all it contained was therefore a picture of the world-system of the new order, and the way in which this system worked was represented by the functioning of the internal organs. These organs absorbed symbolic nourishment which passed along the usual channels of the digestion and the circulation of the blood. From compartments 1 and 2 (stomach and gizzard) the symbolical food passed into compartment 6 (the intestines) and from there into all the others in the form of blood and lastly breath, ending in the liver and the gallbladder. The breath is a vapour, a form of water, which maintains and is indeed the principle of life.

As Ogotemmeli spoke, the deserted granary seemed to come to life, and the setting sun lighting up the west beyond the I gorges heightened the illusion. The walls of the building became tinged with rose colour, and cast gleams of light on the sandstone surfaces and the straw of the dung-heap. On the roof a bunch of purple sorrel stood out like fire. The moment was near when all the western walls of Upper and Lower Ogol would be aflame. All the visible surface of the granary shared in this prodigal display of light, while in the dark interior the wonders of the past came to life again.

Ogotemmeli, his head bowed and his hands on the nape of his neck, was lost in the past history of the heavens. At last he arrived at the final stratum of symbols which showed the universe compressed within the walls of the primal granary, as a body filled with life and absorbing food.

"What is eaten," he said, "is the sunlight. What is excreted is the dark night. The breath of life is the clouds, and the blood is the rain that falls on the world."

—Marcel Griaule. *Conversations with Ogotemmeli.* Oxford: Oxford University Press, 1975, pp. 16–40.

MANDE

The Creation
Polar opposition is also stressed in this retold myth from the Mande-speaking peoples of Mali. God's first attempt to create a single seed ended in failure; thereafter he made everything balanced and twinned. The eight seeds and the two pairs of archetypical twins in the "egg of God" or "egg of the world" eventually contained all the forces that gave rise to people, the world, and nature. Evil resulted from disruptions of this carefully established balance: in prematurely separating himself from his twin, Pemba violated the sacred order and eventually committed incest by planting seeds in the womb of his mother, earth. Only after the other primordial male twin, Faro, atoned for this infraction was fertility restored to the world.

The activities of the ancestors and Faro's journey imply a common origin for many of the peoples of the region. On the one hand, the fact that the religious and social models that they established are still effective among these groups may confirm this. On the other hand, it may reflect political control later won by the

Mande over their neighbors. In either case, the myth validates many of their practices and reveals a system of correspondences between the natural, social, and personal planes that render all aspects of life sacred.

G OD, *Mangala,* first created the *balaza (Acacia albida)* seed, which was, however, a failure. So he abandoned it in order to create twin varieties of eleusine seed, *fani berere* and *fani ba;* thus, as the Keita say, he "made the egg of the world in two twin parts which were to procreate." God then created six more seeds and associated with this group of eight seeds the four elements and the "cardinal points" in order to mark out the organization of the world and its expansion. Thus there was: in the west *(klebi): fani berere* and *fani ba;* in the east *(koro): sano* and *keninge; in the north (Kanaga): so* and *kende;* in the south *(worodugu): kabaro* and *malo.* Finally the whole was enfolded in a hibiscus seed.

The seeds are thus conceived as twins of opposite sex in the "egg of God," which is also called "egg of the world" or "placenta of the world." They are often represented in drawings as an open flower with four petals which are also sometimes called the four "clavicles" of God.

In the same egg, according to the myth, there were in addition two pairs of twins, each consisting of one male and one female, archetypes of the future men. One of the males, Pemba, desiring to dominate the creation, emerged prematurely, before gestation was complete, tearing away a piece of his placenta as he did so. He came down through empty space; the piece of placenta became the earth but it was dry and barren and he could do nothing with it. Seeing this, he went back to heaven and tried to resume his place in the placenta and find his twin. In this he could not succeed, for God had changed the remaining part of his placenta into the sun. So Pemba then stole from one of God's clavicles the eight male seeds which he carried down in a calabash flask *(bara).*

He sowed these seeds in the piece of placenta which had become the earth. In this first field, which the Keita locate near Bounan (a village not far from Lake Debo), only the *fani berere*—one of the eleusine seeds—germinated in the blood of the placenta; the other seeds died for want of water. Because of Pemba's theft and his incestuous act (for Pemba had put the seed in his own placenta, that is, in his mother's womb) the earth became impure and the eleusine seed turned red as it it is today.

The other male twin, Faro, assumed, while in heaven, the form of twin *mannogo* fishes, which are represented in the Niger River today by the *mannogo ble* and the *mannogo fi.* The first represented his strength and his life, the second his body. In order to atone for Pemba's sin and purify the earth, Faro was sacrificed in heaven and his body was cut into sixty pieces which were scattered throughout space. They fell on the earth where they became trees, symbols of vegetal resurrection. God then brought Faro back to life in heaven and, giving him human shape, sent him down to earth on an ark made of his celestial placenta.

The ark came to rest on the mountain called Kouroula, in the area called *kele koroni* "ancient space," which lies between Kri and Kri Koro. This area was then given the name of Mande which the inhabitants translate as "son of the person" *(ma)* or more explicitly "son of the *mannogo*," the "person" being Faro whose first bodily form was that of a silurian fish. The place is also called "the mountain that encircles the world"; it is said that "Faro came out of this mountain, he took his life from the cloudy sky of Mande."

Where the ark came to rest near Kri there was a cave called *kaba koro,* or more commonly *ka*. Near this cave appeared a hollow in the earth which became the first pool, *ko koro* or *ko ba*. On the ark stood Faro, brought back to life, and also the eight original ancestors of men, created from Faro's placenta, that is to say four pairs of male and female twins called *mogo si segi*. The males of these twins were called: Kanisimbo ("from Ka's womb"), Kani yogo simbo ("from the same Ka's womb"), Simboumba Tangnagati ("the big remaining part of the womb which took command"), Nounou (from *nono,* milk). In the ark were also all the animals and plants that were going to multiply on earth.

The first human beings, like Faro himself, had a common vital force *(nyama)* and complementary spiritual forces *ni* and *dya,* each of which had both a male and a female form. Also, in their clavicles were deposited the symbols of the eight seeds created by God. Emerging from the ark they watched, for the first time, the rising of the sun.

The bardic ancestor, Sourakata, then came down from heaven at Kri Koro holding in his hands the skull of the sacrificed Faro. This skull became the first drum. He played on it only once to ask, in vain, for rain. Ke then put the drum in a cave. The ancestral smith then came down to Kri, while Mousso Koroni Koundye, Pemba's female twin, came down "on the wind" at Bounan.

When he saw the prevailing drought the smith struck a rock with his hammer to ask for rain, and water poured down from heaven, filling the hollow *ko koro* with purifying and fertilizing water. Two fishes then came down: *mannogo ble* and *mannogo fi,* manifestations of Faro. *Mannogo fi* is the archetype of man who was to be Faro's "son"; *mannogo ble* represents Faro himself, and on earth and in the water was to be the intermediary between him and mankind. This is why, for the Mande, this fish has become the basic taboo of a great number of people including the Keita.

REVELATION OF THE WORD AND BUILDING OF THE FIRST SANCTUARY Simboumba Tangnagati, one of the male twins, who had entered the pool with the first fall of rain, was then given by Faro the first thirty words and the eight female seeds from God's clavicle. Now, coming out of the water, Simboumba said: "*nko* (I speak)." In order to plant out the seeds he had received, Simboumba Tangnagati left the area of the pool and, that very day at sunset, built a sanctuary on a hill near Kri Koro. This building, called *lu daga blo* (hall of the upper house), stood on the top of a hill; it was regarded as the "egg of the world" and was consecrated to the *mannago ble*. It was made of black earth from the original pool, and its roof was made of a bamboo from the same place which represented Faro's hair. The roof had six edges symbolizing the *mannago ble*'s beard, Faro's speech, and the spilling of water; inside the building Simboumba Tangnagati drew the sign of the *mannogo ble*.

From the door of the sanctuary Simboumba Tangnagati, who thenceforward was to be responsible for the seeds, the rain, and speech, gave men the first thirty words while the seeds were still in the sanctuary. He talked the whole night, ceasing only when he saw the sun and Sirius rising at the same time. This sun was what remained of Pemba's placenta, while Sirius, *sigi dolo*, was the image of Faro's placenta. During this night-long speech, the bard who was present carried a staff, symbol of Faro's resurrection, made of *nogonogo* wood that had grown in the first pool.

The following night the *mannogo ble*, coming out of the Kri pool where he had been hidden among the rice, entered the sanctuary. The next day Simboumba Tangnagati put the seeds on the *mannogo ble*'s head, at a place where there were signs. Then the rain started to pour down on the hill where the *blo* was. The *mannogo ble* then left the sanctuary and went back to the Kri pool. Then the rain, bringing down earth from the hill, spread it out near the pool.

The first human ancestor, Kanisimbo, now sowed in this earth some of the seeds which Simboumba Tangnagati had put in the *blo*. This first field was called *kanisimbo foro*. It was rectangular like the ark and orientated in an east-west direction. Kanisimbo marked off its limits with the rope made of *nogonogo* fibers from which the ark had been suspended during its descent to earth. The field was eighty "cubits" long and sixty "cubits" wide. The "cubits" marked out the work and also represented the length of a man's forearm. Kanisimbo then gave the rope to Simboumba, who used it to tie down the roof of the sanctuary.

In the middle of the field Kanisimbo built a shrine made of three upright stones supporting a fourth. On the east he sowed the *fani berere*, on the west, the *fani ba*, on the north, the small millet *sano*, on the south, rice, *malo*, and in the center, maize, *kaba*. Finally hibiscus seeds, *da*, were sown all around the field.

After the first storm that followed upon the building of the *blo*, two stars began to circle around Sirius *(sigi dolo)*. They represented the two descents of the seeds: the one, called *no dolo*, symbolized Pemba's male seeds, the second, called *dyi dolo*, Faro's female seeds.

THE BUILDING OF THE SECOND SANCTUARY During this period Mousso Koroni Koundye, Pemba's female twin, left Kri and fled to Bounan. There she grew the impure *fani berere* seeds and she and Pemba ate them together. Faro went after her and made her return to Kri, whither she carried back part of the crop. Between Bounan and Kri, however, she dropped seeds all along her way, "sowing at night and cultivating by day." The wild animals sent by Faro tried with varying success to stop her.

Back in Kri, Mousso Koroni, in her fear, hid the *fani berere* brought from Bounan for seven years. Then, on a moonless night *(kalo laba)*, she sowed it "when the sun was in the south." She kept trying "to catch the sun," which was made of the rest of her and Pemba's placenta. By sowing when the sun was in the south, at the time when it looked as if it were going to "fall," she thought "it would dry her field if Faro should attempt to flood it." But the moon when it rose revealed what she had done. The pool *kokoro* overflowed, poured down the hill, and flooded her field, and the *mannogo ble* swallowed the seeds. It sowed part of them on the same spot and turned the rest into fishes' roe.

Men then came down to reap the field which Mousso Koroni had sown and thus, by recovering the seeds, witnessed to Faro's victory. They first built a second Mande *blo* which was an exact copy of the original one. In order to find the right place for it, Simboumba Tangnagati, the third ancestor, took his own seeds in a flask *(bara)* and followed the path the water had made when it flowed out of the pool. The *mannogo ble* showed the way. The place where the water had stopped in Mousso Koroni's field lay between Kaba and Kela and this spot became Faro's first seat *(faro tyn)*. The second *blo* was built near it, at sunset, after rain had fallen. It was dedicated to the *mannogo fi.*

Inside this second sanctuary, also made of earth from the pool, Simboumba Tangnagati drew the sign of the *mannogo ble,* including all the marks he had on his head, and then the sign of the *mannogo fi.* The bamboo roof had six edges representing the beard of the *mannogo fi.*

The two stars which circled around *sigi dolo*—*no dolo* and *dyi dolo*—were symbolized by two balls of earth from the pool, dried and hung from the roof of the sanctuary; other signs represented Sirius, the sun, the moon, and the move from the first to the second sanctuary; each word was associated with a star and also had its sign.

A well *(kolo)* was dug near the sanctuary for Faro and for the *mannogo* which is thought to enter it whenever the roof is being repaired. To draw water from the well and pour it on the sown fields is called "to take the *mannogo* and put it in the field." Around the second sanctuary a field of *fani berere* was made to replace the one made by Mousso Koroni. Afterward it was changed into a maize field, maize *(kaba)* being a basic seed for the Keita. While his brothers went back to the hill, Simboumba Tangnagati, the third ancestor, settled down at the foot of the hill and took command "because of the word."

The first village was laid out at the four cardinal points around the central field which contained the sanctuary and was called Kaba, thus recalling that its center was a maize field, *kaba.* Kaba is also the name of the place where Faro came down to earth in the Kouroula mountains and in other contexts means "cloudy sky."

FARO'S JOURNEY   Faro now traveled east in order to flood all the places where Mousso Koroni had dropped eleusine seeds and he finally reached Bounan and flooded Pemba's field. He was able to recover all the seeds that had been stolen, for he sent the *mannogo ble* everywhere to eat the seeds and it was followed by all the other fishes.

Thus the River Niger, which has been formed from this series of floods, represents Faro's body; and it is said that "Faro lies face downward in the Niger." His head is Lake Debo, his right arm is the Bani, while his body is the Niger itself. The Bani and Niger are also called *bala,* which is male, and *bogolo,* which is female; the river from its source to Sama is Faro's single leg and Sama itself is his genitals. But on the opposite bank Faro, who was androgynous (or a twin), took the opposite sex; thus between Tamani and Sama, from being male on the right bank he became female on the left bank. All along the river a series of *faro tyn* marks the places where he halted: the place where he drowned Mousso Koroni's seeds that the *mannogo ble* had eaten; the place where he left his seeds in the shape of silurian fish for the future birth of men. For Faro is said to be unique and ubiquitous, and procreative.

So, above Koulikoro, Faro himself is responsible for the course of the river; below Koulikoro, one of his descendants is the guardian of each place marked out by the ten *faro tyn.* According to the Keita, as we shall see, the following places are connected with and participate in the myth and ritual of Faro: twenty-two main *faro tyn* between Kaba and Akka connected directly with Faro: these are supposed to represent the twenty-two parts of his body; twenty-two from Koulikoro to Mopti, which are connected with the second generation, i.e., Faro's children; twenty-two from Mopti to Akka connected with the third generation, i.e., Faro's grandchildren. The fourth generation is associated with pools, wells, and streams.

These four generations are also associated with the four ancestors who came down on the ark. The first generation settled in all the places where Mousso Koroni had sown her seeds; the second settled where the *mannogo* "dug in order to stop Mousso Koroni from sowing more seeds"; the third lived in the places where the maize *(kaba)* was sown to mark "the extension of Mande as far as Akka."

With each of these places on the river is connected a wild animal who is believed either to have prevented Mousso Koroni's sowing or to have protected the ritual field of Faro; later on those animals became the totemic taboos *(tne* or *tana)* of the various lineages of Mande.

Each of the *faro tyn* has a special name, connected with the spreading of water and with Faro's expansion on earth: at Kaba, *senebo,* "coming out of cultivation," meaning the fields of *fani berere* taken back from Mousso Koroni in which the seeds from the Kouroula hills were sown; at Kourouba, *kandyi,* "Ka water," meaning the water and rain that Faro brought down onto the earth; at Dangassa, *senebo,* "coming out of cultivation," meaning the field of *fani ba,* that one of the two eleusine seeds which was kept pure and was never eaten by Pemba; this seed also came from the hills. Thus the cultivation of the two original eleusine seeds is separately represented by the first three *faro tyn.* Pemba was the first who sowed, cultivated, and ate the *fani berere;* later, after Faro's arrival, men did the same with *fani ba.* The *kandyi faro tyn,* which is situated between the first and the third, is a sign of the coming of water and of Faro's activities, for "men now grow both sorts of eleusine thanks to Faro's water."

At Samayana, above Bamako, the *faro tyn* is called *sirakuru,* "the ark road." Here Faro changed his direction; in heaven he walked straight but on earth he walked in a sinuous way like a watercourse, and this purifies and regenerates the soil; at Bamako it is called *sutadunu*, "the corpse drum": the whirling water roars and its noise represents the rhythm of Faro's drum, *faro dundun*, which is played for weddings and funerals. The roaring of the water refers to Faro's revelation to men of the second word which happened farther along the river; at Kayo Faro dug a deep hole in the rocks, thus showing his strength; at Koulikoro the *faro tyn* is situated near a sharp rock which juts into the river. Faro placed his first child there to guard the way while he changed to the other bank and became a female; at Mignon, which means "patient," Faro rested after he had dug the hole. He made the river "broader like a wide road." Faro's vital force *(nyama)* is in Nyamina; at Tamani, "soul of the drum," he gave men the second word, which was the symbol of fecundity for it multiplies like birth; at Sama, which means "the delegate," he sent a "delegate of the word."

At Dyafarable, which means "to part the *dya*," Faro's *dya* separated from his body and his *ni* to take its place in the River Dyaka. All human *dya* dwell there along with his. The *faro tyn* is called *gangare*, "horseman," and Faro may be seen on it in the form of a white horse. Faro at last reached Bounan where he vanquished Pemba and ordered the *mannogo ble* to eat the seeds from his field. Then, "spreading the river like a mat *(debe)*," which gave its name to Lake Debo, Faro and the *mannogo ble* stopped in Akka. Akka symbolizes "Faro's clavicles"; the word comes from *hake* "limit" and also signifies the end of Faro's travels.

It is said also that "the place where Faro's ark stopped is situated between Akka and Baka," for the distance between these places represents the length of the ark that came "with the river" from Kaba.

At the end of Lake Debo stand three hills, Gourao, Mamari, and Gambe; they represent, on the one hand, the three main seeds: *fani berere, fani ba,* and *kaba,* and, on the other hand, the three ancestors who stayed in Kaba and the Kri hills that symbolize them in Mande.

According to the Keita, the Bozo are the descendants of the first men who followed Faro along the river and occupied the banks. They are Faro's *dya*. They are said to have been the first to grow and harvest the *fani ba* sown by Faro and the *mannogo ble* in the field taken back from Pemba.

R EVELATION OF THE SECOND WORD   The second word, revealed by Faro to Simboumba Tangnagati, was handed down by him to mankind after Faro's victory and the extending of his power on earth. This revelation occurred at the place on the river which represents his genitals. Faro being essentially procreative, this place is linked with his seed and with the birth of mankind.

The four male ancestors who descended in the ark married by exchanging their twins two by two. In order to transmit the word, Simboumba Tangnagati decided to sacrifice in the sanctuary on the hill *(lu daga blo)* the first twins of mixed sex born of these marriages. He asked the bard to make an arm-drum *(tana)* with the skin of the twins. The tree *gwele,* from which he carved the drum, grew on the hill and symbolized Faro's only leg. Making a double drum of it meant dividing this single member into two legs like those of men, and also re-called Faro's journey on earth with the water. *Tama,* the name of the drum, comes from *ta* (to go away) and refers to this journey. This is also why the bard, since the word was revealed, has, as the Mande say, to go on walking till he reaches Akka, "to follow Faro and testify to the distance he travelled." The two drum skins gave complementary male and female sounds, and the sacrifice was made to ask Faro for the birth of twins in every lineage.

To go from Kaba to Tamani, where the sacrifice was offered, men were led by the *mannogo ble* which entered the sanctuary with the rising water. Thus he showed the way to men, going before them. They went east, along the right bank of the river; by day they walked in the direction of the rising sun, by night, toward Sirius, which, at that time, rose in the east as soon as the sun had set. For the revelation of the word at Tamani, Simboumba Tangnagati carried the seeds from the sanctuary on the hill in order that he might "speak upon them." These seeds were to multiply, as words multiply, in the fertile area of Faro's genitalia. At each *faro tyn* which marked the activities of Faro and the part he played in providing seeds and procreation, twins were sacrificed in order that twin births might be frequent.

When they saw, as on the first occasion by the entrance to the shrine, Sirius rising along with the sun, the first men halted at the place of Faro's fecundity. Then, joined by Mousso Koroni Koundye, they crossed the river on stepping-stones; the bard remained alone on the right bank. Simboumba Tangnagati played on wrought-iron bells *(simbo),* image of Faro's mouth, and said fifty words. These the bard Sourakata repeated on the opposite bank of the river, while he played the drum *tama* on both the male and female sides of the instrument. The fifty words proclaimed the propagation of human beings throughout the earth and the common origin of all lineages from Mande; it is said of them: "black people belong to the millet race and they should all possess the same knowledge."

The place where the bard stood gave its name to the village of Tamani. On the opposite bank the place where the men stood was called Do, "secret"; there is only a small bare hill there and nothing to recall the men's halt because it was to be kept secret from Mousso Koroni, who was still seeking to reach Risius and the sun: "Mousso Koroni must never be able to find the spot."

The men, followed by Mousso Koroni, then went back to Kri along the left bank; Nounou alone went on beyond Kri and along the same bank to Sama, where he crossed the river led by the *mannogo ble,* and stopped at the site of the present Ségou Koro.

Meanwhile the bard went his way along the right bank of the river, walking east to Akka, the *mannogo ble* going before him to show the way. At Akka the bard gave his drum *tama* to the Bozo who were the first to arrive there.

Now the bard had left at Ka the head of Faro which he had been given in heaven after the sacrifice, but he had brought the drum to Akka. So Akka is the head of Faro risen from the dead. The two drum skins recall the two geographical areas, Kaba and Akka, and the narrow central part of the drum is the river itself and hence Faro's journey. The thirty ropes with which it is tied represent the first thirty words and also the thirty lineages. On his way back the bard came to Ka bringing the *simbo* which looks like "the head of Faro alive." It was put aside in the same cave, together with the skull that had become the first drum.

Sourakata's journey, symbol of the continuous traveling of genealogists today, and the revelation of the word of which they have, from that time, been the heralds, gave one of its present names to the river: namely *dyali ba,* "the great bard." The name refers both to Faro, owner of the word, and and to the first bard who was Faro's "spokesman." While he was staying in Akka, the bard saw the ark and, on his return home, he carved a harp of *dogora* or *dura* wood and shaped it like an ark; the four strings of the harp symbolized the four cardinal points.

N OUNOU'S PART Nounou, the fourth human ancestor, who was a hunter and a medicine man, was led by a *mannogo ble* across the river at Sama and followed it "in order to possess both banks and see if the bard's speech could be extended." He carried with him his three medicine shrines. Suddenly he came to a hill called *kulubana* which blocked the road and prevented him from occupying the whole region. This was at a place now called Segou Koro where he settled down.

Mousso Koroni, still trying to find the seeds she had lost and to fight Faro, joined Nounou, "leaving traces wherever she went." Following her treacherous advice, he tried to cross the hill and, to this end, caused the *mannogo ble* to be caught in order that he might sacrifice it and obtain his own *sano* field, with eight plots, on the hill at Segou Koro. Nounon died on account of this; for he had committed sacrilege by killing the *mannogo ble.* He was buried in his house in Segou Sorokimo.

The antelope, *dage,* which Faro had sent to watch the shrines, carried Nounou's vital force in its horns and ran from Segou Koro to Mande, along with Nounou's souls which had come back to life. Using the shrines and the trees that grew in the field and had become the basic medicines, Nounou changed himself into a snake and hid in the Ka cave on the Kouroula hills in Mande. The *dage* and the *mannogo* became taboo for his descendants, who were called Kouloubali (or Koulibali), a name which, according to popular etymology, recalls the name of the hill.

Mousso Koroni, left alone, went wandering about, begging and "leaving traces in all the fields she tried to cultivate." Starving and miserable "she at last went east and was never seen again."

The three ancestors who stayed in Mande, when the time came for them to die, disappeared under the wooden shrine built in the initial field and also became snakes *(mina).* Today in the Ka cave in Kri live four mythical snakes representing the four ancestors.

From the descendants of the ancestors of the ark human beings multiplied. There were first the five mythical generations from whose supposed marriages a complex system of matrimonial alliances derives. The fifth of these gen-

erations consisted of forty-four descendants, among whom twenty-two males symbolically represented the twenty-two *faro tyn;* they are said to be the several ancestors of all the lineages who regard themselves as "coming from Mande."
—Germaine Dieterlen. "The Mande Creation Myth." *Africa,* 1957, *17* (2), 124–138. London: Oxford University Press.

KRACHI

The Separation of God from Man

This fragment of a tale from the Krachi people of Togo envisages a primordial unity between sky and earth, god and man. Because of people's disrespect, the god Wulbari eventually retreated from earth and rose to the sky "where one can admire him but not reach him."

IN THE BEGINNING of days Wulbari and man lived close together and Wulbari lay on top of Mother Earth, Asase Ya. Thus it happened that, as there was so little space to move about in, man annoyed the divinity, who in disgust went away and rose up to the present place where one can admire him but not reach him.

He was annoyed for a number of reasons. An old woman, while making her *fufu* outside her hut, kept on knocking Wulbari with her pestle. This hurt him and, as she persisted, he was forced to go higher out of her reach. Besides, the smoke of the cooking fires got into his eyes so that he had to go farther way. According to others, however, Wulbari, being so close to men, made a convenient sort of towel, and the people used to wipe their dirty fingers on him. This naturally annoyed him. Yet this was not so bad a grievance as that which caused We, the Wulbari of the Kassena people, to remove himself out of the reach of man. He did so because an old woman, anxious to make a good soup, used to cut off a bit of him at each mealtime, and We, being pained at this treatment, went higher.

—Raul Radin (ed.). *African Folktales.* Princeton, N.J.: Princeton University Press, Bollingen Paperback, 1970, p. 28 —Retold from material in A. W. Cardinall. *Tales Told in Togolan.* London: 1931.

FON

The Great Gods

Descendants of the Adja people, the earliest inhabitants of Dahomey who had established a kingdom on the coast by the twelfth century A.D., the Fon achieved supremacy by the sixteenth century. They were conquered in 1738 by the Yoruba, to whom they paid annual tribute for some two hundred years until King Gezo rebelled and won independence. The French negotiated a trade pact with the king in 1851, but later, finding Gezo's successors more difficult to deal with, intervened militarily and annexed the region. Dahomey was incorporated into French West Africa in 1904 and gained independence in 1960.

Although the Fon usually speak of Mawu (moon, female) and Lisa (sun, male) as supreme, this myth tells of a greater God, the hermaphroditic Nana-Buluku who bore them and then retired from the world. Only one cult center for Nanu-Buluku exists; located in Dune, a small village northwest of Abomey, it receives half of certain offerings made to Mawu and Lisa in cult houses all over the country—tribute from worshippers of the divine children to their holy parent.

THE WORLD was created by one god, who is at the same time both male and female. This Creator is neither Mawu nor Liza, but is named Nana-Buluku. In time, Nana-Buluku gave birth to twins, who were named Mawu and Lisa, and to whom eventually dominion over the realm thus created was ceded. To Mawu, the woman, was given command of the night; to Lisa, the man, command of the day. Mawu, therefore, is the moon and inhabits the west, while Lisa, who is the sun, inhabits the east. At the time their respective domains were assigned to them, no children had as yet been born to this pair, though at night the man was in the habit of giving a "rendezvous" to the woman, and eventually she bore him offspring. This is why, when there is an eclipse of the moon, it is said the celestial couple are engaged in love-making; when there is an eclipse of the sun, Mawu is believed to be having intercourse with Lisa.

—Melville J. Herskovits. *Dahomey.* Vol. 2. New York: J.J. Augustin, 1958, p. 101.

NEAR EASTERN MYTHS

ANCIENT EGYPTIAN MYTHS

Theology from Memphis
Around the beginning of the historical period in Egypt (c. 3000 B.C.), the Pharoah Menes united Upper and Lower Egypt and built a new capitol at Memphis. Older cities, like Heliopolis, were close by and still important politically and religiously as cult centers. It was therefore the task of the Memphite theologians to demonstrate the superiority and priority of their new cult. This myth from the First Dynasty attempts to do that by celebrating Ptah, a local Memphite deity and hitherto god only of destiny, as the supreme creator god. Atum, the god of Heliopolis and the old creator god, is reduced in power and envisioned as the child and functionary of Ptah.

The myth describes generative creation in verbal or mental terms: whereas the semiandrogynous Atum had created the world through masturbation (his fingers being the directing agent and his semen forming the raw material of creation), Ptah accomplishes the same end verbally (his heart serving as the directing agent and his mouth forming the raw material of words). After creating all the gods—most importantly the Ennead of nine main deities of the Heliopolitan pantheon—Ptah made ka-spirits (souls) and thus laid the foundation for an ethical order. In addition, he established the religious order by determining the form and functions of the gods, their shrines and appropriate offerings.

At the end of the myth, an attempt is made to assimilate the increasingly popular deity Osiris into the Memphite cult by claiming that he had drowned and was buried in the city.

The ritual use of the myth is evinced not only by its initial praise of Horus (an aspect of Ptah personified by the Pharoah in cult activities), but also by stage directions included for the ritual performers: "Words spoken [by] Geb [to] Seth."

(1) LIVE THE HORUS: Who Prospers the Two Lands; the Two Goddesses: Who Prospers the Two Lands, the Horus of Gold: Who Prospers the Two Lands; the King of Upper and Lower Egypt: Nefer-ka-Re, the Son of

Re: Sha-[ba-ka], beloved of Ptah-South-of-His-Wall, living like Re forever. His majesty copied this text anew in the House of his father Ptah-South-of-His-Wall. Now his majesty had found (it) as (something) which the ancestors had made but which was worm-eaten. It was unknown from beginning to end. Then [his majesty] copied [it] anew, (so that) it is better than its state formerly, in order that his name might endure and his memorial be made to last in the House of his father Ptah-South-of-His-Wall in the course of eternity, through that which the Son of Re: [Sha-ba-ka] did for his father Ptah-tenen, so that he might be given life forever. . . .

(7) The Ennead gathered themselves to him, and he judged Horus and Seth. He prevented them from quarreling (further), and he made Seth the King of Upper Egypt in the land of Upper Egypt, at the place where he was (born), *Su.* Then Geb made Horus the King of Lower Egypt in the land of Lower Egypt, at the place where his father [i.e., Osiris] was drowned, Pezshet-Tawi. Thus Horus stood in (one) place, and Seth stood in (another) place, and they were reconciled about the Two Lands. . . .

(10) Words spoken (by) Geb (to) Seth: "Go to the place in which thou wert born." Seth—Upper Egypt.

Words spoken (by) Geb (to) Horus: "Go to the place in which thy father was drowned." Horus—Lower Egypt.

Words spoken (by) Geb (to) Horus and Seth: "I have judged you." Lower and Upper Egypt.

(But then it became) ill in the heart of Geb that the portion of Horus was (only) equal to the portion of Seth. So Geb gave his (entire) inheritance to Horus, that is, the son of his son, his first-born. . . . (Thus) Horus stood over the (entire) land. Thus this land was united, proclaimed with the great name: "Ta-tenen [another name for Ptah] South-of-His-Wall, the Lord of Eternity." The two Great Sorceresses grew upon his head. So it was that Horus appeared as King of Upper and Lower Egypt, who united the Two Lands in Wall Nome, in the place in which the Two Lands are united.

(15c) It happened that reed and papyrus were set at the great double door of the House of Ptah. That means Horus and Seth, who were reconciled and united, so that they associated and their quarreling ceased in the place which they *reached*, being joined in the House of Ptah' "the Balance of the Two Lands," in which Upper and Lower Egypt have been weighed. . . .

(48) The gods who came into being as Ptah:—

Ptah who is upon the Great Throne . . . ;

Ptah-Nun, the father who [begot] Atum;

Ptah-Naunet, the mother who bore Atum;

Ptah the Great, that is, the heart and tongue of the Ennead;

[Ptah] . . . who gave birth to the gods; . . .

(53) There came into being as the heart and there came into being as the tongue (something) in the form of Atum. The mighty Great One is Ptah, who transmitted [*life* to all gods], as well as (to) their *ka*'s, through this heart, by

which Horus became Ptah, and through this tongue, by which Thoth became Ptah.

(Thus) it happened that the heart and tongue gained control over [every] (other) member of the body, by teaching that he [i.e., Ptah] is in every body and in every mouth of all gods, all men, [all] cattle, all creeping things, and (everything) that lives, by thinking and commanding everything that he wishes.

(55) His Ennead is before him in (the form of) teeth and lips. That is (the equivalent of) the semen and hands of Atum. Whereas the Ennead of Atum came into being by his semen and his fingers, the Ennead (of Ptah), however, is the teeth and lips in this mouth, which pronounced the name of everything, from which Shu and Tefnut came forth, and which was the fashioner of the Ennead.

The sight of the eyes, the hearing of the ears, and the smelling the air by the nose, they report to the heart. It is this which causes every completed (concept) to come forth, and it is the tongue which announces what the heart thinks.

Thus all the gods were formed and his Ennead was completed. Indeed, all the divine order really came into being through what the heart thought and the tongue commanded. Thus the *ka*-spirits were made and the *hemsut*-spirits were appointed, they who make all provisions and all nourishment, by this speech. (*Thus justice was given to*) him who does what is liked, (*and injustice to*) him who does what is disliked. Thus life was given to him who has peace and death was given to him who has sin. Thus were made all work and all crafts, the action of the arms, the movement of the legs, and the activity of every member, in conformance with (this) command which the heart thought, which came forth through the tongue, and which gives value to everything.

(Thus) it happened that it was said of Ptah: "He who made all and brought the gods into being." He is indeed Ta-tenen, who brought forth the gods, for everything came forth from him, nourishment and provisions, the offerings of the gods, and every good thing. Thus it was discovered and understood that his strength is greater than (that of the other) gods. And so Ptah was satisfied, after he had made everything, as well as all the divine order. He had formed the gods, he had made cities, he had founded nomes, he had put the gods in their shrines, (60) he had established their offerings, he had founded their shrines, he had made their bodies like that (with which) their hearts were satisfied. So the gods entered into their bodies of every (kind of) wood, of every (kind of) stone, of every (kind of) clay, or anything which might grow upon him, in which they had taken form. So all the gods, as well as their *ka*'s gathered themselves to him, content and associated with the Lord of the Two Lands.

The Great Seat, which *rejoices* the heart of the gods, which is in the House of Ptah, *the mistress of all life*, is the Granary of the God, through which the sustenance of the Two Lands is prepared, because of the fact that Osiris drowned in his water, while Isis and Nephthys watched. They saw him and they *were distressed at* him. Horus commanded Isis and Nephthys *repeatedly* that they lay hold on Osiris and prevent his drowning. (63) They turned (their) heads in time. So they brought him to land. He entered the mysterious portals in the glory of the lords of eternity, in the steps of him who shines forth on the horizon, on the ways of Re in the Great Seat. He joined with the court and associated with the gods of Ta-tenen Ptah, the lord of years.

Thus Osiris came to be in the land in the "House of the Sovereign" on the north side of this land, which he had reached. His son Horus appeared as King of Upper Egypt and appeared as King of Lower Egypt, in the embrace of his father Osiris, together with the gods who were in front of him and who were behind him.

—John A. Wilson (trans.). "Egyptian Mortuary Texts, Myths, and Tales." In James B. Pritchard (ed.). *Ancient Near Eastern Texts Relating to the Old Testament.* Princeton, N.J.: Princeton University Press, 1950, pp. 4–6.

History of the Creation of the Gods and of the World

One of the very early cult centers in Egypt, Heliopolis produced a cosmology that envisioned Atum ("the complete one") rising up out of the primeval watery chaos and producing the world. By the time of the Pyramid Texts (c. 2400 B.C.), Atum had become closely identified with the sun god Re (or Ra, as it is spelled in this translation), and his emergence out of the water was associated with the rising of the sun and the dispelling of chaotic darkness.

In this "Book of the knowing the evolutions of Re," Neb-er-tcher (Lord-to-the-Limit and one of the forms of the sun god) arises from the waters (Nu) in the aspect of Khepera ("he who comes into existence"). Neither heaven nor earth, nor plants nor animals, existed then, and Khepera was alone. Becoming conscious of his intent, the god "laid a foundation in Maa" (in what is straight and true; that is, according to a careful and just plan). And then, to create all things, in semiandrogynous fashion he masturbated (or "had union with his clenched hand and joined himself in an embrace with his shadow" [his feminine element]) and poured his seed into his mouth (which functions here as a sort of womb). Thus fertilized, he spit forth his son Shu (god of air and the principle of life) and his daughter Tefnut (goddess of moisture and the principle of world order). Speaking through his "father," Khepera notes that in "double henti periods" (technically, 120 years, but used figuratively here to mean a long time) one god had become three.

Atum (or Re or Khepera or Neb-er-tcher—the names all refer to the same god in this context) had only one eye at first, and this capacity to see and judge was depicted as somewhat independent of him. When the great god wept with joy on uniting himself with his two created parts, Shu and Tefnut, his eye raged to find that he had been supplanted by another. To placate it, Neb-er-tcher put it in his forehead and gave it power to rule over all creation.

A splurge of creativity ensued. Men and women had already been made from Neb-er-tcher's tears, and now he came forth in the forms of plants and animals. His offspring Shu and Tefnut (air and moisture) gave birth to Seb and Nut (earth and sky), and these in turn produced the four gods Osiris, Horus, Set (Seth), and Isis.

Shāt   *enti*   *rekh*   *kheperu*   *nu*   *Rā*

The Book   of   knowing   the evolutions   of   Rā,

sekher   *Āpep*   *tchețtu*   *Neb-er-tcher*   *tcheț-f*

[and] of over-throwing   Āpep.   The words of   Neb-er-tcher   [which] he spake

em-khet   *kheper-f*   *nuk*   *pu*   *kheper*

after   he had come into being.   I am   he who   came into being

em   *Kheperà*   *kheper-nà*   *kheper*   *kheperu*

in the form of Kheperà,   I was (or, became)   the creator   of what came into being,

kheper   *kheperu*   *neb*   *em-khet*   *kheper-à*   *āsht*

the creator   of what came into being   all;   after   my coming into being   many

kheperu   *em*   *per*   *em*   *re-à*   *àn*

[were] the things which came into being   coming forth   from   my mouth.   Not

kheper   *pet*   *àn*   *kheper*   *ta*   *àn*   *qemam*

existed heaven,   not   existed earth,   not   had been created

satat	*tchetfet*	*em*	*bet*	*pui*
the things of the earth, (i.e., plants)	and creeping things	in place		that ;

thes - ná	*ám - sen*	*em*	*Nu*
I raised up them	from out of		Nu (i.e., the primeval abyss of water)

em	*enen*	*án*	*qem-ná*	*bet*	*áḥá-ná*
from a state of inactivity.		Not	found I	a place	I could stand

ámi	*khut-ná*	*em*	*ábt-á*
wherein.	I worked a charm	upon (or, with)	my heart.

senti-ná	*em*	*Maā*	*ári-ná*	*áru*	*nebt*
I laid a foundation	in	Maā	[and] I made	attribute	every.

uā-k[uá]	*án*	*áshesh-ná*	*em Shu*	*án*
I was alone,	[for] not	had I spit	in the form of Shu,	not

tef-ná	*em Tefnut*	*án*	*kheper*	*ki*
had I emitted	Tefnut,*	not	existed	another

* I.e., I had not sent forth from my body the emanation which took the form of Shu, nor the moisture which took the form of Tefnut.

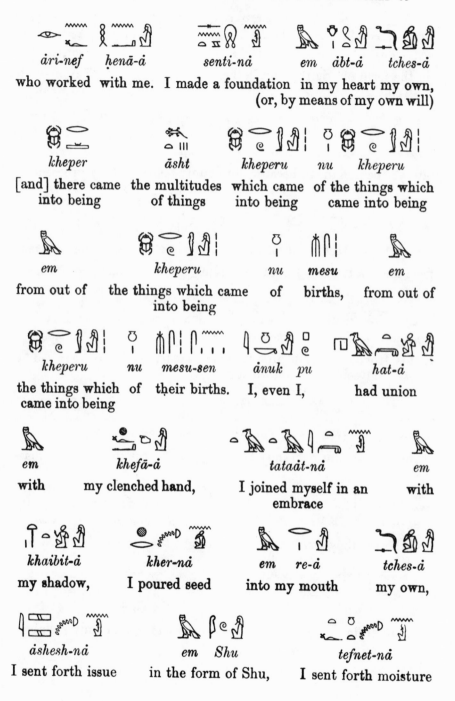

ảri-nef   *ḥenā-ả*   *senti-nả*   *em*   *ảbt-ả*   *tches-ả*

who worked with me.   I made a foundation   in my heart my own,
(or, by means of my own will)

kheper   *āsht*   *kheperu*   *nu*   *kheperu*

[and] there came   the multitudes   which came   of the things which
into being   of things   into being   came into being

em   *kheperu*   *nu*   *mesu*   *em*

from out of   the things which came   of   births,   from out of
into being

kheperu   *nu*   *mesu-sen*   *ảnuk*   *pu*   *ḥat-ả*

the things which   of   their births.   I, even I,   had union
came into being

em   *khefā-ả*   *tataảt-nả*   *em*

with   my clenched hand,   I joined myself in an   with
embrace

khaibit-ả   *kher-nả*   *em*   *re-ả*   *tches-ả*

my shadow,   I poured seed   into my mouth   my own,

ảshesh-nả   *em*   *Shu*   *tefnet-nả*

I sent forth issue   in the form of Shu,   I sent forth moisture *em*   *Ṭafnut*   *àn*   *àtef-à*   *Nu*   *satet-sen*

in the form of Saith my father Nu, "They make to
Tefnut.   be weak

maat-à   *em-sa-sen*   *tcher*   *ḥenḥenti*   *uau-sen*

my eye behind them, because for double *ḥenti* they proceeded
                                 periods

er-à   *em-khet*   *kheper-à*   *em*   *neter*   *uā*   *neter*   *khemt*

from me after I became from god one gods three,

pu   *er-à*   *kheper-nà*   *em*   *ta*   *pen*   *ḥāā*

that is from out of [and after] I came in earth this. Were raised up
      myself,   into being

àref   *Shu*   *Ṭàfnut*   *em*   *enenu*

therefore Shu [and] Tefnut in the inert watery mass

un-sen   *àmi - f*   *àn-sen*   *nà*   *maat-à*

wherein they were, brought they to me my eye

em   *khet-sen*   *em-khet*   *àref*   *sam-nà*   *āt-à*

in their train. After therefore I had united my members

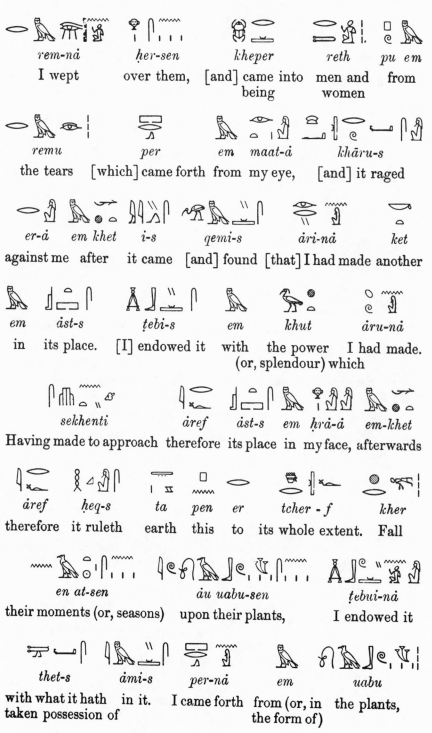

rem-ná   her-sen   kheper   reth   pu em

I wept   over them,   [and] came into   men and   from
being   women

remu   per   em   maat-á   kháru-s

the tears   [which] came forth from   my eye,   [and] it raged

er-á   em khet   i-s   qemi-s   ári-ná   ket

against me after   it came   [and] found [that] I had made another

em   ást-s   ṭebi-s   em   khut   áru-ná

in   its place.   [I] endowed it   with   the power   I had made.
(or, splendour) which

sekhenti   áref   ást-s   em   hrá-á   em-khet

Having made to approach therefore its place in my face, afterwards

áref   ḥeq-s   ta   pen   er   tcher - f   kher

therefore   it ruleth   earth   this   to   its whole extent.   Fall

en at-sen   áu uabu-sen   ṭebui-ná

their moments (or, seasons)   upon their plants,   I endowed it

thet-s   ámi-s   per-ná   em   uabu

with what it hath   in it.   I came forth from (or, in   the plants,
taken possession of   the form of)

tchetfet	nebt	kheper	nebt	ȧm-sen
creeping things	all,	[and] things which came into being	all	[are] in them.

mesu ȧn	Shu Tȧfnut	5.	henȧ	Nut	mesu ȧn
Give birth	Shu [and] Tefnut		[Seb] and	Nut.	Give birth

Seb Nut	Ȧsȧr	Her Khent-ȧn-maa	Set	Ȧst
Seb and Nut	to Osiris,	Horus-Khent-ȧn-maati,	Set,	Isis,

Nebt-het	em	khat	uā em-sa uā	ȧm-sen
Nephthys	from	the womb,	one after the other	of them,

mes-sen	ȧsht-sen	em	ta	pen
they give birth	[and] they multiply	in	earth	this.

—E. A. Wallis Budge. *The Gods of the Egyptians.* Vol. 1. New York: Dover, 1969, pp. 308–313. (Originally published 1904.)

Myth of Ptah from Memphis

Alexander the Great conquered Egypt in 332 B.C. and, on his death, one of his generals founded the Ptolemaic Dynasty. This badly preserved papyrus dates from that time, although it is most probably a reworking of a document from the Eighteenth Dynasty (1550–1350 B.C.).

Ptah was an important creator god whose cult originated in Memphis in late predynastic times. Here he is depicted as establishing the primeval hill (and thus the religious primacy) of Memphis and creating the eight gods of the Ogdoad: Nun and Naunet (water), Heh and Heket (eternity), Kek and Keket (darkness), and Niu and Nit (or Amun and Amaunet, air). Thus personified, these natural forces were portrayed with snake (female) and frog (male) faces, as if they were native to the original waters and muck. In this myth, it is asserted that the Ogdoad arose out of the primeval waters; in other versions, they are credited with creating it.

PTAH found himself in the Primaeval Waters. . .
   He sought a place for his foot.
[The god sought a place for his foot in] the Primaeval Waters
because he had grown old.[. . .
He found], that a place was in [this land
There] came [he] forth from the Primaeval Waters. . . .
He came to Heliopolis.
. . . .

. . . .
[There] said (he) "Land" as the name of Memphis,
. . . .
He desired (himself) [gods,
in order . . . (and) to cause light to exist
and there came into existence the Eight.]
He [gave] four of them a snake's head.
[four of them the head of a frog,
and he gave them names:
Nun and Naunet, Heh and] Hehet,
Kek [and Keket, Niu and Nit.
. . .]
. . .
[. .
So they came into being in the Waters]
"Amun and Amaunet," as he named them another time.
. . .
They were united with those (the Eight),
to complete ten names.

—W. Ericksen and S. Scott. *Fragmente memphitischer Theologie in demotische Schrift* (Pap. demot. Berlin 13603). Wiesbaden: Akademie der Wissenshaften und der Literatur in Mainz, 1954. — Quoted in S. G. F. Brandon. *Creation Legends of the Ancient Near East.* London: Hodder and Stoughton, 1963, pp. 54–55.

The Repulsing of the Dragon and the Creation

As Re, the solar disc, set beneath the horizon each evening and came up triumphantly on the other side of the world in the morning, it was thought that he had to cross the "skies below" during the course of the night. That journey was fraught with danger, because the dragon of darkness and chaos, Apophis, waited in the underworld to capture and destroy him. The repulsing of Apophis and the victorious rising of Re each day is the subject of this myth, which probably came from Thebes.

A vital part of temple ritual was the dramatic presentation of this divine conflict. In performing the ritual and embodying the myth, participants revealed to themselves and others the absolute dimension of their particular situation. As they acted in the temple, Re and Apophis fought in the underworld and, by analogy, as the grand forces of chaos were thwarted by the god in this process, smaller manifestations of disorder were being overcome by them.

This particular myth is an extract from a group of texts—"The Beginning of the Book of the Overthrowing of Apophis, the Enemy of Re and the Enemy of King Win-nofer—life, prosperity, health!—the justified, performed in the course of every day in the temple of Amon-Re, Lord of the Thrones of the Two Lands, Presiding over Karnak." It is special among the texts in its extensive description of the creation.

Although the papyrus dates from c. 310 B.C., its material is much older. Like myths from two thousand years before, it envisions the god alone in Nun (the primeval waters) creating other deities by masturbation. The importance of conceptualization is very explicit, however: "I made (in concept) every form when I was alone, before I had spat out what was Shu . . . and Tefnut . . . and before (any) other had come into being who could act with me." In addition, the myth is very clear about the identity of Re with Being: "When I came into being, being (itself) came into being, and all beings came into being after I came into being."

After Re had created Shu (air) and Tefnut (moisture), his father Nun (the watery chaos) raised them, and his eye (his judging, watching aspect) looked after them. Shu and Tefnut gave birth to Geb (earth) and Nut (sky), and these in turn produced Osiris, Horus Khenti-en-irti, Seth, Isis, Nephthys, and the multitude of divine emanations. All were created to assist in the establishment of being and in the repulsing of the chaotic dragon force, Apophis.

T HE BOOK *of knowing the creations of Re and of overthrowing Apophis. The words to be spoken.*

The All-Lord said, after he had come into being:

"I am he who came into being as Khepri. When I had come into being, being (itself) came into being, and all beings came into being after I came into being. Many were the beings which came forth from my mouth, before heaven came into being, before earth came into being, before the ground and creeping things had been created in this place. I put together (some) of them in Nun as weary ones, before I could find a place in which I might stand. It (seemed) advantageous to me in my heart; I planned with my face; and I made (in concept) every form when I was alone, before I had spat out what was Shu, before I had sputtered out what was Tefnut, and before (any) other had come into being who could act with me.

"I planned in my own heart, and there came into being a multitude of forms of beings, the forms of children and the forms of their children. I was the one who copulated with my fist, I masturbated with my hand. Then I spewed with my own mouth: I spat out what was Shu, and I sputtered out what was Tefnut. It was my father Nun who brought them up, and my Eye followed after them since the ages when they were distant from me.

"After I had come into being as the sole god, there were three gods beside me. I came into being in this land, whereas Shu and Tefnut rejoiced in Nun, in which they were. They brought to me my Eye with them. After I had joined together my members, I wept over them. That is how men came into being from the tears which came forth from my Eye. It was angry with me, after it returned and found that I had made another in its place, having replaced it with the Glorious Eye, which I had made. Then I advanced its place on my head, and after it had ruled this entire land, *its rage fell away to its roots*, for I had replaced what had been taken away from it. I came forth from the roots, and I created all creeping things and whatever lives among them. Then Shu and Tefnut brought forth Geb and Nut. Then Geb and Nut brought forth Osiris, Horus Khenti-en-irti, Seth, Isis, and Nephthys from the body, one of them after another; and they brought forth their multitudes in this land.

"When (these gods) rich in magic spoke, it was the (very) spirit of magic, for they were ordered to annihilate my enemies by the effective charms of their speech, and I sent out these who came into being from my body to overthrow that evil enemy.

"He is one fallen to the flame, Apophis with a knife on his head. He *cannot* see, and his name is no (more) in this land. I have commanded that *a curse* be cast upon him; I have consumed his bones; I have annihilated his soul in the course of every day; I have cut his vertebrae at his neck, severed with a knife which hacked up his flesh and pierced into his hide. . . . I have taken away his heart from its place, his seat, and his tomb. I have made him nonexistent: his name is not; his children are not; he is not and his family is not; he is not and his false-door is not; he is not and his heirs are not. His egg shall not last, nor shall his seed knit together—and vice versa. His soul, his corpse, his state of glory, his shadow, and his magic are not. His bones are not, and his skin is not. He is fallen and overthrown. . . .

". . . See thou, O Re! Hear thou, O Re! Behold, I have driven away thy enemy; I have wiped him out with my feet; I have spat upon him. Re is triumphant over thee—[*variant reading*: over his every fallen enemy]. . . . Drive thou away, consume thou, burn up every enemy of pharaoh—life, prosperity, health!—whether dead or living. . . .

"(Thus) thou shalt be in thy shrine, thou shalt journey in the evening-barque, thou shalt rest in the morning-barque, thou shalt cross thy two heavens in peace, thou shalt be powerful, thou shalt live, thou shalt be healthy, thou shalt make thy states of glory to endure, thou shalt drive away thy every enemy by thy command; for these have done evil against pharaoh—life, prosperity, health!—with all evil words: all men, all folk, all people, all humanity, and so on, the easterners of every desert, and every enemy of pharaoh—life, prosperity, health!—whether dead or living, whom I have driven away and annihilated. Thou dissolvest, fallen, Apophis. Re is triumphant over thee, Apophis—[*to be repeated four times*]. Pharaoh—life, prosperity, health!—is triumphant over his enemies—[*to be repeated four times*]."

This spell is to be recited over Apophis drawn on a new sheet of papyrus in green color and put inside a box on which his name is set, he being tied and bound and put on the fire every day, wiped out with thy left foot and spat upon four times in the course of every day. Thou shalt say as thou puttest him on the fire: "Re is triumphant over thee, O Apophis!"—*four times, and* "Horus is triumphant over his enemy!"—*four times, and* "Pharaoh—life, prosperity, health!—is triumphant over his enemies!"—*four times.*

Now when thou hast written these names of every male and female who is to be overthrown, of whom thy heart is afraid, that is, every enemy of Pharaoh—life, prosperity, health!—whether dead or alive, and the names of their fathers, the names of their mothers, and the names of (their) children, inside the box, they are to be made in wax and put on the fire following the name of Apophis and burned up at the time when Re shows himself. Thus thou shalt do the first time at the height of the sun and (again) when Re sets in the west, when the sunlight is fleeing from the mountain. These things are in truth more advantageous to thee than any (other) procedure. It will go well with him who does them on earth or in the necropolis.

—John A. Wilson (trans.). "Egyptian Mortuary Texts, Myths and Tales." In James B. Pritchard (ed.). *Ancient Near Eastern Texts Relating to the Old Testament*. Princeton, N.J.: Princeton University Press, 1950, pp. 6–7.

Incantation from the Myth of the

Primeval Lotus
One variant of the Hermopolitan cosmology describes the origin of Re from a primeval lotus that floated up out of the chaotic waters of Nun. In this liturgical text from the Ptolemeic Period (300–100 B.C.), Re's eye is that lotus, created by the eight great gods of the Ogdoad. (The Hermopolitan Ogdoad consisted of Nun and Naunet [water], Huh and Hauket [unendingness], Kuk and Kauket [darkness] and Amun and Amaunet [the unseen, or air]—the four basic creative elements.)

By opening his eyes, Re separated day from night and then produced the lesser gods from his mouth (by spitting? speaking?) and mankind from his eyes (from tears?). All things have their source in this lotus child, the sun-god Re.

RECEIVE this god (who is) at the heart of his piece of water, which spouted from your body (O ye Eight!). The great lotus, come forth from the Great Pool, which inaugurated the light, in the First Time. . . . You behold its light, you breathe its perfume, your nostrils are filled with it. It is your son, who produced himself as an infant, illuminating the land with his two eyes. . . . I bring to you the lotus, come from the marsh-land, the eye of Re in person in his marsh-land, he who summed in himself the Ancestors; who created the Former Gods and made all that exists in this land. . . . Opening his two eyes, he illumined the Two Lands, he separated night from day. The gods came forth from his mouth and mankind from his eyes. All things took their birth from him, the child (who shines) in the lotus and whose rays cause all beings to live.

—J. Yoyotte with J. Sauneron. "La naissance du monde selon l'Egypte ancienne." *Sources Orientales*, 1, Paris, 1959.—Quoted in S. G. F. Brandon. *Creation Legends of the Ancient Near East*. London: Hodder and Stoughton, 1963, p. 51.

SUMERIAN, BABYLONIAN, AND ASSYRIAN MYTHS

The Enuma Elish

The *Enuma Elish*—probably the most famous of the ancient Near Eastern texts—is the main source of information concerning Babylonian cosmology. The epic poem was not written primarily as an account of origins, however. Rather, its purposes were to praise Marduk, the main god of Babylon; to explain his rise from a great but local deity to the head of the whole pantheon; and to honor Babylon itself as the most preeminent city. The account of creation is used as a background to the real story of divine struggles and the establishment of Marduk's supremacy.

The Epic of Creation, as it is often called, derived its proper name from the first words of its opening line: *"Enuma elish la nabu shamanu. . . ."*—literally: "When above the heaven had not [yet] been named. . . ." It begins with Apsu (the ocean) and Tiamat (the primeval waters) lying inert together and eventually producing the divine natural forces: Lahmu and Lahamu (silt and slime), Anshar and Kishar (the horizons of sky and earth), Anu (heaven, the principle of authority), and Nudimmud (or Ea, waters of the earth, the principle of wisdom). As the offspring grew, they began to order the chaotic world and become rebellious. Apsu and Tiamat, resentful and angry, tried to reassert themselves. They called on Mummu (mist of the clouds, the principle of entropy) and together conspired to slay the young gods they had begotten. The plan failed, however, as Tiamat withdrew out of motherly concern and the wise Ea (earth water) slew Apsu (ocean) with his art and cunning (as presumably the waters were contained for purposes of irrigation in the first stage of Mesopotamian civilization) and locked Mummu (mist, entropy) away. Later, with his wife Damkina, Ea produced his magnificent son Marduk.

From there, the myth charts Marduk's dramatic rise to power. When Tiamat created monsters and married their chief Kingu in an effort to slay the young gods, Marduk was summoned to control her. In return for his efforts, he demanded and received recognition from the gods as the supreme one. Enthroned and feted, Marduk went forth, slew Tiamat, and then ordered the chaos by fixing the places of the stars, establishing the roles of the gods, separating heaven and earth, and, finally, setting up Babylon as his dwelling place. Almost as an afterthought, the rebellious Kingu was killed and from his blood, the wise Ea made mankind to do the bidding of the gods. The myth ends with elaborate praises of Marduk and a recitation of his fifty names.

Although the *Enuma Elish* was discovered in the ruins of King Ashurbanipal's (668–626 B.C.) library at Nineveh, it probably dates from a much earlier time when Babylon rose to political supremacy and its deity Marduk became a national god. These events took place during the First Babylonian Dynasty (2057–1758 B.C.) and most particularly in the reign of the powerful King Hammurabi (c. 1900 B.C.). But much of the material is even older than that, dating back to the Babylonians' predecessors in the region, the Sumerians. Many of the names in the *Enuma Elish* are Sumerian, and some, such as Apsu, Anu, and Enlil, are Sumerian gods. While a great deal of Babylonian mythology seems derivative of the Sumerians', it is impossible to be exact about the *Enuma Elish,* because no Sumerian prototype has been discovered.

The *Enuma Elish* was written for recitation and was enacted annually on the fourth day of the New Year's festival before a statue of Marduk. In ritually performing the myth, not only was the cosmos symbolically recreated but the order of the world was reconfirmed. The king knelt before the high priest of Marduk and submitted himself (and the state he represented) to humiliation before the god and his power. Rededicating himself in this fashion, the world was reestablished, the divine lease renewed, and the connection between the absolute and the relative, the eternal and the temporal restored.

I When there was no heaven,
no earth, no height, no depth, no name,
when Apsu was alone,
the sweet water, the first begetter; and Tiamat
the bitter water, and that
return to the womb, her Mummu,
when there were no gods—

When sweet and bitter
mingled together, no reed was plaited, no rushes
muddied the water,
the gods were nameless, natureless, futureless, then
from Apsu and Tiamat
in the waters gods were created, in the waters
silt precipitated,

Lahmu and Lahamu,
were named; they were not yet old,
not yet grown tall
when Anshar and Kishar overtook them both,
the lines of sky and earth
stretched where horizons meet to separate
cloud from silt.

Days on days, years
on years passed till Anu, the empty heaven,
heir and supplanter,
first-born of his father, in his own nature
begot Nudimmud-Ea,
intellect, wisdom, wider than heaven's horizon,
the strongest of all the kindred.

Discord broke out among the gods although they were brothers, warring and jarring in the belly of Tiamat, heaven shook, it reeled with the surge of the dance; Apsu could not silence the clamor, their behavior was bad, overbearing and proud.

But still Tiamat lay inert till Apsu, the father of gods, bellowed for that servant who clouds his judgement, his Mummu,

"Dear counsellor, come with me to Tiamat."

They have gone, and in front of Tiamat they sit down and talk together about the young gods, their first-born children; Apsu said,

"Their manners revolt me, day and night without remission we suffer. My will is to destroy them, all of their kind, we shall have peace at last and we will sleep again."

When Tiamat heard, she was stung, she writhed in lonely desolation, her heart worked in secret passion, Tiamat said,

"Why must we destroy the children that we made? If their ways are troublesome, let us wait a little while."

Then Mummu advised Apsu, and he spoke in malice,

"Father, destroy them in full rebellion, you will have quiet in the daytime and at night you will sleep."

When Apsu heard the die was cast against his children, his face flamed with the pleasure of evil; but Mummu he embraced, he hung on his neck, he sat him down on his knees and kissed him.

The decision was known to all their children; confusion seized them and after, a great silence, for they were confounded.

The god who is the source of wisdom, the bright intelligence that perceives and plans, Nudimmud-Ea, saw through it, he sounded the coil of chaos, and against it devised the artifice of the universe.

He spoke the word that charmed the waters, it fell upon Apsu, he lay asleep, the sweet waters slept, Apsu slept, Mummu was overcome, Apsu lay drowned, undone.

Then Ea ripped off his flaming glory coat and took his crown, he set on himself the aureole of the king. When Ea had bound Apsu he killed him, and Mummu, the dark counsellor, he led by the nose and locked away.

Ea had defeated his enemies and trodden them down. Now that his triumph was completed, in deep peace he rested, in his holy palace Ea slept. Over the abyss, the distance, he built his house and shrine and there magnificently he lived with his wife Damkina.

In that room, at the point of decision where what is to come is predetermined, he was conceived, the most sagacious, the one from the first most absolute in action.

In the deep abyss he was conceived, Marduk was made in the heart of the apsu, Marduk was created in the heart of the holy apsu. Ea begot him and Damkina bore him, father and mother; he sucked the paps of goddesses, from his nurses he was fed on the terribleness that filled him.

His body was beautiful; when he raised his eyes great lights flared; his stride was majestic; he was the leader from the first.

When Ea who begot him saw him he exulted, he was radiant, light-hearted, for he saw that he was perfect, and he multiplied his godhead, the one to be first and stand highest.

His limbs were immaculate, the making a fearful mystery beyond comprehension; with four eyes for limitless sight, and four ears hearing all; when his lips moved a tongue of fire burst out. Titanic limbs, standing so high he over-topped the tallest god; he was strong and he wore the glory of ten, and their lightnings played round him. "My son, my son, son of the sun, and heaven's sun!"

Then Anu begot winds and brought them from the four quarters, to be the van and to command the ranks; and he brought the tornado, a wild surf to worry Tiamat.

But now the other gods had no rest any more, tormented by storms, they conspired in their secret hearts and brought to Tiamat the matter of their plot. To their own mother they said, "When they killed Apsu you did not stir, you brought no help to him, your husband. Now Anu has called up from the four quarters this abomination of winds to rage in your guts, and we cannot rest for the pain; Remember Apsu in your heart, your husband, remember Mummu who was defeated; now you are all alone, and thrash around in desolation, and we have lost your love, our eyes ache and we long for sleep. Rouse up, our Mother! Pay them back and make them empty like the wind."

Tiamat approved it, she said, "I approve this advice: we will make mon-sters, and monsters and gods against gods will march into battle together."

Together they jostle the ranks to march with Tiamat, day and night furi-ously they plot, the growling roaring rout, ready for battle, while the Old Hag, the first mother, mothers a new brood.

She loosed the irresistible missile, she spawned enormous serpents with cutting fangs, chock-full of venom instead of blood, snarling dragons wearing their glory like gods. (Whoever sees this thing receives the shock of death, for when they heave those bodies up they never turn them back.)

> She made the Worm
> the Dragon
> the Female Monster
> the Great Lion
> the Mad Dog
> the Man Scorpion
> the Howling Storm
> Kulili
> Kusariqu

There was no pity in their weapons, they did not flinch from battle for her law was binding, irrevocable.

Eleven such monsters she made, but she took from among the gods the clumsy laborer Kingu one of the first generation to be her Captain, War-leader, Assembly-leader, ordering the supplies, leading the van to battle, Supreme Com-mander of the Wars.

All this she gave him when she raised their Company, she said, "Now it is in your hands, my spell will hold them bound, they must obey my will. You are supreme, my one husband, your word will hold the rebel horde."

She gave him the Tables of Fate and fastened them on to his breast,

"Now and for evermore your word is irrevocable, your judgements will last! They will quench the fire and the swinging mace will fail of its power."

When Kingu had received the authority, that belonged before to Anu, in their several natures they confirmed the brood of monsters.

II When her labor of creation was ended, against her children Tiamat began preparations of war. This was the evil she did to requite Apsu, this was the evil news that came to Ea.

When he had learned how matters lay he was stunned, he sat in black silence till rage had worked itself out; then he remembered the gods before him. He went to Anshar, his father's father, and told him how Tiamat plotted, "She loathes us, father, our mother Tiamat has raised up that Company, she rages in turbulence and all have joined her, all those gods whom you begot. Together they jostle the ranks to march with Tiamat, day and night furiously they plot, the growling roaring rout, ready for battle, while the Old Hag, the first mother, mothers a new brood. She has loosed the irresistible missile, spawned enormous serpents with cutting fangs, chock-full of venom instead of blood, snarling dragons wearing their glory like gods. (Whoever sees this thing receives the shock of death, for when they heave those bodies up they never turn them back.)

"She has made the Worm,
the Dragon
the Female Monster
the Great Lion
the Mad Dog
the Man Scorpion
the Howling Storm
Kulili
Kusariqu

"There is no pity in their weapons, they do not flinch from battle for her law is binding, irrevocable.

"Eleven such monsters she has made but she took from among the gods the clumsy laborers Kingu one of the first generation to be her Captain, War-leader, Assembly-leader, ordering the supplies, leading the van to battle, Supreme Commander of the Wars.

"All this she gave him when she raised their Company, she has said,

" 'Now it is in your hands, my spell will hold them bound, they must obey my will. You are supreme, my one husband, your word will hold the rebel horde.'

"She has given to him the Tables of Fate and fastened them on to his breast,

" 'Now and for evermore your word is irrevocable, your judgements will last! They will quench the fire and the swinging mace will fail of its power.'

"So Kingu has received the authority that belonged before to Anu, they have confirmed in their several natures the brood of monsters."

When Anshar heard how the Tiamat-tempest was rising he struck his groin, bit his lip, restless, gloomy and sick at heart, he covered his mouth to stifle his groans.

At last he spoke, urging Ea on to the fight,

"Once you made a snare of words, now go and try it out. You killed Mummu, killed Apsu; kill Kingu who marches in front of Tiamat!"

The sagacious counsellor of all the gods, Nudimmud-Ea, answered Anshar.... [break of eight lines partially reconstructed]

"I will meet Tiamat and calm her spirit, when her heart brims over she will hear my words, and if not mine then yours may appease the waters."

Nudimmud took the short road, went the direct way to Tiamat; but when he saw her whole strategy he could not face her, but he came back cringing.

So Anshar called his son Anu,

"This is the true hero, an irresistible onslaught, a strong god. Go, and face Tiamat, and calm her spirit; when her heart brims over she will listen to you, but if she remains unreconciled my word may appease the waters."

Anu obeyed his father's order, he took the short road, went the direct way to Tiamat; but when he had come so close that he saw her whole strategy, he could not face her, he came back cringing to his father Anshar.

He spoke as though he saw Tiamat still,

"My hands are too weak, I cannot conquer her."

Anshar was dumb; he stared at the ground and his hair stood on end. He shook his head at Ea, all the Anunnaki, the host of gods gathered into that place tongue-tied; they sat with mouths shut for they thought,

"What other god can make war on Tiamat? No one else can face her and come back."

Then the Lord, the father of gods, Anshar rose to his feet majestically. Having considered everything he spoke to the Anunnaki,

"Which one of us is impetuous in battle? The hero Marduk! Only he is strong enough to avenge us."

Then Ea called Marduk into a secret place and gave him subtle advice out of his deep mind,

"You are the dear son who warms my heart, Marduk. When you see Anshar go straight to him as you would go into battle. Stand up when you speak, and when he sees you he will grow calm."

Lord Marduk exulted, he strode forward and stood facing Anshar. When Anshar saw him his heart swelled with joy, he kissed him on the lips and shook off despair.

"Anshar, break your silence, let your words ring out for I will accomplish what you long for most in your heart. What hero has forced the battle on you? Only a female thing, only Tiamat flies at you with all her contrivance. You shall soon straddle Tiamat's neck."

"My son, my wise son, confuse Tiamat with charged words, go quickly now, the storm is your chariot, they will never deflect you from Tiamat, but having done with her, then return."

The Lord exulted, with racing spirits he said to the father of gods,

"Creator of the gods who decides their destiny, if I must be your avenger, defeating Tiamat, saving your lives,

"Call the Assembly, give me precedence over all the rest; and when you sit down to pass your decrees, cheerfully sit in Ubshukinna, the Hall of the Synod; now and forever let my word be law;

"I, not you, will decide the world's nature, the things to come. My decrees shall never be altered, never annulled, but my creation endures to the ends of the world."

III Words broke from the lips of Anshar; he said to his counselor Kaka,

"You are the counselor in whom my heart finds its happiness, the one who judges truly and persuades fairly: go to Lahmu and Lahamu, I am sending you down to primeval sediments, call together the generations of the gods.

"Let them speak, let them sit down to banquet together, they shall eat the feast and drink the new-drawn liquor and then they shall all confirm in his destiny the avenger, Marduk! Kaka, go off, stand in front of them and repeat what I say.

"I am sent here by your son Anshar, I am charged to tell you his secret thoughts,

"She loathes us, our mother Tiamat has raised up that Company, she rages in turbulence and all have joined her, all those gods whom you begot,

"Together they jostle the ranks to march with Tiamat, day and night furiously they plot, the growling roaring rout, ready for battle, while the Old Hag, the first mother, mothers a new brood.

"She has loosed the irresistible missile, spawned enormous serpents with cutting fangs, chock-full of venom instead of blood, snarling dragons wearing their glory like gods. (Whoever sees this thing receives the shock of death, for when they heave those bodies up they never turn them back.)

"She has made the Worm
the Dragon
the Female Monster
the Great Lion
the Mad Dog
the Man Scorpion
the Howling Storm
Kulili
Kusariqu

"There is no pity in their weapons, they do not flinch from battle for her law is binding, irrevocable.

"Eleven monsters she has made, but she took from among the gods the clumsy labourer Kingu one of the first generation to be her Captain, War-leader, Assembly-leader, ordering the supplies, leading the van to battle, Supreme Commander of the Wars.

"All this she gave him when she set up their Company, she had said,

" 'Now it is in your hands, my spell will hold them bound, they must obey my will. You are supreme, my one husband, *your* word will hold the rebel horde.'

"She has given to him the Tables of Fate and fastened them on to his breast,

" 'Now and for evermore your word is irrevocable, your judgements will last! They will quench the fire and the swinging mace will fail of its power.'

"So Kingu has received the authority that belonged before to Anu, they have confirmed in their several natures the brood of monsters.

"I sent Anu but he could not face her, Nudimmud came flying back in terror, then Marduk stood up, a wise god, one of your lineage, his heart has compelled him to set out and face Tiamat, but first he said this,

" 'Creator of the gods who decides their destiny, if I must be your avenger, defeating Tiamat, saving your lives,

" 'Call the Assembly, give me precedence over all the rest; and when you sit down to pass your decrees, cheerfully sit in Ubshukinna, the Hall of the Synod, now and for ever let my word be law;

" 'I, not you, will decide the world's nature, the things to come. My decrees shall never be altered, never annulled, but my creation endures to the ends of the world.'

"Come soon and confirm the destiny of Marduk and the sooner he is off to meet the Great Adversary."

He left and took his way down to Lahmu and Lahamu, stooping he kissed the primeval sediments, bowed to the ground at their feet and delivered the message to old gods,

"I have been sent here by your son Anu, I am charged to tell you his secret thoughts.

"She loathes us, our mother Tiamat has raised up that Company, she rages in turbulence and all have joined her, all those gods whom you begot.

"Together they jostle the ranks to march with Tiamat, day and night furiously they plot, the growling roaring rout, ready for battle, while the Old Hag, the first mother, mothers a new brood.

"She has loosed the irresistible missile, spawned enormous serpents with cutting fangs, chock-full of venom instead of blood, snarling dragons wearing their glory like gods. (Whoever sees this thing receives the shock of death, for when they heave those bodies up they never turn them back.)

"She has made the Worm
the Dragon
the Female Monster
the Great Lion
the Mad Dog
the Man Scorpion
the Howling Storm
Kulili
Kusariqu

"There is no pity in their weapons, they do not flinch from battle for her law is binding, irrevocable. Eleven such monsters she has made, but she took from among the gods the clumsy laborer Kingu one of the first generation to be her Captain, War-leader, Assembly-leader, ordering the supplies, leading the van to battle, Supreme Commander of the Wars.

"All this she gave him when she raised their Company, she has said,

" 'Now it is in your hands, my spell will hold them bound, they must obey my will. You are supreme my one husband, *your* word will hold the rebel horde.'

"She has given to him the Tables of Fate and fastened them on to his breast,

" 'Now and for evermore your word is irrevocable, your judgements will last! They will quench the fire and the swinging mace will fail of its power.'

"So Kingu has received the authority that belonged before to Anu, they have confirmed in their several natures the brood of monsters.

"I sent Anu but he could not face her, Nudimmud came flying back in terror, then Marduk stood up, a wise god, one of your lineage, his heart has compelled him to set out and face Tiamat, but first he said this,

" 'Creator of the gods who decides their destiny, if I must be your avenger, defeating Tiamat, saving your lives,

" 'Call the Assembly, give me precedence over all the rest; and when you sit down to pass your decrees, cheerfully sit in Ubshukinna, the Hall of the Synod, now and forever let my word be law;

" 'I, not you, will decide the world's nature, the things to come. My decrees shall never be altered, never annulled, but my creation endures to the ends of the world.'

"Come soon and confirm the destiny of Marduk and the sooner he is off to meet the Great Adversary."

When Lahmu and Lahamu heard this they muttered together, all the gods moaned with distress,

"What a strange and terrible decision, the coil of Tiamat is too deep for us to fathom."

Then they prepared for the journey, all the gods who determine the nature of the world and of things to come came in to Anshar, they filled Ubshukinna, greeted each other with a kiss.

In the Hall of the Synod the ancestral voices were heard, they sat down to the banquet, they ate the feast, they drank the new-drawn liquor and the tubes through which they sucked dripped with intoxicating wine.

Their souls expanded, their bodies grew heavy and drowsy; and this was the state of the gods when they settled the fate of Marduk.

IV They set up a throne for Marduk and he sat down facing his forefathers to receive the government.

"One god is greater than all great gods,
a fairer fame, the word of command,

the word from heaven, O Marduk,
greater than all great gods, the honour
and the fame, the will of Anu, great
command, unaltering and eternal word!
Where there is action the first to act,
where there is government the first to govern;
to glorify some, to humiliate some,
that is the gift of the god.
Truth absolute, unbounded will;
which god dares question it?
In their beautiful places a place
is kept for you, Marduk, our avenger.

"We have called you here to receive the sceptre, to make you king of the whole universe. When you sit down in the Synod you are the arbiter; in the battle your weapon crushes the enemy.

"Lord, save the life of any god who turns to you; but as for the one who grasped evil, from that one let his life drain out."

They conjured then a kind of apparition and made it appear in front of him, and they said to Marduk, the first-born son,

"Lord, your word among the gods arbitrates, destroys, creates: then speak and this apparition will disappear. Speak again, again it will appear."

He spoke and the apparition disappeared. Again he spoke and it appeared again. When the gods had proved his word they blessed him and cried, "Marduk is King!"

They robed him in robes of a king, the sceptre and the throne they gave him, and matchless war-weapons as a shield against the adversary,

"Be off. Slit life from Tiamat, and may the winds carry her blood to the world's secret ends."

The old gods had assigned to Bel what he would be and what he should do, always conquering, always succeeding;

Then Marduk made a bow and strung it to be his own weapon, he set the arrow against the bow-string, in his right hand he grasped the mace and lifted it up, bow and quiver hung at his side, lightnings played in front of him, he was altogether an incandescence.

He netted a net, a snare for Tiamat; the winds from their quarters held it, south wind, north, east wind, west, and no part of Tiamat could escape.

With the net, the gift of Anu, held close to his side, he himself raised up Imhullu the atrocious wind, the tempest, the whirlwind, the hurricane, the wind of four and the wind of seven, the tumid wind worst of all.

All seven winds were created and released to savage the guts of Tiamat, they towered behind him. Then the tornado Abuba his last great ally, the signal for assault, he lifted up.

He mounted the storm, his terrible chariot, reins hitched to the side, yoked four in hand the appalling team, sharp poisoned teeth, the Killer, the Pitiless, Trampler, Haste, they knew arts of plunder, skills of murder.

He posted on his right the Batterer, best in the melee; on his left the Battle-fury that blasts the bravest, lapped in this armour, a leaping terror, a ghastly aureole; with a magic word clenched between his lips, a healing plant pressed in his palm, this lord struck out.

He took his route towards the rising sound of Tiamat's rage, and all the gods besides, the fathers of the gods pressed in around him, and the lord approached Tiamat.

He surveyed her scanning the Deep, he sounded the plan of Kingu her consort; but so soon as Kingu sees him he falters, flusters, and the friendly gods who filled the ranks beside him—when they saw the brave hero, their eyes suddenly blurred,

But Tiamat without turning her neck roared, spitting defiance from bitter lips,

"Upstart, do you think yourself too great? Are they scurrying now from their holes to yours?"

Then the lord raised the hurricane, the great weapon, he flung his words at the termagant fury,

"Why are you rising, your pride vaulting, your heart set on faction, so that sons reject fathers? Mother of all, why did you have to mother war?

"You made that bungler your husband, Kingu! You gave him the rank, not his by right, of Anu. You have abused the gods my ancestors, in bitter malevolence you threaten Anshar, the king of all the gods.

"You have marshalled forces for battle, prepared the war-tackle. Stand up alone and we will fight it out, you and I alone in battle."

When Tiamat heard him her wits scattered, she was possessed and shrieked aloud, her legs shook from the crotch down, she gabbled spells, muttered maledictions, while the gods of war sharpened their weapons.

Then they met: Marduk, that cleverest of gods, and Tiamat grappled alone in single fight.

The lord shot his net to entangle Tiamat, and the pursuing tumid wind, Imhullu, came from behind and beat in her face. When the mouth gaped open to suck him down he drove Imhullu in, so that the mouth would not shut but wind raged through her belly; her carcass blown up, tumescent, she gaped—And now he shot the arrow that split the belly, that pierced the gut and cut the womb.

Now that the Lord had conquered Tiamat he ended her life, he flung her down and straddled the carcass; the leader was killed, Tiamat was dead, her rout was shattered, her band dispersed.

Those gods who had marched beside her now quaked in terror, and to save their own lives, if they could, they turned their backs on danger. But they were surrounded, held in a tight circle, and there was no way out.

He smashed their weapons and tossed them into the net; they found themselves inside the snare, they wept in holes and hid in corners suffering the wrath of god.

When they resisted he put in chains the eleven monsters, Tiamat's unholy brood, and all their murderous armament. The demoniac band that marched in front of her he trampled into the ground;

But Kingu the usurper, the chief of them, he bound and made death's god. He took the Tables of Fate, usurped without right, and sealed them with his seal to wear on his own breast.

When it was accomplished, the adversary vanquished, the haughty enemy humiliated; when the triumph of Anshar was accomplished on the enemy, and the will of Nudimmud was fulfilled, then brave Marduk tightened the ropes of the prisoners.

He turned back to where Tiamat lay bound, he straddled the legs and smashed her skull (for the mace was merciless), he severed the arteries and the blood streamed down the north wind to the unknown ends of the world.

When the gods saw all this they laughed out loud, and they sent him presents. They sent him their thankful tributes.

The lord rested; he gazed at the huge body, pondering how to use it, what to create from the dead carcass. He split it apart like a cockle-shell; with the upper half he constructed the arc of sky, he pulled down the bar and set a watch on the waters, so they should never escape.

He crossed the sky to survey the infinite distance; he stationed himself above Apsu, that Apsu built by Nudimmud over the old abyss which now he surveyed, measuring out and marking in.

He stretched the immensity of the firmament, he made Esharra, the Great Palace, to be its earthly image, and Anu and Enlil and Ea had each their right stations.

V He projected positions for the Great Gods conspicuous in the sky, he gave them a starry aspect as constellations; he measured the year, gave it a beginning and an end, and to each month of the twelve three rising stars.

When he had marked the limits of the year, he gave them Nebiru, the pole of the universe, to hold their course, that never erring they should not stray through the sky. For the seasons of Ea and Enlil he drew the parallel.

Through her ribs he opened gates in the east and west, and gave them strong bolts on the right and left; and high in the belly of Tiamat he set the zenith.

He gave the moon the lustre of a jewel, he gave him all the night, to mark off days, to watch by night each month the circle of a waxing waning light.

"New Moon, when you rise on the world, six days your horns are crescent, until half-circle on the seventh, waxing still phase follows phase, you will divide the month from full to full.

"Then wane, a gibbous light that fails, until low down on the horizon sun oversails you, drawing close his shadow lies across you, then dark of the moon— at thirty days the cycle's second starts again and follows through for ever and for ever.

"This is your emblem and the road you take, and when you close the sun, speak both of you with justice judgement uncorrupt. . . . [*some lines are missing here*]."

When Marduk had sent out the moon, he took the sun and set him to complete the cycle from this one to the next New Year.... He gave him the Eastern Gate, and the ends of the night with the day, he gave to Shamash.

Then Marduk considered Tiamat. He skimmed spume from the bitter sea, heaped up the clouds, spindrift of wet and wind and cooling rain, the spittle of Tiamat.

With his own hands from the steaming mist he spread the clouds. He pressed hard down the head of water, heaping mountains over it, opening springs to flow: Euphrates and Tigris rose from her eyes, but he closed the nostrils and held back their springhead.

He piled huge mountains on her paps and through them drove water-holes to channel the deep sources; and high overhead He arched her tail, locked-in to the wheel of heaven; the pit was under his feet, between was the crotch, the sky's fulcrum. Now the earth had foundations and the sky its mantle.

When God's work was done, when he had fashioned it all and finished, then on earth he founded temples and made them over to Ea.

But the Tables of Destiny taken from Kingu he returned as a first greeting to Anu; and those gods who had hung up their weapons defeated, whom he had scattered, now fettered, he drove into his presence, the father of the gods.

With the weapons of war broken, he bound to his foot the eleven, Tiamat's monstrous creation. He made likenesses of them all and now they stand at the gate of the abyss, the Apsu Gate; he said,

"This is for recollection for Tiamat shall not be forgotten."

All the generations of the Great Gods when they saw him were full of joy, with Lahmu and Lahamu; their hearts bounded when they came over to meet him.

King Anshar made him welcome with ceremony, Anu and Enlil came carrying presents; but when his mother Damkina sent her present, then he glowed, an incandescence lit his face.

He gave to her servant Usmu, who brought the greeting, charge of the secret house of Apsu; he made him warden of the sanctuaries of Eridu.

All the heavenly gods were there, all the Igigi fell prostrate in front of him, all that were there of the Anunnaki kissed his feet. The whole order came in together to worship.

They stood in front of him, low they bowed and they shouted
"He is king indeed!"

When all the gods in their generations were drunk with the glamour of the manhood of Marduk, when they had seen his clothing spoiled with the dust of battle, then they made their act of obedience....

He bathed and put on clean robes, for he was their king.... A glory was round his head; in his right hand he held the mace of war, in his left grasped the sceptre of peace, the bow was slung on his back; he held the net, and his glory touched the abyss....

He mounted the throne raised up in the temple. Damkina and Ea and all the Great Gods, all the Igigi shouted,

"In time past Marduk meant only 'the beloved son' but now he is king indeed, this is so!"

They shouted together,

"Great Lord of the Universe! this is his name, in him we trust."

When it was done, when they had made Marduk their king, they pronounced peace and happiness for him,

"Over our houses you keep unceasing watch, and all you wish from us, that will be done."

Marduk considered and began to speak to the gods assembled in his presence. This is what he said,

"In the former time you inhabited the void above the abyss, but I have made Earth as the mirror of Heaven, I have consolidated the soil for the foundations, and there I will build my city, my beloved home.

"A holy precinct shall be established with sacred halls for the presence of the king. When you come up from the deep to join the Synod you will find lodging and sleep by night.

"When others from heaven descend to the Assembly, you too will find lodging and sleep by night. It shall be Babylon the home of the gods. The masters of all the crafts shall build it according to my plan."

When the older of the gods had heard this speech they had still one question to ask:

"Over these things that your hands have formed, who will administer law? Over all this earth that you have made, who is to sit in judgement?

"You have given your Babylon a lucky name, let it be our home for ever! Let the fallen gods day after day serve us; and as we enforce your will let no one else usurp our office."

Marduk, Tiamat's conqueror, was glad; the bargain was good; he went on speaking his arrogant words explaining it all to the gods,

"They will perform this service, day after day, and you shall enforce my will as law."

Then the gods worshipped in front of him, and to him again, to the king of the whole universe they cried aloud,

"This great lord was once our son, now he is our king. We invoked him once for very life, he who is the lord, the blaze of light, the sceptre of peace and of war the mace.

"Let Ea be his architect and draw the excellent plan, his bricklayers are we!"

VI Now that Marduk has heard what it is the gods are saying, he is moved with desire to create a work of consummate art. He told Ea the deep thought in his heart.

"Blood to blood
I join,
blood to bone

I form
an original thing,
its name is Man,
aboriginal man
is mine in making.

"All his occupations
are faithful service,
the gods that fell
have rest,
I will subtly alter
their operations,
divided companies
equally blest."

Ea answered with carefully chosen words, completing the plan for the gods' comfort. He said to Marduk,

"Let one of the kindred be taken; only one need die for the new creation. Bring the gods together in the Great Assembly; there let the guilty die, so the rest may live."

Marduk called the Great Gods to the Synod; he presided courteously, he gave instructions and all of them listened with grave attention.

The king speaks to the rebel gods,

"Declare on your oath if ever before you spoke the truth, who instigated rebellion? Who stirred up Tiamat? Who led the battle? Let the instigator of war be handed over; guilt and retribution are on him, and peace will be yours for ever."

The Great Gods answered the Lord of the Universe, the king and counsellor of gods,

"It was Kingu who instigated rebellion, he stirred up that sea of bitterness and led the battle for her."

They declared him guilty, they bound and held him down in front of Ea, they cut his arteries and from his body they created man; and Ea imposed his servitude.

When it was done, when Ea in his wisdom had created man and man's burden, this thing was past comprehension, this marvel of subtlety conceived by Marduk and executed by Nudimmud.

Then Marduk, as king, divided the gods: one host below and another above, three hundred above for the watchers of heaven, watchers of the law of Anu; five times sixty for earth, six hundred gods between earth and heaven.

When universal law was set up and the gods allotted their calling, then the Anunnaki, the erstwhile fallen, opened their mouths to speak to Marduk:

"Now that you have freed us and remitted our labour how shall we make a return for this? Let us build a temple and call it The-Inn-of-Rest-by-Night.

"There we will sleep at the season of the year, at the Great Festival when we form the Assembly; we will build altars for him, we will build the Parakku, the Sanctuary."

When Marduk heard this his face shone like broad day:

"Tall Babel Tower, it shall be built as your desire; bricks shall be set in moulds and you shall name it Parakku, the Sanctuary."

The Anunnaki gods took up the tools, one whole year long they set bricks in moulds; by the second year they had raised its head Esagila, it towered, the earthly temple, the symbol of infinite heaven.

Inside were lodgings for Marduk and Enlil and Ea. Majestically he took his seat in the presence of them all, where the head of the ziggurat looked down to the foot.

When that building was finished the Anunnaki built themselves chapels; then all came in together and Marduk set out the banquet.

"This is Babylon,
'dear city of god'
your beloved home!
The length and breadth
are yours, possess it,
enjoy it, it is your own."

When all the gods sat down together there was wine and feasting and laughter; and after the banquet in beautiful Esagila they performed the liturgy from which the universe receives its structure, the occult is made plain, and through the universe gods are assigned their places.

When the Fifty Great Gods had sat down with the Seven who design the immutable nature of things, they raised up three hundred into heaven. It was then too that Enlil lifted the bow of Marduk and laid it in front of them.

He also lifted the net; they praised the workmanship now that they saw the intricacy of the net and the beauty of the bow.

Anu lifted the bow and kissed it, he said before all the gods, "This is my daughter."

And this was the naming of the bow—

"One is for Long-wood,
two for the Rain-bow,
three is for Starry-bow
glittering above."

And Starry-bow was a god among gods.

When Anu had pronounced the bow's triple destiny he lifted up the king's throne and set Marduk above in the gods' Assembly.

Among themselves they uttered an execration, by oil and by water, pricking their throats, to abide its fate on pain of death.

They ratified his authority as King of Kings, Lord of the Lords of the

Universe. Anshar praised him, he called him Asarluhi, the name that is first, the highest name.

"We will wait and listen, we bend and worship
his name! His word is the last appeal
his writ will run from the zenith to the pit.
All glory to the son, our avenger!
His empire has no end, shepherd of men,
he made them his creatures to the last of time,
they must remember.
He shall command hecatombs, for the gods,
they shall commend food, for the fathers,
and cherish the sanctuary
where the odour of incense and whisper of liturgy
echo on earth the customs of heaven.
Black-headed men will adore him on earth,
the subjected shall remember their god,
at his word they shall worship the goddess.
Let offerings of food not fail
for god and goddess, at his command.
Let them serve the gods, at his command,
work their lands, build their houses.
Let black-headed men serve the gods on earth
without remission; while as for us,
in the multitude of his names
he is our god.
Let us hail him in his names,
let us hail him by his fifty names,
one god."

THE HYMN OF THE FIFTY NAMES OF MARDUK

MARDUK is One,
he is Son of the Sun,
he is the first, the sunburst.
Pasture and pool,
and the byres full,
torrents of rain that hammered the enemy.
Most shining one,
Son of the Sun,
the gods are walking always in the flame of his light.
He created man
a living thing
a labor for ever, and gods go free,
to make to break

to love and to save,
to Marduk all power and praise!
MARUKKA is Two
hammering out the whole creation
to ease the gods in tribulation.
MARUTUKKU is Three,
his praises are heard on every hand,
the armed child who shields the land.
BARASHAKUSHU is Fourth,
who stood at need to bridle earth,
his spirit stoops, his heart is love.
LUGALDIMMERANKIA is Five,
King of the Cosmos!
Over the universe he is acclaimed
by that Great Company his wrath had shamed
Almighty God!
NARI is Six, the Deliverer,
he is our conscience, for once
in our trouble he brought us peace
and a safe haven;
Anunnaki, Igigi, from the pit
and in heaven,
hearing this name secretly quake.
ASARULUDU is Seven,
the Great Magician, this title came from Anu;
in time of peril, their good leader,
by the deadly duel he fetched them rest.
NAMTILLAKU is Eight,
in the shadow of death he discovered life;
it was as though they were made
all new; conjured from death at his word until
the reckless rout submit to his will.
NAMRU is Nine, the gods go a-walking
in the furnace of his beauty.

Voices of older days have spoken: Lahmu, Lahamu, Anshar have spoken,
each of them uttered three names; they said to the children,
"Three names he has from each of us, three names he needs from you."
As once before in Synod in Ubshukinna, at the place of decision, the
young gods eagerly talked together,
"He is the hero, our son, our avenger, we will praise the name of our defender."
They sat down together to shape his destiny, and all of them chanted his
names in the Sanctuary.

VII The Hymn
(*continued*)

ASARU cultivates the sown,
conducts water by small channels
for seed-time, for shooting green
and harvest grain.
ASARUALIM, the gods in fear and hope
at Council turn to him.
He is the light, ASARUALIM NUNNA,
light of the glory of his father;
he is the law of Anu and Enlil and Ea,
he is fullness and plenty,
the gods grow fat on his bounty.
TUTU is life renewed
that sweetens the sanctuary; should wrath
once more rouse up their company
he teaches them to repeat the charm
that lulls to sleep,
he has no peer in that Assembly.
ZIUKKINNA lives in every god,
he made the skies their happiness,
he holds them to their bliss;
below the clouds dull men
remember him,
for this is ZIKU the kernel of life,
sweet breath of grace, abundance,
benevolence, unbelievable wealth
changing famine to plenty;
we breathed his sweetness
in our extremity.
We will speak of the mighty,
we will sing the song of his glory.
AGAKU, the love and the wrath,
with living words he quickens the dead,
he pitied fallen gods,
remitted the labor laid on the adversary.
For your relief he made mankind, his words
endure, he is kind, he has power
of life, it is in the mouth
of black-headed men who remember him.
But also this is TUKU,
they mutter his anathemas

who overwhelmed evil
with mysterious words.
As SHAZU he made the heart,
he sees the marrow,
no sinner escapes his scrutiny.
He has formed the Assembly and spread his protection,
he oversees justice and subdues rebellion,
he has rooted out malice;
wherever he goes the wrong and the right
stand separate.
As one who reads the heart this too
is ZISI, a name that hushed the rebel horde,
out of the body of older gods
drove freezing fear, freeing his fathers, for
SUHRIM is the missile
that extinguished them,
the abject band that cringe from him,
their schemes forestalled, and flying
in the wind.
Be glad you gods, be glad!
He is SUHGURIM who can destroy,
but is an open court to hear all causes;
old gods created new, the enemy erased
and to the children's children
nothing is left of them
or what they did; his name alone
answers the summons of the world.
ZAHRIM, the destroyer, lives!
Iniquity is dead, he has found out
the enemy; when the gods fled
he brought them home, each
to his own, and by this name is known.
ZAHGURIM, savior destroyer,
terrible title, his enemy is fallen
as it were on the field of battle.

ENBILULU, health to the gods and wealth!
He called their names, he called
for hecatombs roast in flames,
he planned the pastures,
sank wells and freed the waters.
He is EPADUN gathering moisture
from sky and earth to wash down the furrows,
watering ploughland with sluices
with dams and dykes in irrigation.

Enbilulu is hymned as GUGAL,
in the orchards of the gods
he watches the canals, he fills
the store-room with sesame, emmer,
abundant grain.
And he is HEGAL,
heaping up wealth for all people,
into the world he sends sweet rain
and greenness . . .
As SIRSIR he seized the carcass,
he carried off Chaos meshed in his snare,
and heaped on her mountains.
Overseer of the world and faithful shepherd,
where his brow is furrowed,
like a shock of hair the corn
waves up; where the vast ocean
rises in anger, he vaults her as a bridge
thrown over the place where duel was fought.
He is also called MALAH, and many another;
the sour sea is his skiff who captains the hulk.
A heap of grain is GIL, barley and sesame
doled out for the land's good.
This is GILMA, the unquenchable fire
that tempers the eternity of their dwelling,
and for their safety is braced as the hoop holding the barrel.
This is AGILMA,
who from the tearing surf creates
over the waters clouds
to guard the unchanging sky.
ZULUM cuts into clay,
allots the acres, grants the tithes.
This MUMMU is the creative word,
the life of the universe.
GISHNUMUNAB, the seed, created
races of men from the world's quarters.
From the wreck of Tiamat's rout,
from the stuff of fallen gods
he made mankind.
He is LUGALABDUBUR
who came as king to confront Chaos,
her forces wither before him for he is steadfast,
the foundations are firm in every direction.
PAPALGUENNA, Lord of Lords,
most sublime god, he rules his brothers.
LUGALDURMAH, at the navel of the world

where heaven and earth are held
by the cord; where the high gods gather,
his greatness ranks higher than all.

ARANUNNA, Counselor, with his father Ea
peerless in his sovereign manner,
he created gods.
DUMUDUKU is the bright mountain,
Dumuduku, the presence in the temple,
at the place of decision where nothing is decided
except with him.
LUGALLANNA, he is strong
with the charge of heaven,
conspicuous among gods
even more than Anshar who called him out,
called one from all.
LUGALUGGA, King Death!
He took them at the crisis, in the maelstrom;
the encompassing intellect, the mind full-stretched.
IRKINGU, in the battle-fury he bore away the bungler;
he created law and law now rules creation.
KINMA, adviser and leader,
his name strikes terror in gods,
the roar of the tornado.
ESIZKUR, up there he sits
in the chapel of prayer, at the Great Festival,
when the gods all come, presents are given, duties imposed.
Unless he is by nothing is created
subtle or beautiful, but when he would
man was made in the quarters of the world,
without him the gods
would not know their hour.
He is GIBIL, the furnace in which the point
is tempered; lightnings forged
the weapons of war against Tiamat;
the gods will never sound
the reaches of his mind.
His name is also ADDU,
wet weather and the welcome storm,
the kindly roar of thunder
hovering over earth.
After the storm the clouds break up
at his word, and under heaven
all people daily have their bread from him.
ASHARU guides the gods of Fate;

all other gods he guards.
As NEBIRU he projected the stars
in their orbit, the wandering gods obey
the laws of passage.
Nebiru, at the still centre,
is the god they adore;
of this starry one they say
    "He who once crossed the firmament tirelessly
    now is the nub of the universe,
    and all the other gods hold course
    on him; he shall fold
    the gods like a flock
    and conquer Tiamat.
    Let her life be narrow and short,
    let her recede into the future
    far-off from man-kind,
    till time is old, keep her
    for ever absent."

Because he had moulded matter and created the ether, Enlil his father, named him BEL MATATI, Lord of this World. With his own name he signed him when the gods of heaven had ended the hymn.

Now too Ea having heard rejoiced,

"The Great Gods have glorified my son, he is Ea, named by my name, he will execute my will and direct my rites." HANSHA!

With fifty names the gods proclaimed him. HANSHA!

With fifty they named him, the one who is first and fares farthest!

EPILOGUE
    Remember the Titles of Marduk!

Rulers will recite them, wise men and sages debate them, father to son repeat them, even shepherds and herdsmen shall hear them.

Let men rejoice in Marduk! The prince of the gods. Man and earth will prosper, for his rule is strong, his command is firm, none of the gods can alter his will; where his eyes have fixed they do not falter.

There is no god can bear his anger, his intellect is vast and his benevolence; sinners and such trash he will blast in his presence; not so the wise teacher to whose words we listen; he wrote it down, he saved it for time to come.

Let the Igigi who built his dwelling, let the gods speak: this was the song of Marduk who defeated Tiamat and attained sovereignty.

—N. K. Sandars. *Poems of Heaven and Hell from Ancient Mesopotamia.* Baltimore, Md.: Penguin Books, 1971, pp. 73–111.

Creation of Man by the Mother

Goddess

In these Old Babylonian (1750–1550 B.C.) and Assyrian (c. 100 B.C.) myths, Ninhursag (or Nintu, goddess of the earth) creates mankind (*Lullu*, the savage, the first man) out of clay and animates it with the blood of a slain god. The metaphors of plastic and generative creation are mixed here: Ninhursag both fashions man and gives birth to him.

Ritual instructions form a substantial part of this text and show that the myth was originally part of a birth incantation. This ritual use underscores the point that the holy birth of all mankind is repeated in time through the birth of each individual. "As the Bearing One gives birth,/ May the mother of the child bring forth by [her]self."

OLD BABYLONIAN TEXT [*obverse; preceding column and top of the present column destroyed*]

"That which is slight shall grow to abundance;
The burden of creation man shall bear!"
The goddess they called, [. . .], [the *mot*]*her*,
The most helpful of the gods, the wise Mami:
"Thou art the mother-womb,
The one who creates mankind.
Create, then Lullu and let him bear the yoke!
The yoke he shall bear, . . . [. . .];
The *burden* of creation man shall bear!"
. [.] . opened her mouth,
Saying to the great gods:
"With me is the *doing* of all that is suitable;
With his . . . let Lullu appear!
He who shall be [. . .] of all [. . .],
Let him *be formed* out of clay, be *animated* with blood!"
Enki opened his mouth,
Saying to the great gods:
"On the . . . and [. . .] of the month
The purification of the land . . . !
Let them slay one god,
And let the gods be purified in the *judgment*.
With his flesh and his blood
Let Ninhursag mix clay.
God and man
Shall [. . .] therein, . . . in the clay!
Unto eternity [. . .] we shall hear."
[*remainder of obverse too fragmentary for translation*]

[*reverse*]
[. . .] her breast,
[. . .] the beard,
[. . .] the cheek of the man.
[. . .] and the raising
[. . .] of both eyes, the wife and her husband.
[Fourteen mother]-wombs were assembled
[Before] Nintu.
[At the ti]me of the new moon
[To the House] of Fates they called the *votaries*.
[*Enkidu . . .*] came and
[*Kneel*]*ed down*, opening the womb.
[. . .] . . . and happy was his countenance.
[. . . bent] the knees [..],
[..] made an opening,
She brought forth issue,
Praying.
Fashion a clay brick into a core,
Make . . . stone in the midst of [. . .];
Let the vexed rejoice in the house of the one in travail!
As the Bearing One gives birth,
May the mo[ther of the ch]ild bring forth by herself!
[*remainder too fragmentary for translation*]

ASSYRIAN VERSION
[*beginning mutilated*]

[. . . they kis]sed her feet,
[Saying: "The creatress of mankind] we call thee;
[The Mistr]ess of all the gods be thy name!"
[They went] to the House of Fate,
[Nin]igiku-Ea (and) the wise Mama.
[Fourteen mother]-wombs were assembled
To tread upon the [c]lay before her.
[. . .] Ea says, as he recites the incantation.
Sitting before her, Ea causes her to recite the incantation.
[Mama reci]ted the incantation; when she completed [her] incantation,
[. . .] she drew upon her clay.
[Fourteen pie]ces she pinched off; seven pieces she placed on the right,
[Seven pie]ces she placed on the left; between them she placed a brick.
[*E*]*a* was kneeling on the *matting*; he opened its navel;
[. . . he c]alled the wise wives.
(Of the) [seven] and seven mother-wombs, seven brought forth males,
[Seven] brought forth females.
The Mother-Womb, the creatress of destiny,

In pairs she completed them,
In pairs she completed before her.
The forms of the people Mami forms.
In the house of the bearing woman in travail,
 Seven days shall the brick lie.
. . . from the house of Mah, the wise Mami.
The vexed shall rejoice in the house of the one in travail.
As the Bearing One gives birth,
May the mother of the child bring forth by [her]self.
[*remainder destroyed*]

—E. A. Speiser (trans.). "Akkadian Myths and Epics." In James B. Pritchard (ed.). *Ancient Near Eastern Texts Relating to the Old Testament.* Princeton, N.J.: Princeton University Press, 1950, pp. 99–100.

When Anu Had Created the Heavens

This Babylonian myth formed part of an incantation that accompanied the rebuilding of the temple. As part of the ceremony, offerings were made, hymns sung, and this creation story recited. Given the importance of the temple as a microcosmic universe, a symbolic home of the gods in human scale modeled on their true universal home, it was necessary ritually to sacralize the building process and to act as the gods acted when they created the world.

This myth devotes itself directly to the sacred process of temple building. It begins by depicting Anu (the sky god) as creator of the heavens and Nudimmud (or Ea, god of waters) as the builder of the Apsu (the abyss of primeval waters) and the maker of men. With these introductions completed, the main part of the myth describes the origin of several minor deities (and the natural elements they represented) that were required in temple construction: gods of carpenters, smiths, and builders (Arazu); goldsmiths, engravers, and miners (Ninkurra); grain (Lakar); offerings and wine (Siris); and finally the god Kusiga (the high priest of the gods). In addition, Ea made a king to maintain the temples (as Anu maintained the world.)

The implication throughout is that the world was created so gods might be properly housed and praised.

WHEN ANU had created the heavens,
 (And) Nudimmud had built the *Apsu*, his dwelling,
Ea nipped off clay in the *Apsu*,
He created the brick-god for the restoration of [temples];
He created the reed and the forest for the work of building [temples];
He created the god of the carpenter, the god of the smith, and Arazu, to complete the work of bu[ilding];
He created the mountains and the seas for all kinds of . [. . .]
He created the god of the goldsmith, the god Ninagal, the god of the engraver, and the god Ninkurra, for the works of [. . . .],

And their great riches for offerings . [. . .];
He created Ashnan, Lahar, Siris, Ningizzida, Ninsar, [. . . .],
To provide abundant regular offe[rings];
He created Umunmutamku (and) Umunmutamnak, to maintain the offe[rings. . . .];
He created the god Kusiga, the high priest of the great gods, for the performance of rites (and) ce[remonies(?)];
He created the king, as the maintainer of [the temples(?)];
[He create]d mankind for the doi[ng of the service of the gods(?)]. [*rest destroyed*]

—Alexander Heidel. *The Babylonian Genesis*. Chicago: University of Chicago Press, 1942, pp. 53–54.

The Worm and the Toothache

The Assyrians recognized the importance of origins in determining the sources and limitations of an enemy's power, and so, in this incantation (c. 1000 B.C.), which accompanied the cure of toothaches, they traced the history of the cause of the pain—the offending worm. When they understood its derivation and place in the universal order, the chanters then could appeal to the appropriate gods for relief. This chant is augmented by remedies for treatment—mixtures of second-grade beer and oil.

The cosmology here includes Anu (the sky god) as the original creator and Shamash (the sun god) and Ea (the god of water) as assigners of function.

AFTER ANU had created the heaven,
(And) the heaven had created the earth,
(And) the earth had created the rivers,
(And) the rivers had created the canals,
(And) the canals had created the morass,
(And) the morass had created the worm,
The worm went before Shamash, weeping,
His tears flowing before Ea.
"What wilt thou give me for my food,
What wilt thou give me for my drink?"
"I will give thee the dried fig
(And) the apricot."
"What are these to me? The dried fig
And the apricot!
Lift me up and among the teeth
And the gums let me dwell!
The blood of the teeth I will suck,
And of the gums I will eat away
The roots of the teeth(?)!"
Fix the pin and seize the foot!
Because thou hast said this, O worm,

May Ea smite thee with the might of
His hand!
Incantation against toothache.
Its treatment: Second-grade beer . . . and oil thou shalt mix together;
The incantation thou shalt recite three times thereon (and) shalt put (the medicine) upon his tooth.

—Alexander Heidel. *The Babylonian Genesis*. Chicago: University of Chicago Press, 1942, pp. 60–61.

Another Version of the Creation

of Man
This fuller version of the Assyrian account of creation of man (c. 800 B.C.) was used in ceremonies for the religiously initiated. It envisions Anu (god of sky), Enlil (god of storms and earth), Shamash (god of sun), Ea (god of water)—air, earth, fire, and water—and the Anunnaki (the great sky gods) sitting in their exalted sanctuary and discussing the progress of creation. Heaven and earth have been created and the water courses established. What remains to be done? The Anunnaki, fixers of destiny in heaven and earth, suggest the creation of man to increase abundance and celebrate festivals. And, as in Babylonian myths, the raw material to be used for this creation is the blood of slain deities.

With this divine heritage, Ulligara ("the establisher of abundance") and Zalgarra ("the establisher of plenty") are created and charged with maintaining and increasing the fertility of earth and its creatures. Day and night they are to "celebrate the festival of the gods" and teach others of this mystery of their origin.

[*obverse*]

WHEN BOTH heaven and earth had been completely finished,
(And) the mother of the goddesses had been brought into being;
When the earth had been brought forth (and) the earth had been shaped;
When the destinies of heaven and earth had been fixed;
(When) trench and canal had been given their right course;
(And) the banks of the Tigris and the Euphrates had been established,
(Then) Anu, Enlil, Shamash, (and) Ea,
The great gods,
Seated themselves (with) the Anunnaki, the great gods,
In the exalted sanctuary
And recounted among themselves what had been created.
"Now that the destinies of heaven and earth have been fixed;
Trench and canal have been given their right course;
The banks of the Tigris and the Euphrates
Have been established;
What (else) shall we do?
What (else) shall we create?
O Anunnaki, ye great gods,
What (else) shall we do?

What (else) shall we create?"
The great gods who were present,
The Anunnaki, who fix the destinies,
Both (groups) of them, made answer to Enlil:
"In Uzumua, the bond of heaven and earth,
Let us slay the Lamga gods.
With their blood let us create mankind;
The service of the gods be their portion,
For all times
To establish the boundary ditch,
To place the spade and the basket
Into their hands
For the dwelling of the great gods,
Which is fit to be an exalted sanctuary,
To mark off field from field;
For all times
To establish the boundary ditch,
To give the trench (its) right course,
To establish the boundary,
To water the four regions of the earth,
To raise the plants,
... [....]."

[*reverse*]

T O ESTABLISH the boundary,
To fill(?) the granary,
[*Destroyed*]
To make the field of the Anunnaki produce,
To increase the abundance in the land,
To celebrate the festival of the gods,
To pour out cold water
For the great house of the gods, which is fit to be an exalted sanctuary,
Ulligarra (and) Zalgarra
They called their names.
(That Ulligarra and Zalgarra should) increase ox, sheep, cattle, fish, and fowl,
The abundance in the land,
Enul (and) Ereshul
Decreed with their holy mouths.
Aruru, the lady of the gods, who is fit for rulership,
Ordained for them mighty destinies:
Skilled worker to produce for skilled worker (and) unskilled worker for unskilled
worker,
Springing up among them like grain from the ground,
A thing which, (like) the star(s) of heaven, shall not be changed forever.
Day and night

To celebrate the festival of the gods,
(These) mighty destinies,
Among themselves
Did Anu, Enlil,
Ea, and Ninmah,
The great gods, decree (for them).
In the place where mankind was created,
There Nisaba was firmly established.
Let the wise teach the mystery to the wise.

—Alexander Heidel. *The Babylonian Genesis*. Chicago: University of Chicago Press, 1942, pp. 56–60.

The Eridu Story of Creation
This myth from the Neo-Babylonian period (c. 600 B.C.) was found in the ruins of Sippar (modern Abu Habba), but probably came from Eridu, at the mouth of the Persian Gulf. There, silt from the Euphrates continually added to the land and presumably gave rise to this explanation of the origin of the earth.

Before any city had been made or any of their great temples (Ekur at Nippur, Eanna at Erech, or Esagila at Eridu) had been constructed, all the lands were sea. The great god Marduk built a reed frame over the waters and poured dirt into it to make the beginning of solid ground. With the goddess Aruru he produced mankind, and then made animals (the beasts of Sumugan, god of cattle and vegetation) and plants, and set the Tigris and Euphrates on their courses. Finally he built the great cities of Mesopotamia and their temples.

This account of the creation was part of an incantation used to purify Ezida, the temple of Nabu at Borsippa.

N O HOLY HOUSE, no house of the gods, had (yet) been made in a holy place;
No reed had sprung up, no tree had been created;
No brick had been laid, no brick-mold had been built;
No house had been made, no city had been built;
No city had been made, no living creature had been placed (therein);
Nippur had not been made, Ekur had not been built;
Erech had not been made, Eanna had not been built;
The *Apsu* had not been made, Eridu had not been built;
No holy house, no house for the gods, its dwelling, had been made;
All the lands were sea;
The spring which is in the sea was a water pipe.
Then Eridu was made, Esagila was built—
Esagila, whose foundation Lugaldukuga laid within the *Apsu*—
Babylon was ma[de], Esagila was completed;
The Anunnaki gods he created at one time.
The holy city, the dwelling of their heart's delight, they called (it)
    solemnly.

Marduk constructed a reed frame on the face of the waters;
He created dirt and poured (it) out by the reed frame.
In order to settle the gods in the dwelling of (their) heart's delight,
He created mankind.
The goddess Aruru created the seed of mankind together with him.
He created the beast of the field (and) the living things of the field;
He created the Tigris and the Euphrates and set (them) in (their) place;
Their names he appropriately proclaimed.
He created the grass, the rush of the marsh, the reed, and the woods;
He created the green herb of the field;
The lands, the marshes, the canebrakes;
The cow (and) her young, the calf; the ewe (and) her young, the sheep of the
   fold;
The orchards and the forests;
The he-goat, the mountain goats. . . .
Lord Marduk piled up a dam at the edge of the sea;
[. . . .] a swamp he made into dry land.
[. . . .] he caused to be;
[. . . . he crea]ted, the tree he created;
[. . . .] in (that) place he created;
[Bricks he laid,] the brick-mold he built;
[The house he built,] the city he built;
[The city he made,] living creature(s) he placed (therein);
[Nippur he built,] Ekur he built;
[Erech he built, Eann]a he built.

—Alexander Heidel. *The Babylonian Genesis*. Chicago: University of Chicago Press, 1942, pp. 50–
52.

From Berossus' Account

of the Babylonian Genesis
Berossus was a priest of Bel Marduk (the Lord Marduk) at Babylon who wrote a history of Babylonia around 250 B.C. Although his writings are now lost, they were recorded by Alexander Polyhistor in the first century B.C., and in turn were noted by the church historian Eusebius of Caesarea, whose work, in its turn, was included in the monk. Synkellos' account, from which we get the following explanation.

Berossus envisions a time when all was a dark, wet chaos ruled over by the sea goddess Omorka (similar to the primordial Tiamat). Strange creatures came into being there—animals with human features and mammals with reptile limbs—as if, in the raw potentiality of the place, creation was going on without direction. Bel provided that direction: he clove Omorka into two parts and made one heaven and the other earth. Having destroyed all the creatures of the dark with this act, he ordered the gods to cut off his own head, to mix its blood with earth, and so to make people and animals capable of living in the ordered world.

H E SAYS there was a time in which all was darkness and water, wherein strange and peculiarly shaped creatures came into being; that there were born men with two wings, some also with four wings and two faces; (some) also having one body but two heads, the one of a man, the other of a woman, being likewise in their genitals both male and female; and that there were other human beings with legs and horns of goats; that some had horses' feet; that others had the limbs of a horse behind, but before were fashioned like men, resembling hippocentaurs; that, likewise, bulls with the heads of men bred there; and dogs with fourfold bodies and the tails of fish; also horses with the heads of dogs; and men and other creatures with the heads and bodies of horses and the tails of fishes; and other creatures with the shapes of every species of animals; that besides these there were fishes, and reptiles, and serpents, and still other wondrous creatures, which had appearances derived from one another; that of these are set up appearances derived from one another; that of these are set up images in the temple of Bel; (and) that over all these (creatures) ruled a woman named Omorka. This in Chaldean is *thamte,* meaning in Greek "the sea," but in numerical value it is equal to "moon."

He says that all things being in this condition, Bel came and clove the woman in two; and that out of one half of her he formed the earth, but with the other half the sky; and that he destroyed the creatures within her; but that this was an allegorical description of nature; for while the whole universe consisted of moisture and such living creatures had been born therein, Bel, who is identified with Zeus, divided the darkness in two, separated heaven and earth from one another, and reduced the universe to order; but that the living things, not being able to bear the strength of the light, perished; that this Bel, upon perceiving that the land was desolate and bearing no fruit, commanded one of the gods to cut off his head, (that he also commanded the other gods) to mix the blood which flowed forth with earth, and to form men and animals capable of bearing the air; that this Bel also formed the stars, the sun, the moon, and the five planets. These things, according to Alexander Polyhistor, Berossus told in his first book: that this god cut off his own head, and that the other gods mixed the blood which flowed forth with earth and formed men; that on this account they are rational and partake of divine understanding.

—*Encyclopedia Britannica.* Vol 3 (14th ed.). London and New York: 1929, p. 460. —Quoted in Alexander Heidel. *The Babylonian Genesis.* Chicago: University of Chicago Press, 1942, pp. 66–67.

OLD AND NEW TESTAMENT MYTHS

Genesis 1–2:3 The first five books of the Old Testament—the Torah or Pentateuch—were compiled and edited over five centuries by four main groups of authors, and Bible scholars have worked arduously to determine which

groups wrote which passages. Each of the four main traditions has certain notable characteristics, and the first account of the creation in Genesis 1–2:3 bears most of the marks of the "P" or Priestly school: among others, a use of *Elohim*—the generic Hebrew term for "divine being"—when referring to God; a great interest in genealogical or other lists (often used to trace the precise line through which God's purpose was effected); a God-centered point of view coupled with little interest in human personalities; and a general flatness of tone and austerity of prose.

Dating the Priestly tradition is difficult, because there seems to have been many separate groups of authors working within it. Most scholars place the tradition after the Babylonian Exile (c. 400 B.C.), but others feel it to be a long process stretching from the post-Exillic period back into pre-Israelite times.

The opening book of the Old Testament was called Genesis by the third-century B.C. Greek translators who made the Septuagint version of the Bible; its proper Hebrew name was Bereshit ("In the beginning. . . ."), referring to its opening words in the same fashion as the Mesopotamian creation epic, the *Enuma Elish*, is named after its first words. The parallels between the first creation account in Genesis and the Mesopotamian epic are not confined to their naming process. Not only are there marked similarities in specific details but also the order of creation events is the same, leading many to presume a dependence of the Old Testament account on that of the *Enuma Elish* or similar Babylonian documents. (The relative ages of the documents and their civilizations precludes dependence of the *Enuma Elish* on Genesis.)

The differences between the two myths are clearly evident as well. Most important, while the *Enuma Elish* is a story of many gods struggling with each other for supremacy through the process of creation, the Old Testament account proclaims simply that Elohim created the world and all its creatures.

When God set out to create the universe, all was in a dark and watery chaos. Out of this, God created day and night, sky, earth and vegetation, the sun, moon and stars, the reptiles and birds, and animals and people by calling them into being. In addition, he ordered the creatures of the earth by making people his overseers and commanded them, "Be fertile and multiply; fill the earth and subdue it; and have dominion over the fish of the sea and over the birds of the air and over every living thing that moves on earth."

(1:1) IN THE BEGINNING God created the heavens and the earth. (2) The earth was without form and void, and darkness was upon the face of the deep; and the Spirit of God was moving over the face of the waters.

(3) And God said, "Let there be light"; and there was light. (4) And God saw that the light was good; and God separated the light from the darkness. (5) God called the light Day, and the darkness he called Night. And there was evening and there was morning, one day.

(6) And God said, "Let there be a firmament in the midst of the waters, and let it separate the waters from the waters." (7) And God made the firmament and separated the waters which were under the firmament from the waters which were above the firmament. And it was so. (8) And God called the firmament Heaven. And there was evening and there was morning, a second day.

(9) And God said, "Let the waters under the heavens be gathered together into one place, and let the dry land appear." And it was so. (10) God called the

dry land Earth, and the waters that were gathered together he called Seas. And God saw that it was good. (11) And God said, "Let the earth put forth vegetation, plants yielding seeds bearing fruit in which is their seed, each according to its kind, upon the earth. And it was so. (12) The earth brought forth vegetation, plants yielding seed according to their own kinds, and trees bearing fruit in which is their seed, each according to its kind. And God saw that it was good. (13) And there was evening and there was morning, a third day.

(14) And God said, "Let there be lights in the firmament of the heavens to separate the day from the night; and let them be for signs and for seasons and for days and years, (15) and let them be lights in the firmament of the heavens to give light upon the earth." And it was so. (16) And God made the two great lights, the greater light to rule the day, and the lesser light to rule the night; he made the stars also. (17) And God set them in the firmament of the heavens to give light upon the earth, (18) to rule over the day and over the night, and to separate the light from the darkness. And God saw that it was good. (19) And there was evening and there was morning, a fourth day.

(20) And God said, "Let the waters bring forth swarms of living creatures, and let birds fly above the earth across the firmament of the heavens." (21) So God created the great sea monsters and every living creature that moves, with which the waters swarm, according to their kinds, and every winged bird according to its kind. And God saw that it was good. (22) And God blessed them, saying, "Be fruitful and multiply and fill the waters in the seas, and let birds multiply on the earth." (23) And there was evening and there was morning, a fifth day.

(24) And God said, "Let the earth bring forth living creatures, according to their kinds: cattle and creeping things and beasts of the earth according to their kinds." And it was so. (25) And God made the beasts of the earth according to their kinds and the cattle according to their kinds, and everything that creeps upon the ground according to its kind. And God saw that it was good.

(26) Then God said, "Let us make man in our image, after our likeness; and let them have dominion over the fish of the sea, and over the birds of the air, and over the cattle, and over all the earth, and over every creeping thing that creeps upon the earth." (27) So God created man in his own image, in the image of God he created him; male and female he created them. (28) And God blessed them, and God said to them, "Be fruitful and multiply, and fill the earth and subdue it; and have dominion over the fish of the sea and over the birds of the air and over every living thing that moves upon the earth." (29) And God said, "Behold, I have given you every plant yielding seed which is upon the face of all the earth, and every tree with seed in its fruit; you shall have them for food. (30) And to every beast of the earth, and to every bird of the air, and to everything that creeps on the earth, everything that has the breath of life, I have given every green plant for food." And it was so. (31) And God saw everything that he had made, and behold, it was very good. And there was evening and there was morning, a sixth day.

(2:1) Thus the heavens and the earth were finished, and all the host of them. (2) And on the seventh day God finished his work which he had done, and he rested on the seventh day from all his work which he had done. (3) So God blessed the seventh day and hallowed it, because on it God rested from all his work which he had done in creation.

—*Holy Bible*. Revised Standard Version. London: Thomas Nelson and Sons, Ltd., 1952.

Genesis 2:4–23 The second creation account in the Old Testament follows directly after the first and offers a very different vision of the beginning. Displaying many characteristic features of the "J" tradition of authorship, it has been so attributed by Bible scholars. "J" uses the personal appelation "Jehovah" (or "Yahweh" as it has come to be transliterated for the name of God) and is the most vivid writer of the four main Pentateuch authors. His style is lively, bold, and economical. And whereas other traditions, such as the "E" or Elohistic one, tend to depict God as remote, filling the distance between him and man with intermediaries like angels or even dreams, "J" envisions the relationship of man and God as very close, almost informal. Unlike the Priestly authors of the opening creation account, "J" is people-oriented: not only are individuals shown in all their complexity, their responses rich in emotion and vividly spontaneous, but God is largely anthropomorphized. "J" 's sophistication in analyzing human motivation, his regard for human freedom with both its strengths and weaknesses, and his flair for revealing the drama of situations are all present in this creation account.

Whereas the "P" tradition has been assumed to be the work of one or more groups of individuals, all the characteristics of "J" point to lone authorship. It is thought that "J" probably wrote in the tenth (or ninth) century B.C.

The difference in focus between the first and second creation accounts is clear from the start: while the subject of the first was God's creation of the universe, here it is his making of man. On the day he made heaven and earth, God fashioned a man, Adam, from the dirt (*'adama*) and breathed life into him. And God planted a garden in Eden (the Sumerian word for "plain" or "steppe") in the East where the four rivers Pishon, Gihon, Tigris, and Euphrates join—presumably at the head of the Persian Gulf, an area known for its fertile, silt-enriched soil. And he placed the tree of life and the tree of the knowledge of good and evil in the middle of the garden.

God also prohibited man's eating from the tree of the knowledge of good and evil, for without its knowledge Adam was indeed innocent. He was unaware even of his own goodness and the purity of his connection with God. Obtaining that knowledge rendered him aware of himself as relative and separate from God and as capable of choosing between good and evil, dualities of the relative world. Ultimately, that knowledge revealed to him his own creatureliness and mortality, and the myth articulates this as God's refusal to let him eat from the tree of life.

To provide Adam with helpers, God first fashioned out of the earth all the animals and birds and had Adam name them (thereby giving them functions and purpose). Finally God made a woman for Adam out of his own rib, and Adam was pleased: "This at last is bone of my bones and flesh of my flesh."

(2:4) IN THE DAY that the Lord God made the earth and the heavens, (5) when no plant of the field was yet in the earth and no herb of the field had yet sprung up—for the Lord God had not caused it to rain upon the earth, and there was no man to till the ground; (6) but a mist went up from the earth and watered the whole face of the ground—(7) then the Lord God formed man of dust from the ground, and breathed into his nostrils the breath of life; and man became a living being. (8) And the Lord God planted a garden in Eden, in the east; and there he put the man whom he had formed. (9) And out of the ground the Lord God made to grow every tree that is pleasant to the sight and good for food, the tree of life also in the midst of the garden, and the tree of the knowledge of good and evil.

(10) A river flowed out of Eden to water the garden, and there it divided and became four rivers. (11) The name of the first is Pishon; it is the one which flows around the whole land of Hav'ilah, where there is gold; (12) and the gold of that land is good; bdellium and onyx stone are there. (13) The name of the second river is Gihon; it is the one which flows around the whole land of Cush. (14) And the name of the third river is Tigris, which flows east of Assyria. And the fourth river is the Euphrates.

(15) The Lord God took the man and put him in the garden of Eden to till it and keep it. (16) And the Lord God commanded the man, saying, "You may freely eat of every tree of the garden; (17) but of the tree of the knowledge of good and evil you shall not eat, for in the day that you eat of it you shall die."

(18) Then the Lord God said, "If it not good that the man should be alone; I will make him a helper fit for him." (19) So out of the ground the Lord God formed every beast of the field and every bird of the air, and brought them to the man to see what he would call them; and whatever the man called every living creature, that was its name. (20) The man gave names to all cattle, and to the birds of the air, and to every beast of the field; but for the man there was not found a helper fit for him. (21) So the Lord God caused a deep sleep to fall upon the man, and while he slept took one of his ribs and closed up its place with flesh; (22) and the rib which the Lord God had taken from the man he made into a woman and brought her to the man. (23) Then the man said,

> This at last is bone of my bones
>   and flesh of my flesh;
> she shall be called Woman,
>   because she was taken out of Man.

—*Holy Bible*. Revised Standard Version. London: Thomas Nelson and Sons, Ltd., 1952.

Psalm 33:6–15

The Psalms of the Old Testament were used in public worship in Israel, probably during the period of the monarchy before the Babylonian Exile (586 B.C.). Their poetic form and many of their themes were borrowed from older Near Eastern cultures, but the individual psalms were adapted and changed by the Hebrews to fit specific circumstances over the centuries. Specific dating and determination of authorship is therefore, in most cases, impossible.

Although the particular theme of Psalm 33—God's creation of the universe by his word—was relatively common in Egyptian and even Babylonian thought, it is emphasized here in a new way: the divine word itself made the world. "He spoke and it came to be; he commanded and it stood forth."

And, after Yahweh created the heavens and gathered the sea, he involved himself in the ordering of political life and the judging of his creatures. Of course, no meaningful separation of political and religious life can be made here. God's involvement in "politics" is one sign of its religious nature, but also it must be remembered that both Israel and the neighboring states were theocracies, religiously grounded and understood. The concept of being the "chosen" people is almost universal and seems to bespeak a feeling of closeness to one's god rather than exclusivity. People are "chosen" to the extent they feel themselves to be in direct relation to their creator.

(33.6) **B**Y the word of the LORD the heavens were made,
　　and all their host by the breath of his mouth.
(7) He gathered the waters of the sea as in a bottle;
　　he put the deeps in storehouses.
(8) Let all the earth fear the LORD,
　　let all the inhabitants of the world stand in awe of him!
(9) For he spoke, and it came to be;
　　he commanded, and it stood forth!

(10) The LORD brings the counsel of the nations to nought;
　　he frustrates the plans of the peoples.
(11) The counsel of the LORD stands for ever,
　　the thoughts of his heart to all generations.
(12) Blessed is the nation whose God is the LORD,
　　the people whom he has chosen as his heritage!

(13) The LORD looks down from heaven,
　　he sees all the sons of men;
(14) from where he sits enthroned he looks forth
　　on all the inhabitants of the earth,
(15) he who fashions the hearts of them all,
　　and observers all their deeds.

—*Holy Bible*. Revised Standard Version. London: Thomas Nelson and Sons, Ltd., 1952.

Psalm 104　Psalm 104 is typical of the "hymn" type of psalms in that it includes a call to worship, an explanation of the reason for worship, and a further statement of praise. It was used in many cultic situations, from sacrifices to festivals and daily worship.

Unlike psalms of lament, where the focus is on the human condition, the hymns are thoroughly God-centered—so much so that it is not for his relation to people nor for his gifts that he is praised, but for what he is and does independent of them. In this case, God is praised for being the creator of the world.

He is envisioned as spreading out the heavens like a tent over the chaotic waters and taming the winds and fires. Most importantly, he controlled the primeval sea, fixing its limits so that earth could appear. Having accomplished these basic acts of creating and ordering, God then provided for the creatures with sustinence (water and food even for the wild beasts), time (night and day), and ultimately life.

(104:1) B LESS THE LORD, O my soul! O LORD my God, thou art very great!
Thou art clothed with honor and majesty,

(2) who coverest thyself with light as with a garment,
who hast stretched out the heavens like a tent,

(3) who hast laid the beams of thy chambers on the waters,
who makest the clouds thy chariot,
who ridest on the wings of the wind,

(4) who makest the winds thy messengers,
fire and flame thy ministers.

(5) Thou didst set the earth on its foundations,
so that it should never be shaken.

(6) Thou didst cover it with the deep as with a garment;
the waters stood above the mountains.

(7) At thy rebuke they fled;
at the sound of thy thunder they took to flight.

(8) The mountains rose, the valleys sank down
to the place which thou didst appoint for them.

(9) Thou didst set a bound which they should not pass,
so that they might not again cover the earth.

(10) Thou makest springs gush forth in the valleys;
they flow between the hills,

(11) they give drink to every beast of the field;
the wild asses quench their thirst.

(12) By them the birds of the air have their habitation;
they sing among the branches.

(13) From thy lofty abode thou waterest the mountains;
the earth is satisfied with the fruit of thy work.

(14) Thou dost cause the grass to grow for the cattle,
and plants for man to cultivate,
that he may bring forth food from the earth,

(15) and wine to gladden the heart of man,
oil to make his face shine,
and bread to strengthen man's heart.

(16) The trees of the LORD are watered abundantly,
the cedars of Lebanon which he planted.

(17) In them the birds build their nests;
the stork has her home in the fir trees.

(18) The high mountains are the the wild goats;
    the rocks are a refuge for the badgers.
(19) Thou hast made the moon to mark the seasons;
    the sun knows its time for setting
(20) Thou makest darkness, and it is night,
    when all the beasts of the forest creep forth.
(21) The young lions roar for their prey,
    seeking their food from God.
(22) When the sun rises, they get them away
    and lie down in their dens.
(23) Man goes forth to his work
    and to his labor until the evening.

(24) O LORD, how manifold are thy works!
    In wisdom hast thou made them all;
    the earth is full of thy creatures.
(25) Yonder is the sea, great and wide,
    which teems with things innumerable,
    living things both small and great.
(26) There go the ships,
    and Leviathan which thou didst form to sport in it.

(27) These all look to thee,
    to give them their food in due season.
(28) When thou givest to them, they gather it up;
    when thou openest thy hand, they are filled with good things.
(29) When thou hidest thy face, they are dismayed;
    when thou takest away their breath, they die
    and return to their dust.
(30) When thou sendest forth thy Spirit, they are created;
    and thou renewest the face of the ground.

(31) May the glory of the LORD endure for ever,
    may the LORD rejoice in his works,
(32) who looks on the earth and it trembles,
    who touches the mountains and they smoke!
(33) I will sing to the LORD as long as I live;
    I will sing praise to my God while I have being.
(34) May my meditation be pleasing to him,
    for I rejoice in the Lord.
(35) Let sinners be consumed from the earth,
    and let the wicked be no more!
    Bless the LORD, O my soul!
    Praise the LORD!

—*Holy Bible*. Revised Standard Version. London: Thomas Nelson and Sons, Ltd., 1952.

From the Book of Job

Both authorship and dating of the Book of Job are in doubt. Partly this is the result of the chaotic structure of the book in which there are not only two basic sections (the prose beginning and end, which seem to derive from older Near Eastern sources; and the poetic middle section, indigenous to Israel) but also evidence of a great many reworkings. Many speeches are confused, with characters taking contrary positions at different points in the text; others seem incomplete or distinctly added.

It is generally agreed that the author was a widely traveled and highly knowledgeable Jew, familiar with Mesopotamian and Egyptian myths, who adapted one of these as a setting for his poetic story. And, although the date of his composition is far from certain, 600–200 B.C. seems a likely period given the prominent role played by Satan (demonstrating perhaps a sixth- or fifth-century B.C. Persian influence) and a questioning of God's presence and concern (common after the Babylonian Exile).

Whoever he was, the author of Job was a person of great artistic talent and religious feeling. The speeches delivered by God to Job, of which Job 38 is a part, are among the most powerful in Old Testament literature. After Job has appealed for a hearing with the Lord to question him about his treatment of a worthy servant, God appears. Rather than answering charges of maltreatment, God questions Job's right to judge him. In this great speech, God proclaims himself the ground of being, the originator of the universe of which Job is only a dependent part. As one mystery of nature is revealed to Job, another unfolds behind it, and God pauses again and again to taunt Job with his ignorance and impotence.

While this speech of God's is in no way a direct answer to the plight of a good man needlessly tormented, the revelation of creation is at least an indirect response. Not only does it represent a communication from God to man and thereby demonstrate his presence and concern, but it also expresses (by its very disregard of Job's charges) the secondary nature of issues of good and evil in comparison with the primary nature of the issue of being. The "how" of the world bows here most clearly to the fact of its being. God's "goodness" is derivative of his creative power, of his *being*. And although modern readers, holding to the primacy of justice over being, are often dissatisfied with this answer, Job is not. Having understood the error of his presumption, he "melts away" and repents in dust and ashes.

(38:1) THEN the LORD answered Job
    out of the whirlwind:
(2) "Who is this that darkens counsel
    by words without knowledge?
(3) Gird up your loins like a man,
    I will question you, and you shall declare to me.

(4) "Where were you when I laid the foundation of the earth?
    Tell me, if you have understanding.
(5) Who determined its measurements—surely you know!
    Or who stretched the line upon it?
(6) On what were its bases sunk,
    or who laid its cornerstone,

(7) when the morning stars sang together,
and all the sons of God shouted for joy?

(8) "Or who shut in the sea with doors,
when it burst forth from the womb;
(9) when I made clouds its garment,
and thick darkness its swaddling band,
(10) and prescribed bounds for it,
and set bars and doors,
(11) and said, 'Thus far shall you come, and no farther,
and here shall your proud waves be stayed'?

(12) "Have you commanded the morning since your days began,
and caused the dawn to know its place,
(13) that it might take hold of the skirts of the earth,
and the wicked be shaken out of it?
(14) It is changed like clay under the seal,
and it is dyed like a garment.
(15) From the wicked their light is withheld,
and their uplifted arm is broken.

(16) "Have you entered into the springs of the sea,
or walked in the recesses of the deep?
(17) Have the gates of death been revealed to you,
or have you seen the gates of deep darkness?
(18) Have you comprehended the expanse of the earth?
Declare, if you know all this.

(19) "Where is the way to the dwelling of light,
and where is the place of darkness,
(20) that you may take it to its territory
and that you may discern the paths to its home?
(21) You know, for you were born then,
and the number of your days is great!

(22) "Have you entered the storehouses of the snow,
or have you seen the storehouses of the hail,
(23) which I have reserved for the time of trouble,
for the day of battle and war?
(24) What is the way to the place where the light is distributed,
or where the east wind is scattered upon the earth?

(25) "Who has cleft a channel for the torrents of rain,
and a way for the thunderbolt,
(26) to bring rain on a land where no man is,
on the desert in which there is no man;

(27) to satisfy the waste and desolate land,
    and to make the ground put forth grass?

(28) "Has the rain a father,
    or who has begotten the drops of dew?
(29) From whose womb did the ice come forth,
    and who has given birth to the hoarfrost of heaven?
(30) The waters become hard like stone,
    and the face of the deep is frozen.

(31) "Can you bind the chains of the Pleiades,
    or loose the cords of Orion?
(32) Can you lead forth the Maźzaroth in their season,
    or can you guide the Bear with its children?
(33) Do you know the ordinances of the heavens?
    can you establish their rule on the earth?

(34) "Can you lift up your voice to the clouds,
    that a flood of waters may cover you?
(35) Can you send forth lightnings, that they may go
    and say to you, 'Here we are'?
(36) Who has put wisdom in the clouds,
    or given understanding to the mists?
(37) Who can number the clouds by wisdom?
    Or who can tilt the waterskins of the heavens,
(38) when the dust runs into a mass
    and the clods cleave fast together?

(39) "Can you hunt the prey for the lion,
    or satisfy the appetite of the young lions,
(40) when they crouch in their dens,
    or lie in wait in their covert?
(41) Who provides for the raven its prey,
    when its young ones cry to God,
    and wander about for lack of food?

(42:1) THEN JOB answered the LORD:
(2)   "I know that thou canst do all things,
    and that no purpose of thine can be thwarted.
(3) 'Who is this that hides counsel
    without knowledge?'
Therefore I have uttered what I did not understand,
    things too wonderful for me, which I did not know.
(4) 'Hear, and I will speak;
    I will question you, and you declare to me.'

(5) I had heard of thee by the hearing of the ear,
   but now my eye sees thee;
(6) therefore I despise myself,
   and repent in dust and ashes."

—*Holy Bible*. Revised Standard Version. London: Thomas Nelson and Sons, Ltd., 1952

From Proverbs

The book of Proverbs in the Old Testament is a collection of educational material written in easily memorizable verse for the instruction of children of the court and upper classes. The "wisdom literature" it contains focuses not on metaphysical speculation, but on pragmatic, utilitarian advice. Like the "wisdom" of Egypt and Mesopotamia by which it was greatly influenced, Proverbs is noticeably universalist in tone and is further marked by a rather simplistic view of divine action and human character and a conservative view of political affairs. So directly was it borrowed from other ancient Near Eastern sources that Proverbs makes no attempt, aside from calling God Yahweh, to integrate its advice into a specifically Hebrew sociopolitical and religious context. That is not the case by the time of the later noncanonical Apocrypha, when "wisdom" had become an essential facet of Hebrew tradition.

Although authorship of Proverbs is conventionally ascribed to Solomon because his court introduced this form of literature into Israel, the actual books were written over the centuries by teachers or "wise men" of the court. In its present form, Proverbs was not collected until after the Babylonian Exile (586 B.C.) and maybe not until the fourth century B.C. While specific sections of the book may be much older, the first nine chapters, forming a kind of general introduction to the whole, probably came from the fourth century.

Given the pragmatic character of most "wisdom literature," it is not surprising that very little speculation of a theological nature is included. Chapter 8:22–31 is a notable exception. Here Wisdom, personified as a goddess, proclaims that she was present with God when the world was created: "The Lord created me the beginning of his works, before all else that he made, long ago" and throughout his creative efforts—as he prepared the heavens, tamed the seas, and created the earth—she was there.

Although seemingly more poetic than metaphysical in import, this depiction of Wisdom as a goddess of great stature and the companion to the creating God was most significant in the later development of a doctrine of Logos found in the New Testament.

(8:22) **T**HE **LORD** created me at the beginning of his work,
   the first of his acts of old.
(23) Ages ago I was set up,
   at the first, before the beginning of the earth.
(24) When there were no depths I was brought forth,
   when there were no springs abounding with water.
(25) Before the mountains had been shaped,
   before the hills, I was brought forth;
(26) before he had made the earth with its fields,
   or the first of the dust of the world.

(27) When he established the heavens, I was there,
    when he drew a circle on the face of the deep,
(28) when he made firm the skies above,
    when he established the fountains of the deep
(29) when he assigned to the sea its limit,
    so that the waters might not transgress his command,
(30) when he marked out the foundations of the earth,
    then I was beside him, like a master workman;
and I was daily his delight,
    rejoicing before him always,
(31) rejoicing in his inhabited world
    and delighting in the sons of men.

—*Holy Bible.* Revised Standard Version. London: Thomas Nelson and Sons, Ltd., 1952.

From the Gospel According to John

The last of the gospels was written in Asia, most probably at Ephesus, after the expulsion of Jewish Christian believers from the synagogues around 90 A.D. The identity of the author is in considerable doubt: some claim he is John, son of Zebedee and one of Jesus' apostles; others cite both the appendix and obvious editorial work in the text in arguing for another, unknown writer. In any case, the author's Jewish origin and Greek training are presumed, and his purpose in writing the gospel is clear: "that you may believe that Jesus is the Christ, the son of God, and that believing you may have life in his name."

The gospel begins with the assertion that "In the beginning was the Word, and the Word was with God and the Word was God," echoing not only Genesis 1:1, where God creates the universe by command, by a word, but also later wisdom literature, which personified wisdom and envisioned her as a distinct but related entity present with God at the creation. The Word of John is associated also with *Logos*, the Greek term signifying God's creative mind. In this instance, the Word is both separate from and identical with God—an aspect of divinity. Personified as "he," the Word is the agent of creation through whom all things were made. And he is identified with both the physical life and light that originated at the beginning and the spiritual life and light that were revealed when the Word transformed itself into flesh as Jesus Christ.

(1:1) IN THE BEGINNING was the Word, and the Word was with God, and the Word was God. (2) He was in the beginning with God; (3) all things were made through him, and without him was not anything made that was made. (4) In him was life, and the life was the light of men. (5) The light shines in the darkness, and the darkness has not overcome it.

(6) There was a man sent from God, whose name was John. (7) He came for testimony, to bear witness to the light, that all might believe through him. (8) He was not the light, but came to bear witness to the light.

(9) The true light that enlightens every man was coming into the world. (10) He was in the world, and the world was made through him, yet the world

knew him not. (11) He came to his own home, and his own people received him not. (12) But to all who received him, who believed in his name, he gave power to become children of God; (13) who were born, not of blood nor of the will of the flesh nor of the will of man, but of God.

(14) And the Word became flesh and dwelt among us, full of grace and truth; we have beheld his glory, glory as of the only Son from the Father. (15) (John bore witness to him, and cried, "This was he of whom I said, 'He who comes after me ranks before me, for he was before me.' ") (16) And from his fulness have we all received, grace upon grace. (17) For the law was given through Moses; grace and truth came through Jesus Christ. (18) No one has even seen God; the only Son, who is in the bosom of the Father, he has made him known.
—*Holy Bible*. Revised Standard Version. London: Thomas Nelson and Sons, Ltd., 1952.

ZOROASTRIAN MYTHS

From the Exegesis of the Good Religion

Although the *Avesta* or sacred book of Zoroastrianism was organized in its present form during the reign of Shahpur II (309–380 A.D.), much of its material is far older. Zarathustra himself (born c. 590 B.C.) is thought to have written one section of it, a collection of seventeen hymns called the Gathas. Unfortunately, given their composition in an ancient form of the Avestan language, translation of them is not certain.

This exegesis (analysis and commentary, c. 350 A.D.) of the *Avesta* depicts creation in abstract physical terms as a kind of birth of matter out of pure "form." In the beginning, only endless light existed. Without external boundaries, it is the One, pure and without other. But within it is twofold: an ideal creation containing the Spirit of the Power of the Word and a material creation with its nucleus of the Spirit of the Power of Nature. After the two spirits were united by the will of the creator (the Light conceived as a whole and personalized?), the material world evolved.

In its first stage, matter was a chaotic mass. Then conception (or hollowing) and formation (or expansion) produced the first body, the first thing with both matter and form. This body then united with the Spirit of the Power of the Word to form the firmament (or, in more philosophical terms, the Wheel of Change). The firmament contained the sun, moon, and stars like embryos within it, and these great natural bodies were the ruling forces in the physical world. All this activity produced "becoming" (expressed in the hot, moist air), which set the elements in motion, revealed the primary physical qualities, and ultimately resulted in the "settling of becoming" or the formation of living things.

While the text of this commentary could apply equally well in terms of its developmental stages to the ancient sacred hymns or to a modern scientific cosmology, the tone is revelatory and religious, for it proclaims the createdness of "ordinary" form and matter, the power of the Holy Word, and the ability to perceive that Spirit, the supernatural, in and through the natural.

CONCERNING the original coming to be of the material creation, from the Exegesis of the Good Religion.

This is what is revealed concerning the instrument which the Creator fashioned from the Endless Light and in which he caused creation to be contained. Its Avestan name is the Endless Form and it is twofold. On the one hand it contains the "ideal" creation; on the other the material creation. In the "ideal" creation the Spirit of the Power of the Word was contained; and in the material creation the Spirit of the Power of Nature was contained, and it settled (in it). The instrument which contains the ideal creation was made perfect and the spiritual (ideal) gods of the Word were separated from it, each for its own function, to perform those activities which were necessary for the creation that was within the instrument. And within the instrument which contains the material creation the marvellous Spirit of the Power of Nature was united to the kingdom of the Spirit of the Power of the Word through the will of the Creator.

In greater detail this is what is revealed concerning the nature of the material world. First was the stage the Avestan name of which is the mass and which is called the . . . mass or conglomeration in the language of the world. From the stage which is called the mass and conglomeration (proceeded) the stage the Avestan name of which is conception and also hollowing and which is called the new phenomenon(?) and also . . . in the language of men. It is (as) an ailment(??) in the mass, and it was inserted into it. From the stage which is called conception, hollowing, the new phenomenon(?) and . . . (proceeded) the stage the Avestan name of which is formation and which is called expansion in the language of men. It is as an ailment(??) in the (former) stage and it was inserted into that stage. From the stage the name of which is formation and expansion (proceeded) the first body united with the Spirit of the Power of the Word; and its Avestan name is the Wheel and it also has the name of Spahr (ﬤwasa) and in the language of men it is called the firmament (*spihr*). In it, like embryos, are the luminaries, the Sun, Moon, and stars, all of the same origin. They control all creation under them and are themselves the highest natural phenomena. From the Wheel proceeded becoming, the hot and the moist of which air is composed: these are connected with the spiritual Word and share in its power: (and from it also proceeded) the elements which are the seed of seeds of material creations and which are the movement of becoming. The elements are called the form of the becoming of the primary qualities. From the movement of becoming (proceeded) the settling of becoming, living things, which include material cattle and men, for they are the form and shape of matter.

—R. C. Zaehner. *Zurvan: A Zoroastrian Dilemma*. Oxford, England: Clarendon Press, 1955, pp. 373–374.

Speaking of the World
After Zarathustra's death (c. sixth century B.C.), Zoroastrianism was changed—probably by the Magi, Median priests who came later to the faith. They incorporated certain deities such as

Mithra, the Indo-Iranian sun god, and Anahitam, the fertility goddess, and absorbed astralism into the cult. In addition, the two primal spirits of Zarathustra's creation myth evolved into Ohrmazd (that is, Ahura Mazdah), the spirit of goodness, and Ahriman, the principle of evil. Largely in this form, Zoroastrianism became the established religion of Iran and lasted until the Islamic conquest in the seventh century A.D.

A Zurvanite strain of Zoroastrianism from which this myth comes competed with this more traditional form of the religion. Zurvan, the god of time, was an ancient deity; there are references to his name as far back as the twelfth century B.C. Evidence of his adoption into the Iranian cult comes in later forms of the Videvat ("Law against the Demons"), where Zurvan appears in two forms: as Infinite Time (Zurvan aharana) and as "Time of the Long Dominion" or finite time (Zurvan deregho-chvadhata). There is an obvious parallel here to the earlier Gathas in which light was conceived in a similar manner, as absolute and unmanifest on the one hand and relative and manifest on the other.

In this Islamic commentary on Zoroastrian cosmology (from the second Ulema i Islam, vv. 6–20), Time is understood as the boundless eternal creator. Time made fire and water and, mixing the two, produced Ohrmazd (goodness). The origin of Ahriman (evil) is not explained here, but as soon as he was seen by Ohrmazd, the two gods proceded to do battle through creation.

Ohrmazd made finite time—the Time of the Long Dominion (12,000 years)—out of Infinite Time and filled it with sky and the stars to ultimately mark its passage. Overwhelmed by Ohrmazd's righteousness, Ahriman was rendered inactive for the first 3,000 years of creation. During the next quarter of the "Long Dominion," Ohrmazd made the sky, water, earth, plants, the Bull, and Gayomart (primal man), and finally Adam and Eve. After he had finished, Evil came into the world and polluted it with his demons of Foulness, Darkness, and Stench. The forces of good finally captured him and bound him in hell under guard.

(6)   **F**IRST I will speak of the world and discuss whether it has (always) existed or whether it was created. If it should be said that it has (always) existed, this opinion is untenable: for ever anew do things wax in the world and then again wane [and wax], decrease and then again increase. Further all that is susceptible of coming to be and passing away and is the effect of a cause is not proper to God. Thus it is established that the world has not (always) existed and that it has been created. Moreover, a created thing necessarily implies a Creator. (7) Now it must be known that in the Pahlavi religion to which the Zoroastrians adhere, the world is said to have been created. After saying that the world has been created we must further say who created it and when, how, and why he created it.

(8) In the religion of Zoroaster it is thus revealed. Except Time all other things are created. Time is the creator; and Time has no limit, neither top nor bottom. It has always been and shall be for evermore. No sensible person will say whence Time has come. In spite of all the grandeur that surrounded it, there was no one to call it creator; for it had not brought forth creation. (9) Then it created fire and water; and when it had brought them together, Ohrmazd came into existence, and simultaneously Time became Creator and Lord with regard to the cre-

ation it had brought forth. (10) Ohrmazd was bright, pure, sweet-smelling, and beneficent, and had power over all good things. Then, he looked down, he saw Ahriman ninety-six thousand parasangs away, black, foul, stinking, and malefi- cent; and it appeared fearful to Ohrmazd, for he was a frightful enemy. (11) And when Ohrmazd saw this enemy, he thought thus: "I must utterly destroy this en- emy," and he considered with what and how many instruments he could destroy him. (12) Then did Ohrmazd begin the work of creation. Whatever Ohrmazd did, he did with the aid of Time; for all the excellence that Ohrmazd needed, had (already) been created. And Ohrmazd made Time of the Long Dominion mani- fest which has the measure of twelve thousand years, and within it he attached the firmament, the artificer (and heaven). (13) And each of the twelve Signs of the Zodiac which are bound to the firmament he appointed for a thousand years. During three thousand years the spiritual creation was made; and Aries, Taurus, and Gemini held sway each for a thousand years. (14) Then Ahriman (with the aid of Time) turned toward the heights that he might do battle with Ohrmazd: he saw an army marshalled and drawn up in ranks, and rushed back to hell. From the foulness, darkness, and stench that was wihin him, he raised an army. This was possible for him. In this matter much has been said. The meaning of this is that when he (saw he) was empty-handed, he rushed back to hell. (15) Because of the righteousness he saw in Ohrmazd for three thousand years he could not move, so that during these thousand years material creation was made. The con- trol of the world passed to Cancer, Leo, and Virgo. In this matter much has been said.

(16) I will say a few words on this subject. In the creation of the material world first he manifested the sky, and the measure of it was twenty-four (thou- sand) by twenty-four thousand parasangs, and its top reached Garooman . . . . After forty-five days he caused the water to appear (from the sky): after sixty days the earth appeared out of the water: after seventy-five days he manifested plants, large and small: after thirty days the Bull and Gayomart appeared: and after eighty days Adam and Eve made their appearance. (17) When the three thousand years we have mentioned (had elapsed) and Man, the material world, and the other creatures we have mentioned had come into existence, the accursed Ahriman again bestirred himself: and (Time brought it about that Ahriman) bored a hole in the sky, the mountains, and the earth, rushed into the material world and defiled everything in it with his wickedness and impurity. (18) As he possessed no spiritual thing, he did battle for ninety days and nights in the mate- rial world; and the firmament was rent, and the spiritual beings came to the as- sistance of the material world. (19) And they seized the seven most evil demons and brought them to the firmament and bound them with unseen (spiritual, *minu*) bonds. And Ahriman afflicted Gayomart with a thousand torments till he passed away. And from him certain things came into existence. About this much has been said. From the Bull too certain things and animals came into existence. About this much has been said. (20) Then they seized upon Ahriman and carried him off to hell by that very hole through which he had entered the world; and

they bound him with unseen bonds. Two angels, even Ardibihist, the Amahra-spand, and Varhram, the god, stood in guard over him.

—R. C. Zaehner. *Zurvan: A Zoroastrian Dilemma.* Oxford, England: Clarendon Press, 1955, pp. 409–411.

On the Mixing of the Bounteous Spirit and the Destructive Spirit

In this Zoroastrian myth from the first chapter of *Selections of Zatspram,* Zurvan (the ancient god of time), Ohrmazd (the principle of goodness), and Ahriman (the principle of Evil) are all active. As a protection against the Lie of the Destructive Spirit, Ohrmazd first fashioned the ideal creation—the incorruptible forms of sky, water, earth, plants, cattle, man, and fire—and with the help of Zurvan managed to fix the temporal boundaries for the coming conflict. For the first half of manifest time (6,000 years), Ohrmazd managed to avoid a confrontation by use of the religious law and prayers. For the next 3,000 years, after he had made the ideal creation manifest and material, he still kept everything pure by withholding motion and thus change. But, since the purpose of creation was to allow evil to express itself and thereby be overcome by good, Ohrmazd asked Zurvan to make motion and animate the world. Ahriman then entered the universe and pulled it down to his dark and evil realm so that only the top of the sky remained close to the light of goodness. According to Zoroastrianism, the subsequent battle between the two great principles is being fought out now in time on earth.

(1) THUS is it revealed in the Religion: the light was above and the darkness beneath; and between the two was the Void. (2) Ohrmazd in the light and Ahriman in the darkness. Ohrmazd knew of the existence of Ahriman and of his coming to do battle: Ahriman knew not of the existence and light of Ohrmazd. (3) In the dismal darkness he wandered to the nether side: then, rushing, he came up and beheld a point of light, and because it was of a different substance from himself, he strove to attain it, and his desire for it waxed so mightily that (it was as great as his desire) for the darkness. (4) When he came to the boundary, Ohrmazd, wishing to hold Ahriman back from his kingdom, advanced to join battle. By the pure word of the Law he laid him low and hurled him back into the darkness. As a protection against the Lie he fashioned in the heights the "ideal" sky, water, earth, plants, cattle, man, and fire—all in ideal form. For three thousand years he held him back. (5) Ahriman too was preparing weapons in the darkness.

At the end of three thousand years he returned to the boundary, and threatening said, "I shall smite thee, I shall smite thy creatures. Art thou of a mind to create a creation, O thou who art the Bounteous Spirit? Verily I shall utterly destroy it." (6) Ohrmazd answered (and said,) "Thou canst not, O Lie, accomplish all."

(7) Again Ahriman threatened (saying), "I shall bring all corporeal existence to hate thee and to love me."

(8) Ohrmazd, in his spiritual wisdom, saw that what Ahriman had threatened he could do unless the time of the conflict were limited. (9) He begged Time to aid him, for he saw that through no intermediary belonging to the light would (Ahriman) desist. Time is a good helper and right orderer of both: there is need of it. (10) (Ohrmazd) made it in three periods, each period three thousand years. (11) Ahriman desisted.

(12) Ohrmazd saw that unless Ahriman were encompassed, he would return to his own principle of darkness whenever he so willed and would prepare more weapons, and the conflict would be without end. After fixing the time, he chanted the Ahunvar. (13) And in the Ahunvar he showed him three things. (14) First that every righteous thing is the will of Ohrmazd: (15) and from this it is plain that since righteousness is the will of Ohrmazd, obviously there are things which are not according to the will of Ohrmazd—and these can only be whatever has its root in Vay who is of a different substance. (16) Secondly this, that he who does the will of Ohrmazd, reward and recompense are his; and he who does not the will of Ohrmazd, punishment and retribution are his. (17) This shows the reward of the virtuous and the punishment of sinners, and thence, too, heaven and hell. (18) Thirdly it shows that the sovereignty of Ohrmazd prospers him who keeps affliction from the poor. (19) This shows that the wealthy are to help the needy: as the learned teach the ignorant, so should the rich generously lend a helping hand to the poor; for the creatures of Ohrmazd are in strife and battle one with another.

(20) For the final rehabilitation will be effected by these three things. (21) First orthodoxy, that is the belief in two principles, in this wise and manner that Ohrmazd is all good and devoid of evil and his will is all-holy; and that Ahriman is all evil and devoid of good. (22) Second, the hope of reward and recompense for the virtuous and the fear of punishment and retribution for sinners, striving after virtue and shunning vice. (23) Third, that creatures should help one another: for from mutual help comes solidarity, from solidarity victory over the enemy, and this is the final rehabilitation.

(24) By this word (Ahriman) was laid low and fell back into the darkness.

(25) (Then) Ohrmazd projected creation in bodily form onto the material plane, first the sky, second water, third earth, fourth plants, fifth cattle, sixth man: and fire permeated all six elements, and the period for which it was inserted into each element lasted, it is said, as much as the twinkling of an eye. (26) For three thousand years creation was corporeal and motionless. Sun, Moon, and stars stood still in the heights and did not move.

(27) At the end of (this) period Ohrmazd considered, "What profit have we from our creation if it neither moves nor walks nor flies?" And with the aid of the firmament and Zurvan he fashioned creation forth. (28) Zurvan had power to set the creation of Ohrmazd in motion without giving motion to the creation of Ahriman, for the (two) principles were harmful to each other and mutually opposed.

(29) Pondering on the end he (Zurvan) delivered to Ahriman an implement (fashioned) from the very substance of darkness, mingled with the power of Zurvan, as it were a treaty, resembling coal (?), black and ashen. (30) And as he handed it to him, he said, "By means of these weapons Az (concupiscence) will devour that which is thine and she herself shall starve, if at the end of nine thousand years thou hast not accomplished that which thou didst threaten, to finish off the treaty, to finish off Time."

(31) Meanwhile Ahriman, together with his powers went to the station of the stars. (32) The bottom of the sky was in the station of the stars: from there he dragged it into the Void which lies between the principles of light and darkness and is the field of battle where both move. (33) And the darkness he had with him he brought into the sky; and he dragged the sky down into the darkness so that within the roof of the sky as much as one third only could reach above the region of the stars.

—R. C. Zaehner. *Zurvan: A Zoroastrian Dilemma.* Oxford, England: Clarendon Press, 1955, pp. 341–343.

Answer of the Spirit of Wisdom

The influence of astrology in later Zoroastrianism, coupled with a recognition of Time (Zurvan) as an independent power, is most evident in this mythical exchange between a wise man and the Spirit of Wisdom (from the eighth chapter of the *Menok i Xrat*).

With the blessing of Time, Ohrmazd (the principle of goodness) fashioned the material world, the spiritual beings (Amahraspands), and the Spirit of Wisdom out of his own essence of light. And, in a vividly described fashion, Ahriman (the principle of evil) committed sodomy on his own person and thereby "gave birth to the demons, lies and other abortions." If procreation is the common metaphor for divine creation, given its usefulness as a way of describing the origin of something out of nothing, this analogy of self-sodomy is an arresting way to point out the self-centeredness and essential uncreativity of Evil's "creative" act.

Numerology becomes important later in the myth as seven—the number of planets and days of the week, and here a symbol of evil—is contrasted with twelve—the number of signs of the zodiac, months in the year, thousands of years in finite time, and the symbol of goodness. The thorough blending of the two in all spheres appropriately reflects the mixture of good and evil found in life—a condition which will exist until Ohriman is defeated and creation dissolves back into the infinite goodness of Ohrmazd.

(1) THE WISE MAN asked the Spirit of Wisdom (saying), "How and in what manner did Ohrmazd create this creation? (2) And how and in what manner did he fashion and create the Amahraspands and the Spirit of Wisdom? (3) How did the accursed Ahriman give birth to the demons and lies and other abortions? (4) And how do all good and bad things come to mankind and other creatures? (5) And can what is destined be changed or not?"

(6) The Spirit of Wisdom made answer (and said), "The Creator Ohr-

mazd fashioned this creation and the Amahraspands and the Spirit of Wisdom from his own light with the blessing of the Infinite Zurvan: (7) for the Infinite Zurvan is unageing, undying, without pain, uncorrupting and undecaying, free from aggression, and for ever and ever no one can violate him nor deprive him of his sovereignty in his proper sphere.

(8) And the accursed Ahriman gave birth to the demons and lies and the other abortions by committing sodomy on his own person. (9) And for nine thousand years he made a treaty with Ohrmazd through infinite Time and till it is completed no one can change it or make it different. (10) And when nine thousand years have fully elapsed, Ahriman will be made powerless; and Sros the Blessed will smite Esm (Wrath); and Mihr, the Infinite Zurvan and the Genius of the Law (justice or order) who lie to no one, and Fate and the divine Fate will smite all the creation of Ahriman, and in the end the demon Az also: (11) and all the creation of Ohrmazd will again be free from aggression as it was fashioned and created in the beginning.

(12) All welfare and adversity that come to man and other creatures come through the Seven and the Twelve. (13) The twelve Signs of the Zodiac, as the Religion says, are the twelve commanders on the side of Ohrmazd; and the seven planets are said to be the seven commanders on the side of Ahriman. (14) And the seven planets oppress all creation and deliver it over to death and all manner of evil: for the twelve Signs of the Zodiac and the seven planets rule the fate of the world and direct it.

(15) Ohrmazd desires welfare and is never susceptible to evil, nor does it beseem him. And Ahriman desires evil and never thinks of anything good nor is he susceptible to it. (16) Sometimes, when he wills, Ohrmazd can change the creation of Ahriman; and sometimes, when he wills, Ahriman can change the creation of Ohrmazd; but he can only change it in such wise that in the end Ohrmazd suffers no loss; for the final victory belongs to Ohrmazd. (17) For it is revealed that Ohrmazd created Yam and Freton and Kayos immortal but Ahriman changed this in the manner that is known. And to Ahriman it seemed that Bevarasp (Dahak) and Frasyak and Alexander were immortal: and Ohrmazd changed this for this greater profit as it is revealed."

—R. C. Zaehner. *Zurvan: A Zoroastrian Dilemma*. Oxford, England: Clarendon Press, 1955, pp. 368–369.

From the Poimandres of Hermes Trismegistus
Popular all over the Graeco-Roman world, Gnosticism was a religious movement comprised of many various sects, most quite independent of each other but nevertheless holding certain ideas in common. All pre-

sumed a fundamental cosmological dualism like that of Zoroastrianism and all not only posited the eternal existence of good and evil spirits but also identified the former with light, mind and spirit and the latter with darkness and materiality. The world was generally seen as the creation of a lesser god (or an evil one) and as the realm in which particles of light were trapped in evil matter. Illusion was common here, and thus "gnosis" or saving knowledge was required to educate souls as to their true origin and the possibility of escape back into pure form. While the origin of Gnosticism is somewhat uncertain (even though it has obvious parallels to Orphism and other eastern cults), its influences on early Christianity are both evident and powerful.

The mostly Gnostic writings of Hermes Trismegistus (the "thrice great," one of Thoth's titles applied to Hermes in the mistaken belief that he and Thoth were the same) originated in Hellenistic Egypt in the second century A.D. In the first book, the Poimandres (shepherd of Men) appears and reveals the nature of the world (transformed from the Will of God), the Demiurge (produced by the Nous, the Mind of God), and man (brought forth by the Nous, like unto himself).

Man's fall into the realm of mindless nature resulted from his love of the divine reflection in earth's waters. Ever after unique among creatures, he has a dual identity: "For though he is immortal and has power over all things, he suffers the lot of mortality." The tragic character of this mixing of light and darkness, of spirit and matter, becomes clearer as the ensnared souls struggle to ascend back out of the material world and rejoin themselves to divinity.

(1) ONCE, when I had engaged in meditation upon the things that are and my mind was mightily lifted up, while my bodily senses were curbed ... I thought I beheld a presence of immeasurable greatness that called my name and said to me:" "What dost thou wish to hear and see and in thought learn and understand?" (2) I said, "Who are thou?" "I am," he said, "Poimandres, the Nous of the Absolute Power. I know what thou wishest, and I am with thee everywhere." (3) I said, "I desire to be taught about the things that are and understand their nature and know God. ..." And he replied, "Hold fast in thy mind what thou wishest to learn, and I shall teach thee."

(4) With these words, he changed his form, and suddenly everything was opened before me in a flash, and I beheld a boundless view, everything became Light, serene and joyful. And I became enamored with the sight. And after a while there was a Darkness borne downward ..., appalling and hateful, tortuously coiled, resembling a serpent. Then I saw this darkness change into some humid nature, indescribably agitated and giving off smoke as from a fire and uttering a kind of sound unspeakable, mournful. Then a roar [or, cry] came forth from it unarticulately, comparable to the voice of a fire. (5) From out of the Light a holy Word [logos] came over the nature, and unmixed fire leapt out of the humid nature upward to the height; it was light and keen, and active at the same time; and the air, being light, followed the fiery breath, rising up as far as the fire from earth and water, so that it seemed suspended from it; but earth and water remained in their place, intermingled, so that the earth was not discernible apart from the water; and they were kept in audible motion through the breath of the Word which was borne over them.

(6) Then Poimandres said to me: ". . . That light is I, Nous, thy God, who was before the humid nature that appeared out of the Darkness. And the luminous Word that issued from Nous is the Son of God. . . . By this understand: that which in thee sees and hears is the Word of the Lord, but the Nous [thy nous?] is God the Father: they are not separate from each other, for Life is the union of these. . . . Now then, fix your mind on the Light and learn to know it."

(7) Having said this, he gazed long at me intently, so that I trembled at his aspect; then when he looked up, I behold in my nous the Light consisting in innumerable Powers and become a boundless Cosmos, and the fire contained by a mighty power and under its firm control keeping its place. . . .

(8) He again speaks to me: "Thou hast seen in the Nous the archetypal form, the principle preceding the infinite beginning.". . . ."Wherefrom then," I ask, "have the elements of nature arisen?" To which he replies: "From the Will of God, who having received into herself the Word and beheld the beautiful [archetypal] Cosmos, imitated it, fashioning herself into a cosmos [or: ordering herself] according to her own elements and her progeny, i.e., the souls.

"(9) But the divine Nous, being androgynous, existing as Life and Light, brought forth by a word another Nous, the Demiurge, who as god over the fire and the breath fashioned seven Governors, who encompass with their circles the sensible world, and their government is called Heimarmene [Destiny]. (10) Forthwith the Word of God leapt out of the downward-borne elements upward into the pure [part of the] physical creation [the demiurgical sphere] and became united with the Nous-Demiurge, for he was of the same substance. And thus the lower elements of Nature were left without reason, so that they were now mere Matter. (11) And together with the Word the Nous-Demiurge, encompassing the circles and whirling them with thunderous speed, set his creations circling in endless revolution, for it begins where it ends. And this rotation of the spheres according to the will of the Nous[-Demiurge] produced out of the lower elements irrational animals, for those elements had not retained the Word. . . . [air, water, earth—the last two now separated—each producing its own animals: androgynous ones, as appears later.]

"(12) Now the Nous, Father of all, being Life and Light, brought forth Man like to himself, of whom he became enamored as his own child, for he was very beautiful, since he bore the Father's image; for indeed even God became enamored of his own form, and he delivered over to him all his works. (13) And Man, beholding the creation which the Demiurge had fashioned in the fire [the celestial spheres], wished himself to create as well, and was permitted by the Father. When he had entered the demiurgical sphere where he was to have full authority, he beheld his brother's works, and they [the seven Governors] became enamored of him, and each gave him a share in his own realm. Having come to know their essence and having received a share of their nature, he then wished to break through the circumference of the circles and to overcome [?] the power of him who rules over the fire. (14) And he [Man] who had full power over the world of things mortal and over the irrational animals bent down through the Harmony and having broken through the vault showed to lower Nature the beautiful form of God. When she beheld him who had in himself inexhaustible beauty and all the forces of the Governors combined with the form of God, she smiled in love; for she had seen the reflection of this most beautiful form of Man in the water and its shadow upon the earth. He too, seeing his likeness present in her, reflected in the water, loved it and desired to dwell in it. At once with the wish it became reality, and he came to inhabit the form devoid of reason. And Nature, having received into herself the beloved, embraced him wholly, and they mingled: for they were inflamed with love. (15) And this is why alone of all the animals on earth man is twofold, mortal through the body, immortal through the essential Man. For though he is immortal and has power over all things, he suffers the lot of mortality, being subject to the Heimarmene; though he was above the Harmony, he has become a slave within the Harmony; though he was androgynous, having issued from the androgynous Father, and unsleeping from the unsleeping one, he is conquered by love and sleep."

Since the Man, now intermingled with Nature, "had in himself the nature of the harmony of the Seven," Nature brought forth seven androgynous men, corresponding to the natures of the seven Governors. We pass over the details of the respective contributions of the elements earth, water, fire, and ether to the constitution of these creatures. As to the contribution of Man as a part of the begetting mixture, he turned "from Life and Light into soul and mind (*nous*), into soul from Life and into mind from Light." (17) This condition of creation lasted to the end of a world-era. The new world-era was initiated by the separation of all the androgynous creatures, animals and men alike, into male and female. And here occurs the only instance in which the author shows his familiarity with the Greek Old Testament in something like a direct quotation: on the model of Gen. 1:22, 28, God admonishes the new bisexual creation, "Be fruitful and multiply," then continues in a very different vein: "and [man] endowed with mind shall recognize that he is immortal and that the cause of death is love" (viz., ultimately the love which drew the Primal Man down into nature). (18) He who has come thus to know himself has come into the supreme good; he, however, who has cherished the body issued from the error of love, he remains in the darkness erring, suffering in his senses the dispensations of death. What then is the sin of those ignorant ones, that they should be deprived of immortality? The first cause of the individual body is the hateful darkness, from which came the humid nature, from which was constituted the body of the sensible world, from which death draws nourishment. Thus the lovers of the body actually are *in* death and deserve death. On the other hand, he who knows himself knows that the Father of all things consists of Light and Life, therefore likewise the Primal Man issued from him, and by this he knows himself to be of Light and Life, and will through this knowledge return to the Life. The knowing ones, filled with love for the Father, before they deliver the body to its own death abhor the senses, whose effects they know; and the Poimandres-Nous assists them in this by acting as a warder at the gates and barring entrance to the evil influences of the body. The unknowing ones are left a prey to all the evil passions, whose insatiability is their torment, always augmenting the flame that consumes them.

[The last part of the instruction (24–26) is devoted to the soul's ascent after death. First at the dissolution of the material body you yield up to the demon your sensuous nature (?) now ineffective, and the bodily senses return each to its source among the elements.] "(25) And thereafter, man thrusts upward through the Harmony, and to the first zone he surrenders the power to grow and to decrease, and to the second the machinations of evil cunning, now rendered powerless, and to the third the deceit of concupiscence, now rendered powerless, and to the fourth the arrogance of dominion, drained of [or: now impotent to achieve] its ambition, and to the fifth the impious audacity and the rashness of impulsive deed, and to the sixth the evil appetites of wealth, now rendered powerless, and to the seventh zone the lying that ensnares. (26) And then denuded of the effects of the Harmony, he enters the nature of the Ogdoas [i.e., the eighth sphere, that of the fixed stars], now in possession of his own power, and with those already there exalts the Father; and those persent rejoice with him at his presence, and having become like his companions he hears also certain powers above the eighth sphere exalting God with a sweet voice. And then in procession they rise up towards the Father and give themselves up to the Powers, and having become Powers themselves, enter the Godhead. This is the good end of those who have attained gnosis: to become God."

—Hans Jonas. *The Gnostic Religion*. Boston: Beacon Press, 1958, pp. 148–153.

The Creation According to Mani
The founder of the most popular form of Gnosticism, Mani was born in Seleucia-Ctesiphon c. 215 A.D. and, until he was flayed to death by the Sassanian king Bahram I some sixty years later, taught a religion combining the theologies of the Buddha, Jesus, and Zoroaster. The last was the most influential in terms of Mani's cosmology as can be seen by the radical dualism of this myth.

Creation is understood only in terms of the continuing battle between good and evil here. After the initial defeat of Primal Man and his helpers by the forces of darkness, the trapped light and good elements tried to escape. Rescue missions by the Living Spirit and the Messenger were only partially successful, although the latter set the world in motion so that matter would ultimately disintegrate and the light be freed. Realizing his only hope for retaining light lay in increasing the amount of matter, the King of Darkness created Adam and Eve and encouraged them to procreate. To counteract that move, the Father of Greatness sent Jesus to reveal the saving knowledge (gnosis) of true origin and identity to Adam. The myth ends with Adam's lament over his alienation from the light—a lament that characterizes the longing for release from relativity and materiality central to Manichaean dualism.

BEFORE the existence of heaven and earth and everything in them there were two natures, the one good and the other evil. Both are separate each from the other. The good principle dwells in the place of Light and is called 'Father of Greatness.' Outside him dwelt his five Sh'kinas: Intelligence,

Knowledge, Thought, Deliberation, Resolution. The evil principle is called 'King of Darkness,' and he dwells in his land of Darkness surrounded by his five Aeons (or, 'Worlds'), the Aeons of Smoke, of Fire, of Wind, of Water, and of Darkness. The world of Light borders on that of Darkness without a dividing wall between the two.

The Darkness was divided against itself—the tree against its fruits and the fruits against the tree. Strife and bitterness belong to the nature of its parts; the gentle stillness is alien to them who are filled with every malignity, and each destroys what is close to him.

Yet it was their very tumult which gave them the occasion to rise up to the worlds of Light. For truly, these members of the tree of death did not even know one another to begin with. Each one had but his own mind, each knew nothing but his own voice and saw but what was before his eyes. Only when one of them screamed did they hear him and turned impetuously towards the sound.

Thus aroused and mutually incited they fought and devoured one another, and they did not cease to press each other hard, until at last they caught sight of the Light. For in the course of the war they came, some pursued and some pursuing, to the boundaries of the Light, and when they beheld the Light—a sight wondrous and glorious, by far superior to their own—it pleased them and they marvelled at it; and they assembled—all the Matter of Darkness—and conferred how they could mingle with the Light. But because of the disorder of their minds they failed to perceive that the strong and mighty God dwelt there. And they strove to rise upward to the height, because never a knowledge of the Good and the Godhead had come to them. Thus without understanding, they cast a mad glance upon it from lust for the spectacle of these blessed worlds, and they thought it could become theirs. And carried away by the passion within them, they now wished with all their might to fight against it in order to bring it into their power and to mix with the Light their own Darkness. They united the whole dark pernicious Hyle and with their innumerable forces rose all together, and in desire for the better opened the attack. They attacked in one body, as it were without knowing their adversary, for they had never heard of the Deity.

As the King of Darkness was planning to mount up to the place of Light, fear spread through the five Sh'kinas. Then the Father of Greatness considered and said:

> "Of these my Aeons, the five Sh'kinas,
> I shall send none forth to battle,
> For I created them for peace and blessedness.
> I myself will go instead
> And will wage war against the enemy."

The Father of Greatness called forth the Mother of Life, and the Mother of Life called forth the Primal Man, and the Primal Man called forth his five Sons, like a man who girds on his armor for battle. The Father charged him with the struggle against the Darkness. And the Primal Man armed himself with the five kinds, and these are the five gods: the light breeze, the wind, the light, the water, and the fire. He made them his armor . . . [we pass over the detailed description of how he clothed himself in these elements one by one, lastly taking the fire for a shield and lance] and plunged rapidly from the Paradises downward until he came to the border of the area adjoining the battlefield. Before him advanced an angel, who spread light ahead of the Primal Man.

The Arch-devil too took his five kinds, namely the smoke, and consuming fire, the darkness, the scorching wind, and the fog, armed himself with them, and went to meet the Primal Man. As the King of Darkness beheld the light of the Primal Man, he took thought and spoke: "What I sought afar I found near by." After they had struggled long with one another, the Arch-devil overcame the Primal Man. Thereupon the Primal Man gave himself and his five Sons as food to the five Sons of Darkness, as a man who has an enemy mixes a deadly poison in a cake and gives it to him. The Arch-devil devoured part of his light [viz., his five sons] and at the same time surrounded him with his kinds and elements. As the Sons of Darkness had devoured them, the five luminous gods were deprived of understanding, and through the poison of the Sons of Darkness they became like a man who has been bitten by a mad dog or a serpent. And the five parts of Light became mixed with the five parts of Darkness.

The Primal Man regained consciousness and addressed seven times a prayer to the Father of Greatness. The Father heard his prayer and called forth as the second creation the Friend of Lights, and the Friend of Lights called forth the Great Architect, and the Great Architect called forth the Living Spirit. And the Living Spirit called forth his five sons [one from each of the five spiritual natures of God; we pass over their names]. And they betook themselves to the Land of Darkness and from the boundary looked down into the abyss of the deep Hell and found the Primal Man swallowed up in the Darkness, him and his five sons. Then the Living Spirit called with a loud voice; and the voice of the Living Spirit became like to a sharp sword and laid bare the form of the Primal Man. And he spoke to him:

> "Peace be unto thee, good one amidst the wicked,
> luminous one amidst the darkness,
> God who dwells amidst the beasts of wrath,
> who do not know his honor."

Thereupon Primal Man answered him and spoke:

> "Come for the peace of him who is dead,
> come, oh treasure of serenity and peace!"

and he spoke further to him:

> "How is it with our Fathers,
> the Sons of Light in their city?"

And the Call said unto him: "It is well with them." And Call and Answer joined each other and ascended to the Mother of Life and to the Living Spirit. The Living Spirit put on the Call and the Mother of Life put on the Answer, her beloved son. The Primal Man was freed from the hellish substances by the Living Spirit who descended and extended to him his right hand, and ascending he became a God again. But the Soul he left behind [for these parts of the Light were too thoroughly mingled with those of the Darkness].

The Living Spirit and his entourage of gods separated the "mixture" from the main mass of Darkness. Then the King of Light ordered him to create the present world and to build it out of these mixed parts, in order to liberate those Light-parts from the dark parts. To this end the Archons who had incorporated the Light (and thereby become weakened) are overcome, and out of their skins and carcasses heaven and earth are made. Though it is said that the Archons are fettered to the firmament (still fastened to their outstretched skins which form the heavens?), and though on the other hand earth and mountains are said to have been formed from their flesh and bones, the sequence makes it clear that by all this neither have they lost their demonic life nor has the Darkness in general lost its power to act.

He spread out all the powers of the abyss to ten heavens and eight earths, he shut them up into this world [cosmos], he made it a prison for all the powers of Darkness. It is also a place of purification for the Soul that was swallowed in them.

Then arose in prayer the Mother of Life, the Primal Man, and the Living Spirit, and besought the Father of Greatness: "Create a new god, and charge him that he go and see that dungeon of the Demons, and that he establish annual revolution and protective escort for sun and moon, and that he be a liberator and savior for that luminosity of gods which from the beginning of all things was beaten by Ahriman, the Demons [etc.], and which they hold captive even now, and also for that luminosity which is retained in the cosmic realms of heaven and earth and there suffers, and that he prepare for the wind, the water, and the fire a way and a path to the Most High." And the Father of Greatness heard them, and called forth as the third creation the Messenger. The Messenger called the Twelve Virgins (according to their names, personified virtues and divine properties), and with them set up an engine of twelve buckets. The Messenger betakes himself to the ships of Light, which up to now have been stationary, and sets them in motion and starts the revolution of the spheres. This revolution becomes the vehicle of the cosmic process of salvation, as distinct from that enacted through the minds of men, since it functions as a mechanism for the separation and upward transportation of the Light entrapped in nature.

First, however, the Messenger tries a shorter way: As the ships moved and came to the middle of the heavens, the Messenger revealed his forms, the male and the female, and became visible to all the Archons, the children of the Darkness, the male and the female. And at the sight of the Messenger, who was beautiful in his forms, all the Archons became excited with lust for him, the male ones for his female appearance and the female ones for his male appearance. And in their concupiscence they began to release the Light of the Five Luminous Gods which they had devoured.... The escaping Light is received by the angels of

Light, purified, and loaded onto the "ships" to be transported to its native realm. But the dubious trick of the Messenger is double-edged in its success, for together with the Light and in the same quantity Dark substance ("sin") also escapes from the Archons and, mingled with the Light, endeavors also to enter the ships of the Messenger. Realizing this, the Messenger conceals his forms again and as far as possible separates out the ejaculated mixture. While the purer parts rise upward, the contaminated parts, i.e., those too closely combined with the "sin," fall down upon the earth, and there this mixed substance forms the vegetable world. Thus all plants, grain, herbs and all roots and trees are creatures of the Darkness, not of God, and in these forms and kinds of things the Godhead is fettered. A similarly miserable origin, only more so, is assigned to the animal world, which springs from abortions of the daughters of Darkness at the sight of the Messenger and similarly keeps Light-substance imprisoned.

The brief revealing of the forms of the Messenger, in addition to leading to these new kinds of imprisonment of the Light, also inspires the Darkness with the idea of a last and most effective means of keeping its threatened spoil, namely, by binding it in the form most adequate to it. That form is suggested to it by the divine form itself which it has seen. Anticipating the eventual loss of all Light through the continual separating effect of the heavenly revolutions; seized by the ambition to create out of himself something equal to that vision; reckoning by this means to devise the safest prison for the alien force; and finally, wishing to have in his world a substitute for the otherwise unattainable divine figure, over which to rule and through which to be sometimes freed from the odious company of his kind, the King of Darkness produces Adam and Eve in the image of the glorious form, and pours into them all the Light left at his disposal.

The creation of Eve had a special purpose. She is more thoroughly subject to the demons, thus becoming their instrument against Adam; to her they imparted of their concupiscence in order to seduce Adam—a seduction not only to carnal lust but through it to reproduction, the most formidable device in Satan's strategy. For not only would it indefinitely prolong the captivity of Light, but it would also through the multiplication so disperse the Light as to render infinitely more difficult the work of salvation, whose only way is to awaken every individual soul. For the Darkness, therefore, everything turned on the seduction of Adam, as for the celestials, on awakening him in time to prevent his seduction.

As the five angels saw the Light of God in its defilement, they begged the Messenger of Good Tidings, the Mother of Light and the Living Spirit that they send someone to this primal creature to free and save him, reveal to him knowledge and justice, and liberate him from the devils. So they sent Jesus.

Jesus the Luminous approached the innocent Adam. He awakened him from the sleep of death, so that he might be delivered from the many demons. And as a man who is just and finds a man possessed by a mighty demon and calms him by his power—so was Adam because that Friend found him sunk in deepest slumber, awakened him, made him stir, shook him awake, drove away from him the seducing Demon and removed the mighty Archon [here female] away from him into bonds. And Adam examined himself and discovered who he was. Jesus showed him the Fathers on high and his own Self cast into all things, to the teeth of panthers and elephants, devoured by them that devour, consumed by them that consume, eaten by the dogs, mingled and bound in all that is, imprisoned in the stench of darkness. He raised him up and made him eat of the tree of life. Then Adam cried and lamented: terribly he raised his voice like a roaring lion, tore [his dress], smote his breast, and spoke: "Woe, woe unto the shaper of my body, unto those who fettered my soul, and unto the rebels that enslaved me!"

—Hans Jonas. *The Gnostic Religion*. Boston: Beacon Press, 1958, pp. 86–87, 210, 213–214, 216–218, 221–222, 224–229.

MYTHS OF ISLAM

The Koran, Sura XLI—The Made Plain

Orthodox Islamic doctrine asserts that the *Koran* (from *qara'a*, to read or recite) is the eternal word of God, written on a tablet in heaven and dictated in a revelation to Mohammed (570–632 A.D.) by the archangel Gabriel. Its theocentric view is most evident throughout. Not only does each section, or "Sura," with one exception begin "In the Name of God, the Compassionate, the Merciful," but the overriding purpose of all of them is to proclaim Allah as the one, true God and to call people to worship him.

Mohammed found little support for his teachings among the tribes of his native Mecca and eventually he emigrated north to Medina and welcoming followers. The importance of this journey (the Hijra) is emphasized by the fact it was chosen as the beginning of the Muslim era (622 A.D., or the year 1 in the Islamic calendar). But the struggles against infidelity did not end there. Throughout his life, Mohammed worked to unify the Arabs in allegiance to the one God, Allah.

In this Sura, he proclaims his revelation to the unfaithful, asking how they can disbelieve in one who created the earth in two days, ordered and blessed it and distributed food in it in four more, made the seven heavens from amorphous smoke in another two days and furnished them with lights and guardian angels. The Sura argues that such a great god should not be confused with lesser, derivative divinities.

HA. Mim. A Revelation from the Compassionate, the Merciful!

A Book whose verses (signs) are MADE PLAIN—an Arabic Koran, for men of knowledge;

Announcer of glad tidings and charged with warnings! But most of them withdraw and hearken not:

And they say, "Our hearts are under shelter from the teachings, and in our ears is a deafness, and between us and thee is a veil. Act as thou thinkest right: we verily shall act as we think right."

Say: I am only a man like you. It is revealed to me that your God is one God: go straight then to Him, and implore his pardon. And woe to those who join gods with God;

Who pay not the alms of obligation, and in the life to come believe not!

But they who believe and do the things that are right shall receive a perfect recompense.

Say: Do ye indeed disbelieve in Him who in two days created the earth? and do ye assign Him peers? The Lord of the worlds is He!

And he hath placed on the earth the firm mountains which tower above it; and He hath blessed it, and distributed food throughout it, for the cravings of all alike, in four days:

Then He applied himself to the Heaven, which then was but smoke; and to it and to the Earth He said, "Come ye, whether in obedience or against your will?" and they both said, "We come obedient."

And He made them seven heavens in two days, and in each heaven made known its office: And we furnished the lower heaven with lights and guardian angels. This, the disposition of the Almighty, the All-knowing.

—J. M. Rodwell (trans.). *The Koran*. London: J. M. Dent, 1909, pp. 192–193

The Koran, Sura XVI—The Bee

In Sura XVI, there is another warning about the risks attendant the worship of false deities who "create nothing, but are themselves created." Mohammed (570–632 A.D.) exhorts people to praise Allah, the true God, who created the world to reveal his truth, made man from a moist germ and ordered the universe for his benefit.

IN THE NAME OF GOD, the Compassionate, the Merciful.

The doom of God cometh to pass. Then hasten it not. Glory be to Him! High let Him be exalted above the gods whom they join with Him!

By His own behest will He cause the angels to descend with the Spirit on whom he pleaseth among his servants, bidding them, "Warn that there is no God but me; therefore fear me."

He hath created the Heavens and the Earth to set forth his truth; high let Him be exalted above the gods they join with Him!

Man hath He created from a moist germ; yet lo! man is an open caviller.

And the cattle! for you hath He created them: in them ye have warm garments and gainful uses; and of them ye eat:

And they beseem you well when ye fetch them home and when ye drive them forth to pasture:

And they carry your burdens to lands which ye could not else reach but with travail of soul: truly your Lord is full of goodness, and merciful:

And He hath given you horses, mules, and asses, that ye may ride them, and for your ornament: and things of which ye have no knowledge hath he created.

Of God it is to point out "the Way." Some turn aside from it: but had He pleased, He had guided you all aright.

It is He who sendeth down rain out of Heaven; from it is your drink; and from it are the plants by which ye pasture.

By it He causeth the corn, and the olives, and the palm-trees, and the grapes to spring forth for you, and all kinds of fruits; verily, in this are signs for those who ponder.

And He hath subjected to you the night and the day; the sun and the moon and the stars too are subjected to you by his behest; verily, in this are signs for those who understand:

And all of varied hues that He hath created for you over the earth: verily, in this are signs for those who remember.

And He it is who hath subjected the sea to you, that ye may eat of its fresh fish, and take forth from it ornaments to wear—thou seest the ships ploughing its billows—and that ye may go in quest of his bounties, and that ye might give thanks.

And He hath thrown firm mountains on the earth, lest it move with you; and rivers and paths for your guidance.

And way marks. By the stars too are men guided.

Shall He then who hath created be as he who hath not created? Will ye not consider?

And if ye would reckon up the favours of God, ye could not count them. Aye! God is right Gracious, Merciful!

And God knoweth what ye conceal, and what ye bring to light,

While the gods whom they call on beside God, create nothing, but are themselves created:

Dead are they, lifeless! and they know not

When they shall be raised!

Your God is the one God.

—J. M. Rodwell (trans.). *The Koran.* London: J. M. Dent, 1909, pp. 200–201.

From the Koran

The order of the passages in the *Koran*, except for the first, is by length from the longest to the shortest. And the suras themselves are, generally speaking, not homogeneous units; they often change subjects abruptly or include unrelated points. In none is there a continuous story of creation; never is the focus solely on cosmological issues. Rather, the creation is alluded to in several places as a sign of God's greatness and as evidence for his meriting worship.

In these brief selections from five different suras, several points are made about that initial divine act. Sura XL: 66–70 claims that God made the heaven and earth and created mankind from dust by decreeing "Be." And Sura VII: 52–57 emphasizes God's ordering of the universe: he made the heavens and earth in six days and ordered all their elements in proper fashion.

Sura LXV: 12 clarifies the structure of the universe with its seven heavens and seven earths through which God continually reveals himself so that people will be faithful. The fourth passage (from Sura XLII: 28) reiterates the notion that the creation serves as a sign for believers, and the fifth (from Sura II: 109–111) stresses again the creative power of God's command.

I T IS GOD who hath given you the earth as a sure foundation, and over it built up the Heaven, and formed you, and made your forms beautiful, and feedeth you with good things. This is God your Lord. Blessed then be God the Lord of the Worlds!

He is the Living One. No God is there but He. Call then upon Him and offer Him pure worship. Praise be the God the Lord of the Worlds!

Say: Verily I am forbidden to worship what ye call on beside God, after that the clear tokens have come to me from my Lord, and I am bidden to surrender myself to the Lord of the Worlds.

He it is who created you of the dust, then of the germs of life, then of thick blood, then brought you forth infants: then he letteth you reach your full strength, and then become old men (but some of you die first), and reach the ordained term. And this that ye may haply understand.

It is He who giveth life and death; and when He decreeth a thing, He only saith of it, "Be," and it is.   [Sura XL, The Believer: 66–70]

Y OUR LORD is God, who in six days created the Heavens and the Earth, and then mounted the throne: He throweth the veil of night over the day: it pursueth it swiftly: and he created the sun and the moon and the stars, subjected to laws by His behest: Is not all creation and its empire His? Blessed be God the Lord of the Worlds!

Call upon your Lord with lowliness and in secret, for He loveth not transgressors.

And commit not disorders on the earth after it hath been well-ordered; and call on Him with fear and longing desire: Verily the mercy of God is nigh unto the righteous.

And He it is who sendeth forth the winds as the heralds of his compassion, until they bring up the laden clouds, which we drive along to some dead land and send down water thereon, by which we cause an upgrowth of all kinds of fruit.— Thus we will bring forth the dead. Haply ye will reflect.

In a rich soil, its plants spring forth abundantly by the will of its Lord, and in that which is bad, they spring forth but scantily. Thus do we diversify our signs for those who are thankful.   [Sura VII, Al Araf: 52–57]

I T IS GOD who hath created seven heavens and as many earths. The Divine command cometh down through them all, that ye may know that God hath power over all things, and that God in his knowledge embraceth all things!   [Sura LXV, Divorce: 12]

A MONG HIS SIGNS is the creation of the Heavens and of the Earth, and the creatures which he hath scattered over both: and, for their gathering together when he will, He is all-powerful.   [Sura XLII, Counsel: 28]

T HE EAST and the West is God's: therefore, whichever way ye turn, there is the face of God: Truly God is immense and knoweth all.

And they say, "God hath a son." No! Praise be to Him! But—His, whatever is in the Heavens and the Earth! All obeyeth Him,

Sole maker of the Heavens and of the Earth! And when he decreeth a thing, He only saith to it, "Be," and it is.   [Sura II, The Cow: 109–111]

—J. M. Rodwell (trans.). *The Koran.* London: J. M. Dent, 1909, pp. 245, 299, 431, 273, 350.

THREE

EUROPEAN MYTHS

ANCIENT GREEK AND ROMAN MYTHS

The Pelasgian Creation Myth
The Pelasgians entered the Greek peninsula from Asia Minor c. 3500 B.C., bringing with them the ubiquitous female figurines of the ancient Near Eastern mother goddess cult. Aside from their possession of these statuettes and their practise of burying the dead with artifacts (suggesting belief in some kind of afterlife), little is known directly of their religion. Robert Graves has constructed this myth out of several fragmentary allusions to Pelasgian cosmology in later texts.

While many of the themes here are similar to those in Near Eastern myths—the creator rising out of Chaos in the beginning, the egg of creation being laid on the primeval waters, the establishment of order by the creation of controlling planetary powers—its most distinct features are the primacy of the mother goddess Eurynome ("wide-wandering") and the rebellion of the snake deity Ophion, her son and consort.

Ophion's primal sin, that of a derivative creature claiming credit for the creation itself, is echoed in several myths around the world. In this case, the events caused by such hubris take on the character of a sexual war as the mother-wife goddess bruises her husband-son's phallic head and banishes him to the underworld.

Throughout the myth, Chaos appears in various forms as an active and barely controlled force. Not only is it depicted as the source of the Goddess of All Things and as the ocean, the resting place for her universal egg, but it is also personified as wind (that which forms but is not formed itself), transformed into the fertilizing snake, and finally symbolized as the dark and womblike caves of the underworld. After tentatively controlling these chaotic forces, Eurynome creates Pelasgus, the ancestor of the Pelasgian people, who teaches all others the rudiments of civilized life.

I N THE BEGINNING, Eurynome, the Goddess of All Things, rose naked from Chaos, but found nothing substantial for her feet to rest upon, and therefore divided the sea from the sky, dancing lonely upon its waves. She danced towards the south, and the wind set in motion behind her seemed something new and apart with which to begin a work of creation. Wheeling about, she caught hold of this north wind, rubbed it between her hands, and behold! the great serpent Ophion. Eurynome danced to warm herself, wildly and more wildly, until Ophion, grown lustful, coiled about those divine limbs and was moved to couple with her. Now, the North Wind, who is also called Boreas, fertilizes; which is why mares often turn their hind-quarters to the wind and breed foals without aid of a stallion. So Eurynome was likewise got with child.

Next she assumed the form of a dove, brooding on the waves and in due process of time, laid the Universal Egg. At her bidding, Ophion coiled seven times about this egg, until it hatched and split in two. Out tumbled all the things that exist, her children: sun, moon, planets, stars, the earth with its mountains and rivers, its trees, herbs and living creatures.

Eurynome and Ophion made their home upon Mount Olympus, where he vexed her by claiming to be the author of the Universe. Forthwith she bruised his head with her heel, kicked out his teeth, and banished him to the dark caves below the earth.

Next, the goddess created the seven planetary powers, setting a Titaness and a Titan over each. Theia and Hyperion for the Sun; Phoebe and Atlas for the Moon; Dione and Crius for the planet Mars; Metis and Coeus for the planet Mercury; Themis and Eurymedon for the planet Jupiter; Tethys and Oceanus for Venus; Rhea and Cronus for the planet Saturn. But the first man was Pelasgus, ancestor of the others, whom he taught to make huts and feed upon acorns, and sew pig-skin tunics such as poor folk still wear in Euboea and Phocis.

—Robert Graves. *Greek Myths.* Vol. 1. Baltimore, Md.: Penguin Books, 1955, p. 27.

Hesiod: From the Theogony

Hesiod lived in Boetia on the Greek mainland in the latter part of the eighth century B.C. and his *Theogony* records, in rough and vivid style, the evolution of the gods and the establishment of the sacred and universal Olympian order with the final triumph of Zeus.

Most striking in this myth is the violent and chaotic manner in which the divine forces struggle among themselves: child killing, incest, castration, destruction, and treachery abound. The gods fight in grand and primitive style, and only Zeus emerges as wise and just. While this is primarily a story of divine succession and final ordering, the creative powers of the gods are emphasized throughout. In the beginning, Chaos, Earth, Tartarus (the underworld), and Eros (love) appear spontaneously, and, in the first generation alone, Chaos produced Night and Erebos (another part of the underworld), who together bore Day and Space; Earth gave birth to Heaven and the Sea by herself and then, with Heaven, produced the Ti-

tans. These and other children of Earth and of Night, endlessly fertile, produced
the generations of the gods who fought together.

C HAOS was first of all, but next appeared
    Broad-bosomed Earth, sure standing-place for all
The gods who live on snowy Olympus' peak,
And misty Tartarus, in a recess
Of broad-pathed earth, and Love, most beautiful
Of all the deathless gods. He makes men weak,
He overpowers the clever mind, and tames
The spirit in the breasts of men and gods.
From Chaos came black Night and Erebos.
And Night in turn gave birth to Day and Space
Whom she conceived in love to Erebos.
And Earth bore starry Heaven, first, to be
An equal to herself, to cover her
All over, and to be a resting-place,
Always secure, for all the blessed gods.
Then she brought forth long hills, the lovely homes
Of goddesses, the Nymphs who live among
The mountain clefts. Then, without pleasant love,
She bore the barren sea with its swollen waves,
Pontus. And then she lay with Heaven, and bore
Deep-whirling Oceanus and Koios; then
Kreius, Iapetos, Hyperion,
Theia, Rhea, Themis, Mnemosyne,
Lovely Tethys, and Phoebe, golden-crowned.
Last, after these, most terrible of sons,
The crooked-scheming Kronos came to birth
Who was his vigorous father's enemy.
Again, she bore the Cyclopes, whose hearts
Were insolent, Brontes and Steropes
And proud-souled Arges, those who found and gave
The thunder and the lightning-bolt to Zeus.
They were like other gods in all respects,
But that a single eye lay in the brow
Of each, and from this, they received the name,
Cyclopes, from the one round eye which lay
Set in the middle of each forehead. Strength
And energy and craft were in their works.
Then Ouranos and Gaia bore three sons
Mighty and violent, unspeakable
Kottos and Gyes and Briareus,
Insolent children, each with a hundred arms

On his shoulders, darting about, untouchable,
And each had fifty heads, standing upon
His shoulders, over the crowded mass of arms,
And terrible strength was in their mighty forms.

And these most awful sons of Earth and Heaven
Were hated by their father from the first.
As soon as each was born, Ouranos hid
The child in a secret hiding-place in Earth
And would not let it come to see the light,
And he enjoyed this wickedness. But she,
Vast Earth, being strained and stretched inside her, groaned.
And then she thought of a clever, evil plan.
Quickly she made grey adamant, and formed
A mighty sickle, and addressed her sons,
Urging them on, with sorrow in her heart,
"My sons, whose father is a reckless fool,
If you will do as I ask, we shall repay
Your father's wicked crime. For it was he
Who first began devising shameful acts."

She spoke, but fear seized all of them, and none
Replied. Then crooked Kronos, growing bold,
Answered his well-loved mother with these words:
"Mother, I undertake to do the deed;
I do not care for my unspeakable
Father, for he first thought of shameful acts."
He spoke, and giant Earth was glad at heart.
She set him in a hiding-place, and put
Into his hands the saw-toothed scimitar,
And told him all the plot she had devised.

Great Heaven came, and with him brought the night.
Longing for love, he lay around the Earth,
Spreading out fully. But the hidden boy
Stretched forth his left hand; in his right he took
The great long jagged sickle; eagerly
He harvested his father's genitals
And threw them off behind. They did not fall
From his hands in vain, for all the bloody drops
That leaped out were received by Earth; and when
The year's time was accomplished, she gave birth
To the Furies, and the Giants, strong and huge,
Who fought in shining armour, with long spears,
And the nymphs called Meliae on the broad earth.

The genitals, cut off with adamant
And thrown from land into the stormy sea,
Were carried for a long time on the waves.
White foam surrounded the immortal flesh,
And in it grew a girl. At first it touched
On holy Cythera, from there it came
To Cyprus, circled by the waves. And there
The goddess came forth, lovely, much revered,
And grass grew up beneath her delicate feet.
Her name is Aphrodite among men
And gods, because she grew up in the foam,
And Cytherea, for she reached that land,
And Cyprogenes from the stormy place
Where she was horn, and Philommedes from
The genitals, by which she was conceived.
Eros is her companion; fair Desire
Followed her from the first, both at her birth
And when she joined the company of the gods.
From the beginning, both among gods and men,
She had this honour and received this power:
Fond murmuring of girls, and smiles, and tricks,
And sweet delight, and friendliness, and charm.

But the great father Ouranos reproached
His sons, and called them Titans, for, he said
They strained in insolence, and did a deed
For which they would be punished afterwards.

And Night bore frightful Doom and the black Ker,
And Death, and Sleep, and the whole tribe of Dreams.

Again, although she slept with none of the gods,
Dark Night gave birth to Blame and sad Distress,
And the Hesperides, who, out beyond
The famous stream of Oceanus, tend
The lovely golden apples, and their trees.
She bore the Destinies and ruthless Fates,
Goddesses who track down the sins of men
And gods, and never cease from awful rage
Until they give the sinner punishment.
Then deadly Night gave birth to Nemesis,
That pain to gods and men, and then she bore
Deceit and Love, sad Age, and strong-willed Strife.
And hateful Strife gave birth to wretched Work,
Forgetfulness, and Famine, tearful Pains,
Battles and Fights, Murders, Killings of men,

Quarrels and Lies and Stories and Disputes,
And Lawlessness and Ruin, both allied,
And Oath, who brings most grief to men on earth
When anyone swears falsely, knowing it.

. . .

And Rhea, being forced by Kronos, bore
Most brilliant offspring to him: Hestia,
Demeter, golden-slippered Hera, strong
Hades, who has his home beneath the earth,
The god whose heart is pitiless, and him
Who crashes loudly and who shakes the earth,
And thoughtful Zeus, father of gods and men,
Whose thunder makes the wide earth tremble. Then,
As each child issued from the holy womb
And lay upon its mother's knees, each one
Was seized by mighty Kronos, and gulped down.
He had in mind that no proud son of Heaven
Should hold the royal rank among the gods
Except himself. For he had learned from Earth
And starry Heaven, that his destiny
Was to be overcome, great though he was,
By one of his own sons, and through the plans
Of mighty Zeus. Therefore he never dropped
His guard, but lay in wait, and swallowed down
His children. Rhea suffered endless grief;
But when she was about to bring forth Zeus,
Father of gods and men, she begged the Earth
And starry Heaven, her parents, to devise
A plan to hide the birth of her dear son
And bring the Fury down on Kronos, for
His treatment of his father and his sons
Whom mighty, crooked Kronos swallowed down.
They heard their daughter and agreed, and told
Her all that fate would bring upon the king
Kronos, and to his mighty-hearted son.
They sent her to the fertile land of Crete,
To Lyctus, when she was about to bear
Her youngest child, great Zeus. And in broad Crete
Vast Earth received the child from her, to raise
And cherish. And she carried him, with speed,
Through the black night, and came to Lyctus first.
She took him in her arms and hid him, deep
Under the holy earth, in a vast cave,
On thickly-wooded Mount Aegeum. Then,

To the great lord, the son of Heaven, the past
King of the gods, she handed, solemnly,
All wrapped in swaddling-clothes, a giant stone.
He seized it in his hands and thrust it down
Into his belly, fool! He did not know
His son, no stone, was left behind, unhurt
And undefeated, who would conquer him
With violence and force, and drive him out
From all his honours, and would rule the gods.

The strength and glorious limbs of the young lord
Grew quickly and the years went by, and Earth
Entrapped great clever Kronos with shrewd words
Advising him to bring his offspring back.
(His son, by craft and power, conquered him.)
And first he vomited the stone, which he
Had swallowed last. At holy Pytho, Zeus
Set firm the stone in broad-pathed earth, beneath
Parnassus, in a cleft, to be a sign
In future days, for men to marvel at.

                    . . .

From tall Mount Othrys came the Titan lords
And from Olympus, those who give us all,
Whom fair-haired Rhea bore, after she lay
With Kronos; they had anger in their hearts
And fought continually for ten full years
With no release nor end to the harsh strife
For either side; the winning of the war
Was balanced evenly between the two.
But when the sons of Ouranos received,
Fittingly, nectar and ambrosia, which
The gods themselves consume, their spirits rose
Proud in their breasts. And then the father of gods
And men spoke to them: "Hear me, glorious sons
Of Ouranos and Gaia, while I speak
As my heart tells me to. For many years
The sons of Kronos and the Titan gods
Have been at war, fighting for victory
And power. Come now, show them your great strength,
Your unapproachable hands, in painful war
Against the Titans, and do not forget
Our kindness and good will, how through our plans
You come back, having suffered, to the light
From gloomy darkness and from painful bonds."

He spoke, and blameless Kottos answered him:
"You do not need to tell us what we know.
We know your mind and thoughts are excellent
And that you keep the gods from chilly harm.
O Lord and Son of Kronos, we came back
From gloomy darkness and from cruel bonds
Because of your intelligence; we find
An unexpected end to suffering.
Now, with our minds intent, and eager hearts,
We will preserve your power in dreadful war
Against the Titans, on the battlefield."

He spoke, and all the gods, givers of gifts,
Applauded him, and lusted for the fight
Even more than before. And on that day
They joined in hateful battle, all of them,
Both male and female, Titan gods and those
Whom Kronos sired and those whom Zeus had brought
To light from Erebos, beneath the earth,
Strange, mighty ones, whose power was immense,
Each with a hundred arms, darting about,
And each had fifty heads standing upon
His shoulders, over the crowded mass of arms.
They stood against the Titans in the grim
Battle, with giant rocks in their strong hands,
While on their side the Titans eagerly
Strengthened their ranks, and both at once displayed
The mightiest efforts which their hands could make;
The boundless sea roared terribly around,
The great earth rumbled, and broad heaven groaned,
Shaken; and tall Olympus was disturbed
Down to its roots, when the immortals charged.
The heavy quaking from their footsteps reached
Down to dark Tartarus, and piercing sounds
Of awful battle, and their mighty shafts.
They hurled their wounding missiles, and the voice
Of both sides, shouting, reached the starry sky,
And when they met, their ALALE! was great.

Then Zeus no longer checked his rage, for now
His heart was filled with fury, and he showed
The full range of his strength. He came from heaven
And from Olympus, lightening as he came,
Continuously; from his mighty hand
The bolts kept flying, bringing thunder-claps

And lightning-flashes, while the holy flame
Rolled thickly all around. The fertile earth
Being burnt, roared out, the voiceless forest cried
And crackled with the fire; the whole earth boiled
And ocean's streams, and the unfruitful sea.
The hot blast reached the earthborn Titans; flame
Unspeakable, rose to the upper air;
The flashing brightness of the thunderbolt
And lightning blinded all, however strong;
The awful heat reached Chaos. To the ear
It sounded, to the eye it looked as though
Broad Heaven were coming down upon the Earth:
For such a noise of crashing might arise
If she were falling, hurled down by his fall.
Just such a mighty crash rose from the gods
Meeting in strife. The howling winds brought on
Duststorm and earthquake, and the shafts of Zeus,
Lightning and thunder and the blazing bolt,
And carried shouting and the battle-cry
Into the armies, and a dreadful noise
Of hideous battle sounded, and their deeds
Were mighty, but the tide of war was turned:
Until that moment, they had kept it up
Continually, in the long, hard fight.

. . .

After Zeus drove the Titans out of heaven
Vast Earth loved Tartarus, and bore a child,
Her last, through golden Aphrodite's work,
Typhoeus, mighty god, whose hands were strong
And feet untiring. On his shoulders grew
A hundred snaky heads, strange dragon heads
With black tongues darting out. His eyes flashed fire
Beneath the brows upon those heads, and fire
Blazed out from every head when he looked round.
Astounding voices came from those weird heads,
All kinds of voices: sometimes speech which gods
Would understand, and sometimes bellowings,
As of a bull let loose, enraged, and proud,
Sometimes that of a ruthless lion; then,
Sometimes the yelp of puppies, marvellous
To hear; and then sometimes he hissed,
And the tall mountains echoed underneath.

Surely that day a thing beyond all help

Might have occurred: he might have come to rule
Over the gods and mortal man, had not
The father of gods and men been quick to see
The danger; but he thundered mightily
And fiercely, and the earth rang terribly,
Broad heaven above, the sea, and Ocean's streams
And Tartarus resounded. As the lord
Arose, mighty Olympus shook beneath
The immortal feet, and Earth gave out a groan.
The purple sea was seized by heat from both,
From thunder and from lightning, and from fire
The monster bore: the burning hurricane
And blazing thunderbolt. The whole earth boiled
And heaven and the sea. The great waves raged
Along the shore, at the immortal's charge,
And endless quakes arose. Hades, the lord
Of dead men down below, trembled for fear,
And the Titans, they who live with Kronos, down
Under Tartarus, shook at the endless din
And fearful battle. Zeus raised up his strength
Seizing his arms, lightning, the blazing bolt,
And thunder, leaped down from Olympus, struck,
And burned the dreadful monster's ghastly heads.
He lashed him with a whip and mastered him,
And threw him down, all maimed, and great Earth groaned.
A flame leaped from the lightning-blasted lord,
When he was struck, on the jagged mountainside.
Great earth was widely scorched by the awful blast
And melted, as tin melts when, skillfully,
Men heat it in the hollow crucibles
Of iron, which is strongest of all things,
But can be conquered by the blazing fire
In mountain hollows, in the holy earth,
And melts, under Hephaistos' clever hands:
Thus earth was melted in the fire's bright flash.
And, angry in his heart, Zeus hurled him down
(To Tartarus. And from Typhoeus come)
The fierce, rain-blowing winds—not Boreas
Or Notos or bright Zephyros, for these
Come from the gods, and they refresh mankind—
But others, reckless gusts, blow on the sea;
Some fall upon the misty sea and bring
Calamity to men; as evil storms
They rage; each blows in season, scattering ships
And killing sailors. Men who meet with them

At sea have no defence against their power.
And sometimes over the vast and blooming earth
They blast the lovely fields of earthborn men
And fill the land with dust and dreadful noise.
But when the blessed gods had done their work
And forcibly put down the Titans' claim
To honour, they fulfilled Earth's plans and urged
Far-seeing Zeus, Olympian, to rule
And be the king of the immortals. Thus
He gave out rank and privilege to each.

—Hesiod. *Theogony: Works and Days*. And Theogonis. *Elegies*. Dorothy Wender (trans.). Baltimore, Md.: Penguin Books, 1973, pp. 622–65.

Hesiod: The Five Ages of Man

Although it is largely an extended admonition to Hesiod's younger brother Perses, *Works and Days* contains some illustrative mythological material. In this section, Hesiod portrays the gradual fall of man from a great and good being to the small-minded and short-lived creature who currently inhabits the earth.

Originally perfect, the first golden race devolved into the second, silver one of moon- and mother-oriented foolish "babies." For their sins, Zeus hid them away in the underworld and produced in their stead the bronze race of warriors, who were mortal and violent, but nonetheless glorious in their strength and power. The fourth race of heroes, the Mycenaean kings, proved more acceptable to the gods and some achieved immortality, but the last and present race of men are a shameless lot, doomed to a harsh and terrible fate.

Behind these descriptions of the ages of man lies Hesiod's faith in the supreme and creative powers of the Olympian deities, led by Kronos in the first and second ages and by Zeus thereafter.

THE GODS, who live on Mount Olympus, first
Fashioned a golden race of mortal men;
These lived in the reign of Kronos, king of heaven,
And like the gods they lived with happy hearts
Untouched by work or sorrow. Vile old age
Never appeared, but always lively-limbed,
Far from all ills, they feasted happily.
Death came to them as sleep, and all good things
Were theirs; ungrudgingly, the fertile land
Gave up her fruits unasked. Happy to be
At peace, they lived with every want supplied,
[Rich in their flocks, dear to the blessed gods.]

And then this race was hidden in the ground.
But still they live as spirits of the earth,
Holy and good, guardians who keep off harm,

Givers of wealth: this kingly right is theirs.
The gods, who live on Mount Olympus, next
Fashioned a lesser, silver race of men:
Unlike the gold in stature or in mind.
A child was raised at home a hundred years
And played, huge baby, by his mother's side.
When they were grown and reached their prime, they lived
Brief, anguished lives, from foolishness, for they
Could not control themselves, but recklessly
Injured each other and forsook the gods;
They did not sacrifice, as all tribes must, but left
The holy altars bare. And, angry, Zeus
The son of Kronos, hid this race away,
For they dishonoured the Olympian gods.

The earth then hid this second race, and they
Are called the spirits of the underworld,
Inferior to the gold, but honoured, too.
And Zeus the father made a race of bronze,
Sprung from the ash tree, worse than the silver race,
But strange and full of power. And they loved
The groans and violence of war; they ate
No bread; their hearts were flinty-hard; they were
Terrible men; their strength was great, their arms
And shoulders and their limbs invincible.
Their weapons were of bronze, their houses bronze;
Their tools were of bronze: black iron was not known.
They died by their own hands, and nameless, went
To Hades' chilly house. Although they were
Great soldiers, they were captured by black Death,
And left the shining brightness of the sun.

But when this race was covered by the earth,
The son of Kronos made another, fourth,
Upon the fruitful land, more just and good,
A god-like race of heroes, who are called
The demi-gods—the race before our own.
Foul wars and dreadful battles ruined some;
Some sought the flocks of Oedipus, and died
In Cadmus' land, at seven-gated Thebes;
And some, who crossed the open sea in ships,
For fair-haired Helen's sake, were killed at Troy.
These men were covered up in death, but Zeus
The son of Kronos gave the others life
And homes apart from mortals, at Earth's edge.

And there they live a carefree life, beside
The whirling Ocean, on the Blessed Isles.
Three times a year the blooming, fertile earth
Bears honeyed fruits for them, the happy ones.
[And Kronos is their king, far from the gods,
For Zeus released him from his bonds, and these,
The race of heroes, well deserve their fame.

Far-seeing Zeus then made another race,
The fifth, who live now on the fertile earth.]
I wish I were not of this race, that I
Had died before, or had not yet been born.
This is the race of iron. Now, by day,
Men work and grieve unceasingly; by night,
They waste away and die. The gods will give
Harsh burdens, but will mingle in some good;
Zeus will destroy this race of mortal men,
When babies shall be born with greying hair.
Father will have no common bond with son,
Neither will guest with host, nor friend with friend;
The brother-love of past days will be gone.
Men will dishonour parents, who grow old
Too quickly, and will blame and criticize
With cruel words. Wretched and godless, they
Refusing to repay their bringing up,
Will cheat their aged parents of their due.
Men will destroy the towns of other men.
The just, the good, the man who keeps his word
Will be despised, but men will praise the bad
And insolent. Might will be Right, and shame
Will cease to be. Men will do injury
To better men by speaking crooked words
And adding lying oaths; and everywhere
Harsh-voiced and sullen-faced and loving harm,
Envy will walk along with wretched man.
Last, to Olympus from the broad-pathed Earth,
Hiding their loveliness in robes of white,
To join the gods, abandoning mankind,
Will go the spirits Righteousness and Shame.
And only grievous troubles will be left
For men, and no defence against our wrongs.

—Hesiod. *Theogony: Works and Days.* And Theoginis. *Elegies.* Dorothy Wenger (trans.). Baltimore, Md.: Penguin Books, 1973, pp. 622–65.

The Orphic Creation Myth

Orphism grew up in the seventh or sixth centuries B.C. and, in contrast to Homer's Olympian religion, was primarily concerned with the destiny of the individual soul, an inner, essential, and immortal self. The concept of man's dual nature—his pure soul entrapped in a material body—led the Orphics to rituals of purification and initiation in which adherents were helped to become free of their bodies and successive incarnations.

Parallels to Iranian religion, with its emphasis on Zurvan, the god of time, are evinced in this version of the Orphic myth where time creates the universal egg from which springs Phanes-Dionysus. The androgynous creator first makes Nyx (Night) and then with her begets Gaea (Earth), Uranus (Heaven), and Cronos.

IN THE BEGINNING time created the silver egg of the cosmos. Out of this egg burst Phanes-Dionysus. For them (the Orphics) he was the first god to appear, the firstborn, whence he early became known as Protogonos. He was bisexual and bore within him the seeds of all gods and men. He was also the creator of heaven and earth, of the sun, the stars, and the dwelling of the gods. The sixth Orphic hymn, dated to be sure in the Christian era but preserving old elements, represented him in epic hexameters:

> O mighty first-begotten, hear my prayer,
> Twofold, egg-born, and wandering through the air;
> Bull-roarer, glorying in thy golden wings,
> From whom the race of Gods and mortals springs.
> Ericapaeus, celebrated power,
> Ineffable, occult, all-shining flower.
> 'Tis thine from darksome mists to purge the sight,
> All-spreading splendor, pure and holy light;
> Hence, Phanes, called the glory of the sky,
> On waving pinions through the world you fly.

Phanes first created his daughter Nyx, the Night; in his bisexual quality, he was her father and mother at once. With Nyx, who alone was privileged to behold him, Phanes at vast intervals of time begat Gaea, Uranus, and Cronus, who after Uranus became lord of the world.

—Walter Wili (trans. of fragments 21, 21a, and 168). "The Orphic Mysteries and the Greek Spirit." *Orphicorum Fragmenta*. Berlin: 1922.—Quoted in Joseph Campbell (ed.). *The Mysteries. Papers from the Eranos Yearbooks*. Vol 2. New York: Pantheon Books, 1955, p. 73.

Ovid: From the Metamorphoses

In Ovid's (43 B.C.–18 A.D.) compendium of mythology, Chaos is depicted as shapeless and discordant, its elements indistinct and mixed. Everything within it is only potentially existent. Land, for instance, is there, "but land on which no man could stand." And all the elements and forces, the polar opposites through whose tension the world is understood, war with each other in uncontrolled fashion.

The identity of the great organizer of this chaotic mass is somewhat uncertain. "God or kindlier Nature" appears unexplained: if it is a god, its origin is unknown and if it is Nature, the method whereby it manifested itself out of Chaos into a distinct power is unclear. But once that feat is accomplished, the divine force uses all the chaotic material to make the world. Sky, air, water, and earth are separated from one another, natural forces are put into operation, and each region of the universe is filled with its proper inhabitants. Finally man is born—either in God's image or from the earth itself—unique among creatures in his ability to reflect back on the sacred world.

B EFORE the ocean was, or earth, or heaven,
   Nature was all alike, a shapelessness,
Chaos, so-called, all ruse and lumpy matter,
Nothing but bulk, inert, in whose confusion
Discordant atoms warred: there was no sun
To light the universe; there was no moon
With slender silver crescents filling slowly;
No earth hung balanced in surrounding air;
No sea reached far along the fringe of shore.
Land, to be sure, there was, and air, and ocean,
But land on which no man could stand, and water
No man could swim in, air no man could breathe,
Air without light, substance forever changing,
Forever at war: within a single body
Heat fought with cold, wet fought with dry, the hard
Fought with the soft, things having weight contended
With weightless things.
                Till God, or kindlier Nature,
Settled all argument, and separated
Heaven from earth, water from land, our air
From the high stratosphere, a liberation
So things evolved, and out of blind confusion
Found each its place, bound in eternal order.
The force of fire, that weightless element,
Leaped up and claimed the highest place in heaven;
Below it, air; and under them the earth
Sank with its grosser proportions; and the water,
Lowest of all, held up, held in, the land.

Whatever god it was, who out of chaos
Brought order to the universe, and gave it
Division, subdivision, he molded earth,
In the beginning, into a great globe,
Even on every side, and bade the waters
To spread and rise, under the rushing winds,
Surrounding earth; he added ponds and marshes,

He banked the river-channels, and the waters
Feed earth or run to sea, and that great flood
Washes on shores not banks. He made the plains
Spread wide, the valleys settle, and the forest
Be dressed in leaves; he made the rocky mountains
Rise to full height, and as the vault of Heaven
Has two zones, left and right, and one between them
Hotter than these, the Lord of Creation
Marked on earth the same design and pattern.
The torrid zone too hot for men to live in,
The north and south too cold, but in the middle
Varying climate, temperature and season.
Above all things the air, lighter than earth,
Lighter than water, heavier than fire,
Towers and spreads; there mist and cloud assemble,
And fearful thunder and lightning and cold winds,
But these, by the Creator's order, held
No general dominion; even as it is,
These brothers brawl and quarrel; though each one
Has his own quarter, still, they come near tearing
The universe apart. Eurus is monarch
Of the lands of dawn, the realms of Araby,
The Persian ridges under the rays of morning.
Zephyrus holds the west that glows at sunset,
Boreas, who makes men shiver, holds the north,
Warm Auster governs the misty southland,
And over them all presides the weightless ether,
Pure without taint of earth.
                    These boundaries given,
Behold, the stars, long hidden under darkness,
Broke through and shone, all over the spangled heaven,
Their home forever, and the gods lived there,
And shining fish were given the waves for dwelling
And beasts the earth, and birds the moving air.

But something else was needed, a linear being,
More capable of mind, a sage, a ruler,
So Man was born, it may be, in God's image,
Or Earth, perhaps, so newly separated
From the old fire of Heaven, still retained
Some seed of the celestial force which fashioned
Gods out of living clay and running water.
All other animals look downward; Man,
Alone, erect, can raise his face toward Heaven.

—Ovid. *Metamorphoses*. Rolfe Humphries (trans.). Bloomington: Indiana University Press, 1973, pp. 3–5.

Earliest (Inferred) Creed of the Celts

The Celts emerged from the Rhinelands as a distinct group c. 500–100 B.C. and spread down and across Europe, the British Isles and Ireland. Because they had no written language of their own, information about their myths derives from archeological finds, Roman commentaries, and later secular literature. Much of what can be inferred about their religious beliefs bears resemblance to the attitudes of the warring Aryans who went into India and the Greek mainland. This reconstructed creation myth in particular is not unlike Hesiod's Theogony with its successive revolutions of divine sons against their fathers.

In the beginning, Heaven and Earth lay so close together that their children, the bright gods and dark Titans, were cramped. To relieve the situation, one daring Titan mutilated and killed his father; with his brothers, he then created the firmament out of the slain god's skull and the seas from his blood.

The identity of the Titan son is a complex one: giver of life and light on the one hand, he is also the lord of the underworld, king of darkness and death. This Janus-like character is a central figure in the Celtic cult, as are the mighty semidivine heroes who later wrest benefits for humanity from the hostile nature gods.

I N THE BEGINNING Earth and Heaven were great world-giants, and they were the parents of a numerous offspring; but the Heaven in those days lay upon the Earth, and their children crowded between them were unhappy and without light, as was also their mother. So she and they took counsel together against Heaven, and one of his sons, who was bolder than the others, undertook shamefully to mutilate Heaven; nay, he and his brothers stayed not their hands till they had cut the world-giant their father into many pieces. Out of his skull they made the firmament, and the spilling of the blood of his body caused a great flood, which, as it settled in the hollows of the earth, made up the sea.

Some of the children of Earth and Heaven were born bright beings or gods, who mostly loved the light and the upper air; and some were Giants or Titans, who were of a darker and gloomier hue. These latter hated the gods, and the gods hated them. The daring son of Earth who began the mutilation of the world-giant was one of the Titans, and he became their king; but the gods did not wish him to rule over them and their abode, so he was driven from his throne by his youngest son, who was born a god. The king, beaten in battle, sailed away to other parts of his realm; and after much wandering on the sea, he was at last received in the country of the happy departed, whence he was afterwards thought to bless the farmer's toil and to help man in other ways.

When the great flood caused by the mangling of the world-giant took place, all men were drowned save a single pair saved in a ship. He who made and owned the ship was not a man, nor did the gods own him as one of them; but he was a Giant or Titan who was kindly disposed towards the race; and when he had safely landed them where they were to dwell, he went away to the same place as the dethroned king. For he was of his kith and kin, unless perhaps those are to be followed who thought the two were but one and the same person, and that person no other than the ruler of the departed himself, the god of all beginning and all end. Viewed through the medium of the latter, he appeared to be the demon of darkness and horror and death, ever busily adding to the number of his victims; but through the former he was seen to be the first father and great parent of all; so it was ever a matter of piety to reckon darkness before light, the night before the day, and winter before summer.

The new king of the gods was of a passing brilliant nature; so they called him Bright and Day and Father Sky. He was a mighty warrior; but he had terrible foes, who forced him to take part in many a fearful struggle. When he fought in summer he always triumphed, but he fared ill in the winter conflicts. On one occasion he was badly wounded, and would never have recovered his former strength and form but for the timely aid of a man who was a cunning leech; and on another he and the other gods would have been hard beset had they not taken care to secure the help of the Sun-hero. This last was not a god, but the youthful son of a mortal. There was, however, no spearman anywhere to equal him, and his father was so wise and crafty that he had forced the gods to treat mankind far better than they had before been wont to do. For the good things bestowed on man were often begrudged by the gods, and most of all by the owners of the wealth of the nether world and the land of the happy dead. They hated this mortal, so kind to his race, and made him suffer untold pain and torture; but he always succeeded in the end in all that he set his mind on achieving, as when, for example, he cheated them of the dog that was to be the hunter's friend and servant; also of the other animals he stole from them as likely to be of use to his kindred. It was from the same nether country that he likewise obtained by craft and falsehood the strong drink that was to cheer man, to give him the dreams of poets and the visions of prophets. These and other boons, too many to name one by one, made him very famous and beloved, more so in some lands than even the king of the gods himself.

—John Rhys. *Lectures on the Origin and Growth of Religion as Illustrated by Celtic Heathendom.* 2nd ed. London: Williams and Norgate, 1862, pp. 669–672.

From the Soothsaying of the Vala

In this cosmological summary from Snorri Sturluson's *Poetic Edda* (c. 1200), the primordial priestess (the Vala) recounts the history of the gods and of the world. When Ymir the frost-giant lived "long ago," there was only a "grinning gap and grass nowhere." The sons of Borr—Odin's generation—built up middle earth and ordered the universe, its times and seasons.

The gods were happy and productive in their courts until the Fates entered the world. "The fearful maidens from Jotunheim (home of the giants)" lived at the roots of Yggdrasil, the ash-tree of the world, which extended through Asgard (home of the gods), Utgard (land of the giants and elves), and Niflheim (the realm of Hel, goddess of death) and supported the universal structure. The power of these Fates to "lay down laws," "choose out life," and "speak the doom of the sons of men" was a central tenet of Scandinavian religion and, as is usually the case when fate is emphasized, led to an interest in divination and augury.

The first man and the first woman were created from the trunks of ash and elm trees which the sky gods (Aesir kinddred) Odin, Honir, and Lodur found on the beach. Out of the same material that formed the essence of the world structure, the gods made the people with life and spirit.

HEARING I ask all holy kindreds,
　　high and low-born, sons of Heimdal!
Thou too, Odin, who bidst me utter
the oldest tidings of men that I mind!

I remember of yore were born the Jötuns,
they who aforetime fostered me:
nine worlds I remember, nine in the Tree,
the glorious Fate Tree that springs 'neath the Earth.

'Twas the earliest of times when Ymir lived;
then was sand nor sea nor cooling wave,
nor was Earth found ever, nor Heaven on high,
there was Yawning of Deeps and nowhere grass:

ere the sons of the god had uplifted the world-plain,
and fashioned Midgarth, the glorious Earth.
Sun shone from the south, on the world's bare stones—
then was Earth o'ergrown with herb of green.

Sun, Moon's companion, out of the south
her right hand flung round the rim of heaven.
Sun knew not yet where she had her hall;
nor knew the stars where they had their place;
nor ever the Moon what might he owned.

Then went all the Powers to their thrones of doom—
the most holy gods— and o'er this took counsel:
to Night and the New-Moons names they gave:
they named the Morning, and named the Mid-day,
Afternoon, Evening, —to count the years.

Gathered the gods on the Fields of Labour;
they set on high their courts and temples;
they founded forges, wrought rich treasures,
tongs they hammered and fashioned tools.

They played at tables in court, were joyous,—

little they wanted for wealth of gold.—
Till there came forth three of the giant race,
all fearful maidens, from Jötunheim.

Then went all the Powers to their thrones of doom,—
the most holy gods,— and o'er this took counsel:
whom should they make the lord of dwarfs
out of Ymir's blood, and his swarthy limbs.

Mead-drinker then was made the highest,
but Durin second of all the dwarfs;
and out of the earth these twain-shaped beings
in form like man, as Durin bade.

New Moon, Waning-moon, All-thief, Dallier,
North and South and East and West.
Corpse-like, Death-like, Niping, Daïnn,
Bifur, Bafur, Bömbur, Nori,
Ann and Onar, Aï, Mead-wolf.

Vigg and Wand-elf, Wind-elf, Thraïnn,
Thekk and Thorin, Thror, Vit, and Lit,
Nyr and Regin, New-counsel, Wise-counsel,—
now have I numbered the dwarfs aright.

Fili, Kili, Fundin, Nali,
Heptifili, Hannar, Sviur,
Frar, Hornbori, Fræg and Loni,
Aurvang, Jari, Oaken-shield.

'Tis time to number in Dallier's song-mead
all the dwarf-kind of Lofar's race,—
who from earth's threshold, the Plains of Moisture,
sought below the Sandy-realms.

There were Draupnir and Dolgthrasir,
Har and Haugspori, Hlevang, Gloin,
Dori, Ori, Duf, Andvari,
Skirfir, Virfir, Skafid, Aï.

Elf and Yngvi, Oaken-shield,
Fjalar and Frost, Fin and Ginar.
Thus shall be told throughout all time
the line who were born of Lofar's race.

Then came three gods of the Aesir kindred,
mighty and blessed, towards their home.

They found on the seashore, wanting power,
with fate unwoven, an Ash and Elm.

Spirit they had not, and mind they owned not,—
blood, nor voice nor fair appearance.
Spirit gave Odin, and mind gave Hönir,
blood gave Lodur, and aspect fair.

An ash I know standing, 'tis called Yggdrasil,
a high tree sprinkled with shining drops;
come dews therefrom which fall in the dales;
it stands ever green o'er the well of Weird.

There are the Maidens, all things knowing,
three in the hall which stands 'neath the Tree.
One is named "Weird," the second "Being"—
who grave on tablets— but "Shall" the third.
They lay down laws, they choose out life,
they speak the doom of the sons of men.

—Olive Bray (ed. and trans.). *The Elder or Poetic Edda. The Mythological Poems*, Part 1. Viking
Club Translation Series, Vol. 2. London: Viking Club, 1908, pp. 277–283.

Kalevala: The Birth of

Väinämöinen
Finno-Ugric peoples of the West (the Finns,
Lapps, and Magyars) came under the influence of the Christians so early that relatively little is known of their indigenous religious beliefs and practices. The Finnish national epic—the *Kalevala*—does contain traditional material, however. Although it was compiled by Elias Lonnrot in 1835, most of its fifty "songs" are
much older.

In this myth, there were only the chaotic waters (that which forms but is not itself formed) and the agent of creation, the beautiful teal, in the beginning. To provide a dry place for a nest, a spot of solidity in the shifting seas, the Mother of
Waters lifted her knee out of the ocean, and the teal laid seven eggs on it. Only by
their immersion in the primordial waters are the pieces of those eggs transformed
into elements of the universe.

SHORT the time that passed thereafter;
  Scarce a moment had passed over,
Ere a beauteous teal came flying
Lightly hovering o'er the water,
Seeking for a spot to rest in,
Searching for a home to dwell in.
Eastward flew she, westward flew she,

Flew to north-west and to southward,
But the place she sought she found not,
Not a spot, however barren,
Where her nest she could establish,
Or a resting-place could light on.
Then she hovered, slowly moving,
And she pondered and reflected,
"If my nest in wind I 'stablish
Or should rest it on the billows,
Then the winds will overturn it,
Or the waves will drift it from me."
Then the Mother of the Waters,
Water-Mother, maid aërial,
From the waves her knee uplifted,
Raised her shoulder from the billows,
That the teal her nest might 'stablish,
And might find a peaceful dwelling.
Then the teal, the bird so beauteous,
Hovered slow, and gazed around her,
And she saw the knee uplifted
From the blue waves of the ocean,
And she thought she saw a hillock,
Freshly green with springing verdure.
There she flew, and hovered slowly,
Gently on the knee alighting,
And her nest she there established,
And she laid her eggs all golden,
Six gold eggs she laid within it,
And a seventh she laid of iron.

O'er her eggs the teal sat brooding,
And the knee grew warm beneath her;
And she sat one day, a second,
Brooded also on the third day;
Then the Mother of the Waters,
Water-Mother, maid aërial,
Felt it hot, and felt it hotter,
And she felt her skin was heated,
Till she thought her knee was burning,
And that all her veins were melting.
Then she jerked her knee with quickness,
And her limbs convulsive shaking,
Rolled the eggs into the water,
Down amid the waves of ocean,
And to splinters they were broken,
And to fragments they were shattered.

In the ooze they were not wasted,
Nor the fragments in the water,
But a wondrous change came o'er them,
And the fragments all grew lovely.
From the cracked egg's lower fragment,
Rose the lofy arch of heaven,
From the yolk, the upper portion,
Now became the sun's bright lustre;
From the white, the upper portion,
Rose the moon that shines so brightly;
Whatso in the egg was mottled,
Now became the stars in heaven,
Whatso in the egg was blackish,
In the air as cloudlets floated.

—W. F. Kirby (trans.). *Kalevala: The Land of the Heroes*. Vol. 1. London: J. M. Dent, 1907, pp. 5–7.

FOUR

MYTHS OF INDIA

HINDU MYTHS

Rig-Veda X, xc: The Sacrifice of Primal

Man   The first of the sacred books of Hinduism, the *Rig-Veda* ("Royal Knowledge") is a collection of 1,028 hymns composed by the warring Aryans who came into India from the Iranian highlands c. 2000–1000 B.C. The theology of the early "books" of the *Rig-Veda* is similar to that found in myths of other Indo-European people to the extent that it is fundamentally polytheistic and nature-oriented. There exists one major difference however: while the polytheism of other Indo-European groups gradually evolved into a kind of modified monotheism with one deity heading the pantheon, Vedism instead raised each deity (frequently credited with the attributes of the others) to a position of supremacy within the context of a given hymn. The individual identities of the gods thus became blurred, and in their place arose the concept of one divine principle expressed in many forms. By the tenth and last book of the *Rig-Veda*, the names of deities are purely functional.

The four Vedas (the *Rig-Veda*, hymns to the gods; the *Sama-Veda*, primarily verses from the *Rig-Veda* arranged for liturgical purposes; the *Yajur-Veda*, sacrificial sentences and verses; and the *Atharva-Veda*, magic spells and incantations) were composed between 2000 and 900 B.C. for use in sacrificial rites, where they were recited by officiating priests.

In this myth from the tenth book, the importance of sacrifice as a creative event is stressed as Parusha (Primal Man) is sacrificed to become the world. Three-quarters of him remains unmanifest and absolute, while the material world, its creatures, and the social classes are all fashioned from the manifest quarter of his immense body.

His mouth becomes the Brahman priest, his arms the prince, his thighs the common people, and his feet the serf. In the end, it is explained that by this grand sacrifice the gods made sacrifice to the principle of sacrifice itself; that is, they made the world holy *(sacer,* "holy;" *facere,* "to make") by creating it out of the process of sacred giving itself. Through the destruction of a body in one form, accomplished in a spirit of offering, the greatest creation of all forms took place. In recognition of this fact and in hopes of imitating the event and thus reestablishing its sacrality, religious rites were born.

A THOUSAND HEADS had [primal] Man,
    A thousand eyes, a thousand feet:
Encompassing the earth on every side,
He exceeded it by ten fingers' [breath].

    [That] Man is this whole universe,—
What was and what is yet to be,
The Lord of immortality
Which he outgrows by eating food.

    This is the measure of this greatness,
But greater yet is [primal] Man:
All beings form a quarter of him,
Three-quarters are the immortal in heaven.

    With three-quarters Man rose up on high,
A quarter of him came to be again [down] here:
From this he spread in all directions,
Into all that eats and does not eat.

    From him was Viraj born,
From Viraj Man again:
Once born, —behind, before,
He reached beyond the earth.

    When with Man as their oblation
The gods performed the sacrifice,
Spring was the melted butter,
Summer the fuel, and autumn the oblation.

    Him they besprinkled on the sacrificial strew,—
[Primeval] Man, born in the beginning:
With him [their victim], gods, Sadhyas, seers
Performed the sacrifice.

    From this sacrifice completely offered
The clotted ghee was gathered up:
From this he fashioned beasts and birds,
Creatures of the woods and creatures of the village.

    From this sacrifice completely offered
Were born the Rig- and Sama-Vedas;
From this were born the meters,
From this was the Yajur-Veda born,

    From this were horses born, all creatures
That have teeth in either jaw:
From this were cattle born,

From this sprang goats and sheep.
When they divided [primal] Man,
Into how many parts did they divide him?
What was his mouth? What his arms?
What are his thighs called? What are his feet?
The Brahman was his mouth,
The arms were made the Prince,
His thighs the common people,
And from his feet the serf was born.
From his mind the moon was born,
And from his eye the sun,
From his mouth Indra and the fire,
From his breath the wind was born.
From his navel arose the atmosphere,
From his head the sky evolved,
From his feet the earth, and from his ear
The cardinal points of the compass:
So did they fashion forth these worlds.
Seven were his enclosing sticks,
Thrice seven were made his fuel-sticks,
When the gods, performing sacrifice,
Bound Man, [their sacrificial] beast.
With sacrifice the gods
Made sacrifice to sacrifice:
These were the first religious rites,
To the firmament these powers went up
Where dwell the ancient Sadhya gods.

—R. C. Zaehner (trans.). *Hindu Scriptures*. London: J. M. Dent, 1966, pp. 8–10.

Rig-Veda X, cxxi: Prajapati (The Golden Embryo)

In another hymn from the tenth book of the *Rig-Veda* (c. 1200 B.C.), the unification of divine power in one functionally named deity is clearly evident. Prajapati (the Golden Embryo) is envisioned as the life-force of all the gods.

Prajapati's origin is somewhat unclear. On the one hand, he is born from the primordial waters that "Moved, conceived the all/as an embryo, giving birth to fire." As such an embryo of fire, Prajapati bears close relation to the chaotic creator forces in that he forms other things but is not formed himself; and his sacrificial connection is well established by this image. But Prajapati is also his own father in the sense that he "looked upon the waters ... with power" and thereby caused them to bring forth the sacrifice that is himself. Once evolved, he created the universe, ordained and sustained the powers of nature and of the gods.

The myth's ritualistic usage is clear from its repetitive nature and its rhythmic appeal, "What god shall we revere with this oblation?"

IN THE BEGINNING the Golden Embryo
[Stirred and] evolved:
Once born he was the one Lord of [every] being;
The heaven and earth did he sustain . . .
What god shall we revere with the oblation?
      Giver of life *(atman),* giver of strength,
Whose behest all [must] obey,
Whose [behests] the gods [obey],
Whose shadow is immortality,
Whose [shadow] death . . .
What god shall we revere with the oblation?
      Who by his might has ever been the One
King of all that breathes and blinks the eye,
Who rules all creatures that have two feet or four . . .
What god shall we revere with the oblation?
      By whose might the snowy peaks,
By whose might, they say, the sea
With Rasa, [the earth-encircling stream],
By whose [might] the cardinal directions
Which are his arms, [exist] . . .
What god shall we revere with the oblation?
      By whom strong heaven and earth are held in place,
By whom the sun is given a firm support,
By whom the firmament, by whom the ether *(rajas)*
Is measured out within the atmosphere . . .
What god shall we revere with this oblation?
      To whom opposing armies, strengthened by his help,
Look up, though trembling in their hearts,
By whom the risen sun sheds forth its light . . .
What god shall we revere with this oblation?
      When the mighty waters moved, conceived the All
As an embryo, giving birth to fire,
Then did he evolve, the One life-force *(asu)* of the gods . . .
What god shall we revere with the oblation?
      Who looked upon the waters, [looked on them] with power,
As they conceived insight, brought forth the sacrifice;
Who, among the gods, was the One God above . . .
What god shall we revere with the oblation?
      May he not harm us, father of the earth,
Who generated heaven, for truth is his law,
Who gave birth to the waters—shimmering, strong . . .
What god shall we revere with the oblation?
      Prajapati! None other than thou hath comprehended
All these [creatures] brought to birth.

Whatever desires be ours in offering up
The oblation to thee, may that be ours!
May we be lords of riches!

—R. C. Zaehner (trans.). *Hindu Scriptures.* London: J. M. Dent, 1966, pp. 10–11.

Rig-Veda X, cxxix: In the Beginning

This hymn from the *Rig-Veda* (c. 1200 B.C.) is one of the most profound and sophisticated of creation myths—profound in its questioning not only of the origin of the world but also of materiality itself, not only of the gods but also of Being-Itself, and sophisticated both in its recognition of the limitations of language and rationality in dealing with this issue and in its tolerance of other possible answers.

The myth asserts that the world did not arise out of being or not-being. Because the two are conceived as polar opposites, they are understood as requiring each other for definition, implying each other for identity. The source that gave rise to either must therefore be prior to both. But language fails here; there are no words for such a condition, and so the Veda inevitably resorts to the negative terminology of "neither this nor that," refusing to fix and limit what is by definition beyond categorization. Linguistic absurdities serve further to demonstrate the difficulties inherent in this task of explanation beyond its limits: only the irreducible and indefinable One breathed, *windless;* above was impulse, below was energy. From this configuration of powers, the world and its gods ultimately evolved.

But "Who knows truly? Who can declare it?" This final admission of humility before the unknowable is unique in cosmologies. By making it, the Veda recognizes that conceptual thinking, which is derivative of being, is insufficient to the task of portraying the origin of being. "Who knows whence this emanation hath arisen?" Perhaps God knows, but since God is the first creation, self-evolved, perhaps even he does not know.

W HEN neither Being nor Not-being was
Nor atmosphere, nor firmament, nor what is beyond.
What did it encompass? Where? In whose protection?
What was water, the deep, unfathomable?
Neither death nor immortality was there then,
No sign of night or day.
That One breathed, windless, by its own energy:
Nought else existed then.
In the beginning was darkness swathed in darkness;
All this was but unmanifested water.
Whatever was, the One, coming into being,
Hidden by the Void,
Was generated by the power of heat.
In the beginning this [One] evolved,
Became desire, first seed of mind.
Wise seers, searching within their hearts.

Found the bond of Being in Not-Being.
Their cord was extended athwart:
Was there a below? Was there an above?
Casters of seed there were, and powers;
Beneath was energy, above was impulse.
Who knows truly? Who can here declare it?
Whence it was born, whence is this emanation.
By the emanation of this the gods
Only later [came to be.]
Who then knows whence it has arisen?
Whence this emanation hath arisen,
Whether [God] disposed it, or whether he did not,—
Only he who is its overseer in highest heaven knows.
[He only knows,] or perhaps he does not know!
—R. C. Zaehner (trans.). *Hindu Scriptures.* London: J. M. Dent, 1966, pp. 11–12.

Brahmanas: Creation from an Egg

The *Brahmanas* (c. 1000 B.C. and later), prose instructions concerning sacrificial ritual, were composed after the *Rig-Veda* and appended to it for use by the officiating priests. The *Satapatha-Brahmana* (the Brahmana of 100 discourses) from which this myth is taken is late enough to have included the *Brhadaranyaka Upanishad,* a philosophical speculation on the meaning of Vedic doctrines.

Here the creator god Prajapati is produced in the form of a golden egg. Rather than the egg being laid upon the primeval waters by a bird or god, as was done in the Finnish and Greek myths, it is produced in this instance by the waters themselves. The creative power of heat is still recognized as an important element, however: in the *Kalevala,* it was generated by the nesting bird; here it results from the churning of the waters.

Additional parallels to Iranian (and Orphic) myths are also present: Prajapati's period of gestation is one year and his life span is one thousand years—facts suggestive of time's connection with being and of the identity of the creator god with time. (If the parallel were carried out, Prajapati could be seen as the equivalent of finite or manifest time; the position of infinite Time in Iranian mythology would here be assumed by the chaotic waters.)

One connection between Indian and Iranian mythology is evidenced here in the reverse. The Asuras or evil ones that Prajapati creates by downward breathing exist as Ahura, the god of Goodness, in Iran; and Iranian devas or evil beings are good divinities when they appear in Indian religion.

VERILY, in the beginning this (universe) was water, nothing but a sea of water. The waters desired, "How can we be reproduced?" They toiled and performed fervid devotions, when they were becoming heated, a golden egg was produced. The year, indeed, was not then in existence: this golden egg floated about for as long as the space of a year.

In a year's time a man, this Prajapati, was produced therefrom; and hence a woman, a cow, or a mare brings forth within the space of a year; for Prajapati was born in a year. He broke open this golden egg. There was then, indeed, no resting-place: only this golden egg, bearing him, floated about for as long as the space of a year.

At the end of a year he tried to speak. He said "bhu*h*": this (word) became this earth;—"bhuva*h*": this became this air;—"sva*h*": this became yonder sky. Therefore a child tries to speak at the end of a year, for at the end of a year Prajapati tried to speak.

When he was first speaking Prajapati spoke (words) of one syllable and of two syllables; whence a child, when first speaking, speaks (words) of one syllable and of two syllables.

These (three words consist of) five syllables: he made them to be the five seasons, and thus there are these five seasons. At the end of the (first) year, Prajapati rose to stand on these worlds thus produced; whence a child tries to stand up at the end of a year, for at the end of a year Prajapati stood up.

He was born with a life of a thousand years: even as one might see in the distance the opposite shore, so did he behold the opposite shore (the end) of his own life.

Desirous of offspring, he went on singing praises and toiling. He laid the power of reproduction into his own self. By (the breath of) his mouth he created the gods: the gods were created on entering the sky; and this is the godhead of the gods (deva) that they were created on entering the sky (div). Having created them, there was, as it were, daylight for him; and this also is the godhead of the gods that, after creating them, there was, as it were, daylight (diva) for him.

And by the downward breathing he created the Asuras: they were created on entering this earth. Having created them there was, as it were, darkness for him.

He knew, "Verily, I have created evil for myself since, after creating, there has come to be, as it were, darkness for me." Even then he smote them with evil, and owing to this it was that they were overcome; whence people say, "Not true is that regarding (the fight between) the gods and Asuras which is related partly in the tale and partly in the legend; for it was even then that Prajapati smote them with evil, and it was owing to this that they were overcome."

Therefore it is with reference to this that the Rishi has said, "Not for a single day hast thou fought, nor hast thou any enemy, O Maghavan: illusion is what they say concerning thy battles; no foe hast thou fought either to-day or aforetime."

Now what daylight, as it were, there was for him, on creating the gods, of that he made the day; and what darkness, as it were, there was for him, on creating the Asuras, of that he made the night: they are these two, day and night.

Prajapati bethought himself, "Everything (sarva), indeed, I have obtained by stealth (tsar) who have created these deities": this became the "sarvatsara," for "sarvatsara," doubtless, is the same as "sa*m*vatsara (year)." And, verily, whosoever thus knows 'sa*m*vatsara' to be the same as "sarvatsara," is not overcome by any evil which, by magic art, steals upon him (tsar); and whosoever thus knows "samvatsara" to be the same as "sarvatsara," overcomes against whomsoever he practises magic art.

Prajapati bethought himself, "Verily, I have created here a counterpart of myself, to wit, the year"; whence they say, "Prajapati is the year"; for he created it to be a counterpart of himself: inasmuch as "samvatsara (year)," as well as "Prajapati," consists of four syllables, thereby it (the year) is a counterpart of him.

Now, these are the deities who were created out of Prajapati—Agni, Indra, Soma, and Parameshthin Prajapatya.

They were born with a life of a thousand years: even as one would see in the distance the opposite shore, so did they behold the opposite shore of their own life.

—Julius Eggeling (trans.). "Satapatha-Brahmana, XI, i, 6." *Sacred Books of the East.* Vol. 44. Max Müller (ed.). Oxford, England: Clarendon Press, 1900, pp. 12–15.

From the Chandogya Upanishad

The *Upanishads* are philosophical instructions—literally "sessions" or "sitting next to"—in which forest-dwelling sages expounded on the nature of Vedic theories. As such, they form the last part of Vedic literature. The thirteen main *Upanishads* were composed c. 800–400 B.C., and scholars fix the Chandogya as one of the oldest (c. 700 B.C.).

The problem of the origin of being and its relation to not-being addressed in *Rig-Veda* X, cxxix, is taken up again here in two different ways. The first passage (III, 19) uses the imagery of the *Brahmanas* to argue that not-being developed itself like the chaotic waters into the egg of the universe. The second (VI, 2) disputes this theory, asking how being could have been derived from not-being. It concludes that being must have been present at the beginning and that it created the world by desiring replication and thereby producing water and heat.

(III, 19) IN THE BEGINNING this world was merely non-being. It was existent. It developed. It turned into an egg. It lay for the period of a year. It was split asunder. One of the two eggshell-parts became silver, one gold.

That which was of silver is this earth. That which was of gold is the sky. What was the outer membrane is the mountains. What was the inner membrane is cloud and mist. What were the veins are the rivers. What was the fluid within is the ocean.

Now, what was born therefrom is yonder sun. When it was born, shouts and hurrahs, all beings and all desires rose up toward it. Therefore at its rising and at its every return shouts and hurrahs, all beings and all desires rise up toward it.

He who, knowing it thus, reverences the sun as Brahma—the prospect is that pleasant shouts will come unto to him and delight him—yea, delight him!

(VI, 2) **I**N **THE BEGINNING,** my dear, this world was just Being, one only, without a second. To be sure, some people say: "In the beginning this world was just Non-being, one only, without a second; that from Non-being Being was produced."

But verily, my dear, whence could this be?, said he. How from Non-being could Being be produced? On the contrary, my dear, in the beginning this world was just Being, one only, without a second.

It bethought itself: "Would that I were many! Let me procreate myself!" It emitted heat. The heat bethought itself: "Would that I were many! Let me procreate myself!" It emitted water. Therefore whenever a person grieves or perspires from the heat, then water [i.e., either tears or perspiration] is produced.

That water bethought itself: "Would that I were many! Let me procreate myself!" It emitted food. Therefore whenever it rains, then there is abundant food. So food for eating is produced just from water.

—Robert Ernest Hume (ed. and trans.). *The Thirteen Principal Upanishads.* London: Oxford University Press, 1971. pp. 214–215, 241.

From the Kena Upanishad   The Kena Upanishad
(800–400 B.C.) is another of the thirteen principal and canonical *Upanishads.* Like the others, it is a philosophical instruction on Vedic themes, particularly in this instance on the nature of the creator Brahman.

The use of many different approaches to religious questions is typical of Vedism. While the second prose part of this Upanishad depicts Brahman in highly anthropomorphic terms and praises him as supreme among the gods, the first verse section included here is far more abstract and philosophical. It cautions against idolatry and argues that Brahman is "not what people here adore." Rather, it defines Brahman as the cause, not the object, of the senses. Brahman is the ground of being and thinking: "What cannot be thought with the mind, but [is] that whereby the mind can think." Beyond both the known and unknown, Brahman cannot be objectified. Thus, while its mystery can be apprehended, it can never be comprehended.

WHO **SENDS** the mind to wander afar? Who first drives life to start on its journey? Who impels us to utter these words? Who is the Spirit behind the eye and the ear?

It is the ear of the ear, the eye of the eye, and the word of words, the mind of mind, and the life of life. Those who follow wisdom pass beyond, and on leaving this world, become immortal.

There the eye goes not, nor words, nor mind. We know not, we cannot understand, how he can be explained: he is above the known, and he is above the unknown. Thus have we heard from the ancient sages who explained the truth to us.

What cannot be spoken with words, but that whereby words are spoken: Know that alone to be Brahman, the Spirit; and not what people here adore.

What cannot be thought with the mind, but that whereby the mind can think: Know that alone to be Brahman, the Spirit; and not what people here adore.

What cannot be seen with the eye, but that whereby the eye can see: Know that alone to be Brahman, the Spirit; and not what people here adore.

What cannot be heard with the ear, but that whereby the ear can hear: Know that alone to be Brahman, the Spirit; and not what people here adore.

What cannot be indrawn with the breath, but that whereby breath is indrawn: Know that alone to be Brahman, the Spirit; and not what people here adore.

—Juan Mascaro (trans.). *The Upanishads.* Baltimore, Md.: Penguin Books, 1965, pp. 51–54.

From the Laws of Manu

Hindu mythology claims that being and time come into existence with Brahma, the creator. Brahma lives for 100 divine years, and each day of his life is represented by a *kalpa,* a period of 4,320 million earthly years. The *kalpas* in turn have fourteen ages, each ruled over by its own Manu, a father of the human race. We now live in the seventh age, and the Manu is Manu Vaivasvata. Manu is thought to have been given the Vedas so that he might construct a system of Hindu law, and it is for this reason that the most important law book is ascribed to him.

The semicanonical lawbooks form part of Smirti or "Human" Tradition (in contrast to the Vedas, Shruti or "Divine" Tradition). Principally based on the Vedas, they sought to present a comprehensive philosophy of life and social organization.

In this passage from the *Lawbook of Manu* (c. 200–100 B.C.), the theme of the golden egg laid in waters is maintained. But in this case Brahman (the Self-Existent) creates both the chaotic waters and the egg (his seed) within them; now manifest, he is born from the egg as Brahman. As such, he is simultaneously Narayana (son of the primal spirit), Purusha (the primal man), and Brahma (the masculine form of Brahman; the creator god). All this complexity serves to demonstrate the mystery that Brahman is both the cause and result of his own creation—both creator and creature, father and son; and secondly, that he is one, although known under different names. Having lived in the egg for one year, Brahman creates the universe out of it by his thought.

H E (that is the Self-existent) desiring to produce beings of many kinds from his own body, first with a thought created the waters and placed his seed in them. That (seed) became a golden egg, in brilliancy equal to the sun; in the (egg) he himself was born as Brahman, the progenitor of the whole world. The waters are called *narah* (for) the waters are, indeed, the offspring of Nara; as they were his first residence, he thence is named Narayana. From that cause, which is indiscernible, eternal, and both real and unreal, was produced that male (Purusha) who is famed in this world (under the appellation of) Brahma. The divine one resided in that egg during a whole year, then he himself by his thought (alone) divided it into two halves; and out of those two halves he formed heaven and earth, between them the middle sphere, the eight points of the horizon, and the eternal abode of the waters.

—G. Buhler (trans.). *The Laws of Manu. Sacred Books of the East.* Vol. 25. In Max Müller (ed.). Oxford, England: Clarendon Press, 1886, p. 5.

From the Vishnu Purana
The *Puranas* or "Ancient Stories" comprise part of the Smirti or "Human" Tradition in the Hindu canon. They are commonly attributed to Vyasa, the legendary author of the great epic, the *Mahabharata,* and were written after 300 A.D., although they contain older material. The *Puranas* generally deal with theological and cosmological issues raised in the *Upanishads* and with Hindu notions of time. Because of their popularity, these books introduced many to ideas that had hitherto been known only by the priestly class.

The distinction between appearance and reality is a complex and troubling one and this myth attempts to simplify it. Brahman is imagined as both the creator and essence of the world. In enlightened reality, all is one, Brahman. In objective appearance, however, things are disparate, and Brahma (the masculine form of Brahman) is their creator. As such, he assumes the form of a boar, raises the earth from the bottom of the primeval seas with his tusks, and orders the universe. Reverting to sacred reality, the passage asserts the identity of Brahman with the mysterious sacred power of sacrifice: "Thou art the person of sacrifice . . . thy mouth is the altar . . . thy name is all the hymns of the Vedas."

MAITREYA: Tell me, mighty sage, how, in the commencement of the (present) Kalpa, Narayana, who is named Brahma, created all existent things.

PARASARA: In what manner the divine Brahma, who is one with Narayana, created progeny, and is thence named the lord of progeny (Prajapati), the lord god, you shall hear.

At the close of the past (of Padma) Kalpa, the divine Brahma, endowed with the quality of goodness, awoke from his night of sleep, and beheld the universe void. He, the supreme Narayana the incomprehensible, the sovereign of all creatures, invested with the form of Brahma, the god without beginning, the creator of all things; of whom, with respect to his name Narayana, the god who has the form of Brahma, the imperishable origin of the world, this verse is repeated: "The waters are called Nara, because they were the offspring of Nara (the supreme spirit); and, as, in them, his first (Ayana) progress (in the character of Brahma) took place, he is thence named Narayan (he whose place of moving was the waters)." He, the lord, concluding that within the waters lay the earth, and being desirous to raise it up, created another form for that purpose; and, as, in preceding Kalpas, he has assumed the shape of a fish or a tortoise, so, in this, he took the figure of a boar. Having adopted a form composed of the sacrifices of the Vedas, for the preservation of the whole earth, the eternal, supreme, and universal soul, the great progenitor of created beings, eulogized by Sanaka and the other saints who dwell in the sphere of holy men (Janaloka); he, the supporter of spiritual and material being, plunged into the ocean. The goddess Earth, beholding him thus descending to the subterranean regions, bowed in devout adoration, and thus glorified the god:—

PRITHIVI (Earth): Hail to thee, who art all creatures; to thee, the holder of the mace and shell: elevate me now from this place, as thou hast upraised me in days of old. From thee have I proceeded; of thee do I consist; as do the skies and all other existing things. Hail to thee, spirit of the supreme spirit; to thee, soul of soul; to thee, who art discrete and indiscrete matter; who art one with the elements and with time. Thou art the creator of all things, their preserver, and their destroyer, in the forms, O lord, of Brahma, Vishnu, and Rudra, at the seasons of creation, duration, and dissolution. When thou hast devoured all things, thou reposest on the ocean that sweeps over the world, meditated upon, O Govinda, by the wise. No one knoweth thy true nature; and the gods adore thee only in the forms it hath pleased thee to assume. They who are desirous of final liberation worship thee as the supreme Brahma; and who that adores not Vasudeva shall obtain emancipation? Whatever may be apprehended by the mind, whatever may be perceived by the senses, whatever may be discerned by the intellect, all is but a form of thee. I am of thee, upheld by thee; thou art my creator, and to thee I fly for refuge: hence, in this universe, Madhavi (the bride of Madhava of Vishnu) is my designation. Triumph to the essence of all wisdom, to the unchangeable, the imperishable: triumph to the eternal; to the indiscrete, to the essence of discrete things: to him who is both cause and effect; who is the universe; the sinless lord of sacrifice; triumph. Thou art sacrifice; thou art the oblation; thou art the mystic Omkara; thou art the sacrificial fires; thou art the Vedas, and their dependent sciences; thou art, Hari, the object of all worship. The sun, the stars, the planets, the whole world; all that is formless, or that has form; all that is visible, or invisible; all. Purushottama, that I have said, or left unsaid; all this, Supreme, thou art. Hail to thee, again and again! hail! all hail!

PARASARA: The auspicious supporter of the world, being thus hymned by the earth, emitted a low murmuring sound, like the chanting of the Sama Veda; and the mighty boar, whose eyes were like the lotus, and whose body, vast as the Nila mountain, was of the dark colour of the lotus-leaves, uplifted upon his ample tusks the earth from the lowest regions. As he reared his head, the waters shed from his brow purified the great sages, Sanandana and others, residing in the sphere of the saints. Through the indentations made by his hoofs, the waters rushed into the lower worlds with a thundering noise. Before his breath the pious denizens of Janaloka were scattered; and the Munis sought for shelter amongst the bristles upon the scriptural body of the boar, trembling as he rose up, supporting the earth, and dripping with moisture. Then the great sages, Sanandana and the rest, residing continually in the sphere of saints, were inspired with delight; and, blowing lowly, they praised the stern-eyed upholder of the earth.

THE YOGINS: Triumph, lord of lords supreme; Kesava, sovereign of the earth, the wielder of the mace, the shell, the discus, and the sword: cause of production, destruction, and existence. THOU ART, O god: there is no other supreme condition but thou. Thou, lord, art the person of sacrifice: for thy feet are the Vedas, thy tusks are the stake to which the victim is bound; in thy teeth are the offerings; thy mouth is the altar; thy tongue is the fire; and the hairs of thy body are the sacrifical grass. Thine eyes, O omnipotent, are day and night; thy head is the seat of all, the place of Brahma; thy name is all the hymns of the Vedas; thy nostrils are all oblations: O thou, whose snout is the ladle of oblation; whose deep voice is the chanting of the Sama Veda; whose body is the hall of sacrifice; whose joints are the different ceremonies; and whose ears have the properties of both voluntary and obligatory rites; do thou, who art eternal, who art in size a mountain be propitious. We acknowledge thee, who hast traversed the world, O universal form to be the beginning, the continuance, and the destruction of all things: thou art the supreme god. Have pity on us, O lord of conscious and unconscious beings. The orb of the earth is seen seated on the tip of thy tusks, as if thou hadst been sporting amidst a lake where the lotus floats, and hadst borne away the leaves covered with soil. The space between heaven and earth is occupied by thy body, O thou of unequalled glory, resplendent with the power of pervading the universe, O lord, for the benefit of all. Thou art the aim of all: there is none other than thee, sovereign of the world: this is thy might, by which all things, fixed or movable, are pervaded. This form, which is now beheld, is thy form, as one essentially with wisdom. Those who have practised devotion conceive erroneously of the nature of the world. The ignorant, who do not perceive that this universe is of the nature of wisdom, and judge of it as an object of perception only, are lost in the ocean of spiritual ignorance. But they who know true wisdom, and whose minds are pure, behold this whole world as one with divine knowledge, as one with thee, O god. Be favourable, O universal spirit: raise up this earth, for the habitation of created beings. Inscrutable deity, whose eyes are like lotuses, give us felicity. O lord, thou art endowed with the quality of goodness: raise up, Govinda, this earth, for the general good. Grant us happiness, O lotus-eyed. May this, thy activity in creation, be beneficial to the earth. Salutation to thee. Grant us happiness, O lotus-eyed.

PARASARA: The supreme being thus eulogized, upholding the earth, raised it quickly, and placed it on the summit of the ocean, where it floats like a mighty vessel, and, from its expansive surface, does not sing beneath the waters. Then, having levelled the earth, the great eternal deity divided it into portions, by mountains. He who never wills in vain created, by his irresistible power, those mountains again upon the earth, which had been consumed at the destruction of the world. Having then divided the earth into seven great portions or continents, as it was before, he constructed, in like manner, the four (lower) spheres, earth, sky, heaven, and the sphere of the sages (Maharloka). Thus Heri, the four-faced god, invested with the quality of activity, and taking the form of Brahma, accomplished the creation. But he (Brahma) is only the instrumental cause of things to be created; the things that are capable of being created arise from nature as a common material cause. With exception of one instrumental cause alone, there is no need of any other cause; for (imperceptible) substance becomes perceptible substance according to the powers with which it is originally imbued.

—H.H. Wilson. *The Vishnu Purana*. Vol. 1. London: Kegan Paul, Trench, Trubner, 1864, pp. 55–57.

A JAIN MYTH

Jinasena: There Is No Creator

A very ancient tradition, Jainism was refounded by Mahavira ("the great hero") in the latter half of the sixth century B.C. Mahavira was considered by his followers to be the twenty-fourth in a series of Tirthamkaras ("one who makes a ford" across the river of existence). Parsva, the twenty-third Tirthamkara, probably lived in the ninth or eight century B.C., but there is doubt as to the historicity of his twenty-two predecessors.

Jainism (from *jina*, "victor") rejects both scripture and divine revelation and, although it admits of a hierarchy of gods residing in various heavens, considers them inferior to the Tirthamkaras and thus denies them relevance and genuine divinity; for this reason, Jainism is usually considered atheistic. Essentially, it is Jainism's goal to free the innately immaterial soul from the karmic matter that accrues to it by involvement with and attachment to the world. Asceticism, both internal and external, is the method adopted for this purpose, and if it is complete the individual *jiva* (soul) is released from the cycle of rebirth to a state of isolated, eternal, and omniscient inactivity.

The Jains hold that no god created the universe, that it is in fact uncreated and indestructible, maintained and changing according to natural principles. This selection from the *Mahapurana* (The Great Legend) was written by the teacher Jinasena in the ninth century A.D. and is modeled on the passages and philosophical discourses of the Hindu *Puranas*.

SOME FOOLISH MEN declare that Creator made the world.
  The doctrine that the world was created is ill-advised, and should be rejected.

If God created the world, where was he before creation?
If you say he was transcendent then, and needed no support, where is he now?

No single being had the skill to make this world—
For how can an immaterial god create that which is material?

How could God have made the world without any raw material?
If you say he made this first, and then the world, you are faced with an endless regression.

If you declare that this raw material arose naturally you fall into another fallacy,
For the whole universe might thus have been its own creator, and have arisen
  equally naturally.

If God created the world by an act of his own will, without any raw material,
Then it is just his will and nothing else—and who will believe this silly stuff?
If he is ever perfect and complete, how could the will to create have arisen in
  him?

If, on the other hand, he is not perfect, he could no more create the universe than
  a potter could.

If he is formless, actionless, and all-embracing, how could he have created the
  world?
Such a soul, devoid of all modality, would have no desire to create anything.

If he is perfect, he does not strive for the three aims of man,
So what advantage would he gain by creating the universe?

If you say that he created to no purpose, because it was his nature to do so, then
  God is pointless.
If he created in some kind of sport, it was the sport of a foolish child, leading to
  trouble.

If he created because of the karma of embodied beings [acquired in a previous
  creation]
He is not the Almighty Lord, but subordinate to something else. . . .

If out of love for living things and need of them he made the world,
Why did he not make creation wholly blissful, free from misfortune?

If he were transcendent he would not create, for he would be free;
Nor if involved in transmigration, for then he would not be almighty.

Thus the doctrine that the world was created by God
Makes no sense at all.

And God commits great sin in slaying the children whom he himself created.
If you say that he slays only to destroy evil beings, why did he create such beings
  in the first place? . . .

Good men should combat the believer in divine creation, maddened by an evil
  doctrine.

Know that the world is uncreated, as time itself is, without beginning and end,
And is based on the principles, life and the rest.

Uncreated and indestructible, it endures under the compulsion of its own nature,
Divided into three sections—hell, earth, and heaven.

—W. Theodore de Bary (ed.). *Sources of Indian Tradition.* Vol. 1. New York: Columbia University
Press, 1966, pp. 76–78.

A BUDDHIST MYTH

The Buddha: How the World Evolved

Siddhartha Gautama, the Buddha or "enlightened one," lived in the sixth century
B.C. (c. 566–486 B.C.) and preached a salvational doctrine called The Middle
Way. Analyzing the human condition and its causes, Buddhism posits a means
whereby people can become "awakened" to the absolute and can escape the otherwise inevitable round of rebirth, suffering, and mortality—their lot in the relative
world.

The Buddha was essentially uninterested in the question of the origin of the
universe, declaring "Inconceivable, O Monks, is this Samsara [wheel of rebirth];
not to be discovered is any first beginnings of beings." Further, he rejected any
idea of a personal creator god, claiming that the world goes through successive periods of expansion and contraction, unaffected by the activities of the gods.

In this excerpt from the third book of the *Digha Niyaka* (3.28ff.)—part of the
Discourse Collection of the Theravada Buddhist Canon—the Buddha argues
against the teachings of the Hindu Brahmanas. He envisions beings rising up into
the World of Radiance or descending into this world of matter depending on the
weight of their acquired karma and mistakenly thinking, as they enter one world
or the other, that they are its creators. By this illustration, he asserts the inaccura-
cy of the Hindu cosmology.

THERE ARE some monks and brahmans who declare as a doctrine received from their teachers that the beginning of all things was the
work of the god *Brahma.* I have gone and asked them whether it was true that
they maintained such a doctrine, and they have replied that it was; but when I
have asked them to explain just how the beginning of things was the work of the
god *Brahma* they have not been able to answer, and have returned the question
to me. Then I have explained it to them thus:

There comes a time, my friends, sooner or later, . . . when the world is dissolved and beings are mostly reborn in the World of Radiance. There they dwell,
made of the stuff of mind, feeding on joy, shining in their own light, flying
through middle space, firm in their bliss for a long, long time.

Now there comes a time when this world begins to evolve, and then the

World of *Brahma* appears, but it is empty. And some being, whether because his allotted span is past or because his merit is exhausted, quits his body in the World of Radiance and is born in the empty World of *Brahma*, where he dwells for a long, long time. Now because he has been so long alone he begins to feel dissatisfaction and longing, and wishes that other beings might come and live with him. And indeed soon other beings quit their bodies in the World of Radiance and come to keep him company in the World of *Brahma*.

Then the being who was born first there thinks: "I am *Brahma*, the mighty *Brahma*, the Conqueror, the Unconquered, the All-seeing, the Lord, the Maker, the Creator, the Supreme Chief, the Disposer, the Controller, the Father of all that is or is to be. I have created all these beings, for I merely wished that they might be and they have come here!" And the other beings ... think the same, because he was born first and they later. And the being who was born first lived longer and was more handsome and powerful than the others.

And it might well be that some being would quit his body there and be reborn in this world. He might then give up his home for the homeless life [of an ascetic]; and in his ardor, striving, intentness, earnestness, and keenness of thought, he might attain such a stage of meditation that with the collected mind he might recall his former birth, but not what went before. Thus he might think: "We were created by *Brahma*, eternal, firm everlasting, and unchanging, who will remain so for ever and ever, while we who were created by the Lord *Brahma* ... are transient, unstable, short-lived, and destined to pass away."

That is how your traditional doctrine comes about that the beginning of things was the work of the god *Brahma*.

—W. Theodore de Bary. *Sources of Indian Tradition.* Vol. 1. New York: Columbia University Press, 1966, pp. 127–128.

TRIBAL MYTHS

DHAMMAI

Before There Was Earth or Sky   One third of
India's vast population belongs to indigenous tribes living outside the social and religious system of Hinduism. One of these groups, the Dhammai come from the northeastern frontier of the country, near Burma and Tibet.

In their creation myth, the Dhammai proclaim the underlying sacrality of the earth and its creatures by recalling the generations of the gods. In a startling evolution, Shuzanghu and Zumiang-Nui conceive the gods of earth and sky, which, after rescue from the primordial worm of chaos, in turn produce divine mountains. The mountains give birth to frogs and finally, in the fifth generation, to human beings still animal-like and hairy.

A T FIRST there was neither earth nor sky, Shuzanghu and his wife Zu-miang-Nui lived above. One day Shuzanghu said to his wife, "How long must we live without a place to rest our feet?" Zumiang-Nui said, "What can I say to you? You always live apart from me and don't love me. But if you truly love me and will stay with me, I will tell you what to do." So Shuzanghu went to his wife and she conceived.

In due time Zumiang-Nui gave birth to a baby-girl, Subbu-Khai-Thung, who is the Earth and to a baby-boy, Jongsuli-Young-Jongbu, who is the Sky. But there was no place for them. So they fell down, down to where Phangnalomang the Worm and his wife were living, and the Worm swallowed them both.

Zumiang-Nui tried to find her children and asked her husband, "What has happened to them? Where have they gone?" But he could not tell her. Then she said, "Next time I have a child, make a clear flat place when I can keep him safely and set traps all round it." Shuzanghu made such a place and when his wife was delivered of her next child, there was somewhere for him to stay. And now when Phangnalomang came to devour the child he was caught in one of the traps. Shuzanghu found him there and split his body open. The two children were still in his belly and the lower part of his body became the Earth and the upper the Sky.

Now Earth and Sky lived together. The Sky went to his wife, the Earth, and she gave birth to a son, Sujang-Gnoi-Rise and a daughter, Jibbi-Jang-Sangne. These were gods but they had the shape of mountains. After they were born Earth and Sky separated and as they were parting Earth gave birth to two other children, a boy, Lujjuphu, and a girl named Jassuju, who had the form of frogs. They mated and from them a boy and a girl in human form, Abugupham-Bumo and Anoi-Diggan-Juje, were born. They were human but were covered with hair. They married each other and in time had three sons, Lubukhanlung, Sangso-Dungso and Kimbu-Sangtung.

—Verrier Elwin. *Myths of the North-East Frontier of India.* Calcutta: Sree Saraswaty Press, 1958, pp. 13–14.

MINYONG

The Separation of Earth and Sky   In this creation myth of the Minyong, a tribal group in northeastern India, the universal problem of the survival of the children under the oppressive weight of the father is dramatized. As in Hesiod's *Theogony* and the Polynesian's Children of Heaven and Earth, the focus here is on the new and younger gods: they conspire and eventually drive the father away, only to produce chaos in the transition period. After prolonged machinations, the creatures of the middle realm—the powerful Wiyus, men and animals—finally arrange things in sufficient order to permit life and light.

SEDI is the earth; Melo is the Sky. The Earth is a woman, the Sky is a man. These two married, and when they came together, Wiyus, men and animals held a Kebang to consider how they could save themselves from being crushed between them. Sedi-Diyor, one of the greatest of the Wiyus, caught hold of the Sky and beat him so that he fled far up into the heavens leaving the Earth behind. As he went away, the Earth gave birth to two daughters. But she was so sad at losing her husband that she could not bear to look at them. Sedi-Diyor, therefore, found a woman to nurse them.

When the little girls were old enough to walk, light began to shine for them, and day by day the light grew brighter. After a while the nurse died and Sedi-Diyor buried her in the ground. The children wept for her as for their mother: they wept so much that they died, and the light they gave died with them.

Now it was dark again, and Wiyus, men and animals were afraid. The Wiyus thought that the nurse must have stolen something from the children and that it was this that had made them weep so much. So they dug up her body to see what it was. They found that it had rotted away, all except the eyes. They saw the eyes great and shining in the darkness, and their own reflection was mirrored in them. They thought that they saw the dead children in the eyes. They took them to a stream and washed them in the water for five days and five nights, and made them shine more brightly. But they could not remove the images looking back at them from the eyes.

The Wiyus sent for a carpenter and he cut the eyes open with great care and removed the reflections, which turned into living children. They called one girl Sedi-Irkong-Bomong and the other Sedi-Irkong-Bong. They did not let them go out of their house.

But one day, when they were grown up, the elder girl, Bomong, dressed herself in gaily-coloured clothes and many ornaments, and went out in her beauty to wander through the world. As she came out of the house, there was light all round her, and it was day. She went across the hills and did not return.

After a long time, her sister Bong went to look for her, tracing the path for her footsteps. But when she came out, there was so much light that she caused the rocks to break, the trees to wither and men to faint in the heat.

Wiyus, men and animals held yet another Kebang and decided that the only thing to do was to kill one of the sisters. They were afraid to do it and argued for a long time, but at last the frog went to sit by the path and waited, bow in hand, for the girl to come. When Bong came shining and lovely he shot her with an arrow in each side and she died. Then it was not so hot, the light was not so dazzling. The trees revived and men went again about their work.

But the girl's body lay where it had fallen. Then there came along Kirte, a Wiyu in the form of a rat; he dragged the corpse to Bomong on his back. As he went along, he fell over and ever since the rat's legs have been crooked. But he got up and took the body to a river where Bomong was due to pass. He showed her sister's body and she wept for sorrow and fear that she herself would be killed. She took a path that no one knew and sat down, placing a big stone on her head. With the shadow of the stone, the world became dark.

At this, Wiyus, men and animals were afraid and they went to search for light. For a long time they found nothing. Then Nginu-Botte caught a rat, a wild bird and a cock and sent them to find Bomong. The cock went first, but its parts were so heavy that it could not walk. It met Banjibanman and told him its trouble, and he cut off its organ and threw it away. Its testes went into its body. This is why the cock has no parts outside its body.

The cock's organ turned into the earthworm.

The cock went on and at last found Bomong and begged her to come back. "No", she said, "they killed my sister and they'll kill me. Tell them that I will only come if they make my sister alive." The cock returned and told Nginu-Botte what the girl had said. He found a carpenter who fashioned Bong's body, making it small and putting life into it. When Bomong heard that her sister was alive again, she threw the stone down from her head and stood up. The day returned and as the light blazed out, the cock cried *"Kokoko-kokoko";* the wild bird sang *"Pengo-pengo";* the rat squeaked *"Taktak-taktak."* For they were glad at the light and heat.

—Verrier Elwin. *Myths of the North-East Frontier of India.* Calcutta: Sree Saraswaty Press, 1958, pp. 48–50.

MYTHS OF CHINA AND JAPAN

MYTHS OF CHINA

Creation Out of Chaos
Although ancient Chinese cosmological thinking tended to be very abstract and philosophical, preferring treatise over myth for its expression, several early legends of creation did exist. One of these concerns Huang-lao ("The Yellow Emperor"), a god of the Taoist pantheon and mythical emperor of the center of the sacred world. Huang-lao is mentioned as early as 200 B.C.; by 200 A.D. he had become the principal deity of the Yellow Turban sect—their divine guide and teacher.

In this retold myth, only chaos (or "no-thing") existed in the beginning; from it light, the sky and earth evolved and brought forth all things (the "ten thousand creations"). Inherent within them were *yang* and *yin*, essential principles of existence that permeate Taoist thinking. Although they recall the sunny (yang) and dark (yin) sides of a riverbank, yang and yin represent much more profound opposition in Chinese thought. Yang is the principle of brightness, activity, and strength; its most obvious symbols are the sky, the masculine, the high, hard, forceful elements. Yin, on the other hand, is the principle of darkness, passivity and weakness, and it is most often associated with the earth, the female, and with what is low, soft, and tranquil. Yin and yang are thus polar opposites, representatives of respective borders of the whole, related and dependent on each other. Through their interaction, all things come to be and can be understood.

Yin and yang mix here to produce the five elements (wood, fire, earth, metal, and water) and eventually a divine man. From the primal light of the universe, a ray shoots down to earth (forming an axis mundi, a center pole to heaven), and a golden god appears. This embodiment of divine light names Huang-lao and instructs him in the ways of the world, ultimately explaining to him its fundamental and pervasive structure: everything—microcosmic and macrocosmic—is constructed on the same principles; the individual has within himself the same forces and elements as the universe. "In this way, everything corresponds to the great in the small and the small in the great."

IN THE BEGINNING there was chaos. Out of it came pure light and built the sky. The heavy dimness, however, moved and formed the earth from itself. Sky and earth brought forth the ten thousand creations, the beginning, having growth and increase, and all of them take the sky and earth as their mode. The roots of Yang and Yin—the male and female principle—also began in sky and earth.

Yang and Yin became mixed, the five elements separated themselves from it and a man was formed. As he looked about he perceived how the sun sank in a red haze in the west and in the east he saw the silver moon ascending, enveloped in the pale fog and all the stars were circling a great star which was in the middle of the world. Out of this illuminating pattern a brilliant ray fell to the earth and standing in front of this amazed man appeared someone like him yet different, he was completely golden in color. The Gold Colored One bowed to the man and honored him. He taught him how to make a garment from grass in order to cover his naked body. He gave him a name, "Huang-lao" (The Yellow Old Man), and showed him how to nourish himself from the roots of plants. He explained to him the journey of the stars, the year long path of sun and moon.

Huang-lao asked about the beginning of all things, about the form of heaven and earth. The Gold Shining form answered:

"In the beginning out of heaven and earth was produced that which is equivalent to blood which flows through the arteries of man. The earth bore fire which produces breath in man. Wind and clouds, rain and snow spread themselves between water and fire. When Yin and Yang diminish or increase in their power, heat and cold are produced. The sun and moon trade their light. This also produces the expiration of the year and the five opposites of the sky: east, south, west, north and midpoint. Thus sky and earth produce the form of man. Yang gives and Yin receives."

Huang-lao asked more questions concerning the nature of that which is beyond the earth and the Gold Colored One answered:

"In the middle of the earth grows a huge boulder which reaches up into the sky and there supports a mighty sphere. At the foot of this mountain flows a source which divides itself into ten thousand rivers and streams and all of these waters empty into the eight seas. The world is encircled by eight poles. The great earth, however, lies in the middle of the world sea in which are found four islands. Thus the water flows around all the sides of the great earth as the juicy meat surrounds the seed of fruit, as the white surrounds the yolk of an egg. In this way everything corresponds to the great in the small and the small in the great. The sun and moon, however, circle the earth in an endless movement and give light to the top and bottom of earth by their brightness."

The story continues from here telling of the populating of the earth and moves from there to the divine-hero, P'an-Ku, who orders the world and teaches men many things and finally vanishes. When he does, suffering appears on earth.

—Claus W. Krieg. *Chinesische Mythen und Legenden*. Zurich: Fritz und Wasmuth, 1946, pp. 7–8.
—Quoted in Charles Long. *Alpha: Myths of Creation*. New York: George Braziller, 1963, pp. 126–128.

Four Versions of the Myth of P'an Ku

From the third to the sixth century A.D., particularly in southern China, a popular creation myth centered around the immense generative power and fertility of the god P'an Ku. While it is claimed in the first of four versions of this myth that P'an Ku arose out of "nothing," that void was indeed a rich one. Given its fecundity, one presumes it was conceived as an indistinct mass—as Chaos or "no-thing," the potentiality of all matter—rather than as the absence or negation of matter. Creation proceeds by the development of increasingly distinct forms out of this original Chaos: first "something" evolves from the "no-thing"; within something, the fundamental creative powers, male and female, are delineated; and finally the creator god P'an Ku is born, a child of Chaos.

A variation of this myth envisages an equally close bond between P'an Ku and Chaos. In this instance, the beginning is depicted as a cosmic egg—a principle of fertility, or wholeness and duality—from which the creator springs forth. As the substance of the egg, Chaos is again the essential basis of creation, here forming the raw material in which the embryonic P'an Ku develops and the stuff from which he makes the basic things of the universe.

The two variant endings of the myth show P'an Ku creating the world by self-sacrifice. In the first, his skull, like the top of the eggshell, becomes the dome of the sky, and his body becomes the elements of the earth. The vermin on his body are transformed into humans who are thus still nourished by his being. (In the second, more local variant, P'an Ku's body forms the five sacred mountains of China.)

The identity of the world with the sacrificed body of a god is a powerful concept. Through it, of course, the sacrality of the world is established, but there is an implicit notion of tremendous sacrifice and loss, the irrevocable end of the golden age when the creator god existed.

I AT FIRST there was nothing. Time passed and nothing became something. Time passed and something split in two: the two were male and female. These two produced two more, and these two produced P'an Ku, the first being, the Great Man, the Creator.

II FIRST there was the great cosmic egg. Inside the egg was Chaos, and floating in Chaos was P'an Ku, the Undeveloped, the divine Embryo. And P'an Ku burst out of the egg, four times larger than any man today, with an adze in his hand (or a hammer and chisel) with which he fashioned the world. Two great horns grew out of his head (the horned head is always the symbol of supernatural power in China); two long tusks grew from his upper jaw, and he was covered with hair.

P'an Ku went to work at once, mightily, to put the world in order. He chiseled the land and sky apart. He piled up the mountains on the earth and dug the valleys deep, and made courses for the rivers.

High above ride the sun and moon and stars in the sky where P'an Ku placed them; below roll the four seas. He taught mankind to build boats and showed him how to throw bridges over rivers, and he told them the secrets of the precious stones.

III THE WORLD was never finished until P'an Ku died. Only his death could perfect the universe: from his skull was shaped the dome of the sky, and from his flesh was formed the soil of the fields; from his bones came the rocks, from his blood the rivers and seas; from his hair came all vegetation. His breath was the wind; his voice made thunder; his right eye became the moon, his left eye, the sun. From his saliva or sweat came rain. And from the vermin which covered his body came forth mankind.

IV WHEN P'AN KU wept his tears became the Yellow River, and when he died his body formed the five sacred mountains of China. T'ai Mountain, in the east, rose from his head; Sung Mountain, in the center, from his body; Heng Mountain of the north rose from his right arm, Heng Mountain of the south from his left; Hua Mountain in the west grew out of his feet.

It is said that P'an Ku's image can still be seen in a cave cherished by the Miao tribe in the Mountains of Kuangsi, and that along with the image of P'an Ku stand also images of the three great sovereigns who followed him: the Lord of Heaven, the Lord of Earth, and the Lord of Man.

—Maria Leach. *The Beginning.* New York: Funk and Wagnalls, 1956, pp. 224–226. —Retold from material in D.A. Mackensie. *Myths of China and Japan.* London: 1923, 260f, 247f.

Lao Tzu: From the Tao Te Ching

Chinese cosmological thinking took the form of philosophical meditations more frequently than that of myth, but as can be seen in these selections from Lao Tzu's *Tao Te Ching*, even the philosophy was evocative and poetic. Along with the *Analects* of Confucius, the *Tao Te Ching* was the most influential book in ancient Chinese history. Although it addressed itself primarily to the proper conduct of rulers, it necessarily included cosmological statements, for it presumed that "Man models himself on earth,/ Earth on heaven,/ Heaven on the way,/ And the way on that which is naturally so."

Lao Tzu (c. 600 B.C.?) was a semi-legendary figure (supposedly the older contemporary of Confucius) who was the greatest of the Taoist sages. He taught a kind of quietism or nonaction that was in fact action in accordance with nature. Lao Tzu emphasized the oneness and eternity of the Tao (the "way" of life), its expression through the polar oppositions of yin and yang (female and male, earth and heaven), and the derivation and development of all creatures and things from this profound duality and even more profound oneness ("The way begets the one; one begets two; two begets three; three begets the myriad creatures").

The essential Tao is "nothing" in that it is "no *thing*"; it is without external distinctions. It is nameless not only because it has no form itself but also because it is the source of all other forms; it is the nonobjectifiable subject. "This essence is quite genuine"; it is the ground of all being and the form of all beings. The oneness of the Tao is visible if sages perceive the oneness in themselves, if they divest themselves of ego and its consequent desires. With ego and desires, the separateness of the sage and the uniqueness of all things are comprehensible as the manifestations of the Tao. "These things are the same," Lao Tzu argues. Oneness and multiplicity, unity and diversity—they diverge in name as they issue forth, "mystery of mysteries—the gateway of the manifold secrets."

T HE WAY that can be told
Is not the constant way;
The name that can be named
Is not the constant name.
The nameless was the beginning of heaven and earth;
The named was the mother of the myriad creatures.
Hence always rid yourself of desires in order to observe its myriad secrets;
But always allow yourself to have desires in order to observe its manifestations.
These two are the same
But diverge in name as they issue forth.
Being the same they are called mysteries.
Mystery upon mystery—
The gateway of the manifold secrets. (I,1)

T HE WAY is for ever nameless....
Only when it is cut are there names.
As soon as there are names
One ought to know that it is time to stop. (I, 32)

T HE WAY conceals itself in being nameless. (II, 41)

T HE WAY begets the one; one begets two; two begets three; three begets the myriad creatures.
The myriad creatures carry on their backs the *yin* and embrace in their arms the *yang* and are the blending of the generative forces of the two. (II, 42)

O F OLD, these came to be in possession of the One:
Heaven in virtue of the One is limpid:
Earth in virtue of the One is settled;
Gods in virtue of the One have their potencies;
The valley in virtue of the One is full;
The myriad creatures in virtue of the One are alive;
Lords and princes in virtue of the One become leaders in the empire.

I T IS THE One that makes these things what they are.
Without what makes it limpid heaven might split;
Without what makes it settled earth might sink;
Without what gives them their potencies gods might spend themselves;
Without what makes it full the valley might run dry;

Without what keeps them alive the myriad creatures might perish;
Without what makes them leaders lords and princes might fall.
Hence the superior must have the inferior as root;
The high must have the low as base. . . .
Turning back is how the way moves;
Weakness is the means the way employs.
The myriad creatures in the world are born from
Something, and something from Nothing. (II, 39)

WHAT CANNOT be seen is called evanescent;
   What cannot be heard is called rarefied;
What cannot be touched is called minute.
These three cannot be fathomed
And so they are confused and looked upon as one.
Its upper part is not dazzling;
Its lower part is not obscure.
Dimly visible, it cannot be named
And returns to that which is without substance.
This is called the shape that has no shape,
The image that is without substance.
This is called indistinct and shadowy.
Go up to it and you will not see its head;
Follow behind it and you will not see its rear.
Hold fast to the way of antiquity
In order to keep in control of the realm of today.
The ability to know the beginning of antiquity
Is called the thread running through the way. (I, 14)

AS A THING the way is
   Shadowy, indistinct.
Indistinct and shadowy,
Yet within it is an image;
Shadowy and indistinct,
Yet within it is a substance.
Dim and dark,
Yet within it is an essence.
This essence is quite genuine
And within it is something that can be tested. (I, 21)

THE WAY is empty, yet use will not drain it.
   Deep, it is like the ancestor of the myriad creatures.
Blunt the sharpness;
Untangle the knots;
Soften the glare;

Let your wheels move only along old ruts.
Darkly visible, it only seems as if it were there.
I know not whose son it is.
It images the forefather of God. (I, 4)

THE SPIRIT of the valley never dies.
This is called the mysterious female.
The gateway of the mysterious female
Is called the root of heaven and earth.
Dimly visible, it seems as if it were there,
Yet use will never drain it. (I, 6)

HEAVEN and earth are enduring. The reason why heaven and earth
can be enduring is that they do not give themselves life. Hence
they are able to be long-lived.
Therefore the sage puts his person last and it comes first,
Treats it as extraneous to himself and it is preserved.
Is it not because he is without thought of self that he is able to accomplish his private ends? (I, 7)

THERE IS a thing confusedly formed,
Born before heaven and earth.
Silent and void
It stands alone and does not change,
Goes round and does not weary.
It is capable of being the mother of the world.
I know not its name
So I style it "the way."
I give it the makeshift name of "the great."
Being great, it is further described as receding,
Receding, it is described as far away,
Being far away, it is described as turning back.
Hence the way is great; heaven is great; earth is great; and the king is also great.
Within the realm there are four things that are great, and the king
counts as one.
Man models himself on earth,
Earth on heaven,
Heaven on the way,
And the way on that which is naturally so. (I, 25)

—Lao Tzu. *Tao Te Ching*. (D. C. Lau, trans.) Baltimore, Md.: Penguin Books, 1963, pp. 57, 91, 102, 103, 100, 70, 78, 60, 62, 63, 82.

The Huai-Nan Tzu:
The Creation of the Universe

The Han period (206 B.C.–220 A.D.) in China was one of syncretism in religious and philosophical thought. Drawing largely on the ethical considerations of Confucius, the political theories of the Legalists, and the mystical doctrines of the Taoists, the "Mixed Schools" emerged. Although the assumptions contained in this passage from the Huai-nan Tzu were primarily Taoist, they were nonetheless accepted by the Confucianists in their attempt to formulate a complete philosophy.

The Huai-nan Tzu asserts, as does Lao Tzu, that being came forth from nonbeing in the Great Beginning of Chaos. Chaos produced emptiness and emptiness produced the universe and matter; thus the infinite conceived the finite. The kinds of matter separated like the yolk and white of an egg to become heaven and earth and, ultimately, the male and female principles. And these then mixed and became seasons and the myriad creatures. Yin in its concentrated form became water, and yang, similarly, became fire.

Beyond or beneath all is the essential oneness of the creator, "No Thing," to which all creatures owe their being.

B EFORE HEAVEN and earth had taken form all was vague and amorphous. Therefore it was called the Great Beginning. The Great Beginning produced emptiness and emptiness produced the universe. The universe produced material-force which had limits. That which was clear and light drifted up to become heaven, while that which was heavy and turbid solidified to become earth. It was very easy for the pure, fine material to come together but extremely difficult for the heavy, turbid material to solidify. Therefore heaven was completed first and earth assumed shape after. The combined essences of heaven and earth became the yin and yang, the concentrated essences of the yin and yang became the four seasons, and the scattered essence of the four seasons became the myriad creatures of the world. After a long time the hot force of the accumulated yang produced fire and the essence of the fire force became the sun; the cold force of accumulated yin became water and the essence of the water force became the moon. The essence of the excess force of the sun and moon became the stars and planets. Heaven received the sun, moon, and stars while earth received water and soil.

When heaven and earth were joined in emptiness and all was unwrought simplicity, then without having been created, things came into being. This was the Great Oneness. All things issued from this oneness but all became different, being divided into the various species of fish, birds, and beasts. . . . Therefore while a thing moves it is called living, and when it dies it is said to be exhausted. All are creatures. They are not the uncreated creator of things, for the creator of things is not among things. If we examine the Great Beginning of antiquity we find that man was born out of nonbeing to assume form in being. Having form, he is governed by things. But he who can return to that form from which he was born and become as though formless is called a "true man." The true man is he who has never become separated from the Great Oneness.

—*Huai-nan Tzu*. 3:1a., 14:1a.—Quoted in W. Theodore de Bary et al. (eds.). *Sources of Chinese Tradition*. Vol. 1. New York: Columbia University Press, 1964, pp. 192–193.

Kuo Hsiang:
Nature and Nonexistence

Chuang Tzu (c. 369–286 B.C.), the great Taoist philosopher and mystic, wrote:

> There is a beginning. There is a not yet beginning to be a beginning. There is a not yet beginning to be a not yet beginning to be a beginning. There is being. There is nonbeing. There is a not yet beginning to be nonbeing. There is a not yet beginning to be a not yet beginning to be nonbeing. Suddenly there is being and nonbeing. But between this being and nonbeing, I don't really know which is being and which is nonbeing. Now I have just said something. But I don't know whether what I have said has really said something or whether it hasn't said something.
>
> There is nothing in the world bigger than the tip of an autumn hair, and Mount T'ai is little. No one has lived longer than a dead child, and P'eng-tsu died young. Heaven and earth were born at the same time I was, and the ten thousand things are one with me.*

Some five hundred years later, after the collapse of the Han dynasty and during the period of social instability in the Three Kingdoms and Six Dynasties (200–589 A.D.) that followed, major religious changes occured in China. Confucianism, which had been so involved in the state cult and so dependent on the state's solidity to carry out its necessary scholarship, began to flounder. By contrast, interest in Taoism and in the newly introduced Buddhism increased and flourished.

For the Neo-Taoists, the writings of Lao Tzu and Chuang Tzu became the sources of scholarship and commentary, the bases of the new thinking. Thus one of the most prominent Neo-Taoists, Kuo Hsiang (d. 312 A.D.) took Chuang Tzu's writings as his starting point, and in this commentary on Chuang Tzu's positions he is primarily concerned with the character of what-was-before-anything-was, before the beginning. Did being and therefore the universe of creatures and things, of matter and mind, derive from non-being? Did being derive from yin and yang? Or from nature or the Tao itself? No, he argues; things merely are, spontaneously, naturally, and so should we be.

T**HE MUSIC** of nature is not an entity existing outside of things. The different apertures, the pipes and flutes and the like, in combination with all living beings, together constitute nature. Since nonexistence is non-

* Chuang Tzu, *Basic Writings* (Burton Watson, trans.). New York: Columbia University Press, 1964, p. 38. The "tip of an autumn hair" is a cliché for a tiny thing; P'eng-tsu was the Chinese Methuselah.

themselves, that is all. By this is not meant that there is an "I" to produce. The "I" cannot produce things and things cannot produce the "I." The "I" is selfexistent. Because it is so by itself, we call it natural. Everything is what it is by nature, not through taking any action. Therefore [Chuang Tzu] speaks in terms of nature. The term nature [literally Heaven] is used to explain that things are what they are spontaneously, and not to mean the blue sky. But someone says that the music of nature makes all things serve or obey it. Now, nature cannot even possess itself. How can it possess things? Nature is the general name for all things.

Not only is it impossible for nonbeing to be changed into being. It is also impossible for being to become nonbeing. Therefore, although being as a substance undergoes infinite changes and transformations, it cannot in any instance become nonbeing. . . . What came into existence before there were things? If I say yin and yang came first, then since yin and yang are themselves entities, what came before them? Suppose I say nature came first. But nature is only things being themselves. Suppose I say perfect Tao came first. But perfect Tao is perfect nonbeing. Since it is nonbeing, how can it come before anything else? Then what came before it? There must be another thing, and so on ad infinitum. We must understand that things are what they are spontaneously and not caused by something else.

Everything is natural and does not know why it is so. The more things differ in corporeal form the more they are alike in being natural. . . . Heaven and earth and the myriad things change and transform into something new every day and so proceed with time. What causes them? They do so spontaneously. . . . What we call things are all that they are by themselves; they did not cause each other to become so. Let us leave them alone and the principle of being will be perfectly realized. The ten thousand things are in ten thousand different conditions, and move forward and backward differently, as though there were a True Lord to make them so. But if we search for evidences for such a true Lord, we fail to find any. We should understand that things are all natural and not caused by something else.

The universe is the general name for all things. They are the reality of the universe while nature is their norm. Being natural means to exist spontaneously without having to take any action. Therefore the fabulous p'eng bird can soar high and the quail can fly low, the cedrela can live for a long time and the mushroom for a short time. They are capable of doing these not because of their taking any action but because of their being natural.

—Kuo Hsiang. *From the Commentary on Chuang Tzu*, Sec. 1, I:8b; Sec. 2, I:21a–23a; Sec. 22, 7:54b–55b: "Nature and Nonexistence." —Quoted in W. Theodore de Bary et al. [eds.]. *Sources of Chinese Tradition*. Vol. 1. New York: Columbia University Press, 1964, pp. 240–243.

Chou Tun-Yi: An Explanation of the Diagram of the Great Ultimate

The major philosophical development of the Sung Dynasty (960–1279 A.D.) was Neo-Confucianism in which thinkers tried to reassert the fundamental doctrines of order and participation in the worldly (the social and political realms) as the means of being united to the world. While Taoism and Buddhism were essentially rejected in their argument that the phenomenal world was illusory and "empty," many of their doctrines were nonetheless adopted into Neo-Confucian systems.

This syncretism is particularly evident here in Chou Tun-Yi's (1017–1073 A.D.) redefinition of Confucian cosmology. He begins with a bow to the Non-Ultimate (Non-Being-Itself, the Nothingness of the Taoists and Buddhists), but quickly asserts that it is the same as the Great Ultimate (Being-Itself, the ground of being) which generates the yin, then the yang, the five material forces (water, fire, wood, metal, and earth), heaven and earth, and all the myriad creatures. In this manner, Chou Tun-Yi manages to assimilate the Taoist and Buddhist positions while still arguing that the source is fundamentally "something" and not "nothing" and that all subsequent developments out of it are fundamentally real and not illusory.

Because at this level of abstraction it is admitted that the positive and negative characterizations of ultimacy are insufficient and falsely limiting—like the chicken and the egg, whichever came first required the other—Chou Tun-Yi's position is difficult to attack. Having united the Non-Ultimate and Great Ultimate as two sides of one coin, he proceeds to declare it full and real and to advise the wise man to order his affairs in accordance with its evolutions in the phenomenal world. Using the five virtues, the sage can live a happy and successful life.

THE NON-ULTIMATE! And also the Great Ultimate (*T'ai-chi*). The Great Ultimate through movement generates the yang. When its activity reaches its limit, it becomes tranquil. Through tranquility the Great Ultimate generates the yin. When tranquility reaches its limit, activity begins again. Thus movement and tranquility alternate and become the root of each other, giving rise to the distinction of yin and yang, and these two modes are thus established.

By the transformation of yang and its union with yin, the five agents of water, fire, wood, metal, and earth arise. When these five material-forces (*ch'i*) are distributed in harmonious order, the four seasons run their course.

The five agents constitute one system of yin and yang, and yin and yang constitute one Great Ultimate. The Great Ultimate is fundamentally the Non-ultimate. The five agents arise, each with its specific nature.

When the reality of the Non-ultimate and the essence of yin and yang and the five agents come into mysterious union, integration ensues. The heavenly principle (*ch'ien*) constitutes the male element, and the earthly principle (*k'un*) constitutes the female element. The interaction of these two material forces engenders and transforms the myriad things. The myriad things produce and reproduce, resulting in an unending transformation.

It is man alone who receives [the material forces] in their highest excellence, and therefore he is most intelligent. His corporeal form appears, and his spirit develops consciousness. The five moral principles of his nature (humanity, righteousness, decorum, wisdom, and good faith) are aroused by, and react to, the external world and engage in activity; good and evil are distinguished and human affairs take place.

The sage orders these affairs by the principles of the Mean, correctness, humanity, and righteousness, considering tranquility to be the ruling factor. Thus he establishes himself as the ultimate standard for man. Hence the character of the sages is "identical with that of Heaven and earth; his brilliance is identical with that of the sun and moon; his order is identical with that of the four seasons; and his good and evil fortunes are identical with those of heavenly and earthly spirits." The gentleman cultivates these moral qualities and enjoys good fortune, whereas the inferior man violates them and suffers evil fortune.

Therefore it is said: "The yin and the yang are established as the way of heaven; the elements of strength and weakness as the way of earth; and humanity and righteousness as the way of man." It is also said there: "If we investigate into the cycle of things, we shall understand the concepts of life and death." Great is the *Book of Changes*! Herein lies its excellence!

—Chou Tun-Yi. "An Explanation of the Diagram of the Great Ultimate." From *T'ai-chi-t'u shuo*, in Chou *Lien-ch'i chi*, I:2a–b. —Quoted in W. Theodore de Bary, et al. [eds.]. *Sources of Chinese Tradition*. Vol. 1. New York: Columbia University Press, 1964, pp. 458–459.

MYTHS OF JAPAN

From the Kojiki
The oldest chronicle in Japanese is the *Kojiki*, or "Records of Ancient Matters." It was compiled in 712 A.D. by the Court Noble Futo no Yasumuro, "an officer in the Upper Division of the First Class of the Fifth Rank and of the Fifth Order of Merit" (d. 723), and includes the earliest doctrines of native Shinto nature worship and polytheism as well as borrowings from Chinese thought.

This short section from the preface outlines the long and complex myth that follows in the body of the text: Heaven and Earth parted, and the Three Deities (Deity Master-of-the-August-Center-of-Heaven, the High-August-Producing-Wondrous Deity, and the Divine-Producing-Wondrous-Deity) created. As in Chinese cosmologies, the dual principles of yin and yang—here the "passive and active elements"—evolved; personified as Izanami ("Female-Who-Invites") and Izanagi ("Male-Who-Invites"), they became the "ancestors of all things."

The subsequent events are only outlined here in the briefest form: "a mirror was hung up" and thereby enticed the Sun-Goddess out of her cave; "jewels were spat out" by Susa-no-Wo (the "Impetuous Male Deity") after he had obtained them from his sister; "a Hundred Kings succeeded each other," presumably in the Japanese Empire; "a blade was bitten" by the Sun-Goddess; "a serpent was slain" by Susa-no-Wo after he was evicted from heaven; and "a Myriad Deities did flourish." Indeed, the sheer number of gods and the chaotic character of their relations are prominent features of the Kojiki, as is the close association between these deities and natural elements. Combined, these features clearly evoke the chaotic relation of powerful, wondrous, and terrible forces of nature in the beginning.

I YASUMARO SAY: Now when chaos had begun to condense, but force and form were not yet manifest, and there was nought named, nought done, who could know its shape? Nevertheless Heaven and Earth first parted, and the Three Deities performed the commencement of creation; the Passive and Active Essences then developed, and the Two Spirits [Izanami, the creatrix, and Izanagi, the creator] became the ancestors of all things. Therefore did he [i.e., Izanagi] enter obscurity and emerge into light, and the Sun and Moon were revealed by the washing of his eyes; he floated on and plunged into the seawater, and Heavenly and Earthly Deities appeared through the ablutions of his person. So in the dimness of the great commencement, we, by relying on the original teaching, learn the time of the conception of the earth and of the birth of islands; in the remoteness of the original beginning, we, by trusting the former sages, perceive the era of the genesis of Deities and of the establishment of men. Truly do we know that a mirror was hung up, that jewels were spat out, and that then an Hundred Kings succeeded each other; that a blade was bitten, and a serpent cut in pieces, so that a Myriad Deities did flourish. By deliberations in the Tranquil River the Empire was pacified; by discussions on the Little Shore the land was purified.

—Yasamuro. *Kojiki, or Records of Ancient Matters.* (W. G. Aston, trans.) Kobe, Japan: J. L. Thompson, 1932, pp. 3–6.

From the Nihongi Like the *Kojiki,* the *Nihongi,* or "Chronicles of Japan" (720 A.D.) begins with a history of the creation and the generations of the gods. Borrowing from Chinese cosmology (particularly from the Huai-nan Tzu of the Han period), the *Nihongi* imagines an initial Chaos. Creation occurs as a matter of internal delineation of hitherto undistinguished elements: what is light and pure rises up to form the heaven, and what is heavier descends to become earth. On its own, heaven created three deities between them (a principle of connection between the separated spheres and two kinds of earth), and then heaven and earth together produced four pairs of deities. It is the last of these that becomes the focus of the myth. Izanagi ("Male-who-invites") and Izanami ("Female-who-invites") wandered about the earth below, still wet, unformed and ungrounded—a primordial slush. They extended downward "the jewel-spear of Heaven" (a symbol both of a phallus and of the axis mundi), and the coagulated brine that emanated from its tip formed an island. On earth, they circled their center pole (a sacred connection between heaven and earth) in a marriage ceremony and mated. From this union of the masculine and feminine principles arose the eight islands, the sea, rivers, mountains, trees, and herbs. Finally they produced the sun, moon, a leech, a bad god ("The Impetuous One"), and fire. (The fourth deity, Susa no o, is often associated with the Izumo people and his banshiment in the myth may reflect the political triumph of the Yamato people over this group.)

Although Izanami was burnt to death by her last child (and her nature thus transformed by that agent of sacrifice and change), her powers of fertility are still apparent. While she is dying, she produces the goddesses of earth and water; fire and earth then mate and give birth to "young growth."

The conclusion of this part of the myth details Izanagi's search for his wife in the underworld, his horror at death, and his flight back to earth. Purified in the powerfully regenerative waters, Izanagi nevertheless retreats from his creation to the land of gloom.

An expression of Shintoism, the *Nihongi* richly expresses that religion's worship of the sacred powers of nature and their many divine personifications.

O F OLD, Heaven and Earth were not yet separated, and the In and Yo (feminine and masculine principles) not yet divided. They formed a chaotic mass like an egg which was of obscurely defined limits and contained germs.

The purer and clearer part was thinly drawn out, and formed Heaven, while the heavier and grosser element settled down and became Earth.

The finer element easily became a united body, but the consolidation of the heavy and gross element was accomplished with difficulty.

Heaven was therefore formed first, and Earth was established subsequently.

Thereafter Divine Beings were produced between them.

Hence it is said that when the world began to be created, the soil of which lands were composed floated about in a manner which might be compared to the floating of a fish sporting on the surface of the water.

At this time a certain thing was produced between Heaven and Earth. It was in form like a reed-shoot. Now this became transformed into a God, and was called Kuni-toko-tachi no Mikoto [Land-eternal-stand-of-August-thing].

Next there was Kuni no sa-tsuchi no Mikoto [Land-of-right-soil-of-Augustness] and next Toyo-kumu-nu no Mikoto, [Rich-form-plain-of-Augustness] in all three deities.

These were pure males spontaneously developed by the operation of the principle of Heaven.

The next Deities who came into being were Uhiji-ni no Mikoto and Suhiji-ni no Mikoto, also called Uhiji-ne no Mikoto [Mud-earth] and Suhiji-ne no Mikoto [Sand-earth].

The next Deities which came into being were Oho-to nochi no Mikoto [Great-after-door] and Oho-to mahe no Mikoto [Great-before-door].

The next Gods which came into being were Omo-taru no Mikoto [Face-pleasing] and Kashiko-ne no Mikoto [awful], also called Aya-kashiko-ne no Mikoto, Imi kashiki no Mikoto, or Awo-kashiki-ne no Mikoto, or Aya-kashiki no Mikoto.

The next Deities which came into being were Izanagi no Mikoto [Male-who-invites] and Izanami no Mikoto [Female-who-invites].

These make eight Deities in all. Being formed by the mutual action of the Heavenly and Earthly principles, they were made male and female. From Kuni no toko-tachi no Mikoto to Izanagi no Mikoto and Izanami no Mikoto are called the seven generations of the age of the Gods.

Izanagi no Mikoto and Izanami no Mikoto stood on the floating bridge of Heaven, and held counsel together, saying: "Is there not a country beneath?"

Thereupon they thrust down the jewel-spear of Heaven, and groping about therewith found the ocean. The brine which dripped from the point of the spear coagulated and became an island which received the name of Ono-goro-jima [Spontaneously-congealed-island].

The two Deities thereupon descended and dwelt in this island. Accordingly they wished to become husband and wife together, and to produce countries.

So they made Ono-goro-jima the pillar of the centre of the land.

Now the male deity turning by the left, and the female deity by the right, they went round the pillar of the land separately. When they met together on one side, the female deity spoke first and said:—"How delightful! I have met with a lovely youth." The male deity was displeased, and said:—"I am a man, and by right should have spoken first. How is it that on the contrary thou, a woman, shouldst have been the first to speak? This was unlucky. Let us go round again." Upon this the two deities went back, and having met anew, this time the male deity spoke first, and said:—"How delightful! I have met a lovely maiden."

Then he inquired of the female deity, saying:—"In thy body is there aught formed?" She answered, and said:—"In my body there is a place which is the source of femininity." The male deity said:—"In my body again there is a place which is the source of masculinity. I wish to unite this source-place of my body to the source-place of thy body." Hereupon the male and female first became united as husband and wife.

Now when the time of birth arrived, first of all the island of Ahaji was reckoned as the placenta, and their minds took no pleasure in it. Therefore it received the name of Ahaji no Shima [the island which is unsatisfactory].

Next there was produced the island of Oho-yamato no Toyo-aki-tsu-shima [rich-harvest-of-island].

Next they produced the island of Iyo no futa-na, and next the island of Tsukushi. Next the islands of Oki and Sado were born as twins. This is the prototype of the twin-births which sometimes take place among mankind.

Next was born the island of Koshi, then the island of Oho-shima, then the island of Kibi no ko.

Hence first arose the designation of the Oho-ya-shima country [great-eight-island country].

Then the islands of Tsushima and Iki, with the small islands in various parts, were produced by the coagulation of the foam of the salt-water.

They next produced the sea, then the rivers, and then the mountains. Then they produced Ku-ku-no-chi, the ancestor of the trees, and next the ancestor of herbs, Kaya no hime.

After this Izanagi no Mikoto and Izanami no Mikoto consulted together, saying:—"We have not produced the Great-eight-island country, with the mountains, rivers, herbs, and trees. Why should we not produce someone who shall be lord of the universe? They then together produced the Sun-Goddess, who was called Oho-hiru-me no muchi [Great-noon-female-of-possessor].

The resplendent luster of this child shone throughout all the six quarters [North, East, South, West, Above and Below]. Therefore the two Deities rejoiced, saying:—"We have had many children, but none of them have been equal to this wondrous infant. She ought not to be kept long in this land, but we ought of our own accord to send her at once to Heaven, and entrust to her the affairs of Heaven."

At this time Heaven and Earth were still not far separated, and therefore they sent her up to Heaven by the ladder of Heaven.

They next produced the Moon-god.

His radiance was next to that of the Sun in splendour. This God was to be the consort of the Sun-Goddess, and to share in her government. They therefore sent him also to Heaven.

Next they produced the leech-child, which even at the age of three years could not stand upright. They therefore placed it in the rock-camphor-wood boat of Heaven, and abandoned it to the winds.

Their next child was Sosa no wo no Mikoto [Impetuous One].

This God had a fierce temper and was given to cruel acts. Moreover he made a practice of continually weeping and wailing. So he brought many of the people of the land to an untimely end. Again he caused green montains to become withered. Therefore the two Gods, his parents, addressed Sosa no wo no Mikoto, saying:—"Thou art exceedingly wicked, and it is not meet that thou shouldst reign over the world. Certainly thou must depart far away to the Netherland" [Hades]. So they at length expelled him.

Their next child was Kagu tsuchi [god of fire].

Now Izanami no Mikoto was burnt by Kagu tsuchi, so that she died. When she was lying down to die, she gave birth to the Earth-Goddess, Hani-yama-hime, and the Water-Goddess, Midzu-ha-no-me. Upon this Kagu tsuchi took to wife Hani-yama-hime, and they had a child named Waka-musubi [young growth]. On the crown of this Deity's head were produced the silkworm and the mulberry tree, and in her navel the five kinds of grain.

Thereafter, Izanagi no Mikoto went after Izanami no Mikoto, and entered the land of Yomi [Hades]. When he reached her they conversed together, and Izanami no Mikoto said: "My lord and husband, why is the coming so late? I have already eaten of the cooking-furnace of Yomi. Nevertheless, I am about to lie down to rest. I pray thee, do not thou look on me." Izanagi no Mikoto did not give ear to her, but secretly took his many-toothed comb and, breaking off its end tooth, made of it a torch, and looked at her. Putrefying matter had gushed up, and maggots swarmed. This is why people at the present day avoid using a single light at night, and also avoid throwing away a comb at night. Izanagi no Mikoto was greatly shocked, and said: "Nay! I have come unawares to a hideous and polluted land." So he speedily ran away back again. Then Izanami no Mikoto was angry, and said: "Why didst thou not observe that which I charged thee? Now am I put to shame." So she sent the eight Ugly Females of Yomi to pursue and stay him. Izanagi no Mikoto therefore drew his sword, and, flourishing it behind him, ran away. Then he took his black head-dress and flung it down. It became changed into grapes, which the Ugly Females seeing, took and ate. When they had finished eating them, they again pursued Izanagi no Mikoto. Then he flung down his many-toothed comb, which forthwith became changed into bamboo-shoots. The Ugly Females pulled them up and ate them, and when they had done eating them, again gave chase. Afterwards, Izanami no Mikoto came herself and pursued him. By this time Izanagi no Mikoto had reached the Even Pass of Yomi.

But, having visited in person the Land of Yomi, he had brought on himself ill-luck. In order, therefore, to wash away the defilement, he visited the Aha gate [a strait famous for its rapid tides] and the Haya-sufu-na [Quick-such-name] gate. But the tide in these two gates was exceeding strong. So he returned and took his way towards Wodo [little gate] in Tachibana. There he did his ablutions. At this time, entering the water, he blew out and produced Iha-tsu-tsu no Mikoto [Rock-of-Elder]; coming out of the water, he blew forth and produced Oho-nawo-bi no Kami [Great Remedy Person]. Entering a second time, he blew out and produced Sokotsutsu no Mikoto [Bottom-elder]; coming out he blew forth and produced Oho-aya-tsu-bi no Kami [Great-Pattern-of-Person]. Entering again, he blew forth and produced Aka-tsutsu no Mikoto [Red Elder], and coming out he blew out and produced the various deities of Heaven and Earth, and of the Sea-plain.

After this, Izanagi no Mikoto, his divine task having been accomplished, and his spirit-career about to suffer a change, built himself an abode of gloom in the island of Ahaji, where he dwelt for ever in silence and concealment.

—W. G. Aston (trans.). *The Nihongi*. London: George Allen and Unwin, 1956, pp. 1–34.

AINU

In the Beginning
the World Was Slush
The Ainu are the native, aboriginal people of Japan. Subjugated by the Japanese in 812 A.D. and forced to retreat to the northern islands of Hokkaido and Sakhalin, the 16,000 remaining Ainu are hunters and fishermen. Not Mongoloid, they are probably remnants of a proto-Nordic people that once spread over western Asia. Their language is unrelated to any other.

Ainu religion is generally classed as animistic, but it has many dualistic features as well. A supreme god dwells in the highest heaven and many lesser deities, including an evil one who created death and disease, populate the lower regions. Ancestor worship, propitiation of evil forces, belief in a future life, and judgment before god with the fire goddess as chief witness are major features of the religion.

Intermarriage with Japanese has caused a decline in both native culture and population, and in this creation myth, a close relation to Japanese cosmologies is clear. As in the *Nihongi,* the primordial earth is slushy and unformed until a wagtail, sacred in the *Nihongi* for his sexual instruction of Izanagi and Izanami, forms dry places by beating the muck with his wings and stamping it into firmness.

IN THE BEGINNING the world was slush, for the waters and the mud were all stirred in together. All was silence; there was no sound. It was cold. There were no birds in the air. There was no living thing.

At last the Creator made a little wagtail and sent him down from his far place in the sky.

"Produce the earth," he said.

The bird flew down over the black waters and the dismal swamp. He did not know what to do. He did not know how to begin.

He fluttered the water with his wings and spashed it here and there. He ran up and down in the slush with his feet and tried to trample it into firmness. He beat on it with his tail, beating it down. After a long time of this treading and tail-wagging a few dry places began to appear in the big ocean which now surrounds them—the islands of the Ainu. The Ainu word for earth is *moshiri*, floating land, and the wagtail is reverenced.

—Retold in Maria Leach. *The Beginning.* New York: Funk and Wagnalls, 1956, p. 205. —Based on material in G. Batchelor. *The Ainu and Their Folklore.* London: 1901, p. 582f. and in "Notes on the Ainu." *Transactions of the Asiatic Society of Japan.* Vol. 10. Yokohama: 1882.

SIX

SIBERIAN AND ESKIMO MYTHS

TUNGUS

God Triumphs Over the Devil

The Tungus (or Evenki) are a native Siberian group now numbering about 30,000. The vast majority live in the USSR, mainly in the Evenki National Okrug, while the rest are in China. Before the Russians moved into Siberia in the latter part of the sixteenth century and before the Soviets eventually established control of the region, the Tungus practiced a shamanistic religion.

In many Siberian creation myths such as this one, God created the earth by setting fire to the primordial ocean. Using one creative force to overcome and order another, he triumphed over the powers of chaos and formed the land.

Once on earth, God met the devil, Buninka, who had designs of his own. Buninka broke God's twelve-stringed musical instrument (one string for each month), and in response to this challenge God offered a test of respective power. The creation of the pine tree, the focus of the subsequent contest, is significant for several reasons: at a psychosexual level, it is an obvious phallic symbol, evocative of fertility and creative power; it is also, religiously, an axis mundi, a symbolic connection between the absolute and relative realms, heaven and earth. In addition, given its properties as an evergreen, the pine symbolizes immortal and unchanging life. When the devil's tree proved weak and ungrounded in comparison to God's, the superior might of God was established.

G OD sent fire into the primordial ocean. In the course of time the fire vanquished the power of the water and burnt up a part of the ocean, so that it became quite hard. Thus the present land and sea were formed.

When God stepped down upon the earth he met the devil, Buninka, who also desired to create a world. Thus a dispute arose between God and the devil. The devil wished to destroy God's earth and broke the latter's twelve-stringed musical instrument. Then God was angry and said: "If thou canst command a pine-tree to grow out of the lake I will recognize thy power, but if I can do it, thou must admit that I am omnipotent." The devil agreed to God's proposal. At once, when God commanded, a tree arose from the water and began to grow, but the devil's pine would not stand erect but tottered from one side to the other. Thus the devil saw that God was mightier than he.

—Uno Holmberg. *Finno-Ugric, Siberian Mythology*. In MacCulloch (ed.), *The Mythology of All Races*. Vol. 4. Boston: Marshall Jones, 1927, p. 329.

MONGOLIAN

A Lama Came Down from Heaven

The simultaneous conquest of northern India by the Moslems and of northern China by the Mongols under Genghis Khan (1167?–1227 A.D.) forced the Tibetan Buddhists to turn away from the religious life of India to which they had been attached and to look toward the Mongolians. The missionary work they did among these people even after the fall of the Mongol (Yuan) Dynasty in China is evident in this creation myth fragment.

Here a *Lama* ("superior one," the ideal of Tibetan Buddhism) stirs the primeval waters with an iron rod much as Izanagi and Izanami did in the Japanese myth, the *Nihongi*. Affected by this powerful connection to the source of creative power, the chaos orders itself into land and the surrounding sea.

The Mongolians, currently numbering around 3,250,000, now live in Mongolia, northern and western Manchuria, and in the Buryat-Mongol Autonomous SSR in the USSR.

IN THE BEGINNING, when there was yet no earth, but water covered everything, a Lama came down from Heaven, and began to stir the water with an iron rod. By the influence of the wind and fire thus brought about, the water on the surface in the middle of the ocean thickened and coagulated into land.

—Uno Holmberg. *Finno-Ugric, Siberian Mythlology*. In MacCulloch (ed.), *The Mythology of All Races*. Vol. 4. Boston: Marshall Jones, 1927, pp. 328–329.

ALARSK BURYATS

When Burkhan Came Down from Heaven

Closely related to the Mongols linguistically and culturally, the Buryats are another people indigenous to Siberia. Currently numbering about 250,000, they live in the Buryat Autonomous SSR, north of Mongolia. While most Buryats are Russian Orthodox today, a strong Buddhist influence is apparent in this older creation myth.

With the devil acting as an earth diver, God scatters the earth over the surface of the water and commands the world to be born. And then, in a strongly dualistic development, the devil is rewarded for his service with a piece of land for himself. Thrusting his staff into the fertile ground (an imitative sexual act), he causes the earth to give birth to all the harmful creatures.

WHEN BURKHAN (=Buddha) came down from Heaven to create the earth, the devil (Sholmo) appeared beside him to give advice how the earth was to be made from the earth-matter and stones under the water, offering at the same time to fetch the earth-matter. God scattered the earth-matter, which the devil had brought him, on the surface of the ocean and said: "Let the world be born!" As a reward for his trouble the devil begged for a part of the land, receiving enough to plant his staff on. The devil at once pushed his staff into this, and from the hole there crept forth all manner of reptiles, snakes, etc. Thus he created the harmful creatures of the world.

—Uno Holmberg. *Finno-Ugric, Siberian Mythology*. In MacCulloch (ed.), *The Mythology of All Races*. Vol. 4. Boston: Marshall Jones, 1927, p. 315.

ALTAIC

God and First Man   The Altaic peoples are a linguistically related group including Turks, Mongols, and Tungus-Manchus. Religious influences on these originally shamanistic, nomadic people come from Buddhism, Islam, Iranian religion, Nestorian Christianity, and Manichaeism. In this myth, the nascent or developed dualism of these creeds is clear. God and the Devil—identified here with the "First Man," the first of the ancestors and eventual ruler of the underworld—act together to create land out of the watery chaos. Through his attempt to trick God and retain some earth for himself, the Devil inadvertently creates the boggy, unformed places.

IN THE BEGINNING when there was nothing but water, God and the "First Man" moved about in the shape of two black geese over the waters of the primordial ocean. The devil, however, could not hide his nature, but endeavoured ever to rise higher, until he finally sank down into the depths. Nearly suffocating, he was forced to call to God for help, and God raised him again into the air with the power of his word. God then spoke: "Let a stone rise from the bottom of the ocean!" When the Stone appeared, "Man" seated himself upon it, but God asked him to dive under the water and bring land. Man brought earth in his hand and God scattered it on the surface of the water saying: "Let the world take shape!" Once more God asked Man to fetch earth. But Man then decided to take some for himself and brought a morsel in each hand. One handful he gave to God but the other he hid in his mouth, intending to create a world of his own. God threw the earth which the devil had brought him beside the rest on the water, and the world at once began to expand and grow harder, but with the growing of the world the piece of earth in Man's mouth also swelled until he was about to suffocate so that he was again compelled to seek God's help. God inquired: "What was thy intention? Didst thou think thou couldst hide earth from me in thy mouth?" Man now told his secret intentions and at God's request spat the earth out of his mouth. Thus were formed the boggy places upon the earth.

—Uno Holmberg. *Finno-Ugric, Siberian Mythology.* In MacCulloch (ed.), *The Mythology of All Races.* Vol. 4. Boston: Marshall Jones, 1927, pp. 317–318.

ESKIMO

The Creation
The 55,000 Eskimo who live in the vast arctic and subarctic regions of the north are remarkably similar in language, physical appearance, and religion. Elements of this myth are common among Eskimo from the Chuckchi Peninsula in Siberia to Greenland, where they migrated by the thirteenth century A.D.; indeed, the latter sequences involving two brothers quarreling over the sun is characteristic of Finno-Ugric and Turko-Mongolian mythology as well.

This myth was related by an old Unalit man from Kigitauik. Although its scope is typically limited and it does not focus on the creation of the universe as such, it does tell of the origin of people and society. Particularly, the myth evokes a connection between the trickster god, Raven, who travels frequently between the three worlds of heaven, earth, and the sea floor, and the shaman, a priest or medicine man basic to Eskimo and other religions whose function it is to mediate between the worlds of spirits and men. Like the Raven, the shaman is an outsider beyond the ordered realms of natural and human society. And, like the shaman, the Raven has great sacred powers; by his cunning and intelligence, he easily changes form and instructs people in the proper way of life.

This myth describes the origin of people (born from a plant, which surprises Raven), the differences between the inland and coastal peoples, the three worlds of the sky, earth, and water and the sacred spirits that inhabit all of them. In the end, it recalls the conflict between two Raven brothers over the proper placement of the sun and, as the world grows older and more ordered, the gradual loss of sacred power. As the Raven brother settles down to marriage and earthly life, he loses his ability to ascend from earth to the spirit world. Thus the separation of the two, so palpable now, is established.

I T WAS in the time when there were no people on the earth plain. During four days the first man lay coiled up in the pod of a beach-pea. On the fifth day he stretched out his feet and burst the pod, falling to the ground, where he stood up, a full-grown man. He looked about him, and then moved his hands and arms, his neck and legs, and examined himself curiously. Looking back, he saw the pod from which he had fallen, still hanging to the vine, with a hole in the lower end, out of which he had dropped. Then he looked about him again and saw that he was getting farther away from his starting place, and that the ground moved up and down under his feet and seemed very soft. After a while he had an unpleasant feeling in his stomach, and he stooped down to take some water into his mouth from a small pool at his feet. The water ran down into his stomach and he felt better. When he looked up again he saw approaching, with a waving motion, a dark object which came on until just in front of him, when it stopped, and, standing on the ground, looked at him. This was a raven, and, as soon as it stopped, it raised one of its wings, pushed up its beak, like a mask, to the top of its head, and changed at once into a man. Before he raised his mask Raven had stared at the man, and after it was raised he stared more than ever, moving about from side to side to obtain a better view. At last he said: "What are you? Whence did you come? I have never seen anything like you." Then Raven looked at Man, and was still more surprised to find that this strange new being was so much like himself in shape.

Then he told Man to walk away a few steps, and in astonishment exclaimed again: "Whence did you come? I have never seen anything like you before." To this Man replied: "I came from the pea-pod." And he pointed to the plant from which he came. "Ah!" exclaimed Raven, "I made that vine, but did not know that anything like you would ever come from it. Come with me to the high ground over there; this ground I made later, and it is still soft and thin, but it is thicker and harder there."

In a short time they came to the higher land, which was firm under their feet. Then Raven asked Man if he had eaten anything. The latter answered that he had taken some soft stuff into him at one of the pools. "Ah!" said Raven, "you drank some water. Now wait for me here."

Then he drew down the mask over his face, changing again into a bird, and flew far up into the sky where he disappeared. Man waited where he had been left until the fourth day, when Raven returned, bringing four berries in his claws. Pushing up his mask, Raven became a man again and held out two salmonberries and two heathberries, saying, "Here is what I have made for you to eat. I also wish them to be plentiful over the earth. Now eat them." Man took the berries and placed them in his mouth one after the other and they satisfied his hunger, which had made him feel uncomfortable. Raven then led Man to a small creek near by and left him while he went to the water's edge and molded a couple of pieces of clay into the form of a pair of mountain sheep, which he held in his hand, and when they became dry he called Man to show him what he had done. Man thought they were very pretty, and Raven told him to close his eyes. As soon as Man's eyes were closed Raven drew down his mask and waved his wings four times over the images, when they became endowed with life and bounded away as full-grown mountain sheep. Raven then raised his mask and told Man to look. When Man saw the sheep moving away, full of life, he cried out with pleasure. Seeing how pleased Man was, Raven said, "If these animals are numerous, perhaps people will wish very much to get them." And Man said he thought they would. "Well," said Raven, "it will be better for them to have their home among the high cliffs, so that every one can not kill them, and there only shall they be found."

Then Raven made two animals of clay which he endowed with life as before, but as they were dry only in spots when they were given life, they remained brown and white, and so originated the tame reindeer with mottled coat. Man thought these were very handsome, and Raven told him that they would be very scarce. In the same way a pair of wild reindeer were made and permitted to get dry and white only on their bellies, then they were given life; in consequence, to this day the belly of the wild reindeer is the only white part about it. Raven told Man that these animals would be very common, and people would kill many of them.

"You will be very lonely by yourself," said Raven. "I will make you a companion." He then went to a spot some distance from where he had made the animals, and, looking now and then at Man, made an image very much like him. Then he fastened a lot of fine water grass on the back of the head for hair, and after the image had dried in his hands, he waived his wings over it as before and a beautiful young woman arose and stood beside Man. "There," cried Raven, "is a companion for you," and he led them back to a small knoll near by.

In those days there were no mountains far or near, and the sun never ceased shining brightly; no rain ever fell and no winds blew. When they came to the knoll, Raven showed the pair how to make a bed in the dry moss, and they slept there very warmly; Raven drew down his mask and slept near by in the form of a bird. Waking before the others, Raven went back to the creek and made a pair each of sticklebacks, graylings, and blackfish. When these were swimming about in the water, he called Man to see them. When the latter looked at them and saw the sticklebacks swim up the stream with a wriggling motion he was so surprised that he raised his hand suddenly and the fish darted away. Raven then showed him the graylings and told him that they would be found in clear mountain streams, while the sticklebacks would live along the seacoast and that both would be good for food. Next the shrew-mouse was made, Raven saying that it would not be good for food but would enliven the ground and prevent it from seeming barren and cheerless.

In this way Raven continued for several days making birds, fishes, and animals, showing them to Man, and explaining their uses.

After this he flew away to the sky and was gone four days, when he returned, bringing back a salmon for the use of Man. Looking about he saw that the ponds and lakes were silent and lonely, so he created many water insects upon their surfaces, and from the same clay he made the beaver and the muskrat to frequent their borders. Then, also, were made flies, mosquitoes, and various other land and water insects, it being explained to Man that these were made to enliven and make cheerful the earth. At that time the mosquito was like the house-fly in its habits and did not bite as it does now.

Man was shown the muskrat and told to take its skin for clothing. He was also told that the beavers would live along the streams and build strong houses and that he must follow their example, and likewise that the beavers would be very cunning and only good hunters would be able to take them.

At this time the woman gave birth to a child, and Raven directed Man how to feed and care for it, telling him that it would grow into a man like himself. As soon as the child was born, Raven and Man took it to a creek, rubbed it over with clay, and then returned with it to his stopping place on the knoll. The next morning the child was running about pulling up grass and other plants which Raven had caused to grow near by; on the third day the child became a full-grown man.

After this Raven thought that if he did not create something to make men afraid they would destroy everything he had made to inhabit the earth. Then he went to a creek near by, where he formed a bear and gave it life, jumping to one side quickly as the bear stood up and looked fiercely about. Man was then called and told that the bear would be very fierce and would tear him to pieces if he disturbed it. Then were made different kinds of seals, and their names and habits were explained to man. Raven also taught Man to make rawhide lines from sealskin, and snares for deer, but cautioned him to wait until the deer were abundant before he snared any of them.

In time the woman was with child again, and Raven said it would be a girl and they must rub her over with clay as soon as she was born, and that after she was grown she must marry her brother. Then Raven went away to the place of the pea vine, where the first man was found. While he was gone a girl was born and the pair did as they were told, and the next day the girl walked about. On the third day she became a full-grown woman, and was married to the young man as directed by Raven, in order that the earth might be peopled more rapidly.

When Raven reached the pea vine he found three other men had just fallen from the pea pod that gave the first one. These men, like the first, were looking about them in wonder, and Raven led them away in an opposite direction from that in which he had taken the first man, afterward bringing them to firm land close to the sea. Here they stopped, and Raven remained with them a long time, teaching them how to live. He taught them how to make a fire drill and bow from a piece of dry wood and a cord, taking the wood from the bushes and small trees he had caused to grow in hollows and sheltered places on the hillside. He made for each of the men a wife, and also made many plants and birds such as frequent the seacoast, but fewer kinds than he had made in the land where the first man lived. He taught the men to make bows and arrows, spears, nets, and all the implements of the chase and how to use them; also how to capture the seals which had now become plentiful in the sea. After he had taught them how to make kaiaks, he showed them how to build houses of drift logs and bushes covered with earth. Now the three wives of the last men were all pregnant, and Raven went back to the first man, where he found the children were married; then he told Man about all he had done for the people on the seacoast. Looking about here he thought the earth seemed bare; so, while the others slept, he caused birch, spruce, and cottonwood trees to spring up in low places, and then awoke the people, who were much pleased at seeing the trees. After this they were taught how to make fire with the fire drill and to place the spark of tinder in a bunch of dry grass and wave it about until it blazed, then to place dry wood upon it. They were shown how to roast fish on a stick, to make fish traps of splints and willow bark, to dry salmon for winter use, and to make houses.

Raven then went back to the coast men again. When he had gone Man and his son went down to the sea and the son caught a seal which they tried to kill with their hands but could not, until, finally, the son killed it by a blow with his fist. Then the father took off its skin with his hands alone and made it into lines which they dried. With these lines they set snares in the woods for reindeer. When they went to look at these the next morning, they found the cords bitten in two and the snares gone, for in those days reindeer had sharp teeth like dogs. After thinking for a time the young man made a deep hole in the deer trail and hung in it a heavy stone fastened to the snare so that when it caught a deer the stone would slip down into the hole, drag the deer's neck down to the ground, and hold it fast. The next morning when they returned they found a deer entangled in the snare. Taking it out they killed and skinned it, carrying the skin home for a bed; some of the flesh was roasted on the fire and found to be very good to eat.

One day Man went out seal hunting along the seashore. He saw many seals, but in each case after he had crept carefully up they would tumble into the water before he could get to them, until only one was left on the rocks; Man crept up to it more carefully than before, but it also escaped. Then he stood up and his breast seemed full of a strange feeling, and the water began to run in drops from his eyes and down his face. He put up his hand and caught some of the drops to look at them and found that they were really water; then, without any wish on his part, loud cries began to break from him and the tears ran down his face as he went home. When his son saw him coming, he called to his wife and mother to see Man coming along making such a strange noise; when he reached them they were still more surprised to see water running down his face. After he told them the story of his disappointment they were all stricken with the same strange ailment and began to wail with him, and in this way people first learned how to cry. After this the son killed another seal and they made more deer snares from its hide.

When the deer caught this time was brought home, Man told his people to take a splint bone from its foreleg and to drill a hole in the large end. Into this they put some strands of sinew from the deer and sewed skins upon their bodies to keep themselves warm when winter came; for Raven had told them to do this, so that the fresh deerskins dried upon them. Man then showed his son how to make bows and arrows and to tip the latter with points of horn for killing deer; with them the son killed his first deer. After he had cut up this deer he placed its fat on a brush and then fell asleep; when he awoke he was very angry to find that mosquitoes had eaten all of it. Until this time mosquitoes had never bitten people, but Man scolded them for what they had done and said, "Never eat meat again, but eat men," and since that day mosquitoes have always bitten people.

Where the first man lived there had now grown a large village, for the people did everything as Raven directed them, and as soon as a child was born it was rubbed with clay and so caused to grow to its full stature in three days. One day Raven came back and sat by Man, and they talked of many things. Man asked Raven about the land he had made in the sky. Raven said that he had made a fine land there, whereupon Man asked to be taken to see it. This was agreed to and they started toward the sky where they arrived in a short time. There Man found himself in a beautiful country with a very much better climate than that on earth; but the people who lived there were very small. Their heads reached only to his thigh when they stood beside him. Man looked about as they journeyed and saw many strange animals; also that the country was much finer than the one he had left. Raven told him that this land, with its people and animals, was the first he had made.

The people living here wore handsomely made fur clothing, worked in ornamental patterns, such as people now wear on earth; for Man, on his return, showed his people how to make clothes in this manner, and the patterns have been retained ever since. After a time they came to a large kashim, and went in; a very old man, the first made by Raven in the sky land, came out from his place of honor at the head of the room, opposite the door, and welcomed them, telling the people to bring food for the guest from the lower land, who was his friend. Then boiled flesh of a kind which Man had never eaten before was brought to him. Raven told him that it was from the mountain sheep and the tame reindeer. After Man had eaten Raven led him on again to show him other things which he had made, and told him not to try to drink from any of the lakes they might pass, for in them he had made animals that would seize and destroy him if he went near.

On the way they came to a dry lake bed in which tall grass was growing thickly. Lying upon the very tips of this grass, which did not bend under its weight, was a large, strange-looking animal, with a long head and six legs. The two hind-legs were unusually large; the forelegs were short, and a small pair extended down from the belly. All over the animal's body grew fine, thick hair, like that on the shrew-mouse, but it was longer about the feet. From the back of the head grew a pair of thick, short horns, which extended forward and curved back at the tips. The animal had small eyes and was of very dark color or blackish.

Raven told Man that when people wished to kill one of these animals they first placed logs on the ground under them, for, if they did not, the animal would sink into the earth when he fell and be lost. In order to kill one of them many people were needed, and when the animal fell on the logs other logs must be thrown over it and held down, while two men took large clubs and beat in its skull between the eyes.

Next they came to a round hole in the sky, around the border of which grew a ring of short grass, glowing like fire. This, Raven said, was a star called the Moon-dog *(i-gha-lum ki-mukh-ti)*. The tops of the grass bordering the hole were gone, and Raven said that his mother had taken some, and he had taken the rest to make the first fire on earth. He added that he had tried to make some of this same kind of grass on the earth but could not.

Man was now told to close his eyes and he would be taken to another place. Raven took him upon his wings and, dropping through the star hole, they floated down for a long time, until at last they entered something that seemed to resist their course. Finally they stopped, and Raven said they were standing at the bottom of the sea. Man breathed quite easily there, and Raven told him that the foggy appearance was caused by the water. He said, "I will make some new kinds of animals here; but you must not walk about; you must lie down, and if you become tired you may turn over upon the other side."

Raven then left Man lying on one side, where he rested for a long time; finally he awoke, but felt very tired, so he tried to turn over, but could not. Then Man thought, "I wish I could turn over;" and in a moment he turned without effort. As he did this he was surprised to see that his body had become covered with long, white hairs and that his fingers had become long claws, but he quickly fell asleep again. He awoke, and turned over and fell asleep three times more. When he awoke the fourth time Raven stood beside him and said, "I have changed you into a white bear. How do you like it?" Man tried to answer, but could not make a sound until the Raven waved his magic wing over him, when he replied that he did not like it, for he would have to live on the sea while his son would be on the shore, and he would feel badly. Then Raven made a stroke with his wings and the bearskin fell from Man and lay empty at one side while he sat up in his original form. Then Raven took one of his tail-feathers, placing it inside the bearskin for a spine, and, after waving his wing over it, a white bear arose. Then they passed on, and ever since white bears have been found on the frozen sea.

Raven asked Man how many times he had turned over, and he answered, "four." "That was four years," said Raven, "for you slept there just four years." They had gone only a short distance beyond this, when they saw a small animal like a shrew-mouse; this was a *wi-lu-gho-yuk*. It is like the shrew that lives on the land, but this one always lives at sea on the ice. When it sees a man it darts at him, and, entering the toe of his boot, crawls all over his body, after which, if he keeps perfectly quiet, it will leave him unharmed and the man will become a successful hunter. In case the man moves even a finger while this animal is on him, it instantly burrows into his flesh and goes directly to his heart, causing death.

Then Raven made the *a-mi-kik*, a large, slimy, leathery-skin animal, with four long, wide-spreading arms. This is a fierce animal, living in the sea, which wraps its arms about a man or a kaiak and drags them under the water; if the man tries to escape from it by leaving his kaiak and getting on the ice it will dart underneath, breaking the ice beneath his feet, and even pursuing him on shore by burrowing through the earth as easily as it swims in the water, so that no one can escape from it when it once pursues him.

Beyond this, they saw two large dark-colored animals, around which swam a smaller one. Raven hurried forward and sat upon the head of the smaller animal, and it became quiet. When Man drew near, Raven showed him two walrus, and said that the animal upon whose head he was borne was a walrus dog (*az-i-wu-gumki-mukh-ti*). This animal, he said, would always go with large herds of walrus and would kill people. It was long and rather slender, covered with black scales which were not too hard to be pierced by a spear. Its head and teeth were somewhat like those of a dog; it had four legs and a long, round tail covered with scales like those on the body; with a stroke of this tail it could kill a man.

Some whales and grampus were seen next. Raven told Man that only good hunters could kill them, and that when one was killed an entire village could feast. Then they saw the *i-mum ka-bvi-a-ga,* or sea fox, an animal very much like the red fox, except that it lives in the sea and is so fierce that it kills men. Near this were two *i-mum isni-kak* or *i-mum pikh-tukh-chi,* the sea otter, which is like the land otter, but has much finer fur, tipped with white, and is very scarce, only the best hunters being able to capture it. They passed many kinds of fish and then the shore rose before them, and overhead could be seen the ripples on the surface of the water. "Close your eyes, and hold fast to me," said Raven. As soon as he had done this, Man found himself standing on the shore near his home, and was very much astonished to see a large village where he had left only a few huts; his wife had become very old and his son was an old man. The people saw him and welcomed him back, making him their headman; he was given the place of honor in the kashim, and there told the people what he had seen and taught the young men many things. The villagers would have given Raven a seat by the old man in the place of honor, but he refused it and chose a seat with the humble people near the entrance.

After a time the old man began to wish to see the fine sky land again, but his people tried to induce him to stay with them. He told his children that they must not feel badly at his absence, and then, in company with Raven, he returned to the sky land. The dwarf people welcomed them, and they lived there for a long time, until the villagers on the earth had become very numerous and killed a great many animals. This angered Man and Raven so much that one night they took a long line and a grass basket with which they descended to the earth. Raven caught ten reindeer, which he put into the basket with the old man; then one end of the cord was fastened to the basket and Raven returned to the sky, drawing it up after him. The next evening they took the reindeer and went down close to Man's village; the deer were then told to break down the first house they came to and destroy the people, for men were becoming too numerous. The reindeer did as they were told and ate up the people with their sharp, wolf-like teeth, after which they returned to the sky; the next night they came back and destroyed another house with its people in the same manner. The villagers had now become much frightened and covered the third house with a mixture of deer fat and berries. When the reindeer tried to destroy this house they filled their mouths with the fat and sour berries, which caused them to run off, shaking their heads so violently that all their long, sharp teeth fell out. Afterward small teeth, such as reindeer now have, grew in their places, and these animals became harmless.

Man and Raven returned to the sky after the reindeer ran away, Man saying, "If something is not done to stop people from taking so many animals they will continue until they have killed everything you have made. It is better to take away the sun from them so that they will be in the dark and will die."

To this Raven agreed, saying, "You remain here and I will go and take away the sun." So he went away and, taking the sun, put it into his skin bag and carried it far away to a part of the sky land where his parents lived, and it became very dark on earth. In his father's village Raven took to himself a wife from the maidens of the place and lived there, keeping the sun hidden carefully in the bag.

The people on earth were very much frightened when the sun was taken away, and tried to get it back by offering Raven rich presents of food and furs, but without effect. After many trials the people propitiated Raven so that he let them have the light for a short time. Then he would hold up the sun in one hand for two days at a time, so that the people could hunt and get food, after which it would be taken away and all would become dark. After this a long time would pass and it required many offerings before he would let them have light again. This was repeated many times.

Raven had living in this village an older brother who began to feel sorry for the earth people and to think of means by which he could get the sun and return it to its place. After he had thought a long time he pretended to die, and was put away in a grave box, as was customary. As soon as the mourners left his grave he arose and went out a short distance from the village, where he hid his raven mask and coat in a tree; then he went to the spring where the villagers got their water, and waited. In a short time his brother's wife came for water, and after she had filled her bucket she took up a ladle full of water to drink. As she drank, Raven's brother, by a magic spell, changed himself into a small leaf, falling into the ladle, and was swallowed with the water. The woman coughed and then hastened home, where she told her husband that she had swallowed some strange thing while drinking at the spring, to which he paid little attention, saying it was probably a small leaf.

Immediately after this the woman became with child, and in a few days gave birth to a boy, who was very lively and crept about at once and in a few days was running about. He cried continually for the sun, and, as the father was very fond of him, he frequently let the child have it for a plaything, but was always careful to take it back again. As soon as the boy began to play out of doors he cried and begged for the sun more than ever. After refusing for a long time, his father let him take the sun again and the boy played with it in the house, and then, when no one was looking, he carried it outside, ran quickly to the tree, put on his raven mask and coat, and flew far away with it. When he was far up from the sky he heard his father crying out to him, "Do not hide the sun. Let it out of the bag to make some light. Do not keep it always dark." For he feared his son had stolen it to keep it for himself.

Then Raven went home and the Raven boy flew on to the place where the sun belonged. There he tore off the skin covering and put the sun in its place again. From this place he saw a broad path leading far away, which he followed. It led him to the side of a hole surrounded by short grass glowing with light, some of which he plucked. He remembered that his father had called to him not to keep it always dark, but to make it partly dark and partly light. Thinking of this, he caused the sky to revolve, so that it moved around the earth, carrying the sun and stars with it, thus making day and night.

While he was standing close by the edge of the earth, just before sunrise, he stuck into the sky a bunch of the glowing grass that he held in his hand, and it has stayed there ever since, forming the brilliant morning star. Going down to the earth he came at last to the village where the first people lived. There the old people welcomed him, and he told them that Raven had been angry with them and had taken the sun away, but that he had put it back himself so that it would never be moved again.

Among the people who welcomed him was the headman of the sky dwarfs, who had come down with some of his people to live on the earth. Then the people asked him what had become of Man, who had gone up to the sky with Raven. This was the first time the Raven boy had heard of Man, and he tried to fly up to the sky to see him, but found that he could rise only a short distance above the earth. When he found that he could not get back to the sky, he wandered away until he came to a village where lived the children of the other men last born from the pea-vine. There he took a wife and lived a long time, having many children, all of whom became Raven people like himself and were able to fly over the earth, but they gradually lost their magic powers until finally they became ordinary ravens like the birds we see now on the tundras.

—E. W. Nelson. *The Eskimo About Bering Strait. 18th Annual Report of the Bureau of American Ethnology*. Washington, D.C.: 1899, pp. 452–462.

CHUCKCHI ESKIMO

Creator Makes Men and Animals About

1,600 Eskimo live on the Chuckchi Peninsula at the northeastern tip of Siberia, the westernmost boundary of Eskimo-inhabited territory, which stretches through arctic and subarctic regions all the way to Greenland. Re'mkilin, a Reindeer Chuckchi man, related this creation myth at his camp on the Omolon River during the summer of 1895. It tells of two lands—Lu'ren and Qe'nieven—the ancestral homes respectively of the Maritime and Reindeer branches of the Chuckchi.

While Raven is one of the primary creators in many Eskimo myths, here he is portrayed as an incompetent assistant of the creator. But even though he fails to peck through the sky to the light above and is punished for that failure, Raven is nevertheless still recognized as the first of God's creatures, closest to the creator and therefore honored for his primacy.

Most Eskimo myths presume the existence of land and therefore express the drama of creation through the opposition of darkness and light rather than through the more common opposition of liquid and solid. Order is established along with the day, when the wagtail finally pecks through the crust of the sky.

The rest of the myth involves the creation and education of human beings. Creator descended to earth and made people out of seal bones, emphasizing the continued dependency of the Eskimo on these sea mammals. Retreating back to his sacred realm, Creator searched for worthy messengers capable of traveling between heaven and earth. Birds were obvious choices, but Ptarmigan failed; so Creator made the foxes and wolves and sent them down in turn, but these too did not fulfill their purpose. To punish all these creatures, Creator made them scavengers, as he had made Raven—outlaws to himself and the human community. Finally descending to earth himself, he instructed people in their sexuality, thus making them creators in their own right, and gave them fire, food, and appropriate occupations.

The bear created at the end of the myth is reminiscent of the Ainu bears, sacrificed at annual festivals so that their spirits may be released to guard villages at night. Here the bear fails to find a fire-drill, which, by the time Creator locates it, has transformed itself into a Russian (a Chuckchi pun connects the words for "fire-drill" and "Russian"). Self-transformed—that is, existing in a different system from the Chuckchis—the Russian is nonetheless given social and economic function by the creator.

ONCE UPON A TIME it was quite dark. There existed only two lands, Lu'ren and Qe'nievin. Creator sat on the noonday-side of these lands, and considered how he could make the sunshine. So he created Raven and said to him, "Go and peck; and with your pecking set free the morning-dawn." The Raven flew eastward and pecked, but he could do nothing. So he came back to Creator and said to him, "I could do nothing." Creator was angry. He caught Raven and cast him aside. "No need of you. Be off. I will not give you food; go find it for yourself."

Then Creator made Wagtail, and he was a large, fine bird. Wagtail flew away and pecked and pecked. He wore out his beak pecking. At last he made a tiny hole, and came back to Creator. Creator asked him, "How far did you succeed?" I succeeded in making a very tiny hole." "Go back and make a bigger one," said Creator. So Wagtail went back and pecked again. At last, pecking and pecking, he made a large hole. The dawn spurted through, and it was light.

Wagtail had worn off all his beak with pecking. His body was skin and bones and all his feathers dropped out. He had no wings to fly with. Wagtail went back on foot to Creator. There was nothing to eat along the way, and even his bones became brittle and thin; he grew quite small and weak. At last he came to Creator, "How is it? Have you done the task?" "Yes, I have done it. There is light over the earth." "Ah, ah." Creator clothed him with new feathers and made his beak sharp-pointed again. Then he gave him a new house under a grass hummock, and he said, "Live here and bring forth children; your food shall be the worms in the ground."

After that Creator descended to the earth. He scattered seal bones and said to them, "Be living human creatures!" Then he came back. After a while he thought, "Who will bring me news from the earth?" He sent Ptarmigan, "Go and visit the earth and humankind." Ptarmigan went for a short distance. He came back and said to Creator, "Oh, it is too far away, I could not reach it." Creator caught Ptarmigan and cast him way off into the thick willow bushes. "I do not want you. Live alone in the open. I will not give you food. Go find it for yourself." After that Creator made a large Polar Owl. He said to Owl, "Go and visit the land of Lu'ren." Owl set off and came to Lu'ren. He looked from afar. Four human beings, two men and two men, were standing there upon the ground. They did not dare to sit down.

The other land, Qe'nievin, was a ridge of mountains, quite long and high. Four men were there made of four little stones. Creator thought about this land also and said to himself, "How shall I know the news of Qe'nievin?" He created Yellow Fox and sent him there. "Go and bring news from Qe'nievin." Yellow Fox went, but he could not reach it. So he came back and tried to deceive Creator. Yellow Fox said, "There is no such land; there are no men; nothing at all." Creator caught him and cast him aside. "No need of you. Live in the open. I shall not give any more food. Find it for yourself."

Then Creator made an Arctic Fox and sent him likewise. "Go and bring news from Qe'nievin." Arctic Fox started off and indeed he reached Qe'nievin. He looked from a great distance. Four men were there standing upon their feet.

They did not dare to sit down. Arctic Fox was sorely frightened. He ran back and came to Creator panting for breath. "Well now?" "Ah, men, men." Creator was very angry. He caught Arctic Fox and threw him aside. "Oh, you good-for-nothing. Why are you so afraid? Why have you brought me no news? Be off. I shall give you no more food. Live in the open. Feed by yourself!"

After that he thought again, "Oh, whom shall I send to fetch news from Qe'nievin?" He plucked some dry grass of the last year, and of the year before that. Of this he made a Wolf. He said "Go and visit Qe'nievin. See the people who are there." Wolf went and looked also from a distance and saw the men. They were standing on their feet, as they were afraid to sit down. Wolf was frightened. He ran away and came back to Creator. "Ah, I saw men," he said. "They had eyes and eye-brows and hair upon their heads. They were standing on their feet, as they were afraid to sit down. They are half-crazy, quite awful to look upon." Creator retorted, "Why did you not go nearer?" "I was afraid." Creator caught Wolf and cast him aside. "Why are you so full of vain fright? Be off. I do not want you. Neither shall I give you any more food. Find it for yourself!"

Creator lost all patience and went himself. He came to the men and took the male by the shoulder. "Sit down!" Then he made the female sit down close by the male's side. He said to both, "Lie down." Then to the woman again, "Turn upon your back, face upward." And she did. "Now spread your legs." And she did. "Wider." He took the man and put him upon the woman. So they copulated, and multiplied and became humankind.

Creator made reindeer of some willow sprigs. "These are for your food," he said. "Slaughter them and live on them!" He prepared clothes for the Maritime people of sealskin, and for the Reindeer people, of reindeer skin. Then he made a fire-drill of hard wood of drifted pine. He produced fire by drilling. He made the reindeer multiply. The first fawn was born. They killed a reindeer buck, cooked the brisket whole and threw into the fire some raw fat and some tallow. The reindeer fawn sucked its mother. After that man and woman moved off and they forgot the fire-drill in their former camping place. They pitched a new camp. The woman fetched some fuel and wanted to make a fire, but she had nothing to start it with. They asked Creator about it. He thought for a while; then he took a handful of black soil and created the Black One who walks barefooted (the Bear). "Go and fetch the fire-drill. See what has become of it." Bear set off, but when he had gone half-way, he was so tired he lay down and fell asleep right in the path. A ptarmigan fluttered up gibbering. Bear started up and ran off back to Creator. "Where is the fire-drill?" "I could not find it." Something white and awful fluttered up on the very road and drove me back." Creator struck Bear. "Be off. No need of you, if even a ptarmigan frightens you off. Oh, you lazy sleeper, Heavy-Walking-One." Creator went himself, and lo, the fire-drill had turned into a man. He said, "What then? Since it is so, be a man, be a Russian. Produce tea and sugar, tobacco and salt, hardware and calico. Be rich. Possess yourself of iron, and let all the tribes be your slaves, but let the Reindeer and the Maritime Chuckchee people have a fair trade with you."

—Waldemar Borgoras. "Chuckchee Tales." *Journal of American Folklore,* 1928, *41,* 297–300. New York: G. E. Stechert, for the American Folklore Society.

SEVEN

NORTH AMERICAN MYTHS

JOSHUA

Xowalaci and His Companion

Like many northwest Pacific Coast Indians, the Joshua lived at the mouth of a river (in this case, the Rogue River in southern Oregon) where they could safely beach their huge dugout canoes and find protection from warring neighbors. This myth was related by Charlie DePoe in the early 1900s.

The fallibility of the creator (Xowalaci, "The Giver") is a remarkable feature of this myth. Twice he attempts to create human beings, and twice he fails, producing dogs (sea mammals and dogs) and snakes (those powerful symbols of fertility and chaos, two of which eventually surround and contain the ordered world). Only by the intervention of the first man, Xowalaci's companion, is a woman finally created out of his dream, and it is again in a dream that he mates with her and produces the first child.

Other notable elements in this myth include a variation on the earth diver motif (here the creator drops clods of mud down on the bottom of the water rather than diving down and bringing mud to the surface), and the presence of a mysterious and troublesome man who walks the primordial earth unknown and uncontrolled.

IN THE BEGINNING there was no land. There was nothing but the sky, some fog, and water. The water was still; there were no breakers. A sweat-house stood on the water, and in it there lived two men,—Xowalaci (The Giver) and his companion. Xowalaci's companion had tobacco. He usually stayed outside watching, while Xowalaci remained in the sweat-house.

One day it seemed to the watcher as if daylight were coming. He went inside and told Xowalaci that he saw something strange coming. Soon there appeared something that looked like land, and on it two trees were growing. The man kept on looking, and was soon able to distinguish that the object, that was approaching, was white land. Then the ocean began to move, bringing the land nearer. Its eastern portion was dark. The western part kept on moving until it struck the sweat-house, where it stopped. It began to stretch to the north and to the south. The land was white like snow. There was no grass on it. It expanded like the waves of the ocean. Then the fog began to disappear, and the watcher could look far away.

He went into the sweat-house, and asked, "Xowalaci, are you ready?" and Xowalaci said, "Is the land solid?"—"Not quite," replied the man. Then Xowalaci took some tobacco and began to smoke. He blew the smoke on the land, and the land became motionless. Only two trees were growing at that time,—redwood to the south, and ash to the north. Five times Xowalaci smoked, while discussing with his companion various means of creating the world and the people. Then night came, and after that daylight appeared again. Four days Xowalaci worked; and trees began to bud, and fell like drops of water upon the ground. Grass came up, and leaves appeared on the trees. Xowalaci walked around the piece of land that had stopped near his sweat-house, commanding the ocean to withdraw and to be calm.

Then Xowalaci made five cakes of mud. Of the first cake he made a stone, and dropped it into the water, telling it to make a noise and to expand, as soon as it struck the bottom. After a long while he heard a faint noise, and knew then that the water was very deep. He waited some time before dropping the second cake. This time he heard the noise sooner, and knew that the land was coming nearer to the surface. After he had dropped the third cake, the land reached almost to the surface of the water. So he went into the sweat-house and opened a new sack of tobacco. Soon his companion shouted from the outside, "It looks as if breakers were coming!" Xowalaci was glad, because he knew now that the land was coming up from the bottom of the ocean. After the sixth wave the water receded, and Xowalaci scattered tobacco all over. Sand appeared. More breakers came in, receding farther and farther westward. Thus the land and the world were created. To the west, to the north, and to the south there was tide-water; to the east the land was dry. The new land was soft, and looked like sand. Xowalaci stepped on it, and said, "I am going to see if the great land has come;" and as he stepped, the land grew hard.

Then Xowalaci looked at the sand, and saw a man's tracks. They seemed to have come from the north, disappearing in the water on the south. He wondered what that could mean, and was very much worried. He went back to his first piece of land, and told the water to overflow the land he had created out of the five cakes of mud. Some time afterwards he ordered the water to recede, and looked again. This time he saw the tracks coming from the west, and returning to the water on the north side. He was puzzled, and ordered the water to cover up his new land once more. Five times he repeated this process. At last he became discouraged, and said, "This is going to make trouble in the future!" and since then there has always been trouble in the world.

Then Xowalaci began to wonder how he could make people. First he took some grass, mixed it with mud, and rubbed it in his hands. Then he ordered a house to appear, gave the two mud figures to his companion, and told him to put them into the house. After four days two dogs—a male and a bitch—appeared.

They watched the dogs, and twelve days later the bitch gave birth to pups. Xowa-laci then made food for the dogs. All kinds of dogs were born in that litter of pups. They were all howling. After a while Xowalaci went to work again. He took some white sand from the new land, and made two figures in the same way as before. He gave the figures to his companion, and ordered a house for them. Then he warned the dogs not to go to the new house, as it was intended for the new people. After thirteen days Xowalaci heard a great hissing; and a big snake came out of the house, followed by a female snake and by many small snakes. Xowalaci felt bad when he saw this, and went to his companion, telling him that this trouble was due to the tracks that had first appeared in the world. Soon the land became full of snakes, which, not having seen Xowalaci, wondered how everything had come about. The world was inhabited by dogs and snakes only. One day Xowalaci wished three baskets to appear, gave them to his companion, and told him to fill them partly with fresh water and partly with salt water. Then he put ten of the biggest snakes into the baskets, crushed them, and threw them into the ocean. Two bad snakes got away from him; and all snake-like animals that live to-day come from these snakes. Xowalaci said to these two snakes, "You two will live and surround the world like a belt, so that it won't break!" Then he crushed five bad dogs in the same way, made a great ditch with his finger, and threw the dogs into the ditch. These dogs became water-monsters. All animals that raise their heads above the water and smell, and then disappear quickly under the water, came from these five dogs.

Pretty soon Xowalaci began to think again, "How can I make people? I have failed twice!" Now, for the first time his companion spoke. He said, "Let me smoke tonight, and see if people will not come out (of the smoke)." For three days he smoked, at the end of which a house appeared with smoke coming out of it. The man told Xowalaci, "There is a house!" After a while a beautiful woman came out of the house, carrying a water-basket. Then Xowalaci was glad, and said, "Now we shall have no more trouble in creating people." The woman did not see Xowalaci and his companion, as they were watching her. After nine days the woman became sad, and wondered who her father and relatives were. She had plenty of food.

One day Xowalaci said to his companion, "Stay here and take this woman for your wife! You shall have children and be the father of all the people. I am leaving this world. Everything on it shall belong to you." And the man answered, "It is well; but, perchance, I too may have troubles." Then Xowalaci asked him, "How are you going to be troubled?" So the man said, "Do you make this woman sleep, so that I can go to her without her seeing me." The woman found life in the house very easy. Whenever she wished for anything, it appeared at once. About noon she felt sleepy for the first time. When night came, she prepared her bed and lay down. As soon as she was sound asleep, the man went in to her. She was not aware of this, but dreamed that a handsome man was with her. This was an entirely new dream to her. At daybreak she woke up and looked into the blanket. No one was there, although she was sure that someone had been with her. She wished to know who had been with her that night. So next evening she prepared her bed again, hoping that the same would happen; but no one came to her. She did the same every night without any one coming near her.

Soon the woman became pregnant. Xowalaci and his companion were still on the land, watching her; but she could not see them, because they were invisible to her. After a while the child was born. It was a boy. He grew very fast. The young woman made a cradle for him. After six months the boy could talk. The woman still wanted to know who the father of her child was. So one day she wrapped the child in blankets, and said, "I will neglect the boy and let him cry, and, perchance, his father may come. I will go and look at the country." She started south, carrying the baby on her back. She travelled for ten years, seeing no one and never looking at the child. After a long time she could hear only a faint sound coming from behind. Nothing remained of the boy but skin and bones. Finally she stopped at Saloma, and here for the first time she took the child from her back and looked at it. Its eyes were sunken and hollow; the boy was a mere skeleton. The woman felt bad and began to cry. She took the boy out of the cradle and went to the river to bathe. After she had put on her clothes, she felt of the child's heart. It was still beating! The boy urinated, and was dirty all over. His body was covered with maggots, and he had acquired various diseases. The woman took him to the water and washed his body. She had no milk with which to feed him: so she sang a medicine-song, and milk came to her. She gave the breast to the child, but it was too weak to suck: hence she had to feed it gradually. As the days went by, the boy grew stronger. After three days his eyes were better. Then they went back to their house, where they found plenty of food. The boy grew soon into a strong and handsome man, and was helping his mother with her work. One day he asked her, "Mother, where is your husband?" and she replied, "I only dreamed of my husband." Then she told him all that had happened before he was born; and the boy said, "Oh! perchance my father may turn up some day."

Then Xowalaci said to his companion, "The woman is home now." That night the woman longed for her husband. She had been dreaming all the time that he was a handsome man, and that her boy looked just like him. At dusk it seemed to her as if some one were coming. Her heart began to beat. Soon she heard footsteps. The door opened, and her boy exclaimed, "Oh, my father has come!" She looked and saw the man of her dreams. At first she was ashamed and bashful. The man told her all that had happened before, and claimed her as his wife.

One day Xowalaci told the man that all the world had been made for him. Then he instructed him how to act at all times and under all conditions. He also admonished him to have more children, and the man had sixteen children. The first one was a boy, then came a girl, then another boy, and so on. Half of his children went to live north of the Rogue River, while the other half settled down south of the river. Xowalaci told the man that hereafter he would obtain everything by wishing. Then he straightened out the world, made it flat, and placed the waters. He also created all sorts of animals, and cautioned the man not to cut down more trees or kill more animals than he needed. And after all this had been done, he bade him farewell and went up to the sky, saying, "You and your wife and your children shall speak different languages. You shall be the progenitors of all the different tribes."

—L. Ferrand and L. J. Frachtenberg. "Shasta and Athapascan Myths from Oregon." *Journal of American Folklore*, 1915, *28*, pp. 224–228.

SALINAN

After the Flood
Conflict between the forces of chaos and order is the focus of this Salinan Indian myth from California. Eagle, like Raven and Coyote in related myths, plays the role of the defender of creation. Jealous of his power, the old woman of the sea (ancient in her primordiality, feminine in her passivity and formlessness-which-forms, and watery to symbolize the nature of the preexistent chaos) attacks the creation with a flood. By cunning and inventiveness, Eagle saves the world; and by his creative power, ritual purgation (the sweat house) and breath of life, he molds people from elder twigs and animates them.

T HE OLD WOMAN of the Sea was jealous of Eagle and wished to be more powerful than he. So she came towards him with her basket in which she carried the sea. Continually she poured the water out of the basket until it covered all the land. It rose nearly to the top of Santa Lucia Peak where were gathered Eagle and the other animals. Then Eagle said to Puma, "Lend me your whiskers to lassoo the basket." He made a lariat out of the whiskers of Puma and lassoed the basket. Then the sea ceased rising and the old woman died.

Then said Eagle to Dove, "Fetch some earth!" Then Eagle made the world of the mud brought by the dove. Then he took three sticks of elder and formed from these a woman and two men. But still they had no life. They all entered the sweat-house. Then said Prairie-Falcon, "Fetch my *barsalilo!* Coyote went to bring it but brought a load of different wood. "No!" said Prairie-Falcon. "That is not my *barsalilo*," and Coyote had to go again. Then they all sweated. After sweating the eagle blew on the elder-wood people and they lived. Then they made a bower of branches and held a great fiesta.

—J. A. Mason. "The Language of the Salinan Indians." *University of California Publications in American Archeology and Ethnology*, 1918, *14* (1), 105.

WYOT

The Origin of Man
The development of human beings from animals is depicted in this Wyot myth from California. In the beginning, Above-Old-Man (a symbolic representation common in Pacific Northwest myths) was displeased with his creation and planned to destroy it. The people were too animalistic; they were still furry, and their speech was indistinct. (In related myths, the cause of God's displeasure is man's constant fighting.)

To avoid the oncoming flood (a reversion to the chaos of not-being), the hero

Condor wove a basket and hid in it with his sister. After the destruction of the old world and its purification in the waters, Condor and his sister emerged, mated, and produced the first proper people.

The way in which God is portrayed here and the use of the flood motif are sufficiently similar to Christian mythology to suggest that this myth may have been affected by missionary influence.

THE FIRST PEOPLE born not right they talked. It was not right. They were furry. He began to hear Above-Old-Man. He began to think about it, "How am I going to get rid of them?" In time he knew it. Condor knew it what was going to happen. Water was going to come. That is why it was woven. No one knew anything about it. Long time it was made basket was finished. Water came. His sister got in. It began to be tossed by waves. They knew nothing any more. Suddenly it no longer moved. He thought it was (floating) at anchor. That is when they pushed it (opening) aside. They looked around. Land they saw. He knew (that) people were no more. He started to look for them. He saw no one. Birds he saw. He saw wild pigeons, birds, turtle doves. He began to fly about. Then he saw coon his track. He came upon arrival he called her sister (kin). She did not look right. He kept on going. He came back. Upon arrival he-spoke again to her his sister. She did not like it. He began to study about it. He decided, "When I come back this way I intend to speak to her 'My wife?'" She laughed. A long time of that word she had been thinking his sister. They were married. Not long after she became pregnant. Person was born child was born. From then on people kept on being born. Good they were, good it was they began to use good talk. Very nice people they were. Above-Old-Man knew it they were good. He liked them. He was content. That is why he liked them.

—Gladys A. Reichard. "Wyot Grammar and Texts." *University of California Publications in American Archeology and Ethnology,* 1925, 22 (1), p. 175.

MAIDU

In the Beginning
Like the Joshua creation myth, this California Maidu myth has as its creator a marvelous guide and helper, Earth-Initiate. Descending from heaven, shining like the sun, this dazzling power brings order to the world, forming land and calling forth his sister sun, brother moon, and the stars until the watery, dark chaos of the beginning is dispelled.

Self-emergent, along with Rattlesnake, Coyote takes the place of Raven here as a trickster deity; he alone among the creatures can see the face of Earth-Initiate and understand what he is doing. But, although he is a great and powerful mediator between the sacred and profane realms, Coyote is morally ambivalent. Like the gods of many other cultures, he is *prior* to good and evil. Thus while Earth-Initiate plans for a gentle and easy world complete with a lake of renewal for the aged, Coyote wants work, suffering, and death to be the human lot. In a sequence common in Plains Indian mythology, Coyote causes death only to have his son be the first victim.

Although Coyote has great power, it is finally limited and earth-bound. He cannot create on his own: he can make the shape of people, but he cannot animate them. Nor can he conquer death and join the first man and his own son in the spirit house or in heaven. Thus the structure of the world is set until Earth-Initiate comes again and makes it all over.

I N THE BEGINNING there was no sun, no moon, no stars. All was dark, and everywhere there was only water. A raft came floating on the water. It came from the north, and in it were two persons—Turtle and Father-of-the-Secret-Society. The stream flowed very rapidly. Then from the sky a rope of feathers, was let down, and down it came Earth-Initiate. When he reached the end of the rope, he tied it to the bow of the raft, and stepped in. His face was covered and was never seen, but his body shone like the sun. He sat down, and for a long time said nothing.

At last Turtle said, "Where do you come from?" and Earth-Initiate answered, "I come from above." Then Turtle said, "Brother, can you not make for me some good dry land, so that I may sometimes come up out of the water?" Then he asked another time, "Are there going to be any people in the world?" Earth-Initiate thought awhile, then said, "Yes." Turtle asked, "How long before you are going to make people?" Earth-Initiate replied, "I don't know. You want to have some dry land: well, how am I going to get any earth to make it of?"

Turtle answered, "If you will tie a rock about my left arm, I'll dive for some." Earth-Initiate did as Turtle asked, and then, reaching around, took the end of a rope from somewhere, and tied it to Turtle. When Earth-Initiate came to the raft, there was no rope there: he just reached out and found one. Turtle said, "If the rope is not long enough, I'll jerk it once, and you must haul me up; if it is long enough, I'll give two jerks, and then you must pull me up quickly, as I shall have all the earth that I can carry." Just as Turtle went over the side of the boat, Father-of-the-Secret-Society began to shout loudly.

Turtle was gone a long time. He was gone six years; and when he came up, he was covered with green slime, he had been down so long. When he reached the top of the water, the only earth he had was a very little under his nails: the rest had all washed away. Earth-Initiate took with his right hand a stone knife from under his left armpit, and carefully scraped the earth out from under Turtle's nails. He put the earth in the palm of his hand, and rolled it about till it was round; it was as large as a small pebble. He laid it on the stern of the raft. By and by he went to look at it: it had not grown at all. The third time that he went to look at it, it had grown so that it could be spanned by the arms. The fourth time he looked, it was as big as the world, the raft was aground, and all around were mountains as far as he could see. The raft came ashore at Ta'doiko, and the place can be seen to-day.

When the raft had come to land, Turtle said, "I can't stay in the dark all the time. Can't you make a light, so that I can see?" Earth-Initiate replied, "Let us get out of the raft, and then we will see what we can do." So all three got out. Then Earth-Initiate said, "Look that way, to the east! I am going to tell my sister to come up." Then it began to grow light, and day began to break; then Father-of-the-Secret-Society began to shout loudly, and the sun came up. Turtle said, "Which way is the sun going to travel?" Earth-Initiate answered, "I'll tell her to go this way, and go down there." After the sun went down, Father-of-the-Secret-Society began to cry and shout again, and it grew very dark. Earth-Initiate said, "I'll tell my brother to come up." Then the moon rose. Then Earth-Initiate asked Turtle and Father-of-the-Secret-Society, "How do you like it?" and they both answered, "It is very good." Then Turtle asked, "Is that all you are going to do for us?" and Earth-Initiate answered, "No, I am going to do more yet." Then he called the stars each by its name, and they came out. When this was done, Turtle asked, "Now what shall we do?" Earth-Initiate replied, "Wait, and I'll show you." Then he made a tree grow at Ta'doiko—the tree called Hu'kimtsa; and Earth-Initiate and Turtle and Father-of-the-Secret-Society sat in its shade for two days. The tree was very large, and had twelve different kinds of acorns growing on it.

After they had sat for two days under the tree, they all went off to see the world that Earth-Initiate had made. They started at sunrise, and were back by sunset. Earth-Initiate travelled so fast that all they could see was a ball of fire flashing about under the ground and the water. While they were gone, Coyote and his dog Rattlesnake came up out of the ground. It is said that Coyote could see Earth-Initiate's face. When Earth-Initiate and the others came back, they found Coyote at Ta'doiko. All five of them then built huts for themselves, and lived there at Ta'doiko, but no one could go inside of Earth-Initiate's house. Soon after the travellers came back, Earth-Initiate called the birds from the air, and made the trees and then the animals. He took some mud, and of this made first a deer; after that, he made all the other animals. Sometimes Turtle would say, "That does not look well: can't you make it some other way?"

Some time after this, Earth-Initiate and Coyote were at Marysville Buttes. Earth-Initiate said, "I am going to make people." In the middle of the afternoon he began, for he had returned to Ta'doiko. He took dark red earth, mixed it with water, and made two figures—one a man, and one a woman. He laid the man on his right side, and the woman on his left, inside his house. Then he lay down himself, flat on his back, with his arms stretched out. He lay thus and sweated all the afternoon and night. Early in the morning the woman began to tickle him in the side. He kept very still, did not laugh. By and by he got up, thrust a piece of pitch-wood into the ground, and fire burst out. The two people were very white. No one to-day is as white as they were. Their eyes were pink, their hair was black, their teeth shone brightly, and they were very handsome. It is said that Earth-Initiate did not finish the hands of the people, as he did not know how it would be best to do it. Coyote saw the people, and suggested that they ought to have hands like his. Earth-Initiate said, "No, their hands shall be like mine." Then he finished them. When Coyote asked why their hands were to be like that, Earth-Initiate answered, "So that, if they are chased by bears, they can climb trees." This first man was called Ku'ksu; and the woman, Morning-Star Woman.

When Coyote had seen the two people, he asked Earth-Initiate how he had made them. When he was told, he thought, "That is not difficult. I'll do it myself." He did just as Earth-Initiate had told him, but could not help laughing, when, early in the morning, the woman poked him in the ribs. As a result of his failing to keep still, the people were glass-eyed. Earth-Initiate said, "I told you not to laugh," but Coyote declared he had not. This was the first lie.

By and by there came to be a good many people. Earth-Initiate had wanted to have everything comfortable and easy for people, so that none of them should have to work. All fruits were easy to obtain, no one was ever to get sick and die. As the people grew numerous, Earth-Initiate did not come as often as formerly, he only came to see Ku'ksu in the night. One night he said to him, "Tomorrow morning you must go to the little lake near here. Take all the people with you. I'll make you a very old man before you get to the lake." So in the morning Ku'ksu collected all the people, and went to the lake. By the time he had reached it, he was a very old man. He fell into the lake, and sank down out of sight. Pretty soon the ground began to shake, the waves overflowed the shore, and there was a great roaring under the water, like thunder. By and by Ku'ksu came up out of the water, but young again, just like a young man. Then Earth-Initiate came and spoke to the people, and said, "If you do as I tell you, everything will be well. When any of you grow old, so old that you cannot walk, come to this lake, or get some one to bring you here. You must then go down into the water as you have seen Ku'ksu do, and you will come out young again." When he had said this, he went away. He left in the night, and went up above.

All this time food had been easy to get, as Earth-Initiate had wished. The women set out baskets at night, and in the morning they found them full of food, all ready to eat, and lukewarm. One day Coyote came along. He asked the people how they lived, and they told him that all they had to do was to eat and sleep. Coyote replied, "That is no way to do: I can show you something better." Then he told them how he and Earth-Initiate had had a discussion before men had been made; how Earth-Initiate wanted everything easy, and that there should be no sickness or death, but how he had thought it would be better to have people work, get sick, and die. He said, "We'll have a burning." The people did not know what he meant; but Coyote said, "I'll show you. It is better to have a burning, for then the widows can be free." So he took all the baskets and things that the people had, hung them up on poles, made everything all ready. When all was prepared, Coyote said, "At this time you must always have games." So he fixed the moon during which these games were to be played.

Coyote told them to start the games with a foot-race, and every one got ready to run. Ku'ksu did not come, however. He sat in his hut alone, and was sad, for he knew what was going to occur. Just at this moment Rattlesnake came to Ku'ksu, and said, "What shall we do now? Everything is spoiled!" Ku'ksu did not answer, so Rattlesnake said, "Well, I'll do what I think is best." Then he went out and along the course that the racers were to go over, and hid himself, leaving his head just sticking out of a hole. By this time all the racers had started, and among them Coyote's son. He was Coyote's only child, and was very quick. He soon began to outstrip all the runners, and was in the lead. As he passed the spot where Rattlesnake had hidden himself, however, Rattlesnake raised his head and bit the boy in the ankle. In a minute the boy was dead.

Coyote was dancing about the home-stake. He was very happy, and was shouting at his son and praising him. When Rattlesnake bit the boy, and he fell dead, every one laughed at Coyote, and said, "Your son has fallen down, and is so ashamed that he does not dare to get up." Coyote said, "No, that is not it. He is dead." This was the first death. The people, however, did not understand, and picked the boy up, and brought him to Coyote. Then Coyote began to cry, and every one did the same. These were the first tears. Then Coyote took his son's body and carried it to the lake of which Earth-Initiate had told them, and threw the body in. But there was no noise, and nothing happened, and the body drifted about for four days on the surface, like a log. On the fifth day Coyote took four sacks of beads and brought them to Ku'ksu, begging him to restore his son to life. Ku'ksu did not answer. For five days Coyote begged, then Ku'ksu came out of his house bringing all his bead and bear-skins, and calling to all the people to come and watch him. He laid the body on a bear-skin, dressed it, and wrapped it up carefully. Then he dug a grave, put the body into it, and covered it up. Then he told the people, "From now on, this is what you must do. This is the way you must do till the world shall be made over."

About a year after this, in the spring, all was changed. Up to this time everybody spoke the same language. The people were having a burning, everything was ready for the next day, when in the night everybody suddenly began to speak a different language. Each man and his wife, however, spoke the same. Earth-Initiate had come in the night to Ku'ksu; and had told him about it all, and given him instructions for the next day. So, when morning came, Ku'ksu called all the people together, for he was able to speak all the languages. He told them each the names of the different animals, etc., in their languages, taught them how to cook and to hunt, gave them all their laws, and set the time for all their dances and festivals. Then he called each tribe by name, and sent them off in different directions, telling them where they were to live. He sent the warriors to the north, the singers to the west, the flute-players to the east, and the dancers to the south. So all the people went away, and left Ku'ksu and his wife alone at Ta'doiko. By and by his wife went away, leaving in the night, and going first to Marysville Buttes. Ku'ksu staid a little while longer, and then he also left. He too went to the Buttes, went into the spirit house, and sat down on the south side. He found Coyote's son there, sitting on the north side. The door was on the west.

Coyote had been trying to find out where Ku'ksu had gone, and where his own son had gone, and at last found the tracks, and followed them to the spirit house. Here we saw Ku'ksu and his son, the latter eating spirit food. Coyote wanted to go in, but Ku'ksu said, "No, wait there. You have just what you wanted, it is your own fault. Every man will now have all kinds of troubles and accidents, will have to work to get his food, and will die and be buried. This must go on till the time is out, and Earth-Initiate comes again, and everything will be made over. You must go home, and tell all the people that you have seen your son, that he is not dead." Coyote said he would go, but that he was hungry, and wanted some of the food. Ku'ksu replied, "You cannot eat that. Only ghosts may eat that food." Then Coyote went away and told all the people, "I saw my son and Ku'ksu, and he told me to kill myself." So he climbed up to the top of a tall tree, jumped off, and was killed. Then he went to the spirit house, thinking he could now have some of the food; but there was no one there, nothing at all, and so he went out, and walked away to the west, and was never seen again. Ku'ksu and Coyote's son, however, had gone up above.

—Roland B. Dixon. "The Maidu Creation Myth." *Bulletin of the American Museum of Natural History,* xvii, 39, no. 1. —Quoted in Stith Thompson (ed.). *Tales of the North American Indians.* Bloomington: Indiana University Press, 1968 (originally published 1929), pp. 24–30.

CUPENO

A Bag Hung in Space   In a second, fragmentary California myth—this one from the Cupeno tribe—Coyote has a more elevated origin. Both temporally (he is one of the first creatures) and spacially (he emerges from a bag suspended in space), the myth shows him to be most proximate to the creator. Even Coyote's language is special: emanating from a creature of the middle realm between the earth and the sky, it serves shamans from the lower world to transcend their muddy origin and communicate with the high gods.

Lévi-Strauss and other structuralists have used characters like Coyote to explain the function of myths as a reconciliation of opposites. They point out that while the primary opposition is that existing between the sacred and profane (heaven and earth, immortality and mortality, life and death), it is often expressed at a more mundane level as the distinction between farmers (those who do not kill what they eat) and hunters (those who do kill what they eat). Because Coyote and other scavengers (such as Raven, his more northern mythological counterpart) eat meat but do not kill it, they act to reconcile these opposites and, by extension, the grand oppositions life and death and heaven and earth.

I N THE BEGINNING all was dark and void. A bag hung in space. In time it opened out into two halves. From one half came coyote (isil), from the other came wild cat (tukut). They immediately fell to arguing as to which was the older. Coyote was the older because he spoke first. People had been created, but they could not see. They were in mud and darkness. They heard coyote call first and they knew that he was older. The people were not in the bag with coyote and wild cat. They arose from the mud and started to sing. Shamans today understand coyote, because people heard him first.

—E. W. Gifford. "Clans and Minorities of Southern California." *University of California Publications in American Archaeology and Ethnology,* 1918, *14* (2), 192.

OKANAGON

Origin of the Earth and People

The Okanagon Tribe from the northern forests (in the northwestern United States and British Columbia) is part of the Salishan subdivision of the Algonquin language family. Once paleolithic hunters and fishermen, the Okanagon developed a new mythology when they turned to farming under the influence of white settlers.

White influence is recognizable in this creation myth, where earlier belief in the earth as a divine mother is shadowy and adapted to a rather Christian framework. It is now the Chief who made the earth and then fashioned people from her soil, and it is he who established the significance of the directions.

The Okanagon informant assumes his people's primacy even in this largely borrowed myth, and concludes that Indians are the finest of races, closest to the true, pure color of earth.

THE CHIEF (or God) made seven worlds, of which the earth is the central one. There are three worlds above, and three below. Maybe the first priests or white people told us this, but some of us believe it now. When the Chief made the earth, he stretched it out with its head to the west, therefore the west is the head of the earth. Heaven, or the place of the dead, is in that direction, and the great rivers all flow westward. West is the direction the souls take. Some say they follow the course the waters take. Perhaps in the beginning the earth was a woman. Some Indians say so, and state that the Chief stretched her body across the world (probably the water), and that she lay with her feet east and her head west. He transformed her into the earth we live on, and he made the first Indians out of her flesh (which is the soil). Thus the first Indians were made by him from balls of red earth or mud, and this is why we are reddish-colored. Other races were made from soil of different colors. Afterwards some of these different races met at certain points and intermingled, and thus the intermediate shades of color have arisen. As red earth is more nearly related to gold and copper than other kinds of earth, therefore the Indians are nearer to gold, and finer than other races.

—James A. Teit. *Folk-Tales of the Salishan and Sahaptin Tribes. Memoirs of the American Folk-Lore Society,* 1917, II, 84. New York: G. E. Stechert, for the American Folk-Lore Society.

SALISHAN–SAHAPTIN

Making the World and People

Foreign influence is also evident in this Salishan-Sahaptin myth from Similkameen, but the merging of Judeo-Christian and native Indian features is more subtle here than in the Okanagon myth. While one great Chief still makes the earth, he does so in typical earth-diver fashion, rolling it out from a single small ball and connecting the realms of the world by an axis mundi. Even the "Adam and Eve" motif of derivative feminine creation is modified here: the first people are wolves, kin to all animals, and the first wolf-woman is made from the wolf-man's tail. The Old Testament assertions of separate animal and human creations and of the superiority of people over all other creatures is hard to maintain in this Indian myth where all creatures are finally related. Although the form of this myth may be Judeo-Christian, the message is still Indian.

T HE CHIEF ABOVE made the earth. It was small at first, and he let it increase in size. He continued to enlarge it, and rolled it out until it was very large. Then he covered it with a white dust, which became the soil. He made three worlds, one above another,—the sky world, the earth we live on, and the underworld. All are connected by a pole or tree which passes through the middle of each. Then he created the animals. At last he made a man, who, however, was also a wolf. From this man's tail he made a woman. These were the first people. They were called "Tai'en" by the old people, who knew the story well, and they were the ancestors of all the Indians.

—James A. Teit. *Folk-Tales of the Salishan and Sahaptin Tribes. Memoirs of the American Folk-Lore Society,* 1917, II, 84. New York: G. E. Stechert, for the American Folk-Lore Society.

BLOOD

The Creation of Man   J. MacLean recorded this myth
from the Blood Tribe of the Blackfoot Indian Confederacy (including the Piegan, Blackfoot, and Blood tribes) in Alberta, Canada, in the early 1880s. And he described his difficulties even then in finding genuine Indian myths: "The separation of the tribes, the rapid settlement of the country by the white people, the death of many of the old chiefs, and the depressed spirits of the people have seriously impaired the purity of the folk-lore of the natives. The following fragments were gathered from the lips of Blood Indians as I sat in their lodges with note-books in hand. The younger members of the tribe could not be relied on to relate these myths accurately. Those I have given have been repeatedly verified by the aged members of the tribe."

The disordered state of the world in the beginning is clearly dramatized in this myth: Napioa, the old creator, sent four creatures to look for earth in the bottom of the waters, but only the fourth, turtle, ever returned. And after he had made solid ground, he found on it strange, two-headed people, the untamable and monstrous remnants of chaos. Even in making human beings, Napioa had trouble distinguishing women's sexual and oral apertures. (Since both are sources of creation, physical and verbal, their connection here is not accidental.) Finally, Napioa created men and encouraged them to overcome their fear and have relations with the women.

The unsettled character of Blood Indian life and the disassociation from their religious roots is reflected not only in the myth's general tone of sadness and anxiety, but in its uncertainties about the origin of Napioa himself and of white people.

NAPIOA, the *Old Man,* floated upon a log in the waters, and had with him four animals: Mameo, the fish; Matcekupis, the frog; Maniskeo, the lizard; and Spopeo, the turtle. He sent them down into the waters in the order named, to see what they could find. The first three descended, but never returned; the turtle, however, arose with his mouth full of mud. Napioa took the mud from the mouth of the turtle, rolled it around in the hollow of his hand, and in this manner made the earth, which fell into the waters, and afterward grew to its present size.

There was only one person named Napioa. He lived in the world when the people who dwelt with him had two heads. He did not make these people, although he made the world, and how they came upon the earth no one knows. The Bloods do not know where Napioa came from. They do not know whether he was an Indian or not. He was not the ancestor of the Blackfeet, but the Creator of the Indian race. He was double-jointed. He is not dead, but is living in a great sea in the south. He did not make the white people, and the Indians do not know who made them.

After he made the earth, he first made a woman. Her mouth was slit vertically, and he was not satisfied, so he closed it, and recut it in the same shape as it has remained till to-day. Afterward he made several women, and then he made several men. The men lived together, but separate from the women, and they did not see the women for some time. When the men first saw the women they were astonished and somewhat afraid. Napioa told them to take one woman each, but they were afraid. He encouraged them, and then they each took a wife.

Napioa made the buffalo. They were quite tame. He gave bows and arrows to the Indians and told them to shoot the buffalo. They did so; and as the buffalo were tame, they killed a large number.

—J. MacLean. "Blackfoot Mythology." *Journal of American Folklore,* 1883, *6,* 166–167.

HURON

The Making of the World
The Huron Confederation of four tribes speaking the Wyandot language (of the Hokan-Siouan family) lived in Ontario and numbered about 20,000 until their continuing war with the Iroquois reached a climax in the late 1640s. Strengthened by firearms, the Iroquois attacked in 1648, decimated the Huron, and destroyed the Confederation. Remnants of the Huron joined others (the Tobacco Nation, the Neutral Nation, and the Erie Indians), but were still pursued by the Iroquois until they moved west. (A small group of Huron fled to Quebec and were ultimately given a reservation at Lorette.) Eventually the Huron who had joined with the Tobacco Nation settled in Ohio and fought with the British in the American Revolution and the War of 1812. In 1842, they moved to Kansas and in 1867 to northeastern Oklahoma, where they now reside as citizens.

These forced migrations are not reflected in the Huron's creation myth, which is typical of the tribes of the eastern woodlands. Although a Catholic mission was established amongst them in 1642 by Father Jean de Brébuff, the strong dualistic nature of this myth presumably did not derive from Christianity. Rather, it seems a development of the double characteristics of most culture heroes and tricksters gods. Instead of both good and evil forces being contained in one hero, here they are externalized and separated into two individuals.

In the beginning, when the world was chaotic, all the creatures were present and welcoming to the sacred woman who fell from heaven. It was they who saved her and dove for earth so that she could make land. (As in some Buddhist myths, the turtle holds up the earth here; when he moves, the earth will crumble.) Although killed by the birth of her evil son, the continuing creativity of the fallen goddess is emphasized by the transformation of her body into essential plants. Her power is echoed by that of her sons: after creating all the good and bad creatures in their separate domains, the malevolent twin is visited by his opposite. The good hero subdues all the monsters (cutting them down to an appropriate size), and agrees to a final combat with his brother.

Although they are anthropomorphized here, the twins are called Good Mind and Evil Mind in some Huron cosmologies. That kind of sophistication is evident even in the depiction of their struggle in this myth, where each understands the specific vulnerability of the other. When Good (being) ultimately wins, Evil (not-being) departs to the west to establish a land of the dead.

I N THE BEGINNING there was nothing but water, a wide sea, which was peopled by various animals of the kind that live in and upon the water. It happened then that a woman fell down from the upper world. It is supposed that she was, by some mischance, pushed down by her husband through a rift in the sky. Though styled a woman, she was a divine personage. Two loons, which were flying over the water, happened to look up and see her falling. To save her from drowning they hastened to place themselves beneath her, joining their bodies together so as to form a cushion for her to rest on. In this way they held her up, while they cried with a loud voice to summon the other animals to their aid. The cry of the loon can be heard to a great distance, and the other creatures of the sea heard it and assembled to learn the cause of the summons. Then came the tortoise (or "snapping turtle," as Clarke called it), a mighty animal, which consented to relieve the loons of their burden. They placed the woman on the back of the tortoise, charging him to take care of her. The tortoise then called the other animals to a grand council, to determine what should be done to preserve the life of the woman. They decided that she must have earth to live on. The tortoise directed them all to dive to the bottom of the sea and endeavor to bring up some earth. Many attempted it,—the beaver, the musk-rat, the diver, and others,—but without success. Some remained so long below that when they rose they were dead. The tortoise searched their mouths, but could find no trace of earth. At last the toad went down, and after remaining a long time rose, exhausted and nearly dead. On searching his mouth the tortoise found in it some earth, which he gave to the woman. She took it and placed it carefully around the edge of the tortoise's shell. When thus placed, it became the beginning of dry land. The land grew and extended on every side, forming at last a great country, fit for vegetation. All was sustained by the tortoise, which still supports the earth.

When the woman fell she was pregnant with twins. When these came forth they evinced opposite dispositions, the one good, the other evil. Even before they were born the same characters were manifested. They struggled together, and their mother heard them disputing. The one declared his willingness to be born in the usual manner, while the other malignantly refused, and, breaking through his mother's side, killed her. She was buried, and from her body sprang the various vegetable productions which the earth required to fit it for the habitation of man. From her head grew the pumpkin-vine; from her breasts the maize; from her limbs the bean and the other useful esculents. Meanwhile the twins grew up, showing in all they did their opposing inclinations. The name of the good one was Tijuskeha, which means, Clarke said, something like saviour, or good man. The evil brother was named Tawiskarong, meaning flinty, or flint-like, in allusion probably to his hard and cruel nature. They were not men, but supernatural beings, who were to prepare the world to be the abode of men. Finding that they could not live together, they separated, each taking his own portion of the earth. Their first act was to create animals of various kinds. The bad brother made fierce and monstrous creatures, proper to terrify and destroy mankind,—serpents, panthers, wolves, bears, all of enormous size, and huge mosquitoes, "as large as turkeys." Among other things he made an immense toad, which drank up all the fresh water that was on the earth. In the mean time the good brother, in his province, was creating the innocent and useful animals. Among the rest he made the partridge. To his surprise, the bird rose in the air and flew toward the territory of Tawiskarong. Tijuskeha asked him whither he was going. The bird replied that he was going to look for water, as there was none left in that land, and he heard there was some in the dominion of Tawiskarong. Tijuskeha then began to suspect mischief. He followed the course which the partridge had taken, and presently reached the land of his evil brother. Here he encountered the snakes, ferocious brutes, and enormous insects which his brother had made, and overcame them. Finally he came to the monstrous toad, which he cut open, letting the water flow forth. He did not destroy the evil animals,—perhaps had not the power to do so,—but he reduced them in size, so that men would be able to master them.

The spirit of his mother warned him in a dream to beware of his evil brother, who would endeavor to destroy him by treachery. Finally they encountered, and as it was evident that they could not live together on the earth, they determined to decide by a formal combat (a duel, as Clarke styled it) which of them should remain master of the world. It was further agreed that each should make known to the other the only weapon by which he could be overcome. This extraordinary article of their agreement was probably made necessary by the fact that without such a disclosure the contest would have lasted forever. The good brother declared that he could be destroyed only by being beaten to death with a bag full of corn, beans, or some other product of the bread kind; the evil brother rejoined that he could be killed only by the horn of a deer or of some other wild animal. (In these weapons it seems evident that there is some reference to the different characters or attributes of the brothers.) They set off a fighting-ground, or "list," within which the combat was to take place. Tawiskarong had the first turn, or, as duellists would say, the first fire. He set upon his brother with a bag of corn or beans, chased him about the ground, and pounded him until he was nearly lifeless and lay as if dead. He revived, however (perhaps through the aid of his mother's spirit), and, recovering his strength, pursued in turn his evil brother, beating him with a deer's horn until he killed him. But the slain combatant was not utterly destroyed. He reappeared after death to his brother, and told him that he had gone to the far west, and that thenceforth all the races of men after death would go to the west, like him. "And," said Clarke, "it is the belief of all the pagan Indians that after death their spirits will go to the far west, and dwell there."

—Horatio Hale. "Huron Folklore." *Journal of American Folklore*, 1888, *1e*, 175–183. Boston: Houghton Mifflin, for the American Folklore Society, 1888. Reprinted by Kraus Publishing, New York, 1963.

MANDAN

First Creator and Lone Man

When North American Indian tribes were not destroyed by white men, they were often decimated by their weapons and diseases: the Mandan were ultimately victims of cholera and smallpox. Tradition describes a more eastern origin, but by the middle of the eighteenth century they resided in nine villages near the mouth of the Heart River in the southern part of central North Dakota. Suffering severely from attacks by the Assiniboine and Sioux and finally all but wiped out by smallpox, they moved westward along to Missouri to the Knife River. When Lewis and Clarke visited in 1804, the Mandan numbered about 1,250; by 1837, after another outbreak of smallpox and cholera, there were only 150 left. Joining with the Hidatsa and eventually the Arikara tribes, they moved north to Fort Berthold, where they now live on a reservation.

Related by the mother of Arthur Mandan who recorded it at a Catholic mission in the late 1920s, the Mandan myth combines many Indian and Christian features. In an Arikara myth, Lone Man was born from a plant, but here he walks over the newly created earth with the First Creator. The earth-diver motif, Lone Man's birth, and his thwarting of the evil and chaotic monsters are typically Indian. Even his claim of connection between his body and the cedar tree, possibly echoed in the cross of Christ, is related to other Plains Indian myths: in another Arikara myth, Corn Mother left a cedar tree to represent her when she departed from the people. Here it is constructed with hoops, forming a kind of basket protection against the flood to come; and, with its characteristics as a pointer to the heavens and a source of life, it is a perfect religious symbol of the axis mundi. (It was around this cedar tree, called the Great Canoe, that the Mandan conducted their most sacred Okipa ceremony, in which great warriors sacrificed themselves through dances and pain for the good of the world and the placation of evil spirits.)

The total goodness of Lone Man, however, introduces a rather Christian element into the myth. This is particularly evident in his refusal to marry, in his rebuke of the evil spirits, and in his claims of creation. (In related Arikara myths, he fights with evil spirits, but these are more typically primordial, personifications of the recently thwarted chaos.)

I N THE BEGINNING the surface of the earth was all water and there was darkness. The First Creator and Lone Man were walking on the top of the waters and as they were walking along they happened to see a small object which seemed to have life and upon investigation they found it to be a small bird of the duck family—the kind that is very fond of diving.—"Well!" they said, "Let us ask this creature where it gets its subsistence. We don't see any kind of food on the waters and she must have something to keep her alive." So they asked her and she told them that she got her food in the bed of the waters. They asked her to show them a sample of the food. She told them she would be very glad to do so and at once she dived down to the bed of the waters and up she came with a small ball of sand. Upon seeing the sand they said, "Well! if this keeps the bird alive it must be good for other creatures also. Let us create land out of this substance, and living creatures, and let us make the land productive that it may bear fruit for the subsistence of the creatures that we shall create. Let us choose therefore the directions where each shall begin." So Lone Man chose the northern part and the First Creator the southern, and they left a space between in the water which is the Missouri river. Then, after agreeing to compare results, they began the creation.

The First Creator made broad valleys, hills, coulees with timber, mountain streams, springs, and, as creatures, the buffalo elk, black-tailed and white-tailed antelope, mountain sheep and all other creatures useful to mankind for food and clothing. He made the valleys and coulees as shelter for the animals as well as for mankind. He set lakes far apart. Lone Man created for the most part level country with lakes and small streams and rivers far apart. The animals he made lived some of them in the water, like beaver, otter, and muskrat. Others were the cattle of many colors with long horns and long tails, moose, and other animals.

After all this was ended they met as agreed upon to compare their creations. First they inspected what Lone Man had created and then they went on to what First Creator had made, then they began to compare results. First Creator said, "The things you have created do not meet with my approval. The land is too level and affords no protection to man. Look at the land I have created. It contains all kinds of game, it has buttes and mountains by which man can mark his direction. Your land is so level that a man will easily lose his way for there are no high hills as signs to direct him. Look at the waters I have created,—the rivers, brooks, springs with running water always pure and refreshing for man and beast. In summer the springs are always cool, in winter they are always warm. The lakes you have made have most of them no outlet and hence become impure. The things I have made are far more useful to man. Look at the buffalo,—they are all black save here and there a white one so rare as to be highly prized. In winter their hair grows long and shaggy to combat the cold; in warm weather they shed their hair in order to endure the heat more comfortably. But look at the cattle you have created with long horns and tail, of all colors, and with hair so short and smooth that they cannot stand the cold!" Lone Man said, "These things I have created I thought were the very things most useful to man. I cannot very well change them now that they are once created. So let us make man use first the things that you have made until the supply is exhausted and then the generations to come shall utilize those things which I have created." So it was agreed between them and both blessed their creation and the two parted.

In the course of time Lone Man looked upon the creation and saw mankind multiplying and was pleased, but he also saw evil spirits that harmed mankind and he wanted to live among the men that he had created and be as one of them. He looked about among all nations and peoples to find a virgin to be his mother and discovered a very humble family consisting of a father, mother and daughter. This virgin he chose to be his mother. So one morning when the young woman was roasting corn and eating it he thought this would be the proper time to enter into the young woman. So he changed himself into corn and the young woman ate it and conceived the seed. In the course of time the parents noticed that she was with child and they questioned her, saying, "How is it, daughter, that you are with child when you have not known man? Have you concealed anything from us?" She answered, "As you say, I have known no man. All I know is that at the time when I ate roast corn I thought that I had conceived something, then I did not think of the matter again until I knew I was with child." So the parents knew that this must be a marvel since the child was not conceived through any man, and they questioned her no more.

In course of time the child was born and he grew up like other children, but he showed unusual traits of purity and as he grew to manhood he despised all evil and never even married. Everything he did was to promote goodness. If a quarrel arose among the people he would pacify them with kind words. He loved the children and they followed him around wherever he went. Every morning he purified himself with incense, which fact goes to show that he was pure.

The people of the place where he was born were at that time Mandans. They were in the habit of going to an island in the ocean off the mouth of a river to gather *ma-ta-ba-ho*. For the journey they used a boat by the name of *I-di-he* (which means Self Going); all they had to do was to strike it on one side and tell it to go and it went. This boat carried twelve persons and no more; if more went in the boat it brought ill luck. On the way to the island they were accustomed to meet dangerous obstacles.

One day there was a party setting out for the island to get some *ma-ta-ba-ho* and everyone came to the shore to see them off and wish them good luck. The twelve men got into the boat and were about to strike the boat on the side for the start when Lone Man stepped into the boat, saying that he wanted to go too. The men in the boat as well as the people on the shore objected that he would bring ill luck, but he persisted in accompanying them and finally, seeing that they could not get rid of him, they proceeded on the journey.

Now on the way down the river, evil spirits that lived in the water came out to do them harm, but every time they came to the surface Lone Man would rebuke them and tell them to go back and never show themselves again. As they neared the mouth of the river, at one place the willows along the bank changed into young men who were really evil spirits and challenged the men in the boat to come ashore and wrestle with them. Lone Man accepted the challenge. Everyone with whom he wrestled he threw and killed until the wrestlers, seeing that they were beaten, took to their heels. Then he rebuked the willows, saying that he had made them all and they should not turn themselves into evil spirits any more. When they reached the ocean they were confronted by a great whirlpool, into which the men in the boat began to cast trinkets as a sacrifice in order to pacify it, but every time they threw in a trinket Lone Man would pick it up saying that he wanted it for himself. Meanwhile, in spite of all they could do, the whirlpool sucked them in closer. Then the men began to murmur against Lone Man and complain that he brought them ill luck and lament that they were to be sucked in by the whirlpool. Then Lone Man rebuked the whirlpool saying, "Do you not know that I am he who created you? Now I command you to be still." And immediately the waters became smooth. So they kept on the journey until they came to a part of the ocean where the waves were rough. Here the men again began to offer sacrifices to pacify the waves, but in spite of their prayers and offerings the waves grew ever more violent. And this time Lone Man was picking up the offerings and the men were trying to persuade him not to do so, but he kept right on,—never stopped! By this time the boat was rocking pretty badly with the waves and the men began to murmur again and say that Lone Man was causing their death. Then he rebuked the waves, saying, "Peace, be still," and all at once the sea was still and calm and continued so for the rest of the trip.

Upon the island there were inhabitants under a chief named Ma-na-ge (perhaps water of some kind). On their arrival, the chief told the inhabitants of his village to prepare a big feast for the visitors at which he would order the visitors to eat all the food set before them and thus kill them. Lone Man foresaw that this would happen and on his way he plucked a bulrush and inserted it by way of his throat through his system. So when the feast was prepared and all were seated in a row with the food placed before them, he told the men each to eat a little from the dish as it passed from one man to the next until it reached Lone Man, when he would empty the whole contents of the dish into the bulrush, by which means it passed to the fourth strata of the earth. When all the food was gone, Lone Man looked about as if for more and said, "Well! I always heard that these people were very generous in feeding visitors. If this is all you have to offer I should hardly consider it a feast." All the people looked at the thirteen men and when they saw no signs of sickness they regarded them as mysterious.

Next Ma-na-ge asked the visitors if they wanted to smoke. Lone Man said "Certainly! for we have heard what good tobacco you have." This pleased Ma-na-ge, for he thought he would surely kill the men by the effects of the tobacco. So he called for his pipe, which was as big as a pot. He filled the pipe and lighted it and handed it over to the men. Each took a few puffs until it came to Lone Man, who, instead of puffing out the smoke, drew it all down the bulrush to the fourth strata of the earth. So in no time the whole contents of the pipe was smoked. Then he said he had always heard that Ma-na-ge was accustomed to kill his visitors by smoking with them but if this was the pipe he used it was not even large enough to satisfy him. From that time on Ma-na-ge watched him pretty closely.

(You may put in about the women if you want to).

Now Lone Man was in disguise. The chief then asked his visitors for their bags to fill with the ma-ta-ba-ho, as much as each man had strength to carry, and each produced his bag. Lone Man's was a small bag made of two buffalo hides sewed together, but they had to keep putting in to fill it. The chief watched them pretty closely by this time and thought, "If he gets away with that load he must be Lone Man!" So when the bag was filled, Lone Man took the bag by the left hand, slung it over his right shoulder and began to walk away. Then Ma-na-ge said, "Lone Man, do you think that we don't know you?" Said Lone Man as he walked away, "Perhaps you think that I am Lone Man!" Ma-na-ge said, "We shall come over to visit you on the fourth night after you reach home." By this he meant, in the fourth year.

When they reached home, Lone Man instructed his people how to perform ceremonies as to himself and appointed the men who were to perform them. He told them to clear a round space in the center of the village and to build a round barricade about it and to take four young cottonwood trees as a hoop. In the center of the barricade they were to set up a cedar and paint it with red earth and burn incense and offer sacrifices to the cedar. Lone Man said, "This cedar is my body which I leave with you as a protection from all harm, and this barricade will be a protection from the destruction of the water. For as Ma-na-ge said, they are coming to visit you. This shall be the sign of their coming. There will be a heavy fog for four days and four nights, then you may know that they are coming to destroy you. But it is nothing but water. When it comes, it will rise no higher than the first hoop next to the ground and when it can get no higher it will subside.

After he had instructed them in all the rites and ceremonies they should perform he said, "Now I am going to leave you—I am going to the south—to other peoples—and shall come back again. But always remember that I leave with you my body." And he departed to the south. And after four years Ma-na-ge made his visit in the form of water and tried in every way to destroy the inhabitants of the village, but when he failed to rise higher than the first hoop he subsided.

—Martha Warren Beckwith. *Mandan-Hitatsa Myths and Ceremonies. Memoirs of the American Folklore Society,* 1938, 1–7. New York: J. J. Augustin, for the American Folklore Society, 1937.

ASSINIBOINE

The Making of Men and Horses
Many Plains Indians tell of a great sky god and many lesser, intermediary spirits (thunder, lightning, sun, moon, and stars) who travel through their sacred world in search of

game until one falls down a hole into the chaos of earth below and creates the world. This Assiniboine myth is missing that preface: it begins with a flood, a state of chaotic potentiality, and Inktonmi, the orderer who caused dirt to be brought out of the water and land to be made.

The creation of horses is an interesting part of the myth. The Assiniboine, like other tribes, did not have horses in any number until the eighteenth century, and yet they still credit the creation of horses to the wolf-god Inktonmi in the beginning of the world. The overwhelming importance of horses to relatively modern Assiniboine culture is thus expressed mythologically as essential, original, and determined from the start. What is essential becomes "first" when temporalized.

A particularly charming feature of this myth is its portayal of determination: having been silenced and even killed by the creator in an argument over the length of winter, the frog still makes his point with body language.

ALL THE EARTH was flooded with water. Inktonmi sent animals to dive for dirt at the bottom of the sea. No animal was able to get any. At last he sent the Muskrat. It came up dead, but with dirt in its claws. Inktonmi saw the dirt, took it, and made the earth out of it.

Inktonmi was wearing a wolf-skin robe. He said, "There shall be as many months as there are hairs on this skin before it shall be summer." Frog said, "If the winter lasts as long as that, no creature will be able to live. Seven months of winter will be enough." He kept on repeating this, until Inktonmi got angry, and killed him. Still Frog stuck out seven of his toes. Finally, Inktonmi consented, and said there should be seven winter months.

Inktonmi then created men and horses out of dirt. Some of the Assiniboine and other northern tribes had no horses. Inktonmi told the Assiniboine that they were always to steal horses from other tribes.

—R. H. Lowie. "The Assiniboine." *Anthropological Papers of the American Museum of Natural History.* New York, 1909, *4* (1), 1.

CHEROKEE

How the World Was Made The Cherokee were

the largest tribe in the southeastern part of the United States, inhabiting the mountainous regions of North and South Carolina, Georgia, Alabama, and Tennessee, until gold was discovered on their lands and they were forcibly removed by military troops in 1838. Several thousand Cherokee died on that long march to the Indian Territory (in what is now Oklahoma); those who survived it established a new community with its own public school system, newspapers, and so on.

When De Soto visited the Cherokee in 1540, he found a settled and advanced agricultural society. The smoky river pearls he was given as a welcoming gift had been part of the finery associated with the great Mound Builder cultures of the Mississippi and Ohio regions. Several rituals, such as the Cherokee's sacred ball game, attest to connections between these civilizations and the people who eventually established the Aztec empire, but contact seems to have been broken off before the Aztec era. The religion and myths of these southeastern Indian cultures gradually devolved under pressure from white settlers, disease, and war, and many of their important religious figures became, like Br'er Rabbit (once a powerful trickster deity), the heroes only of "children's fairy tales."

This Cherokee myth bears little stamp of the specifically southeastern Indian culture. It envisages a three-tiered universe held together by five cords, the formation of land by the earth-diver Water-Beetle and its hardening by the Great Buzzard (similar to the Ainu myth), the proper positioning of the sun and the creation of plants, animals, and people. Uncertainty of origins, most understandable in a brutalized and resettled people cut off from their land and traditions, is evident in the myth's confusion about the identity of the creator.

THE EARTH is a great island floating in a sea of water, and suspended at each of the four cardinal points by a cord hanging down from the sky vault, which is of solid rock. When the world grows old and worn out, the people will die and the cords will break and let the earth sink down into the ocean, and all will be water again. The Indians are afraid of this.

When all was water, the animals were above in Galun'lati, beyond the arch; but it was very much crowded, and they were wanting more room. They wondered what was below the water, and at last Dayuni'si, "Beaver's Grandchild," the little Water-beetle, offered to go and see if it could learn. It darted in every direction over the surface of the water, but could find no firm place to rest. Then it dived to the bottom and came up with some soft mud, which began to grow and spread on every side until it became the island which we call the earth. It was afterward fastened to the sky with four cords, but no one remembers who did this.

At first the earth was flat and very soft and wet. The animals were anxious to get down, and sent out different birds to see if it was yet dry, but they found no place to alight and came back again to Galun'lati. At last it seemed to be time, and they sent out the Buzzard and told him to go and make ready for them. This was the Great Buzzard, the father of all the buzzards we see now. He flew all over the earth, low down near the ground, and it was still soft. When he reached the Cherokee country, he was very tired, and his wings began to flap and strike the ground, and wherever they struck the earth there was a valley, and where they turned up again there was a mountain. When the animals above saw this, they were afraid that the whole world would be mountains, so they called him back, but the Cherokee country remains full of mountains to this day.

When the earth was dry and the animals came down, it was still dark, so they got the sun and set it in a track to go every day across the island from east to west, just overhead. It was too hot this way, and Tsiska'gili, the Red Crawfish, had his shell scorched a bright red, so that his meat was spoiled; and the Cherokee do not eat it. The conjurers put the sun another hand-breadth higher in the air, but it was still too hot. They raised it another time, and another, until it was seven handbreadths high and just under the sky arch. Then it was right, and they left it so. This is why the conjurers call the highest place Gulkwa'gine Di'galun'latiyun, "the seventh height," because it is seven hand-breadths above the earth. Every day the sun goes along under this arch, and returns at night on the upper side to the starting place.

There is another world under this, and it is like ours in everything—animals, plants, and people—save that the seasons are different. The streams that come down from the mountains are the trails by which we reach this underworld, and the springs at their heads are the doorways by which we enter it, but to do this one must fast and go to water and have one of the underground people for a guide. We know that the seasons in the underworld are different from ours, because the water in the springs is always warmer in winter and cooler in summer than the outer air.

When the animals and plants were first made—we do not know by whom—they were told to watch and keep awake for seven nights, just as young men now fast and keep awake when they pray to their medicine. They tried to do this, and nearly all were awake through the first night, but the next night several dropped off to sleep, and the third night others were asleep, and then others, until, on the seventh night, of all the animals only the owl, the panther, and one or two more were still awake. To these were given the power to see and to go about in the dark, and to make prey of the birds and animals which must sleep at night. Of the trees only the cedar, the pine, the spruce, the holly, and the laurel were awake to the end, and to them it was given to be always green and to be greatest for medicine, but to the others it was said: "Because you have not endured to the end you shall lose your hair every winter."

Men came after the animals and plants. At first there were only a brother and sister until he struck her with a fish and told her to multiply, and so it was. In seven days a child was born to her, and thereafter every seven days another, and they increased very fast until there was danger that the world could not keep them. Then it was made that a woman should have only one child in a year, and it has been so ever since.

—J. Mooney. *Myths of the Cherokee. 19th Annual Report of the Bureau of Ethnology*, Part 1. Washington, D.C.: 1897–1898, pp. 239–240.

YUCHI

Creation of the Earth
Along with the "Five Civilized Tribes" (Cherokee, Chichasaw, Choctaw, Creek, and Seminole)—60,000 in all—the Yuchi people were also deported from their lands in Georgia to the Indian Territory in Oklahoma in 1838. In addition to the real severities of the march itself, the experience of resettlement was deeply wrenching. The Yuchi had a matrilineal social structure, but in Oklahoma assignments of land were made to men, food was rationed to men as heads of their households, election of male officials was accomplished on a territorial and not kinship basis, and inheritance was determined on the male, not the female, line. Gradually those of the tribe who survived changed their way of being and adopted a patrilineal structure more common among whites and the local Plains Indians.

This Yuchi creation myth, recorded in the early 1900s, still retains some matrilineal features: the Sun is deified, as is common in many planting cultures, but when anthropomorphized appears atypically as a woman, the mother of people who sprang from a drop of her blood. This myth is also distinguished by its recognition of the life-giving power of chaos not only as the source of matter, the stuff of the creation, but also as the basis for healing medicine. The great serpent of fertility and infinity (he is often shown swallowing his own tail, thereby forming an unending circle) is finally killed on a cedar tree, usually sacred to Plains Indians, and the great medicine is found there.

I N THE BEGINNING the waters covered everything. It was said "Who will make the land appear?"

Lock-chew, the Crawfish, said: "I will make the land appear."

So he went down to the bottom of the water and began to stir up the mud with his tail and hands. He then brought up the mud to a certain place and piled it up.

The owners of the land at the bottom of the water said:

"Who is disturbing our land?" They kept watch and discovered the Crawfish. Then they came near him, but he suddenly stirred the mud with his tail so that they could not see him.

"Lock-chew continued his work. He carried mud and piled it up until at last he held up his hands in the air, and so the land appeared above the water.

The land was soft. It was said: "Who will spread out the land and make it dry and hard?" Some said: "Ah-yok, the Hawk, should spread out the soft land and make it dry." Others said "Yah-tee, the Buzzard, has larger wings; he can spread out the land and make it dry and hard."

Yah-tee undertook to spread out and dry the earth. He flew above the earth and spread out his long wings over it. He sailed over the earth; he spread it out. After a long while he grew tired of holding out his wings. He began to flap them, and thus he caused the hills and valleys because the dirt was still soft.

"Who will make the light?" it was said. It was very dark.

Yohah, the Star, said, "I will make the light."

It was so agreed. The Star shone forth. It was light only near him.

"Who will make more light?" it was said.

Shar-pah, the Moon, said: "I will make more light." Shar-pah made more light, but it was still dark.

T-cho, the Sun, said: "You are my children, I am your mother, I will make the light. I will shine for you."

She went to the east. Suddenly light spread over all the earth. As she passed over the earth a drop of blood fell from her to the ground, and from this blood and earth sprang the first people, the children of the Sun, the Uchees.

The people wished to find their medicine. A great monster serpent destroyed the people. They cut his head from his body. The next day the body and head were together. They again slew the monster. His head again grew to his body.

Then they cut off his head and placed it on top of a tree, so that the body could not reach it. The next morning the tree was dead and the head was united to the body. They again severed it and put it upon another tree. In the morning the tree was dead and the head and body were reunited.

The people continued to try all the trees in the forest. At last they placed the head over the Tar, the cedar tree, and in the morning the head was dead. The cedar was alive, but covered with blood, which had trickled down from the head. Thus the Great Medicine was found.

Fire was made by boring with a stick into a hard weed.

The people selected a second family. Each member of this family had engraved on his door a picture of the sun.

In the beginning all the animals could talk, and but one language was used. All were at peace. The deer lived in a cave, watched over by a keeper and the people were hungry. He selected a deer and killed it. But finally the deer were set free and roved over the entire earth.

All animals were set free from man, and names were given to them, so that they could be known.

—John R. Swanton. "Creek Stories," No. 90. *U.S. Bureau of American Ethnology Bulletin 88 (Myths and Tales of the South Eastern Indians)*. Washington, D.C.: Government Printing Office, 1929, pp. 84–85.

FOUR APACHE CREATION MYTHS

The ancestors of the Apache entered the southwestern part of what is now the United States around 1000 A.D. from the north, following the herds of buffalo and other game they hunted. At the time of contact with the Spanish, they were still dividing into separate subtribes: among them, the Jicarilla and Lipan lived east of the Rio Grande, while the White Mountain (an aggregate of subtribes) and the Chiricahua moved to the west. Social organization remained simple, because the harsh desert conditions required living in small groups. With the acquisition of horses and firearms, intertribal warface escalated and ultimately permitted the raiding of neighboring settlements to become a way of life. Although their own name for themselves was *Tinde* ("the people"), they were called *Apache* ("enemy") by the Zuni.

Renowned for their fighting ability, the Apache successfully resisted Spanish and later Mexican and American incursions until the middle of the nineteenth century when the United States obtained the region and began large-scale migrations westward through their lands. Strong Apache resistance lasted until 1886 when Geronimo and his Chiricahua followers surrendered. Remnants of the tribes now live on reservations in Arizona and New Mexico.

CHIRICAHUA APACHE

When the Earth Was New After the Indian War of 1886, the Chiricahua were removed from Arizona and imprisoned first in Florida, then Alabama, and finally Fort Sill, Oklahoma, where they were released in 1913. The majority of those remaining joined the Mescalero Reservation in New Mexico, where this myth was recorded.

Strongly influenced by the punitive aspects of Christian doctrine, the myth recalls a flood sent to destroy the people who worshipped Indian—now *false*—gods. The creators of the Indians presumably escaped, but pottery and arrowheads were all that remained of their creations. When the waters receded and people again populated the earth, they were offered a choice of weapons. That the white man took the gun and the Indian was left with bow and arrow signifies to the informant the unfortunate turn of events that led to his present situation.

THERE WERE many people on earth. They did not know God. They prayed to the Gahe (mountain-dwelling gods), Lightning, and Wind. They did not know about the living God. So the ocean began to rise and covered the earth. These people of ancient times were drowned. Just a few were saved.

South of Deming, New Mexico, is a tall mountain, "White-ringed Mountain." It was the only mountain which was not covered. About a half mile of it was sticking out. They have showed me the place where the water stopped. There is a circle of white like white paint all around this spot. It looks pretty.

When the flood came the turkey ran up this mountain ahead of it. The water followed and got his tail wet. That's why the turkey has white at the tips of the tail feathers.

When the water started to go down, the people, animals, and birds on the mountain top were saved and increased again from these few. I guess White-Painted Woman and Child-of-the-Water went up [to the sky] before this happened. I don't know whether the people who left pottery and arrowheads were the ones killed off by this flood.

After the water had gone down, a bow and arrow and a gun were put before two men. The man who had the first choice took the gun and he became the white man. The other had to take the bow and he became the Indian. If the second man had got the gun, he would have been the white man, they say.

—Morris Edward Opler. *Myths and Tales of the Chiricahua Apache Indians. Memoirs of the American Folklore Society,* 1942, 37, 1–2. New York: The American Folklore Society, 1942.

WHITE MOUNTAIN APACHE

The Earth Is Set Up   Believing in a universe alive with

spiritual power, the Apache recognized shamans or medicine men as people capable of bridging the gap between the sacred and profane dimensions. Possessed of great power and wise in the ways of nature, the shamans could forecast future events, counteract evil spirits, heal the sick, and guide their people in matters of proper conduct. Palmer Valor, a ninety-five-year-old shaman who related this myth in 1932 warned that: "Tales are to be told during the night, at any time from dusk to dawn. The sun should not see you doing it. They are meant to be heard only during the cold months, from November to February. In the spring, summer and fall too much danger is abroad—snakes, poisonous insects and lightning. For this reason people will wait until such evil things are absent so they will not hear themselves spoken of and punish the narrator or his family." Like his explanation, Valor's myth is full of respect for the sacred and ambivalent powers of nature. Both they and the four "people" who ordered them are described personally and with drama, reflecting the close relation between the Apaches and their world.

The White Mountain Tribe consists of several groups of Apache subtribes, including the Mimbreno, Mogollon, Pinaleno, Chiricahua, and Arivaipa. Numbering around 4,000, the tribe lives on a reservation in Arizona.

F OUR PEOPLE started to work on the earth. When they set it up, the wind blew it off again. It was weak like an old woman. They talked together about the earth among themselves. "What shall we do about this earth, my friends? We don't know what to do about it." Then one person said, "Pull it from four different sides." They did this, and the piece they pulled out on each side they made like a foot. After they did this the earth stood all right. Then on the east side of the earth they put big black cane, covered with black metal thorns. On the south side of the earth they put big blue cane covered with blue metal thorns. Then on the west side of the earth they put big yellow cane covered with yellow metal thorns. Then on the north side of the earth they put big white cane covered with white metal thorns.

After they did this the earth was almost steady, but it was still soft and mixed with water. It moved back and forth. After they had worked on the earth this way Black Wind Old Man [the wind of the east] came to this place. He threw himself against the earth. The earth was strong now and it did not move. Then Black Water Old Man threw himself against the earth. When he threw himself against the earth, thunder started in the four directions. Now the earth was steady, and it was as if born already.

But the earth was shivering. They talked about it: "My friends, what's the matter with this earth? It is cold and freezing. We better give it some hair." Then they started to make hair on the earth. They made all these grasses and bushes and trees to grow on the earth. This is its hair.

But the earth was still too weak. They started to talk about it: "My friends, let's make bones for the earth." This way they made rocky mountains and rocks sticking out of the earth. These are the earth's bones.

Then they talked about the earth again: "How will it breathe, this earth?" Then came Black Thunder to that place, and he gave the earth veins. He whipped the earth with lightning and made water start to come out. For this reason all the water runs to the west. This way the earth's head lies to the east, and its water goes to the west.

They made the sun so it traveled close over the earth from east to west. They made the sun too close to the earth and it got too hot. The people living on it were crawling around, because it was too hot. Then they talked about it: "My friends, we might as well set the sun a little further off. It is too close." So they moved the sun a little higher. But it was still too close to the earth and too hot. They talked about it again. "The sun is too close to the earth, so we better move it back." Then they moved it a little higher up. Now it was all right. This last place they set the sun is just where it is now.

Then they set the moon so it traveled close over the earth from east to west. The moon was too close to the earth and it was like daytime at night. Then they talked about it: "My friends, we better move the moon back, it is like day."

So they moved it back a way, but it was still like daylight. They talked about it again: "It is no good this way, we better move the moon higher up." So they moved it higher up, but it was still a little light. They talked about it again and moved it a little further away. Now it was just right, and that is the way the moon is today. It was night time.

This is the way they made the earth for us. This is the way all these wild fruits and foods were raised for us, and this is why we have to use them because they grow here.

—Granville Goodwin. *Myths and Tales of the White Mountain Apache. Memoirs of the American Folklore Society,* 1939, *33,* 1–2. New York: J. J. Augustin, for The American Folklore Society.

LIPAN APACHE

The Way of the Indian
Differing from Chiricahua and White Mountain peoples, the Lipan Apache envisage a chaotic beginning in which they existed, embryonic and animalistic, in the womb of the earth. With the same moral ambivalence encountered in trickster gods of other American Indian myths, the first two explorers sent up by the people betrayed and forgot them; only the badger returned and reported the existence of land.

The combined forces of two great chaotic powers, wind and water, had revealed the earth, but it was left to four "Indians" (one for each direction, a totality of power) to order it. Using one as earth material, and thus reemphasizing the symbiotic relation between the Indians and the earth, the three formed the land and made it habitable. The "people"—animals, birds and trees—then emerged from Mother Earth in a grand imitation of birth, and journeying across her surface under the direction of sun and moon (as the Lipan had on their migrations) established their new homes. This great march of the family of nature, of which human beings are only a part, emphasizes the essential unity evident in the Apache world view.

The Lipan were scattered and all but annihilated on the eve of the southwestern reservation period.

I N THE BEGINNING they were going to create human beings. The part about that is not very long. Then comes the part about Killer-of-Enemies, and that is longer. The white men have their way and the Indians have theirs. I am going to do my best to explain the way of the Indian.

Down in the lower world, at the beginning, there was no light; there was only darkness. Down there, at the bottom, were some people. They knew of no other places; they lived there.

They held a council down there. They discussed whether there was another world. They decided to send someone above to find out. They looked at each other and asked who should be sent out.

One said, "How about Wind?"

They asked him. Wind agreed to go.

Wind went upward. He was a whirlwind. He came up to this earth. Nothing but water covered the earth then. He rolled back the water like a curtain.

After the wind had rolled back the water, land appeared. The water was all at one side.

Then they sent Crow out to look over the dry land. Crow saw the dead fish that had been left on the dry land. He stayed there and picked the eyes out of the fish. He didn't come back as he had promised to do.

At that time the land was very level. There were no mountains on earth. The ground was just like ashes or like the places where there is white alkali on the earth's suface now.

The crow never came back. The people below wondered what had happened to him. They wanted news. So they sent Beaver out.

The water was getting low now. Instead of going back to his people Beaver busied himself building dams. He went around from stream to stream. The people below wondered what had happened to him.

Then, because the beaver didn't come back, they sent Badger out. He was faithful to his fellows in the lower world. He came up and looked around. He saw that it was all dry up there. He went back and told the others. Then they were all happy, for he was the only one who did faithful work.

Then they sent four others after that, four men, to look over this world above. These first four who came up on earth to prepare it were called by the word that means Indians. I know of no other name for them. These four chose one from whom were to be made the things of the earth as we know it now. They selected Mirage. They put up Mirage in the form of a ball. They walked away from Mirage and looked. It looked very pretty. That ball of mirage became a part of this earth.

Now they fixed the world. They were going to make hills and mountains. They made a little lightning. They made little arroyos, and water came running to them. That is the way the earth and the mountains, the hills and the water were made. At first it was all level, but of Mirage they made all the things of the earth.

Now all was ready on the earth. Springs and channels were made. All was prepared for the people of the lower world. Then the people of the lower world prepared to ascend. They came up to the upper world. They are here now.

After they came up, they moved around the edge of the earth clockwise. All those people were animals, birds, trees, and bushes. The real humans were not here yet. Animals, birds, grass, and trees were people at that time and could talk as humans do. They had one language and all understood each other. These were the first people. Even the rocks and the plants that are on the earth now were among these people. All these were the first people, those who were first on this earth. The animal and tree people came out first. Then the real humans came out after them. The different kinds of animals and birds, the different grasses and trees,—each represents a different tribe.

When they started from the place of emergence, the first to stop were the western people, the Chiricahua perhaps. As they went along clockwise, different people dropped off. As they stopped they became different tribes and had different languages. "You shall be such and such a people and speak this language," they were told. That is how all these different tribes and languages were made.

All the northern tribes use the dog for a horse. They used the dog for a horse at this time as they moved north.

At the very end of the journey the Tonkawa dropped off with the Lipan. The Lipan were the very last to stop the journey and find a home.

Now the people were all fixed.

When the people first came out and were going clockwise, they came to a certain stream. There the willow people stopped. "We'll stay and live here," they said. That is why the willow tree is both green and grey. It stands for the old and young at the same time.

Then a little later the alligator-barked juniper stopped. "I shall live here," he said. He was wearing turquoise beads which became his berries.

Later on another of the juniper people stopped. He too had turquoise beads which he still wears. Another juniper stopped next. He selected his place and stands there wearing turquoise. These beads became his berries.

There was still another kind of juniper who stopped next. He was wearing reddish beads and they turned to his berries.

Next oak stopped. He was wearing black stones on his head. These are his acorns now. As they went along another kind of oak stopped. He too wore black stones for decoration.

The next was an oak too. This one was also wearing black stones which are now his acorns. Next a fourth oak found a place he liked. He too wore black stones.

As they went along the chokecherry stopped. It has red berries now, for it was wearing red beads that day.

Then another tree stopped at some little hills on the east side of the Pecos. The hills run from south to southeast.

When they were moving they did not stop to sleep. They just kept moving all the time. At this place they decided to sleep, however. Someone put down a white walking cane over them. Then they went to sleep. One night passed. Then the people woke up the next day and journeyed again. They moved clockwise.

The moon and the sun took the lead then. They were with the people. The sun is the man, the moon is the woman. The moon they call Changing Woman.

These two said, "We'll go ahead. We will separate but we will meet each other." And when they meet there is an eclipse. Before they left the people they said, "Nothing will disturb you people. Everything ahead is good for you people." The sun and the moon said, "We will take the lead now. We will keep on going. We will never stop, no matter what happens here on earth; we will always keep going." The moon is Changing Woman and the sun is Killer-of-Enemies. When he left this world he went back to the sun and he is there now.

—Morris Edward Opler. *Myths and Legends of the Lipan Apache Indians. Memoirs of the American Folklore Society,* 1940, 34, 13–26, 29, 33–37. New York: J. J. Augustin, for the American Folklore Society, 1940.

JICARILLA APACHE

In the Beginning Nothing Was Here

Like the Lipan creation myth, that of the Jicarilla depicts a beginning of chaos ruled by its three great powers: Darkness, Water, and Cyclone. Shapers without shape themselves, they exist in pure potentiality, in loneliness. And the Hactcin, the divine life forces of nature, personifications of the power of things, formed Mother Earth, the underworld, and Father Sky from the chaos.

The dreamlike quality of the timeless time of the beginning is clear here: the Jicarilla Apache lived in the womb of the earth, potential and shadowy. Black Hactcin—the divine and joyous force of the east—first formed the creatures, and then the animals, birds and trees all appealed for a younger brother, a companion, and brought special things (now used in sacred ceremonies) for his making. Appealing to the powers of the world (standing to the east, south, and so on) and planning his work (tracing an outline in pollen, and so on), Black Hactcin formed his creation and inspired it with the breath of life. With the power to move and speak and laugh and shout, the man was now complete but for the wife he created in his own dream. Right, left, right, left—in steps still repeated by young girls being initiated (being created as adults), the people walked and celebrated their being with all the other creatures.

I N THE BEGINNING nothing was here where the world now stands; there was no ground, no earth,—nothing but Darkness, Water, and Cyclone. There were no people living. Only the Hactcin [personifications of the powers of objects and natural forces] existed. It was a lonely place. There were no fishes, no living things.

All the Hactcin were here from the beginning. They had the material out of which everything was created. They made the world first, the earth, the underworld, and then they made the sky. They made Earth in the form of a living woman and called her Mother. They made Sky in the form of a man and called him Father. He faces downward, and the woman faces up. He is our father and the woman is our mother.

In the beginning there were all kinds of Hactcin living in the underworld, in the place from which the emergence started. The mountains had a Hactcin, the different kinds of fruit each had one, everything had a Hactcin.

It was then that the Jicarilla Apache dwelt under the earth. Where they were there was no light, nothing but darkness. Everything was perfectly spiritual and holy, just like a Hactcin.

Everything there was as in a dream. The people were not real; they were not flesh and blood. They were like the shadows of things at first.

The most powerful Hactcin down there was Black Hactcin. The Hactcin were all there already but in the darkness Black Hactcin was the leader. It was there, before anything else was made, that Black Hactcin made all the animals.

We dwelt for many years there. It was not a few minutes or a few days. But we do not know how long it was.

This is how animals and men first came to be made. Black Hactcin first tried to make an animal. He made it with four legs of clay and put a tail on it. He looked at it. He said, "It looks rather peculiar." Then he spoke to the mud image. "Let me see how you are going to walk with those four feet." That is why little children always like to play with clay images. Then it began to walk.

"That's pretty good," said Black Hactcin. "I think I can use you in a beneficial way."

He spoke to the image. "You have no help; you are all alone. I think I will make it so that you will have others from your body."

Then all sorts of animals came out from that same body. Black Hactcin had the power; he could do anything.

Now there were all kinds of animals. Black Hactcin stood and looked. He laughed to see all those different kinds of animals; he just couldn't help it when he saw those animals with all their different habits. That is why people laugh today at the habits of animals. They see a hog and laugh at it, saying, "See that dirty animal lying in the mud." All animals were there, some with horns, like the deer and elk, some with big horns like the mountain sheep. All were present. But at that time all those animals could speak, and they spoke the Jicarilla Apache language.

And those animals spoke to Black Hactcin. Each one came to speak to him. They asked him many questions. Each asked him what he should eat and where he should go to live, and questions of that order.

The Hactcin spoke to them. He divided all foods among them. To the horse, sheep, and cow he gave grass. "That is what you shall eat," he said. To some he gave brush, to some pine needles. Some he told to eat certain kinds of leaves but no grass.

"Now you can spread over the country," he told them. "Go to your appointed places and then come back and tell me where you want to stay all your lives."

He sent some to the mountains, some to the desert, and some to the plains. That is why you find the animals in different places now. The animals went out and chose their places then. So you find the bear in the mountains and other animals in different kinds of country.

Hactcin said, "It is well. It looks well to see you in the places you have chosen."

So all the animals were set apart.

Then Black Hactcin held out his hand and asked for water to come to his hand. A drop of rain fell into his palm. He mixed it with earth and it became mud. Then he fashioned a bird from the mud. He made the head, body, wings, and two legs.

He spoke in the same way to the image he had made. "Let me see how you are going to use those wings to fly," he said. He didn't know whether he would like it. Then the mud turned to a bird. It flew around. Black Hactcin liked it. "Oh, that is fine!" he said. He enjoyed seeing the difference between this one and the ones with four legs.

"I think you need companions and someone to help you. By yourself alone you will never be satisfied. From your body there will come others with wings."

When Hactcin said this the bird became lonesome. He flew to the east, south, west, and north and came back saying, "I can find no one to help me."

The Hactcin took the bird and whirled it around rapidly in a clockwise direction. The bird grew dizzy, and, as one does when he is dizzy, this bird saw many images around. He saw all kinds of birds there: eagles, hawks, and small birds too. He could hardly believe his sight, but when he was himself again, there were really all kinds of birds there. And because Black Hactcin turned the bird around and made him dizzy, birds now circle when they rise in the air.

All different birds were there now. Birds like the air, dwell high, and seldom light on the ground because that drop of water which became the mud from which the first bird was made fell from the sky.

Then the birds came to Black Hactcin. "What shall we eat? Where shall we dwell? Where shall we rest?" they asked.

He sent them all in different directions. "Find the place you like best and tell me about it," he said.

The birds flew in all directions. All came back. Each one told of the place it liked.

"That is all right," Black Hactcin told each of them. "You may have that place for your home."

Then they asked about food. Black Hactcin held his hand up to the east, south, west, and north in turn, and because he had so much power, all kinds of seeds fell into his hand. He scattered the seeds before them. The birds were going to pick them up.

"All right, now pick them up," he said.

The birds went to do it, but the seeds turned to worms, grasshoppers, and all insects. The Hactcin was trying to tease them. They couldn't catch them at first.

Then Black Hactcin said, "Oh, it's hard work to catch those flies and grasshoppers. You can do it though."

Then they all chased the grasshoppers and other insects around. That is why many birds today use the insects for food and chase the grasshoppers around.

At the time when Black Hactcin threw the seeds down he said to Turkey, "You must be the one who takes charge of all these seeds." That is why Turkey has control of the crops now. That is why some of these Indians and the white people too use the turkey at Thanksgiving. The white people put the turkey in the middle of the table and have the fruits and vegetables all around it. The Indians use the turkey feathers too. When they plant a crop they put one turkey feather in each corner of the field. The turkey is striped just like corn. The head is like the corn tassel. Every part of the turkey's body stands for some part of the corn plant.

There was a river nearby. "You must drink from that river," Black Hactcin told them. The birds thought that was a beautiful place.

"Now I'm going to make something to scare you," Black Hactcin said. He was always teasing them.

He picked up some moss and began to roll it between his hands. Then he threw it into the water. And it became frogs, fish, and all that live in the water. That is why, often, when the birds come to drink at the water, something sticks its nose out of the water and frightens them and they jump back. Sometimes even humans are frightened in this way.

While the birds were flying around some of their feathers fell out and into the water, and these turned to water birds such as the duck, heron, sandhill crane, and others.

Now the birds and animals had everything, food and a place to stay and rest.

Black Hactcin started to make more images of animals and birds. The ones who were already made called a council and came together. The birds and animals were together at this council, for they all spoke the same language in those days.

"Now what are we going to do?" they asked Black Hactcin. "We need a companion, we need man."

"What do you mean?" asked Black Hactcin. "Why do you need another companion?"

The birds and animals said, "You are not going to be with us all the time; you will go elsewhere some of the time."

"I guess that's true. Perhaps some day I'll go away to a place where no one will see me."

So all the birds and animals gathered all different objects: pollen, specular iron ore, water scum, all kinds of pollen, from corn, tule, and the trees. They put these all together. They added red ochre, white clay, white stone, jet, turquoise, red stone, Mexican opal, abalone, and assorted valuable stones. They put all these before Black Hactcin.

He told them, "You must stay a little distance from me. I don't want you to see what I make."

He stood to the east, then to the south, then to the west, then to the north. He traced an outline of a figure on the ground, making it just like his own body, for the Hactcin was shaped just as we are today. He traced the outline with pollen. The other objects and the precious stones he placed around on the inside, and they became the flesh and bones. The veins were of turquoise, the blood of red ochre, the skin of coral, the bones of white rock, the fingernails were of Mexican opal, the pupil of the eye of jet, the whites of the eyes of abalone, the marrow in the bones of white clay, and the teeth, too, were of Mexican opal. He took a dark cloud and out of it fashioned the hair. It becomes a white cloud when you are old.

This was a man which Black Hactcin was making. And now the man came to life. "Black Hactcin sent Wind into the body of man to render him animate. The whorls at the ends of the fingers indicate the path at the time of the creation of man." He was lying down, face downward, with his arms outstretched. The birds tried to look but could not make out what it was.

"Do not look," said Black Hactcin.

Then the man braced himself up, leaning on his arms which were outstretched.

"Don't look," said Hactcin to the birds, who were very much excited now.

It was because the animals were so eager to see what Black Hactcin was making that people are so curious today, just as you were eager to know this story.

"Sit up," commanded Black Hactcin to the man, and he was sitting up now. This was the third time Black Hactcin had spoken to him.

Then Black Hactcin went over to him and facing him, picked him up. Now Hactcin tried to teach him to speak.

"Speak to me, speak, speak, speak." Black Hactcin said it four times. Then the man spoke.

Then Black Hactcin said to him four times, "Laugh, laugh, laugh, laugh," and the man laughed.

"Shout, shout, shout, shout," and the man did so.

Now Black Hactcin was teaching him to walk. "Step forward," he said and made him step with his right foot first, then with his left, then right, and then left again. Now the man could walk.

Then Black Hactcin said, "Run," and made him run four times in a clockwise arc. That is why they have to run at the girl's puberty rite just like that.

When the birds saw what Black Hactcin had made they sang and chirped as though it were early morning. That is why, when the girl who has come of age runs at the time of her puberty ceremony, an old woman stands there and makes that noise in her ear.

Now the man could talk and he understood what the birds were singing and what Black Hactcin was saying, for all had one language then. The man was the only human being living; he was by himself.

The birds and the animals thought it was not good that he should be by himself and they all came together and spoke to Black Hactcin.

Black Hactcin asked the birds and animals for some lice. "Who has lice? You must bring some to me."

They brought some. Black Hactcin put some on the man's head. He scratched and scratched. Then his eyes became heavy and he went to sleep. He was dreaming and dreaming. He dreamt that someone, a girl, was sitting beside him.

He woke up. The dream had come true. A woman was there. He spoke to his wife and she answered. He laughed and she laughed too.

He said. "Let us both get up."

They both arose.

"Let's walk," he told her. "Right, left, right, left." He led her for four steps.

"Run!" he said, and they both ran.

Now another person was there. The birds sang and chirped. They wanted to make pleasant music for them so they wouldn't become lonesome.

The names of these first two were Ancestral Man and Ancestral Woman.

—Morris Edward Opler. *Myths and Tales of the Jicarilla Apache Indians.* New York: G. E. Stechert, for the American Folklore Society, 1938, 1–6.

HOPI

The Emergence "Who are we? Why are we here?" are the questions central to this Hopi myth of emergence, and the answer expressed directly and also implied throughout is to live and be happy by respecting the love of the creater in wisdom and harmony. But the people continually forget this basic religious command, and the myth charts their journey from the beginning through failures to new hope.

Originally, there was only Taiowa and the first world of endless space existed in his mind. "Then he, the infinite, conceived the finite," and so creation began. Delineating a dependent and active force within himself, Taiowa created his "nephew" Sotuknang and had him arrange the nine-tiered world. Then Sotuknang formed Spider Woman who, with a mixture of earth, saliva (raw material and a fertilizing agent), and creative wisdom (a forming principle) made twin gods to harden the earth, to animate it with vibration and sound, and finally to guard it at the two poles. After having formed plants, birds, and animals in the same manner, she made the four colors of people in three stages, and the dawn broke, and the sun (Taiowa's symbol) rose to greet its creatures. Only Sotuknang, however, could make people independently creative, and this he did by giving them speech, reproductive power, and the wisdom to use them well.

Physically complete, the people's spiritual development was just beginning. In stages appropriate to psychosexual development as well as to cultural and religious development, the people moved from one stage or world to another in a manner imitative of birth. (Just so do the Hopi initiates emerge from the roof of their *kivas* on the last night of the year when the fires have been extinguished and the new ones are about to be lit. Having listened to the Emergence Story, they climb up the ladder of the *kiva* into the new world of adulthood and membership into the group.)

From the first world of harmony and unity with its sins of attention to differences and consequent warring, to the second world of culture and commerce and its sins of greed and acquisitiveness, and finally through the third world of civilization and technology and its sins of hatred and warfare, the faithful finally emerge to journey northeastward across water (implying a southern Asian origin) to the new, present, fourth world of migrations and final settlement. It is a spiritual odyssey from the worldly back to the world, and signs of sacrality permeate it. The myth eloquently proclaims the holiness of all, the fundamental unity of spirit and matter and the relation of all things through endless correspondences. The four types of life-giving corn, the colors, sounds, plants, animals, minerals, and directions—all resonate with the same holy vibrations as the world itself. Microcosms within macrocosms, the individual's body is to the society what the society is to the world, and all are ordered in the same fashion, dependent on the holy power of the creator.

The Hopi (or "peaceful ones") live in nine villages in a reservation on the mesas of northeastern Arizona. Although visited by the Spanish under Pedro de Tovar in 1540, their remote location saved them from major colonist influence. They repulsed the Franciscan attempt to establish Christian missions among them in the seventeenth century and have remained one of the least white-influenced of the American Indian peoples.

TOKPELA: THE FIRST WORLD   The first world was Tokpela [Endless Space].

But first, they say, there was only the Creator, Taiowa. All else was endless space. There was no beginning and no end, no time, no shape, no life. Just an immeasurable void that had its beginning and end, time, shape, and life in the mind of Taiowa the Creator.

Then he, the infinite, conceived the finite. First he created Sotuknang to make it manifest, saying to him, "I have created you, the first power and instrument as a person, to carry out my plan for life in endless space. I am your Uncle. You are my Nephew. Go now and lay out these universes in proper order so they may work harmoniously with one another according to my plan."

Sotuknang did as he was commanded. From endless space he gathered that which was to be manifest as solid substance, molded it into forms, and arranged them into nine universal kingdoms: one for Taiowa the Creator, one for himself, and seven universes for the life to come. Finishing this, Sotuknang went to Taiowa and asked, "Is this according to your plan?"

"It is very good," said Taiowa. "Now I want you to do the same thing with the waters. Place them on the surfaces of these universes so they will be divided equally among all and each."

So Sotuknang gathered from endless space that which was to be manifest as the waters and placed them on the universes so that each would be half solid and half water. Going now to Taiowa, he said, "I want you to see the work I have done and if it pleases you."

"It is very good," said Taiowa. "The next thing now is to put the forces of air into peaceful movement about all."

This Sotuknang did. From endless space he gathered that which was to be manifest as the airs, made them into great forces, and arranged them into gentle ordered movements around each universe.

Taiowa was pleased. "You have done a great work according to my plan, Nephew. You have created the universes and made them manifest in solids, waters, and winds, and put them in their proper places. But your work is not yet finished. Now you must create life and its movement to complete the four parts, Tuwaquachi, of my universal plan."

SPIDER WOMAN AND THE TWINS   Sotuknang went to the universe wherein was that to be Tokpela, the First World, and out of it he created her who was to remain on that earth and be his helper. Her name was Kokyangwuti, Spider Woman.

When she awoke to life and received her name, she asked, "Why am I here?"

"Look about you," answered Sotuknang. "Here is this earth we have created. It has shape and substance, direction and time, a beginning and an end. But there is no life upon it. We see no joyful movement. We hear no joyful sound. What is life without sound and movement? So you have been given the power to help us create this life. You have been given the knowledge, wisdom, and love to bless all the beings you create. That is why you are here."

Following his instructions, Spider Woman took some earth, mixed with it some *tuchvala* [liquid from mouth: saliva], and molded it into two beings. Then she covered them with a cape made of white substance which was the creative wisdom itself, and sang the Creation Song over them. When she uncovered them the two beings, twins, sat up and asked, "Who are we? Why are we here?"

To the one on the right Spider Woman said, "You are Poqanghoya and you are to help keep this world in order when life is put upon it. Go now around all the world and put your hands upon the earth so that it will become fully solidified. This is your duty."

Spider Woman then said to the twin on the left, "You are Palongawhoya and you are to help keep this world in order when life is put upon it. This is your duty now: go about all the world and send out sound so that it may be heard throughout all the land. When this is heard you will also be known as 'Echo,' for all sound echoes the Creator."

Poqanghoya, traveling throughout the earth, solidified the higher reaches into great mountains. The lower reaches he made firm but still pliable enough to be used by those beings to be placed upon it and who would call it their mother.

Palongawhoya, traveling throughout the earth, sounded out his call as he was bidden. All the vibratory centers along the earth's axis from pole to pole resounded his call; the whole earth trembled; the universe quivered in tune. Thus he made the whole world an instrument of sound, and sound an instrument for carrying messages, resounding praise to the Creator of all.

"This is your voice, Uncle," Sotuknang said to Taiowa. "Everything is tuned to your sound."

"It is very good," said Taiowa.

When they had accomplished their duties, Poqanghoya was sent to the north pole of the world axis and Palongawhoya to the south pole, where they were jointly commanded to keep the world properly rotating. Poqanghoya was also given the power to keep the earth in a stable form of solidness. Palongawhoya was given the power to keep the air in gentle ordered movement, and instructed to send out his call for good or for warning through the vibratory centers of the earth.

"These will be your duties in time to come," said Spider Woman.

She then created from the earth trees, bushes, plants, flowers, all kinds of seed-bearers and nut-bearers to clothe the earth, giving to each a life and name.

In the same manner she created all kinds of birds and animals—molding them out of earth, covering them with her white-substance cape, and singing over them. Some she placed to her right, some to her left, others before and behind her, indicating how they should spread to all four corners of the earth to live.

Sotuknang was happy, seeing how beautiful it all was—the land, the plants, the birds and animals, and the power working through them all. Joyfully he said to Taiowa, "Come see what our world looks like now!"

"It is very good," said Taiowa. "It is ready now for human life, the final touch to complete my plan."

CREATION OF MANKIND So Spider Woman gathered earth, this time of four colors, yellow, red, white, and black; mixed with *tuchvala,* the liquid of her mouth; molded them; and covered them with her white-substance cape which was the creative wisdom itself. As before, she sang over them the Creation Song, and when she uncovered them these forms were human beings in the image of Sotuknang. Then she created four other beings after her own form. They were *wuti,* female partners, for the first four male beings.

When Spider Woman uncovered them the forms came to life. This was at the time of the dark purple light, Qoyangnuptu, the first phase of the dawn of Creation, which first reveals the mystery of man's creation.

They soon awakened and began to move, but there was still a dampness on their foreheads and a soft spot on their heads. This was at the time of the yellow light, Sikangnuqua, the second phase of the dawn of Creation, when the breath of life entered man.

In a short time the sun appeared above the horizon, drying the dampness on their foreheads and hardening the soft spot on their heads. This was the time of the red light, Talawva, the third phase of the dawn of Creation, when man, fully formed and firmed, proudly faced his Creator.

"That is the Sun," said Spider Woman. "You are meeting your Father the Creator for the first time. You must always remember and observe these three phases of your Creation. The time of the three lights, the dark purple, the yellow, and the red reveal in turn the mystery, the breath of life, and warmth of love. These comprise the Creator's plan of life for you as sung over you in the Song of Creation:

SONG OF CREATION

The dark purple light rises in the north,
A yellow light rises in the east.
Then we of the flowers of the earth come forth
To receive a long life of joy.
We call ourselves the Butterfly Maidens.

Both male and female make their prayers to the east,
Make the respectful sign to the Sun our Creator.

The sounds of bells ring through the air,
Making a joyful sound throughout the land,
Their joyful echo resounding everywhere.

Humbly I ask my Father,
The perfect one, Taiowa, our Father,
The perfect one creating the beautiful life
Shown to us by the yellow light,
To give us perfect light at the time of the red light.

The perfect one laid out the perfect plan
And gave to us a long span of life,
Creating song to implant joy in life.
On this path of happiness, we the Butterfly Maidens
Carry out his wishes by greeting our Father Sun.

The song resounds back from our Creator with joy,
And we of the earth repeat it to our Creator.
At the appearing of the yellow light,
Repeats and repeats again the joyful echo,
Sounds and resounds for times to come.

The First People of the First World did not answer her; they could not speak. Something had to be done. Since Spider Woman received her power from Sotuknang, she had to call him and ask him what to do. So she called Palonga-whoya and said, "Call your Uncle. We need him at once."

Palongawhoya, the echo twin, sent out his call along the world axis to the vibratory centers of the earth, which resounded his message throughout the universe. "Sotuknang, our Uncle, come at once! We need you!"

All at once, with the sound as of a mighty wind, Sotuknang appeared in front of them. "I am here. Why do you need me so urgently?"

Spider Woman explained. "As you commanded me, I have created these First People. They are fully and firmly formed; they are properly colored; they have life; they have movement. But they cannot talk. That is the proper thing they lack. So I want you to give them speech. Also the wisdom and the power to reproduce, so that they may enjoy their life and give thanks to the Creator."

So Sotuknang gave them speech, a different language to each color, with respect for each other's difference. He gave them the wisdom and the power to reproduce and multiply.

Then he said to them, "With all these I have given you this world to live on and to be happy. There is only one thing I ask of you. To respect the Creator at all times. Wisdom, harmony, and respect for the love of the Creator who made you. May it grow and never be forgotten among you as long as you live."

So the First People went their directions, were happy, and began to multiply.

THE NATURE OF MAN   With the pristine wisdom granted them, they understood that the earth was a living entity like themselves. She was their mother; they were made from her flesh; they suckled at her breast. For her milk was the grass upon which all animals grazed and the corn which had been created specially to supply food for mankind. But the corn plant was also a living entity with a body similar to man's in many respects, and the people built its flesh into their own. Hence corn was also their mother. Thus they knew their mother in two aspects which were often synonymous—as Mother Earth and the Corn Mother.

In their wisdom they also knew their father in two aspects. He was the Sun, the solar god of their universe. Not until he first appeared to them at the time of the red light, Talawva, had they been fully firmed and formed. Yet his was but the face through which looked Taiowa, their Creator.

These universal entities were their real parents, their human parents being but the instruments through which their power was made manifest. In modern times their descendants remembered this.

When a child was born his Corn Mother was placed beside him, where it was kept for twenty days, and during this period he was kept in darkness; for while his newborn body was of this world, he was still under the protection of his universal parents. If the child was born at night, four lines were painted with cornmeal on each of the four walls and ceiling early next morning. If he was born during the day, the lines were painted the following morning. The lines signified that a spiritual home, as well as a temporal home, had been prepared for him on earth.

On the first day the child was washed with water in which cedar had been brewed. Fine white cornmeal was then rubbed over his body and left all day. Next day the child was cleaned, and cedar ashes were rubbed over him to remove the hair and baby skin. This was repeated for three days. From the fifth day until the twentieth day, he was washed and rubbed with cornmeal for one day and covered with ashes for four days. Meanwhile the child's mother drank a little of the cedar water each day.

On the fifth day the hair of both child and mother was washed, and one cornmeal line was scraped off each wall and ceiling. The scrapings were then taken to the shrine where the umbilical cord had been deposited. Each fifth day thereafter another line of cornmeal was removed from walls and ceiling and taken to the shrine.

For nineteen days now the house had been kept in darkness so that the child had not seen any light. Early on the morning of the twentieth day, while it was still dark, all the aunts of the child arrived at the house, each carrying a Corn Mother in her right hand and each wishing to be the child's godmother. First the child was bathed. Then the mother, holding the child in her left arm, took up the Corn Mother that had lain beside the child and passed it over the child four times from the navel upward to the head. On the first pass she named the child; on the second she wished the child a long life; on the third, a healthy life. If the child was a boy, she wished him a productive life in his work on the fourth pass; if a girl, that she would become a good wife and mother.

Each of the aunts in turn did likewise, giving the child a clan name from the clan of either the mother or father of the aunt. The child was then given back to its mother. The yellow light by then was showing in the east. The mother, holding the child in her left arm and the Corn Mother in her right hand, and accompanied by her own mother—the child's grandmother—left the house and walked toward the east. Then they stopped, facing east, and prayed silently, casting pinches of cornmeal toward the rising sun.

When the sun cleared the horizon the mother stepped forward, held up the child to the sun, and said, "Father Sun, this is your child." Again she said this, passing the Corn Mother over the child's body as when she had named him, wishing for him to grow so old he would to have lean on a crook for support, thus proving that he had obeyed the Creator's laws. The grandmother did the same thing when the mother had finished. Then both marked a cornmeal path toward the sun for this new life.

The child now belonged to his family and the earth. Mother and grandmother carried him back to the house, where his aunts were waiting. The village crier announced his birth, and a feast was held in his honor. For several years the child was called by the different names that were given him. The one that seemed most predominant became his name, and the aunt who gave it to him became his godmother. The Corn Mother remained his spiritual mother.

For seven or eight years he led the normal earthly life of a child. Then came his first initiation into a religious society, and he began to learn that, although he had human parents, his real parents were the universal entities who had created him through them—his Mother Earth, from whose flesh all are born, and his Father Sun, the solar god who gives life to all the universe. He began to learn, in brief, that he too had two aspects. He was a member of an earthly family and tribal clan, and he was a citizen of the great universe, to which he owed a growing allegiance as his understanding developed.

The First People, then, understood the mystery of their parenthood. In their pristine wisdom they also understood their own structure and functions—the nature of man himself.

The living body of man and the living body of the earth were constructed in the same way. Through each ran an axis, man's axis being the backbone, the vertebral column, which controlled the equilibrium of his movements and his functions. Along this axis were several vibratory centers which echoed the primordial sound of life throughout the universe or sounded a warning if anything went wrong.

The first of these in man lay at the top of the head. Here, when he was born, was the soft spot, kopavi, the "open door" through which he received his life and communicated with his Creator. For with every breath the soft spot moved up and down with a gentle vibration that was communicated to the Creator. At the time of the red light, Talawva, the last phase of his creation, the soft spot was hardened and the door was closed. It remained closed until his death, opening then for his life to depart as it had come.

Just below it lay the second center, the organ that man learned to think with by himself, the thinking organ called the brain. Its earthly function enabled man to think about his actions and work on this earth. But the more he understood that his work and actions should conform to the plan of the Creator, the more clearly he understood that the real function of the thinking organ called the brain was carrying out the plan of all Creation.

The third center lay in the throat. It tied together those openings in his nose and mouth through which he received the breath of life and the vibratory organs that enabled him to give back his breath in sound. This primordial sound, as that coming from the vibratory centers of the body of earth, was attuned to the universal vibration of all Creation. New and diverse sounds were given forth by these vocal organs in the forms of speech and song, their secondary function for man on this earth. But as he came to understand its primary function, he used this center to speak and sing praises to the Creator.

The fourth center was the heart. It too was a vibrating organ, pulsing with the vibration of life itself. In his heart man felt the good of life, its sincere purpose. He was of One Heart. But there were those who permitted evil feelings to enter. They were said to be of Two Hearts.

The last of man's important centers lay under his navel, the organ some people now call the solar plexus. As this name signifies, it was the throne in man of the Creator himself. From it he directed all the functions of man.

The first People knew no sickness. Not until evil entered the world did persons get sick in the body or head. It was then that a medicine man, knowing how man was constructed, could tell what was wrong with a person by examining these centers. First, he laid his hands on them: the top of the head, above the eyes, the throat, the chest, the belly. The hands of the medicine man were seer instruments; they could feel the vibrations from each center and tell him in which life ran strongest or weakest. Sometimes the trouble was just a bellyache from uncooked food or a cold in the head. But other times it came "from outside," drawn by the person's own evil thoughts, or from those of a Two Hearts. In this case the medicine man took out from his medicine pouch a small crystal about an inch and a half across, held it in the sun to get it in working order, and then looked through it at each of the centers. In this manner he could see what caused the trouble and often the very face of the Two Hearts person who had caused the illness. There was nothing magical about the crystal, medicine men always said. An ordinary person could see nothing when he looked through it; the crystal merely objectified the vision of the center which controlled his eyes and which the medicine man had developed for this very purpose. . . .

Thus the First People understood themselves. And this was the First World they lived upon. Its name was Tokpela, Endless Space. Its direction was west; its color *sikyangpu*, yellow; its mineral *sikyasvu*, gold. Significant upon it were *kato'ya*, the snake with a big head; *wisoko*, the fat-eating bird; and *muha*, the little four-leaved plant. On it the First People were pure and happy.

TOKPA: THE SECOND WORLD   So the First People kept multiplying and spreading over the face of the land and were happy. Although they were of different colors and spoke different languages, they felt as one and understood one another without talking. It was the same with the birds and animals. They all suckled at the breast of their Mother Earth, who gave them her milk of grass, seeds, fruit, and corn, and they all felt as one, people and animals.

But gradually there were those who forgot the commands of Sotuknang and the Spider Woman to respect their Creator. More and more they used the vibratory centers of their bodies solely for earthly purposes, forgetting that their primary purpose was to carry out the plan of Creation.

There then came among them Lavaihoya, the Talker. He came in the form of a bird called Mochni [bird like a mocking bird], and the more he kept talking the more he convinced them of the differences between them: the difference between people and animals, and the differences between the people themselves by reason of the colors of their skins, their speech, and belief in the plan of the Creator.

It was then that animals drew away from people. The guardian spirit of animals laid his hands on their hind legs just below the tail, making them become wild and scatter from the people in fear. You can see this slightly oily spot today on deer and antelope—on the sides of their back legs as they throw up their tails to run away.

In the same way, people began to divide and draw away from one another—those of different races and languages, then those who remembered the plan of Creation and those who did not.

There came among them a handsome one, Kato'ya, in the form of a snake with a big head. He led the people still farther away from one another and their pristine wisdom. They became suspicious of one another and accused one another wrongfully until they became fierce and warlike and began to fight one another.

All the time Mochni kept talking and Kato'ya became more beguiling. There was no rest, no peace.

But among all the people of different races and languages there were a few in every group who still lived by the laws of Creation. To them came Sotuknang. He came with the sound as of a mighty wind and suddenly appeared before them. He said, "I have observed this state of affairs. It is not good. It is so bad I talked to my Uncle, Taiowa, about it. We have decided this world must be destroyed and another one created so you people can start over again. You are the ones we have chosen."

They listened carefully to their instructions.

Said Sotuknang, "You will go to a certain place. Your *kopavi* [vibratory center on top of the head] will lead you. This inner wisdom will give you the sight to see a certain cloud, which you will follow by day, and a certain star, which you will follow by night. Take nothing with you. Your journey will not end until the cloud stops and the star stops."

So all over the world these chosen people suddenly disappeared from their homes and people and began following the cloud by day and the star by night. Many other people asked them where they were going and, when they were told, laughed at them. "We don't see any cloud or any star either!" they said. This was because they had lost the inner vision of the *kopavi* on the crown of their head; the door was closed to them. Still there were a very few who went along anyway because they believed the people who did see the cloud and the star. This was all right.

After many days and nights the first people arrived at the certain place. Soon others came and asked, "What are you doing here?" And they said, "We were told by Sotuknang to come here." The other people said, "We too were led here by the vapor and the star!" They were all happy together because they were of the same mind and understanding even though they were of different races and languages.

When the last ones arrived Sotuknang appeared. "Well, you are all here, you people I have chosen to save from the destruction of this world. Now come with me."

He led them to a big mound where the Ant People lived, stamped on the roof, and commanded the Ant People to open up their home. When an opening was made on top of the anthill, Sotuknang said to the people, "Now you will enter this Ant kiva, where you will be safe when I destroy the world. While you are here I want you to learn a lesson from these Ant People. They are industrious. They gather food in the summer for the winter. They keep cool when it is hot and warm when it is cool. They live peacefully with one another. They obey the plan of Creation."

So the people went down to live with the Ant People. When they were all safe and settled Taiowa commanded Sotuknang to destroy the world. Sotuknang destroyed it by fire because the Fire Clan had been its leaders. He rained fire upon it. He opened up the volcanoes. Fire came from above and below and all around until the earth, the waters, the air, all was one element, fire, and there was nothing left except the people safe inside the womb of the earth.

This was the end of Tokpela, the First World.

EMERGENCE TO THE SECOND WORLD While this was going on the people lived happily underground with the Ant People. Their homes were just like the people's homes on the earth-surface being destroyed. There were rooms to live in and rooms where they stored their food. There was light to see by, too. The tiny bits of crystal in the sand of the anthill had absorbed the light of the sun, and by using the inner vision of the center behind their eyes they could see by its reflection very well.

Only one thing troubled them. The food began to run short. It had not taken Sotuknang long to destroy the world, nor would it take him long to create another one. But it was taking a long time for the First World to cool off before the Second World could be created. That was why the food was running short.

"Do not give us so much of the food you have worked so hard to gather and store," the people said.

"Yes, you are our guests," the Ant People told them. "What we have is yours also." So the Ant People continued to deprive themselves of food in order to supply their guests. Every day they tied their belts tighter and tighter. That is why ants today are so small around the waist.

Finally that which had been the First World cooled off. Sotuknang purified it. Then he began to create the Second World. He changed its form completely, putting land where the water was and water where the land had been, so the people upon their Emergence would have nothing to remind them of the previous wicked world.

When all was ready he came to the roof of the Ant kiva, stamped on it, and gave his call. Immediately the Chief of the Ant People went up to the opening and rolled back the *nuta. "Yung-ai!* Come in! You are welcome!" he called.

Sotuknang spoke first to the Ant People. "I am thanking you for doing your part in helping to save these people. It will always be remembered, this you have done. The time will come when another world will be destroyed; and when wicked people know their last day on earth has come, they will sit by an anthill and cry for the ants to save them. Now, having fulfilled your duty, you may go forth to this Second World I have created and take your place as ants."

Then Sotuknang said to the people, "Make your Emergence now to this Second World I have created. It is not quite so beautiful as the First World, but it is beautiful just the same. You will like it. So multiply and be happy. But remember your Creator and the laws he gave you. When I hear you singing joyful praises to him I will know you are my children, and you will be close to me in your hearts."

So the people emerged to the Second World. Its name was Tokpa [Dark Midnight]. Its direction was south, its color blue, its mineral *qochasiva,* silver. Chiefs upon it were *salavi,* the spruce; *kwahu,* the eagle; and *kolichiyaw,* the skunk.

It was a big land, and the people multiplied rapidly, spreading over it to all directions, even to the other side of the world. This did not matter, for they were so close together in spirit they could see and talk to each other from the center on top of the head. Because this door was still open, they felt close to Sotuknang and they sang joyful praises to the Creator, Taiowa.

They did not have the privilege of living with the animals, though, for the animals were wild and kept apart. Being separated from the animals, the people tended to their own affairs. They built homes, then villages and trails between them. They made things with their hands and stored food like the Ant People. Then they began to trade and barter with one another.

This was when the trouble started. Everything they needed was on this Second World, but they began to want more. More and more they traded for things they didn't need, and the more goods they got, the more they wanted. This was very serious. For they did not realize they were drawing away, step by step, from the good life given them. They just forgot to sing joyful praises to the Creator and soon began to sing praises for the goods they bartered and stored. Before long it happened as it had to happen. The people began to quarrel and fight, and then wars between villages began.

Still there were a few people in every village who sang the song of their Creation. But the wicked people laughed at them until they could sing it only in their hearts. Even so, Sotuknang heard it through their centers and the centers of the earth. Suddenly one day he appeared before them.

"Spider Woman tells me your thread is running out on this world," he said. "That is too bad. The Spider Clan was your leader, and you were making good progress until this state of affairs began. Now my Uncle, Taiowa, and I have decided we must do something about it. We are going to destroy this Second World just as soon as we put you people who still have the song in your hearts in a safe place."

So again, as on the First World, Sotuknang called on the Ant People to open up their underground world for the chosen people. When they were safely underground, Sotuknang commanded the twins, Poqanghoya and Palongawhoya, to leave their posts at the north and south ends of the world's axis, where they were stationed to keep the earth properly rotating.

The twins had hardly abandoned their stations when the world, with no one to control it, teetered off balance, spun around crazily, then rolled over twice. Mountains plunged into seas with a great splash, seas and lakes sloshed over the land; and as the world spun through cold and lifeless space it froze into solid ice.

This was the end of Tokpa, the Second World.

EMERGENCE TO THE THIRD WORLD For many years all the elements that had comprised the Second World were frozen into a motionless and lifeless lump of ice. But the people were happy and warm with the Ant People in their underground world. They watched their food carefully, although the ants' waists became still smaller. They wove sashes and blankets together and told stories.

Eventually Sotuknang ordered Poqanghoya and Palongawhoya back to their stations at the poles of the world axis. With a great shudder and a splintering of ice the planet began rotating again. When it was revolving smoothly about its own axis and stately moving in its universal orbit, the ice began to melt and the world began to warm to life. Sotuknang set about creating the Third World: arranging earths and seas, planting mountains and plains with their proper coverings, and creating all forms of life.

When the earth was ready for occupancy, he came to the Ant kiva with the proper approach as before and said, "Open the door. It is time for you to come out."

Once again when the *nuta* was rolled back he gave the people their instructions. "I have saved you so you can be planted again on this new Third World. But you must always remember the two things I am saying to you now. First, respect me and one another. And second, sing in harmony from the tops of the hills. When I do not hear you singing praises to your Creator I will know you have gone back to evil again."

So the people climbed up the ladder from the Ant kiva, making their Emergence to the Third World.

KUSKURZA: THE THIRD WORLD Its name was Kuskurza, its direction east, its color red. Chiefs upon it were the mineral *palasiva,* copper; the plant *piva,* tobacco; the bird *angwusi,* crow; and the animal *choovio,* antelope.

Upon it once more the people spread out, multiplied, and continued their progress on the Road of Life. In the First World they had lived simply with the animals. In the Second World they had developed handicrafts, homes, and villages. Now in the Third World they multiplied in such numbers and advanced so rapidly that they created big cities, countries, a whole civilization. This made it difficult for them to conform to the plan of Creation and to sing praises to Taiowa and Sotuknang. More and more of them became wholly occupied with their own earthly plans.

Some of them, of course, retained the wisdom granted them upon their Emergence. With this wisdom they understood that the farther they proceeded on the Road to Life and the more they developed, the harder it was. That was why their world was destroyed every so often to give them a fresh start. They were especially concerned because so many people were using their reproductive power in wicked ways. There was one woman who was becoming known throughout the world for her wickedness in corrupting so many people. She even boasted that so many men were giving her turquoise necklaces for her favors she could wind them around a ladder that reached to the end of the world's axis. So the people with wisdom sang louder and longer their praises to the Creator from the tops of their hills.

The other people hardly heard them. Under the leadership of the Bow Clan they began to use their creative power in another evil and destructive way. Perhaps this was caused by that wicked woman. But some of them made a *patuwvota* [shield made to hide] and with their creative power made it fly through the air. On this many of the people flew to a big city, attacked it, and returned so fast no one knew where they came from. Soon the people of many cities and countries were making *patuwvotas* and flying on them to attack one another. So corruption and war came to the Third World as it had to the others.

This time Sotuknang came to Spider Woman and said, "There is no use wating until the thread runs out this time. Something has to be done lest the people with the song in their hearts are corrupted and killed off too. It will be difficult, with all this destruction going on, for them to gather at the far end of the world I have designated. But I will help them. Then you will save them when I destroy this world with water."

"How shall I save them?" asked Spider Woman.

"When you get there look about you," commanded Sotuknang. "You will see these tall plants with hollow stems. Cut them down and put the people inside. Then I will tell you what to do next."

Spider Woman did as he instructed her. She cut down the hollow reeds; and as the people came to her, she put them inside with a little water and *hurusuki* [white cornmeal dough] for food, and sealed them up. When all the people were thus taken care of, Sotuknang appeared.

"Now you get in to take care of them, and I will seal you up," he said. "Then I will destroy the world."

So he loosed the waters upon the earth. Waves higher than mountains rolled in upon the land. Continents broke asunder and sank beneath the seas. And still the rains fell, the waves rolled in.

The people sealed up in their hollow reeds heard the mighty rushing of the waters. They felt themselves tossed high in the air and dropping back to the water. Then all was quiet, and they knew they were floating. For a long, long time—so long a time that it seemed it would never end—they kept floating.

Finally their movement ceased. The Spider Woman unsealed their hollow reeds, took them by the tops of their heads, and pulled them out. "Bring out all the food that is left over," she commanded.

The people brought out their *hurusuki;* it was still the same size, although they had been eating it all this time. Looking about them, they saw they were on a little piece of land that had been the top of one of their highest mountains. All else, as far as they could see, was water. This was all that remained of the Third World.

"There must be some dry land somewhere we can go to," they said. "Where is the new Fourth World that Sotuknang has created for us?" They sent many kinds of birds, one after another, to fly over the waters and find it. But they all came back tired out without having seen any sign of land. Next they planted a reed that grew high into the sky. Up it they climbed and stared over the surface of the waters. But they saw no sign of land.

Then Sotuknang appeared to Spider Woman and said, "You must continue traveling on. Your inner wisdom will guide you. The door at the top of your head is open."

So Spider Woman directed the people to make round, flat boats of the hollow reeds they had come in and to crawl inside. Again they entrusted themselves to the water and the inner wisdom to guide them. For a long time they drifted with the wind and the movement of the waters and came to another rocky island.

"It is bigger than the other one, but it is not big enough," they said, looking around them and thinking they heard a low rumbling noise.

"No. It is not big enough," said Spider Woman.

So the people kept traveling toward the rising sun in their reed boats. After awhile they said, "There is that low rumbling noise we heard. We must be coming to land again.

So it was. A big land, it seemed, with grass and trees and flowers beautiful to their weary eyes. On it they rested a long time. Some of the people wanted to stay, but Spider Woman said, "No. It is not the place. You must continue on."

Leaving their boats, they traveled by foot eastward across the island to the water's edge. Here they found growing some more of the hollow plants like reeds or bamboo, which they cut down. Directed by Spider Woman, they laid some of these in a row with another row on top of them in the opposite direction and tied them all together with vines and leaves. This made a raft big enough for one family or more. When enough rafts were made for all, Spider Woman directed them to make paddles.

"You will be going uphill from now on and you will have to make your own way. So Sotuknang told you: The farther you go, the harder it gets."

After long and weary traveling, still east and a little north, the people began to hear the low rumbling noise and saw land. One family and clan after another landed with joy. The land was long, wide, and beautiful. The earth was rich and flat, covered with trees and plants, seed-bearers and nut-bearers, providing lots of food. The people were happy and kept staying there year after year.

"No. This is not the Fourth World," Spider Woman kept telling them. "It is too easy and pleasant for you to live on, and you would soon fall into evil ways again. You must go on. Have we not told you the way becomes harder and longer?"

Reluctantly the people traveled eastward by foot across the island to the far shore. Again they made rafts and paddles. When they were ready to set forth Spider Woman said, "Now I have done all I am commanded to do for you. You must go on alone and find your own place of Emergence. Just keep your doors open, and your spirits will guide you."

"Thank you, Spider Woman, for all you have done for us," they said sadly. "We will remember what you have said."

Alone they set out, traveling east and a little north, paddling hard day and night for many days as if they were paddling uphill.

At last they saw land. It rose high above the waters, stretching from north to south as far as they could see. A great land, a mighty land, their inner wisdom told them. "The Fourth World!" they cried to each other.

As they got closer, its shores rose higher and higher into a steep wall of mountains. There seemed no place to land. "Let us go north. There we will find our Place of Emergence," said some. So they went north, but the mountains rose higher and steeper.

"No! Let us go south! There we will find our Place of Emergence!" cried others. So they turned south and traveled many days more. But here too the mountain wall reared higher.

Not knowing what to do, the people stopped paddling, opened the doors on top of their heads, and let themselves be guided. Almost immediately the water smoothed out, and they felt their rafts caught up in a gentle current. Before long they landed and joyfully jumped out upon a sandy shore. "The Fourth World!" they cried. "We have reached our Place of Emergence at last!"

Soon all the others arrived and when they were gathered together Sotuknang appeared before them. "Well, I see you are all here. That is good. This is the place I have prepared for you. Look now at the way you have come."

Looking to the west and the south, the people could see sticking out of the water the islands upon which they had rested.

"They are the footprints of your journey," continued Sotuknang, "the tops of the high mountains of the Third World, which I destroyed. Now watch."

As the people watched them, the closest one sank under the water, then the next, until all were gone, and they could see only water.

"See," said Sotuknang, "I have washed away even the footprints of your Emergence; the stepping-stones which I left for you. Down on the bottom of the seas lie all the proud cities, the flying *patuwvotas,* and the worldly treasures corrupted with evil, and those people who found no time to sing praises to the Creator from the tops of their hills. But the day will come, if you preserve the memory and the meaning of your Emergence, when these stepping-stones will emerge again to prove the truth you speak."

This at last was the end of the Third World, Kuskurza [an ancient name for which there is no modern meaning].

T UWAQACHI: THE FOURTH WORLD   "I have something more to say before I leave you," Sotuknang told the people as they stood at their Place of Emergence on the shore of the present Fourth World. This is what he said:

"The name of this Fourth World is Tuwaqachi, World Complete. You will find out why. It is not all beautiful and easy like the previous ones. It has height and depth, heat and cold, beauty and barrenness; it has everything for you to choose from. What you choose will determine if this time you can carry out the plan of Creation on it or whether it must in time be destroyed too. Now you will separate and go different ways to claim all the earth for the Creator. Each group of you will follow your own star until it stops. There you will settle. Now I must go. But you will have help from the proper deities, from your good spirits. Just keep your own doors open and always remember what I have told you. This is what I say."

Then he disappeared.

The people began to move slowly off the shore and into the land, when they heard the low rumbling noise again. Looking around, they saw a handsome man and asked, "Are you the one who has been making these noises we have heard?"

"Yes. I made them to help you find the way here. Do you not recognize me? My name is Masaw. I am the caretaker, the guardian and protector of this land."

The people recognized Masaw. He had been appointed head caretaker of the Third World, but, becoming a little self-important, he had lost his humility before the Creator. Being a spirit, he could not die, so Taiowa took his appointment away from him and made him the deity of death and the underworld. This job Below was not as pleasant as the one Above. Then when the Third World was destroyed, Taiowa decided to give him another chance, as he had the people, and appointed him to guard and protect this Fourth World as its caretaker.

He was the first being the people had met here, and they were very respectful to him. "Will you give us your permission to live on this land?" they asked.

"Yes, I will give you my permission as owner of the land."

"Will you be our leader?" the people then asked.

"No," replied Masaw. "A greater one than I has given you a plan to fulfill first. When the previous parts of the world were pushed underneath the water, this new land was pushed up in the middle to become the backbone of the earth. You are now standing on its *atvila* [west side slope]. But you have not yet made your migrations. You have not yet followed your stars to the place where you will meet and settle. This you must do before I can become your leader. But if you go back to evil ways again I will take over the earth from you, for I am its caretaker, guardian, and protector. To the north you will find cold and ice. That is the Back Door to this land, and those who may come through this Back Door will enter without my consent. So go now and claim the land with my permission."

When Masaw disappeared, the people divided into groups and clans to begin their migrations.

"May we meet again!" they all called back to one another.

This is how it all began on this, our present Fourth World. As we know, its name is Tuwaqachi, World Complete, its direction north, its color *sikyangpu,* yellowish white. Chiefs upon it are the tree *kneumapee,* juniper; the bird *mongwau,* the owl; the animal *tohopko,* the mountain lion; and the mixed mineral *sikyapala.*

Where all the people went on their migrations to the ends of the earth and back, and what they have done to carry out the plan of Creation from this Place of Beginning to the present time, is to be told next by all the clans as they came in.

—Frank Waters. *The Book of the Hopi.* New York: Ballantine Books, 1963, pp. 3–28.

ZUNI

The Beginning of Newness

Like the Hopi, the Zuni Pueblo Indians also managed to escape pervasive foreign influence. Although they were attacked by Francisco Vasquez de Coronado in 1540, on the mistaken assumption that their villages were the fabled Seven Cities of Cibola, repositories of fabulous gold stores, they repulsed attempts to Christianize them in the centuries that followed.

While the Zuni have a long myth of emergence and migrations like other Indians of the Southwest, this first part of their cosmology describes the origin of the world. In the beginning, only Awonawilona, the Father of Fathers, existed. The ground of being, or Being-Itself, Awonawilona conceived within himself and in effect divided himself into chaos and order, not-being and being: he conceived a thought within himself and thereby gave birth first to the "mists of increase" and "streams potent of growth"—to creative potentiality, the primordial waters, chaos; and secondly to himself as the sun—creative reality, fire, order. As the sun, he mated with the waters (that is, being merged with not-being) and produced heaven and earth and, as parallel Chinese myths relate, "all the myriad creatures."

BEFORE the beginning of the new-making, Awonawilona (the Maker and Container of All, the All-father Father), solely had being. There was nothing else whatsoever throughout the great space of the ages save everywhere black darkness in it, and everywhere void desolation.

In the beginning of the new-made, Awonawilona conceived within himself and thought outward in space, whereby mists of increase, steams potent of growth, were evolved and uplifted. Thus, by means of his innate knowledge, the All-container made himself in person and form of the Sun whom we hold to be our father and who thus came to exist and appear. With his appearance came the brightening of the spaces with light, and with the brightening of the spaces the great mist-clouds were thickened together and fell, whereby was evolved water in water; yea, and the world-holding sea.

With his substance of flesh outdrawn from the surface of his person, the Sun-father formed the seed-stuff of twain worlds, impregnating therewith the great waters, and lo! in the heat of his light these waters of the sea grew green and scums rose upon them, waxing wide the weighty until, behold! they became Awitelin Tsita, the "Four-fold Containing Mother-earth," and Apoyan Ta'chu, the "All-covering Father-sky."

From the lying together of these twain upon the great world-waters, so vitalizing, terrestrial life was conceived; whence began all beings of earth, men and the creatures, in the Four-fold womb of the World.

Thereupon the Earth-mother repulsed the Sky-father, growing big and sinking deep into the embrace of the waters below, thus separating from the Sky-father in the embrace of the waters above. As a woman forebodes evil for her first-born ere born, even so did the Earth-mother forebode, long withholding from birth her myriad progeny and meantime seeking counsel with the Sky-father. "How," said they to one another, "shall our children when brought forth, know one place from another, even by the white light of the Sun-father?"

Now like all the surpassing beings the Earth-mother and the Sky-father were changeable, even as smoke in the wind; transmutable at thought, manifesting themselves in any form at will, like as dancer may by mask-making.

Thus, as a man and woman, spake they, one to the other. "Behold!" said the Earth-mother as a great terraced bowl appeared at hand and within it water, "this is as upon me the homes of my tiny children shall be. On the rim of each world-country they wander in, terraced mountains shall stand, making in one region many, whereby country shall be known from country, and within each, place from place. Behold, again!" said she as she spat on the water and rapidly smote and stirred it with her fingers. Foam formed, gathering about the terraced rim, mounting higher and higher. "Yea," said she, and from my bosom they shall draw nourishment, for in such as this shall they find the substance of life whence we were ourselves sustained, for see!" Then with her warm breath she blew across the terraces; white flecks or the foam broke away, and, floating over above the water, were shattered by the cold breath of the Sky-father attending, and forthwith shed downward abundantly fine mist and spray! "Even so, shall white clouds float up from the great waters at the borders of the world, and clustering about the mountain terraces of the horizons be borne aloft and abroad by the breaths of the surpassing of soul-beings, and of the children, and shall hardened and broken be by thy cold, shedding downward, in rain-spray, the water of life, even into the hollow places of my lap! For therein chiefly shall nestle our children mankind and creature-kind, for warmth in thy coldness."

Lo! even the trees on high mountains near the clouds and the Sky-father crouch low toward the Earth-mother for warmth and protection! Warm is the Earth-mother, cold the Sky-father, even as woman is the warm, man the cold being!

"Even so!" said the Sky-father; "Yet not alone shalt thou helpful be unto our children, for behold!" and he spread his land abroad with the palm downward and into all the wrinkles and crevices thereof he set the semblance of shining yellow corn-grains; in the dark of the early world-dawn they gleamed like sparks of fire, and moved as his hand was moved over the bowl, shining up from and also moving in the depths of the water therein. "See!" said he, pointing to the seven grains clasped by his thumb and four fingers, "by such shall our children be guided; for behold, when the Sun-father is not nigh, and thy terraces are as the dark itself (being all hidden therein), then shall our children be guided by lights—like to these lights of all the six regions turning round the midmost one—as in and around the midmost place, where these our children shall abide, lie all the other regions of space! Yea! and even as these grains gleam up from the water, so shall seedgrains like to them, yet numberless, spring up from thy bosom when touched by my waters, to nourish our children." Thus and in other ways many devised they for their offspring.

—F. H. Cushing. *Outlines of Zuni Creation Myths. Thirteenth Annual Report of the Bureau of American Ethnology*. Washington, D.C.: 1896, pp. 379-381.

EIGHT

CENTRAL AND SOUTH AMERICAN MYTHS

QUICHÉ MAYA

From the Popol Vuh

The *Popol Vuh* (Book of the Community) is the sacred history of the Quiché Maya, the most powerful tribe in the western highlands, which form the southern branch of the great Mayan civilization. After the Quiché were conquered in 1524 by Pedro de Alvarado and their religious books destroyed, the Popol Vuh was rewritten in native language but with Latin letters by a converted member of the tribe. Although this manuscript is now lost, a copy made by Father Ximénez in the late 1600s survived.

The Popol Vuh recounts the history of the Quiché from the beginning of creation down through the Mayan kings in 1550. At times wandering and interrupted with side issues, it is a difficult myth to interpret. Not only was it written several centuries after the decline of the Mayan civilization (whose classic age spanned 317–889 A.D.), leading to questions of interpolation and changes, but also the significance of many names and the precise nature and relationship of many deities are now confused. Nevertheless, the outlines of the first, cosmological section of the myth are clear: in the beginning, only Tepeu and Gucumatz existed as sun-fire powers in the middle of the dark waters of the void. They thought and spoke together and then, joined in agreement, created the world by command: "Let the emptiness be filled!" and it was. The earth rose out of the water, and the gods made all the animals and birds to live on it. But these creatures were flawed in that they could not speak to praise their creators, so the gods set out to make people.

The first attempt failed because the clay they were using melted in the waters. By contrast, the second race of people, carved wooden creatures, were too solid and inflexible; they were without souls and minds. Destroyed by monsters and by all the things in their world that they had offended in the course of their existence, the second race of people devolved into monkeys and fled to the forests.

So the gods tried a third time, and with greater haste, because the dawn of the world was approaching. Aided by the animals, they gathered plants (mostly varieties of corn and beans, the main diet of the Maya) and made four people (one for each cardinal direction) out of these. While the names of the first four men are difficult to translate with certainty, they seem to be kinds of sorcerers or wizards, that is, men of very great power. And indeed they were. Gifted with great vision and understanding, they frightened even the gods, who limited the wizards' powers somewhat before proceeding with creation. Next the gods formed four women (whose names all indicate affinity with water, the passive and receptive side of the primary duality).

The first people then produced all the ancestors of the Quiché and other Central American tribes. After many migrations, they finally stood on the top of a sacred mountain and waited for the dawn (both physical and spiritual light). And when the sun arose, its heat hardened the earth and turned the fearsome animals to helpless stone, and all the people rejoiced.

(I.1) THIS is the account of how all was in suspense, all calm, in silence; all motionless, still, and the expanse of the sky was empty.

This is the first account, the first narrative. There was neither man, nor animal, birds, fishes, crabs, trees, stones, caves, ravines, grasses, nor forests; there was only the sky.

The surface of the earth had not appeared. There was only the calm sea and the great expanse of the sky.

There was nothing brought together, nothing which could make a noise, nor anything which might move, or tremble, or could make noise in the sky.

There was nothing standing; only the calm water, the placid sea, alone and tranquil. Nothing existed.

There was only immobility and silence in the darkness, in the night. Only the Creator, the Maker, Tepeu, Gucumatz, the Forefathers, were in the water surrounded with light. They were hidden under green and blue feathers, and were therefore called Gucumatz. By nature they were great sages and great thinkers. In this manner the sky existed and also the Heart of Heaven, which is the name of God and thus He is called.

Then came the word. Tepeu and Gucumatz came together in the darkness, in the night, and Tepeu and Gucumatz talked together. They talked then, discussing and deliberating; they agreed, they united their words and their thoughts.

Then while they meditated, it became clear to them that when dawn would break, man must appear. Then they planned the creation, and the growth of the trees and the thickets and the birth of life and the creation of man. Thus it was arranged in the darkness and in the night by the Heart of Heaven who is called Huracan.

The first is called Caculha Huracan. The second is Chipi-Caculha. The third is Raxa-Caculha [all forms of lightning and thunder]. And these three are the Heart of Heaven.

Then Tepeu and Gucumatz came together; then they conferred about life and light, what they would do so that there would be light and dawn, who it would be who would provide food and sustenance.

Thus let it be done! Let the emptiness be filled! Let the water recede and make a void, let the earth appear and become solid; let it be done. Thus they spoke. Let there be light, let there be dawn in the sky and on the earth! There shall be neither glory nor grandeur in our creation and formation until the human being is made, man is formed. So they spoke.

Then the earth was created by them. So it was, in truth, that they created the earth. Earth! they said, and instantly it was made.

Like the mist, like a cloud, and like a cloud of dust was the creation, when the mountains appeared from the water; and instantly the mountains grew.

Only by a miracle, only by magic art were the mountains and valleys formed; and instantly the groves of cypresses and pines put forth shoots together on the surface of the earth.

And thus Gucumatz was filled with joy, and exclaimed: "Your coming has been fruitful, Heart of Heaven; and you, Huracan, and you Chipi-Caculha, Raxa-Caculha!"

"Our work, our creation shall be finished," they answered.

First the earth was formed, the mountains and the valleys; the currents of water were divided, the rivulets were running freely between the hills, and the water was separated when the high mountains appeared.

Thus was the earth created, when it was formed by the Heart of Heaven, the Heart of Earth, as they are called who first made it fruitful, when the sky was in suspense, and the earth was submerged in the water.

So it was that they made perfect the work, when they did it after thinking and meditating upon it.

(I.2) THEN they made the small wild animals, the guardians of the woods, the spirits of the mountains, the deer, the birds, pumas, jaguars, serpents, snakes, vipers, guardians of the thickets.

And the Forefathers asked: "Shall there be only silence and calm under the trees, under the vines? It is well that hereafter there be someone to guard them."

So they said when they meditated and talked. Promptly the deer and the birds were created. Immediately they gave homes to the deer and the birds. "You, deer, shall sleep in the fields by the river bank and in the ravines. Here you shall be amongst the thicket, amongst the pasture; in the woods you shall multiply, you shall walk on four feet and they will support you. Thus be it done!" So it was they spoke.

Then they also assigned homes to the birds big and small. "You shall live in the trees and in the vines. There you shall make your nests; there you shall multiply; there you shall increase in the branches of the trees and in the vines." Thus the deer and the birds were told; they did their duty at once, and all sought their homes and their nests.

And the creation of all the four-footed animals and the birds being finished, they were told by the Creator and the Maker and the Forefathers: "Speak, cry, warble, call, speak each one according to your variety, each, according to your kind." So was it said to the deer, the birds, pumas, jaguars, and serpents.

"Speak, then, our names, praise us, your mother, your father. Invoke then, Huracan, Chipi-Caculha, Raxa-Caculha, the Heart of Heaven, the Heart of Earth, the Creator, the Maker, the Forefathers; speak, invoke us, adore us," they were told.

But they could not make them speak like men; they only hissed and screamed and cackled; they were unable to make words, and each screamed in a different way.

When the Creator and the Maker saw that it was impossible for them to talk to each other, they said: "It is impossible for them to say our names, the names of us, their Creators and Makers. This is not well," said the Forefathers to each other.

Then they said to them: "Because it has not been possible for you to talk, you shall be changed. We have changed our minds: your food, your pasture, your homes, and your nests you shall have; they shall be the ravines and the woods, because it has not been possible for you to adore us or invoke us. There shall be those who adore us, we shall make other [beings] who shall be obedient. Accept your destiny: your flesh shall be torn to pieces. So shall it be. This shall be your lot." So they said, when they made known their will to the large and small animals which are on the face of the earth.

They wished to give them another trial; they wished to make another attempt; they wished to make [all living things] adore them.

But they could not understand each other's speech; they could succeed in nothing, and could do nothing. For this reason they were sacrificed, and the animals which were on earth were condemned to be killed and eaten.

For this reason another attempt had to be made to create and make men by the Creator, the Maker, and the Forefathers.

"Let us try again! Already dawn draws near: let us make him who shall nourish and sustain us! What shall we do to be invoked, in order to be remembered on earth? We have already tried with our first creations, our first creatures; but we could not make them praise and venerate us. So, then, let us try to make obedient, respectful beings who will nourish and sustain us." Thus they spoke.

Then was the creation and the formation. Of earth, of mud, they made [man's] flesh. But they saw that it was not good. It melted away, it was soft, did not move, had no strength, it fell down, it was limp, it could not move its head, its face fell to one side, its sight was blurred, it could not look behind. At first it spoke, but had no mind. Quickly it soaked in the water and could not stand.

And the Creator and the Maker said: "Let us try again because our creatures will not be able to walk nor multiply. Let us consider this," they said.

Then they broke up and destroyed their work and their creation. And they said: "What shall we do to perfect it, in order that our worshipers, our invokers, will be successful?"

Thus they spoke when they conferred again: "Let us say again to Xpiya-coc, Xmucane, Hunahpu-Vuch, Hunahpu-Utiu: 'Cast your lot again. Try to create again.' " In this manner the Creator and the Maker spoke to Xpiyacoc and Xmucane.

Then they spoke of those soothsayers, the Grandmother of the day, the Grandmother of the Dawn, as they were called by the Creator and the Maker, and whose names were Xpiyacoc and Xmucane.

And said Huracan, Tepeu, and Gucumatz when they spoke to the soothsayer, to the Maker, who are the diviners: "You must work together and find the means so that man, whom we shall make, man, whom we are going to make, will nourish and sustain us, invoke and remember us.

"Enter, then, into council, grandmother, grandfather, our grandmother, our grandfather, Xpiyacoc, Xmucane, make light, make dawn, have us invoked, have us adored, have us remembered by created man, by made man, by mortal man. Thus be it done.

"Let your nature be known, Hunahpu-Vuch, Hunahpu-Utiu, twice mother, twice father, Nim-Ac, Nima-Tziis, the master of emeralds, the worker in jewels, the sculptor, the carver, the maker of beautiful plates, the maker of green gourds, the master of resin, the master Toltecat, grandmother of the sun, grandmother of dawn, as you will be called by our works and our creatures.

"Cast the lot with your grains of corn and the *tzite*. Do it thus, and we shall know if we are to make or carve his mouth and eyes out of wood." Thus the diviners were told.

They went down at once to make their divination, and cast their lots with the corn and the *tzite*. "Fate! Creature!" said an old woman and an old man. And this old man was the one who cast the lots with Tzite, the one called Xpiyacoc. And the old woman was the diviner, the maker, called Chiracan Xmucane.

Beginning the divination, they said: "Get together, grasp each other! Speak, that we may hear." They said, "Say if it is well that the wood be got together and that it be carved by the Creator and the Maker, and if this [man of wood] is he who must nourish and sustain us when there is light when it is day!

"Thou, corn; thou, *tzite;* thou, fate; thou, creature; get together, take each other," they said to the corn, to the *tzite,* to fate, to the creature. "Come to sacrifice here, Heart of Heaven; do not punish Tepeu and Gucumatz!"

Then they talked and spoke the truth: "Your figures of wood shall come out well; they shall speak and talk on earth."

"So may it be," they answered when they spoke.

And instantly the figures were made of wood. They looked like men, talked like men, and populated the surface of the earth.

They existed and multiplied; they had daughters, they had sons, these wooden figures; but they did not have souls, nor minds, they did not remember their Creator, their Maker; they walked on all fours, aimlessly.

They no longer remembered the Heart of Heaven and therefore they fell out of favor. It was merely a trial, an attempt at man. At first they spoke, but their face was without expression; their feet and hands had no strength; they had no blood, nor substance, nor moisture, nor flesh; their cheeks were dry, their feet and hands were dry, and their flesh was yellow.

Therefore, they no longer thought of their Creator nor their Maker, nor of those who made them and cared for them.

These were the first men who existed in great numbers on the face of the earth.

(I.3) IMMEDIATELY the wooden figures were annihilated, destroyed, broken up, and killed.

A flood was brought about by the Heart of Heaven; a great flood was formed which fell on the heads of the wooden creatures.

Of *tzite,* the flesh of man was made, but when woman was fashioned by the Creator and the Maker, her flesh was made of rushes. These were the materials the Creator and the Maker wanted to use in making them.

But those that they had made, that they had created, did not think, did not speak with their Creator, their Maker. And for this reason they were killed, they were deluged. A heavy resin fell from the sky. The one called Xecotcovach came and gouged out their eyes; Camalotz came and cut off their heads; Cotzbalam came and devoured their flesh. Tucumbalam came, too, and broke and mangled their bones and their nerves, and ground and crumbled their bones.

This was to punish them because they had not thought of their mother, nor their father, the Heart of Heaven, called Huracan. And for this reason the face of the earth was darkened and a black rain began to fall, by day and by night.

Then came the small animals and the large animals, and sticks and stones struck their faces. And all began to speak: their earthen jars, their griddles, their plates, their pots, their grinding stones, all rose up and struck their faces.

"You have done us much harm; you ate us, and now we shall kill you," said their dogs and birds of the barnyard.

And the grinding stones said: "We were tormented by you; every day, every day, at night, at dawn, all the time our faces went *boli, boli, buqui, buqui,* because of you. This was the tribute we paid you. But now that you are no longer men, you shall feel our strength. We shall grind and tear your flesh to pieces," said their grinding stones.

And then their dogs spoke and said: "Why did you give us nothing to eat? You scarcely looked at us, but you chased us and threw us out. You always had a stick ready to strike us while you were eating.

"Thus it was that you treated us. You did not speak to us. Perhaps we shall not kill you now; but why did you not look ahead, why did you not think about yourselves? Now we shall destroy you, now you shall feel the teeth of our mouths; we shall devour you," said the dogs, and then, they destroyed their faces.

And at the same time, their griddles and pots spoke: "Pain and suffering you have caused us. Our mouths and our faces were blackened with soot; we were always put on the fire and you burned us as though we felt no pain. Now you shall feel it, we shall burn you," said their pots, and they all destroyed their [the wooden men's] faces. The stones of the hearth, which were heaped together, hurled themselves straight from the fire against their heads causing them pain.

The desperate ones [the men of wood] ran as quickly as they could; they wanted to climb to the tops of the houses, and the houses fell down and threw them to the ground; they wanted to climb to the treetops, and the trees cast them far away; they wanted to enter the caverns, and the caverns repelled them.

So was the ruin of the men who had been created and formed, the men made to be destroyed and annihilated; the mouths and faces of all of them were mangled.

And it is said that their descendants are the monkeys which now live in the forests; these are all that remain of them because their flesh was made only of wood by the Creator and the Maker.

And therefore the monkey looks like man, and is an example of a generation of men which were created and made but were only wooden figures. . . .

(III.1) HERE, then, is the beginning of when it was decided to make man, and when what must enter into the flesh of man was sought.

And the Forefathers, the Creators and Makers, who were called Tepeu and Gucumatz said: "The time of dawn has come, let the work be finished, and let those who are to nourish and sustain us appear, the noble sons, the civilized vassals; let man appear, humanity, on the face of the earth." Thus they spoke.

They assembled, came together and held council in the darkness and in the night; then they sought and discussed, and here they reflected and thought. In this way their decisions came clearly to light and they found and discovered what must enter into the flesh of man.

It was just before the sun, the moon, and the stars appeared over the Creators and Makers.

From Paxil, from Cayala, as they were called, came the yellow ears of corn and the white ears of corn.

These are the names of the animals which brought the food: *yac* (the mountain cat), *utiu* (the coyote), *quel* (a small parrot), and *bob* (the crow). These four animals gave tidings of the yellow ears of corn and the white ears of corn, they told them that they should go to Paxil and they showed them the road to Paxil.

And thus they found the food, and this was what went into the flesh of created man, the made man; this was his blood; of this the blood of man was made. So the corn entered [into the formation of man] by the work of the Forefathers.

And in this way they were filled with joy, because they had found a beautiful land, full of pleasures, abundant in ears of yellow corn and ears of white corn, and abundant also in *pataxte* and cacao, and in innumerable *zapotes, anonas, jocotes, nantzes, matasanos,* and honey. There was an abundance of delicious food in those villages called Paxil and Cayala. There were foods of every kind, small and large foods, small plants and large plants.

The animals showed them the road. And then grinding the yellow corn and the white corn, Xmucane made nine drinks, and from this food came the strength and the flesh, and with it they created the muscles and the strength of man. This the Forefathers did, Tepeu and Gucumatz, as they were called.

After that they began to talk about the creation and the making of our first mother and father; of yellow corn and of white corn they made their flesh; of corn-meal dough they made the arms and the legs of man. Only dough of corn meal went into the flesh of our first fathers, the four men, who were created.

(III.2) THESE are the names of the first men who were created and formed: the first man was Balam-Quitze [sorcerer of fatal laughter], the second, Balam-Acab [sorcerer of the night], the third, Mahucutah [not brushed], and the fourth was Iqui-Balam [black sorcerer].

These are the names of our first mothers and fathers.

It is said that they only were made and formed, they had no mother, they had no father. They were only called men. They were not born of woman, nor were they begotten by the Creator nor by the Maker, nor by the Forefathers. Only by a miracle, by means of incantation were they created and made by the Creator, the Maker, the Forefathers, Tepeu and Gucumatz. And as they had the appearance of men, they were men; they talked, conversed, saw and heard, walked, grasped things; they were good and handsome men, and their figure was the figure of a man.

They were endowed with intelligence; they saw and instantly they could see far, they succeeded in seeing, they succeeded in knowing all that there is in the world. When they looked, instantly they saw all around them, and they contemplated in turn the arch of heaven and the round face of the earth.

The things hidden [in the distance] they saw all, without first having to move; at once they saw the world, and so, too, from where they were, they saw it.

Great was their wisdom; their sight reached to the forests, the rocks, the lakes, the seas, the mountains, and the valleys. In truth, they were admirable men, Balam-Quitze, Balam-Acab, Mahucutah, and Iqui-Balam.

Then the Creator and the Maker asked them: "What do you think of your condition? Do you not see? Do you not hear? Are not your speech and manner of walking good? Look, then! Contemplate the world, look [and see] if the mountains and the valleys appear! Try, then, to see!" they said to [the four first men].

And immediately they [the four first men] began to see all that was in the world. Then they gave thanks to the Creator and the Maker: "We really give you thanks, two and three times! We have been created, we have been given a mouth and a face, we speak, we hear, we think, and walk; we feel perfectly, and we know what is far and what is near. We also see the large and the small in the sky and on earth. We give you thanks, then, for having created us, oh, Creator and Maker! for having given us being, oh, our grandmother! oh, our grandfather!" they said, giving thanks for their creation and formation.

They were able to know all, and they examined the four corners, the four points of the arch of the sky and the round face of the earth.

But the Creator and the Maker did not hear this with pleasure. "It is not well what our creatures, our works say; they know all, the large and the small," they said. And so the Forefathers held counsel again. "What shall we do with them now? Let their sight reach only to that which is near; let them see only a little of the face of the earth! It is not well what they say. Perchance, are they not by nature simple creatures of our making? Must they also be gods? And if they do not reproduce and multiply when it will dawn, when the sun rises? And what if they do not multiply?" So they spoke.

"Let us check a little their desires, because it is not well what we see. Must they perchance be the equals of ourselves, their Makers, who can see afar, who know all and see all?"

Thus spoke the Heart of Heaven, Huracan, Chipi-Caculha, Raxa-Caculha, Tepeu, Gucumatz, the Forefathers, Xpiyacoc, Xmucane, the Creator and the Maker. Thus they spoke, and immediately they changed the nature of their works, of their creatures.

Then the Heart of Heaven blew mist into their eyes, which clouded their sight as when a mirror is breathed upon. Their eyes were covered and they could see only what was close, only that was clear to them.

In this way the wisdom and all the knowledge of the four men, the origin and beginning [of the Quiché race], were destroyed.

In this way were created and formed our grandfathers, our fathers, by the Heart of Heaven, the Heart of Earth.

(III.3) THEN their wives had being, and their women were made. God himself made them carefully. And so, during sleep, they came, truly beautiful, their women, at the side of Balam-Quitze, Balam-Acab, Mahucutah, and Iqui-Balam.

There were their women when they awakened, and instantly their hearts were filled with joy because of their wives.

Here are the names of their wives: Caha-Paluna [falling water] was the name of the wife of Balam-Quitze; Chomiha [beautiful water] was the wife of Balam-Acab; Tzununiha [water of hummingbirds], the wife of Mahucutah; and Caquixaha [water of the macaw] was the name of the wife of Iqui-Balam. These are the names of their wives, who were distinguished women.

They conceived the men, of the small tribes and of the large tribes, and were the origin of us; the people of Quiché.

There were many priests and sacrificers; there were not only four, but those four were the Forefathers of us, the people of the Quiché.

The names of each one were different when they multiplied there in the East, and there were many names of the people: Tepeu, Oloman, Cohah, Quenech, Ahau, as they called those men there in the East, where they multiplied.

The beginning is known, too, of those of Tamub and those of Ilocab who came together from there in the East.

Balam-Quitze was the grandfather and the father of the nine great houses of the Cavec; Balam-Acab was the grandfather and father of the nine great houses of the Nimhaib; Mahucutah, the grandfather and father of the four great houses of Ahau-Quiché.

Three groups of families existed; but they did not forget the name of their grandfather and father, those who propagated and multiplied there in the East.

The Tamub and Ilocab also came, and thirteen branches of peoples, the thirteen of Tecpan, and those of Rabinal, the Cakchiquel, those from Tziquinaha, and the Zacaha and the Lamaq, Cumatz, Tuhalha, Uchabaha, those of Chumilaha, those of Quibaha, of Batenaba, Acul-Vinac, Balamiha, the Canchahel, and Balam-Colob.

These are only the principal tribes, the branches of the people which we mention; only of the principal ones shall we speak. Many others came from each group of the people, but we shall not write their names. They also multiplied there in the East.

Many men were made and in the darkness they multiplied. Neither the sun nor the light had yet been made when they multiplied. All lived together, they existed in great number and walked there in the East.

Nevertheless, they did not sustain nor maintain [their God]; they only raised their faces to the sky, and they did not know why they had come so far as they did.

There they were then, in great number, the black men and the white men, men of many classes, men of many tongues, that it was wonderful to hear them.

There are generations in the world, there are country people, whose faces we do not see, who have no homes, they only wander through the small and large woodlands, like crazy people. So it is said scornfully of the people of the wood. So they said there, where they saw the rising of the sun.

The speech of all was the same. They did not invoke wood nor stone, and they remembered the word of the Creator and the Maker, the Heart of Heaven, the Heart of Earth.

In this manner they spoke, while they thought about the coming of the dawn. And they raised their prayers, those worshipers of the word [of God], loving, obedient, and fearful, raising their faces to the sky when they asked for daughters and sons:

"Oh thou, Tzacol, Bitol [Creator and Maker]! Look at us, hear us! Do not leave us, do not forsake us, oh, God, who art in heaven and on earth, Heart of Heaven, Heart of Earth! Give us our descendants, our succession, as long as the sun shall move and there shall be light. Let it dawn; let the day come! Give us many good roads, flat roads! May the people have peace, much peace, and may they be happy; and give us good life and useful existence! Oh, thou Huracan, Chipi-Caculha, Raxa-Caculha, Chipi-Nanauac, Raxa-nanauac, Voc, Hunahpu, Tepeu, Gucumatz, Alom, Qaholom, Xpiyacoc, Xmucane, grandmother of the sun, grandmother of the light, let there be dawn, and let the light come!"

Thus they spoke while they saw and invoked the coming of the sun, the arrival of day; and at the same time that they saw the rising of the sun, they contemplated the Morning Star, the Great Star, which comes ahead of the sun, that lights up the arch of the sky and the surface of the earth, and illuminates the steps of the men who had been created and made. . . .

(III.9) **H**ERE, then, is the dawn, and the coming of the sun, the moon, and the stars.

Balam-Quitze, Balam-Acab, Mahucutah, and Iqui-Balam were very happy when they saw the Morning Star. It rose first, with shining face, when it came ahead of the sun.

Immediately they unwrapped the incense which they had brought from the East, and which they had planned to burn, and then they untied the three gifts which they had planned to offer.

The incense which Balam-Quitze brought was called Mixtan-Pom; the incense which Balam-Acab brought was called Cavixtan-Pom; and that which Mahucutah brought was called Cabauil-Pom. The three had their incense and burned it when they began to dance facing toward the East.

They wept for joy as they danced and burned their incense, their precious incense. Then they wept because they did not yet behold nor see the sunrise.

But, then, the sun came up. The small and large animals were happy; and arose from the banks of the river, in the ravines, and on the tops of the mountains, and all turned their eyes to where the sun was rising.

Then the puma and the jaguar roared. But first the bird called Queletzu burst into song. In truth, all the animals were happy, and the eagle, the white vulture; the small birds and the large birds stretched their wings.

The priests and the sacrificers were kneeling; great was the joy of the priests and sacrificers and of the people of Tamub and Ilocab and the people of Rabinal, the Cakchiquel, those from Tziquinaha, and those from Tuhalha, Uchabaha, Quibaha, from Batena, and the Yaqui Tepeu, all those tribes which exist today. And it was not possible to count the people. The light of dawn fell upon all the tribes at the same time.

Instantly the surface of the earth was dried by the sun. Like a man was the sun when it showed itself, and its face glowed when it dried the surface of the earth.

Before the sun rose, damp and muddy was the surface of the earth, before the sun came up; but then the sun rose, and came up like a man. And its heat was unbearable. It showed itself when it was born and remained fixed [in the sky] like a mirror. Certainly it was not the same sun which we see, it is said in their old tales.

Immediately afterward Tohil, Avilix, and Hacavitz were turned to stone, together with the deified beings, the puma, the jaguar, the snake, the *cantil,* and the hobgoblin. Their arms became fastened to the trees when the sun, the moon, and the stars appeared. All alike, were changed into stone. Perhaps we should not be living today because of the voracious animals, the puma, the jaguar, the snake, and the *cantil,* as well as the hobgoblin; perhaps our power would not exist if these first animals had not been turned into stone by the sun.

When the sun arose, the hearts of Balam-Quitze, Balam-Acab, Mahucutah, and Iqui-Balam were filled with joy. Great was their joy when it dawned. And there were not many men at that place; only a few were there on the mountain Hacavitz. There dawn came to them, there they burned their incense and danced, turning their gaze toward the East, whence they had come. There were their mountains and their valleys, whence had come Balam-Quitze, Balam-Acab, Mahucutah, and Iqui-Balam, as they were called.

—*The Popol Vuh.* Adrián Recinos, trans.; Delia Goetz and Sylvanus G. Morley, English trans. Norman: University of Oklahoma Press, 1950, pp. 81–92, 165–173, 186–190.

MAYA

Our Father God
This modern creation myth from the Mayan Indians of Guatemala shows the effect of centuries of missonary work and the complex way in which Christian doctrines were assimilated into a basically Indian framework. In a similar Aztec myth, the Great Mother of the universe protects her unborn child, Tezcatlipoca, from the jealous star gods, her other children. When Tezcatlipoca is born, he destroys all his persecutors, transforms his sister into the moon, and becomes the sun himself.

In this Guatemalan myth, once Our Father God demonstrates his great powers, his uncles (the ancestors or "Ancient Men," called "Jews" by the Indians) plot his destruction. Beaten and burned, he miraculously survives, outwits his opponents, and transforms them into monkeys (as in the Popol Vuh). Although finally betrayed and crucified by the Jewish kings, Our Father God escapes up a ladder (another axis mundi connecting the profane and sacred realms) to the heavens and becomes the sun. Then, like the hero of the Popol Vuh, he destroys the ancient beings (here the kings, there the great animals) with his heat and "clears the world."

Not only are the Indian and Christian myths sufficiently similar in basic structure to permit easy merging, but also the experience of Christianity as a new religion supplanting an older Judaism in its own history seems easily translatable into this new culture. The Mayans thus identify their own ancestors with the "unbelieving" Jews, and describe the religious struggle and final victory of the new young god with personal conviction.

WHEN OUR FATHER GOD was born of Our Virgin Mother, He was born there in the pasture. The ox gave him breath that he should live.

"How did it happen that our sister [the Virgin Mother] gave birth to a son?" [asked the Ancient Men, brothers of the Virgin Mother]. "Whose is the son that our sister has?"

Three days after birth Our Father spoke, and when the brothers [the Ancient Men] heard him speak they took him away to work. "Come with us," they said to him. "You will be our companion, we will look after you, we will give you your food and your drink, when we have finished working we will carry you."

They arrived at the working place, placed an axe in the hand of Our Father God so that He should work, beat him, and then set him to clear away some trees standing in a field. He chopped at the trees only twice to clear the field, thereby winning over the brothers [who had to work all day to cut down one tree].

"This brother [i.e., God] will become more powerful than we are," said the brothers. "Later he will annoy us more, this fatherless orphan."

When they returned from work they beat him and did not give him any food; instead they handed him an axe, a cutting knife with a long wooden shaft, a machete, and a hoe, and made this brother [God] walk in front of them. They left him with his mother, saying, "Here is our brother, we will come to get him tomorrow."

She said, "He will not go with you again because he is very small, my son."

God said, "I am going with my brothers. I am going to see how they burn a field [i.e., prepare a field for cultivation]."

[The next day] on the way [to the field] there is a volcano that is hidden from view. They beat him [God] with a whip, shouting, "You are going to be more knavish than we are. You are a son of a widow." Then they carried him to the field, tied him to a tree by means of twenty-two new ropes, set fire to the field, and [they] the Ancient Men formed a circle around the fire. They believed that he was burned and said, "Hear how his stomach has already burst. Now we have won."

"Our Father God then called the "cotusa" [an animal]. The earth opened and the cotusa came to cut the ropes. Then God went with the cotusa into the earth and escaped free [from the burning field]. When the field was cold, they [the Ancient Men] went to look. God had left a kind of tree which resembles human bones at the foot of the tree to which he had been tied. "Now he is burned, now he is dead," they cried.

During their journey home the Ancient Men came to a volcano and there they saw him [God] playing in his hut, there with his mother. "It appears that our brother is playing there; now we are not going to win. Let us inquire if our brother has already arrived."

"We ordered him to leave sooner than we did," [the Ancient Men told the Virgin Mother]. "Do not burn yourself, we said."

They, her brothers, returned to their houses. "Let us make a fiesta, we are sad, we did not conquer the son of the widow." Then they searched for a drum and a chirimía [flageolet], donned their jackets, put on their masks, placed their weapons, a squirrel pelt and the pelt of a wildcat under their arms and they, the Ancient Men, danced.

"I am going to see how my brothers dance," said she, the Mother of Our God. "I will carry a bit of my cotton; I will arrange it [the cotton] in my basket."

"I am going with you, Mama."

"Do not go, son, they might trample on you."

"I can go in the basket under the cotton, and watch [them]."

He observed what they did and then returned to his hut with his mother. Having finished dancing, the brothers of the Mother of Our Father God ate.

"I am going to see what they are eating, Mama," said God. He watched from the door of the house. Then they threw the bones [from the food] in the face of Our Father God. He picked them up and gathered them together, those meat bones, in his hat and carried them to his hut. Then he planted [the bones], erected a corral, closed the corral and returned to his hut. Three days after planting he went to see it and found there good [i.e., well grown] cattle, the beast, the pig, the deer, the sheep, the goat, the armadillo, the chickens, the rabbit, the turkey, the fox, the coyote, the badger, the raccoon, the "pisote," the poodle, the "taquazin," the squirrel, the snake, the mouse, the bird, the lizard, the toad, the frog, the iguana, the crab, the goose, the turtle [tortoise], the buzzard, the widow [red-beaked buzzard], the sparrow hawk, the raven, the songbird, the owl, the barn owl, the cockroach, the dog, the cat, the fish, the scorpion, the butterfly, the ant, the louse, the white louse, the flea, the woodpecker [three kinds], the sparrow, the tiger, and the lion. Our Father God planted all the animals there are in the world.

When the Ancient Men saw the corral, they opened it. [Later] when Our Father God arrived to look at it again, no more than one half of the animals were left. Yes, only the horse, the sheep, the cattle, the pig, the chickens, the duck, the turkey, the dog, and the goat, only these was Our Father God able to seize. The wild animals had already fled to the woods when he arrived.

Our Father God went to see how they [the Ancient Men] perform their dances. He said to his mother, "I am going to form one [dance] too, like that of my brothers."

The mother said to him, "Liar, you can hardly do it. A gathering is necessary, there is money and food to be spent."

He formed it [the dance] in just one night, arranging [the performance] for midnight. When his dance began, they [the Ancient Men] heard the skyrockets. They went to watch it and saw that the dance was much better [than their dance]. Then they consulted with their companions [?], to whom the older brothers admitted that they were shamed. They threw away their dance costumes and said to the younger brother [God], "Yes, we have behaved badly to you. Excuse us, we ask pardon. Show us where you went to get your costumes."

"If you like," [answered God]. "But they come from very far away. You will hardly endure it [the trip], it costs much, there is cramp on the road, there is catarrh, there is custom. Gather yourselves together and we will go; I will show you."

They went on their way until they arrived at the seat of a very great tree. God told them to climb up [the tree]; [when] he saw that they had already ascended, he went up behind them. The tree continued to grow, going very far up. Then he [God] stripped the bark from the tree, formed a lagoon at the base of the tree, and he, Our Father God, commanded that once for all they should remain there [in the tree] because they had behaved very badly to him. Then he [left and] arrived at his mother's place.

"Where did you leave your brothers?" asked the mother.

"They come from far away," [he answered].

"Who knows where you left them?" [she remarked].

"They remained there; I will go [with you] if you wish to see them."

Our Mother arrived [there] and saw that they had become animals.

"Liar," she said. "These cannot be they. They of whom you speak are animals."
She questioned [the animals]. "Is it you?" They shook the tree in reply.
[They could not talk now because they were animals.] Then some refuse fell in
her eye, and [in anger] she commanded that they should remain like animals for
all time.

"Now you will eat the fruit of the tree," [she ordered]. "You do not wish
to be good."

Then the kings [of the Jews] gathered together against Our Father God.
They ran after him; he ran away. [On the way] there was a man working.

"What are you doing?" [asked God]. "What are you planting?"

"I am planting some stones."

"Within three days these stones will become very large," [said God].
"Some men are following me; if they question you, do not tell them that I passed
by."

"There was one who passed by when I was planting my stones sixty days
ago," [the man told the kings]. From there they followed God, with machete,
with weapon, with lance. "Until we have killed him," said the kings.

There was another man planting beans [on the route over which God was
fleeing]. Our Father God asked, "What are you doing?"

"I am planting a little of my beans."

"Within three days your beans will be dry," [God told him]. "There are
some men following me; if they question you, don't tell them anything."

"There was one who passed by when I was planting my beans about sixty
days ago," he told them [the kings].

He [God] now walked very little. The kings seized him and killed him.
Then, when they had finished killing him, they, the kings, nailed him to the cross,
opening his arms and putting nails through them. Then they went away.

He [God] placed a ladder on the cross and went away by means of this
ladder. He arrived in heaven. Then began the light in the seat of heaven, the cock
crowed, the beasts and the cattle howled. The world [that God formed] became
clear, and then the sun lit up and the kings were burned.

—Morris Siegel. "The Creation Myth and Acculturation in Acatan, Guatemala." *Journal of American Folklore*, 1943, *56*, 121–124. Philadelphia: American Folklore Society.

INCA

Ordering the World
The great Inca Empire succeeded a
long series of prehistoric Peruvian cultures when it came to prominence c. 1200
A.D. and became powerful enough to take over neighboring tribes by force c. 1440.
When Pizarro conquered the Inca in 1553, he found an Empire stretching from
Quito, Ecuador, to the Rio Maule in Chile. It was a highly organized and disci-
plined socialist society, capable of monumental building projects, an extraordinary
road system, and even a messenger service that could cover 150 miles a day. The
upper class worshipped a high god with no name, who was most commonly referred to by one of his titles ("Wiraqoca" to the Inca, "Viracocha" to the Span-

ish). Perceived as the ground of being, the source of all power, this personification of the Holy had neither special function nor particular cult, and popular religious attention was therefore focused on his more immanent servants, the gods and goddesses of the sun, thunder, moon, sea, and the *huacas,* local sacred places and things.

This myth was recounted by one of the last Incas to Garcilaso de la Vega, the son of an Inca princess and a Spanish conquistador, around 1556 when he was a young man. It later became part of *The Royal Commentaries* Garcilaso wrote about the history of Peru. Appropriate to a culture so highly organized, the myth recalls the primitive animalistic state of people before "our father Sun" sent two of his children by the moon goddess to earth. The young Inca (emperor) and his sister-bride moved about until they found a place where they could easily plunge the golden rod their father had given them (that is, in mythological language, until they could find a place where Earth was properly receptive to sun's fertilization; or, in agricultural language, until they could find rich soil and good climate.) There they stopped, organized all the local people, and eventually ruled an empire of such size and power it could reach out and conquer others. The social order was essential to the empire's success: cities were divided into upper and lower halves; men and women were instructed in appropriate tasks. Thus the myth proclaims the divinity of all rulers descending from the first Inca and their divine sanction of the basic social structure.

"AT ONE TIME, all the land you see about you was nothing but mountains and desolate cliffs. The people lived like wild beasts, with neither order nor religion, neither villages nor houses, neither fields nor clothing, for they had no knowledge of their wool or cotton. Brought together haphazardly in groups of two and three, they lived in grottoes and caves and, like wild game, fed upon grass and roots, wild fruits, and even human flesh. They covered their nakedness with the bark and leaves of trees, or with the skins of animals. Some even went unclothed. And as for women, they possessed none who were recognized as their very own.

"Seeing the condition they were in, our father the Sun was ashamed for them, and he decided to send one of his sons and one of his daughters from heaven to earth, in order that they might teach men to adore him and acknowledge him as their god; to obey his laws and precepts as every reasonable creature must do; to build houses and assemble together in villages; to till the soil, sow the seed, raise cattle, and enjoy the fruits of their labors like human beings.

"Our father the Sun set his two children down at a place eighty leagues from here, on Lake Titicaca, and he gave them a rod of gold, a little shorter than a man's arm and two fingers in thickness.

" 'Go where you will,' he said to them, 'and whenever you stop to eat or to sleep, plunge this rod into the earth. At the spot where, with one single thrust, it disappears entirely, there you must establish and hold your court. And the peoples whom you will have brought under your sway shall be maintained by you in a state of justice and reason, with piety, mercy, and mildness.

" 'To the entire world,' added our father the Sun, 'I give my light and my brilliance; I give men warmth when they are cold; I cause their fields to fructify and their cattle to multiply; each day that passes I go all around the world in order to have a better knowledge of men's needs and to satisfy these needs: follow my example. Do unto all of them as a merciful father would do unto his well-beloved children; for I have sent you on earth for the good of men, that they might cease to live like wild animals. You shall be the kings and lords of all the peoples who accept our law and our rule.'

"Having thus declared his will to his two children, our father the Sun dismissed them. They then left Lake Titicaca and walked northwards, trying vainly each day to thrust their rod of gold into the earth. And so they came to a little shelter about seven or eight leagues from here. Day was breaking when they left it and that is why the Inca called this spot Caparec Tempu, which means: the Inn of Morning. Later, he filled it with people and, to this day, the inhabitants of that village take pride in this name that comes from our first king. From there, the Inca and his bride, our queen, entered into Cuzco valley which, at that time, was nothing but wild, mountainous country.

"The first halt they made in this valley," my uncle said, "was at a place called Huanacauri, a half-day's walk from here. There they tried their rod and not only did it sink into the earth, but it disappeared entirely. Then our Inca turned to his sister-bride:

" 'Our father the Sun,' he said, 'has commanded us to remain in this valley, to settle here and make it our home. You then go your way, and I shall go mine, to call together and assemble the inhabitants of these regions, in order that we might teach them good, as we have been ordered to do.'

"Now they left the hill of Huanacauri, each going his own way; and this spot being the first to have been trod on by their feet, you will understand," my uncle said, "that we built a temple there, so that our father the Sun should be perpetually adored in recognition of the signal favor he showed us on that day. The prince set out for the north and the princess for the south. They explained to all whom they met that their father the Sun had sent them on earth to be the rulers and benefactors of this country, to teach them all how to live, how to clothe and feed themselves like men, instead of like animals.

"The savages to whom they spoke these promising words marveled as much at what they saw as at what they heard: for the Inca and his sister-bride were both arrayed in garments and ornaments that had been given to them by our father the Sun, and both of them had ears that were pierced and open the way we, their descendants, wear ours today. Never had the inhabitants of this region seen anything like it; therefore, they believed all that was told them, they worshiped our ancestors as the children of the Sun, and obeyed them as their kings. The news of this wonderful event began to spread from place to place and a great gathering of men and women was soon assembled about the two Incas, ready to follow them wherever they might lead.

"Our sovereigns then distributed the necessary tasks amongst this crowd of persons, ordering some to go seek food for all, whilst others, following their instructions, were to begin to build huts and houses. Thus our imperial city came into existence, and was divided into two halves: *Hanan-Cuzco,* or Upper-Cuzco, and *Hurin-Cuzco,* or Lower-Cuzco. Hanan-Cuzco was founded by our king and Hurin-Cuzco by our queen, and that is why the two parts were given these names, without the inhabitants of one possessing any superiority over those of the other, but simply to recall the fact that certain of them had been originally brought together by the king, and certain others by the queen. There existed only one single difference between them, a difference in accordance with the king's desire, and that was, that the inhabitants of Upper-Cuzco were to be considered as the elder, and those of Lower-Cuzco as the younger brothers. Indeed, it was as it is in the case of a living body, in which there always exists a difference between the right and the left hands, for the reason that those from above had been brought together by the male, and those from below by the female element. All the cities and all the villages in our Empire were subsequently divided in this way into upper and lower lineages, as well as into upper and lower districts.

"While peopling the city, our Inca taught the male Indians the tasks that were to be theirs, such as selecting seeds and tilling the soil. He taught them how to make hoes, how to irrigate their fields by means of canals that connected natural streams, and even to make these same shoes that we still wear today. The queen, meanwhile, was teaching the women how to spin and weave wool and cotton, how to make clothing, as well as other domestic tasks.

"In short, our sovereigns, the Inca king, who was master of the men, and Queen Coya, who was mistress of the women, taught their subjects everything that had to do with human living.

"The first subjects of the Inca were soon well aware of the numerous benefits they derived from their new situation and they went immediately into the mountains to proclaim to all their neighbors the arrival on earth of the marvelous children of the Sun. In proof of their statements, they displayed their clothing and their foodstuffs, explaining that now they lived in houses, grouped together in villages. Soon, the savages began to marvel, too, and they came in droves to join the Inca and his sister, remaining to serve and obey them. After six or seven years, they had become so numerous that the Inca possessed armed troops for his defense and for subjugating those who did not come of their own accord. He had taught them to make bows, lances, arrows, and bludgeons.

"In order to shorten this account of the exploits of our first king, we shall say simply that he extended his rule towards the east as far as the river which we call Paucartampu, that he conquered eight leagues of land to the west, as far as the great Apurimac river, and nine leagues to the south, as far as the Queque-sana. In this latter direction, he had more than one hundred villages built, the most important of which contained a hundred homes.

"Such then," my uncle concluded, "were the beginnings of our city which, today, as you can see, is rich and populous; such were those of the great, illustrious Empire that your father and his companions [i.e., the Spaniards] took from us; and such were our first Incas, our first kings, those who came here during the first centuries of the world and from whom all our other kings are descended, in the same way that all of us, all your relatives, are. I am unable to say exactly at what date the Sun sent his first children down to earth, because that demands calculation that is beyond my memory; let us say that it was at least four hundred years ago. Our Inca's name was Manco Capac and our Coya Mama, Occlo Huaco. They were brother and sister, as I explained to you before, the children of the Moon and the Sun.

"I believe now that I have answered all your questions and, in order not to make you weep, I have held back from my own eyes the tears of blood wrung from my heart by sorrow at the spectacle of our Inca's downfall and our lost Empire."

—Garcilaso de la Vega. *The Incas.* Alain Gheerbrant, ed., Maria Jolas, trans. New York: Avon Books, 1964, pp. 43–47.

YARURO

Eight Versions of the Creation

Legend
The Yaruros live along the Rio Capanaparo in Venezuela and worship a mother goddess, Kuma, the consort or mother of the sun and source and establisher of all. Kuma came into being with her brothers Puana (the water serpent) and Itciai (the jaguar), who created water and earth respectively and who still serve as identifications of the two exogamous matrilineal moieties into which Yaruro society is divided.

Only the shamans among the Yaruros can contact Kuma now and visit her land of giants (a heaven in which perfect, huge forms of every creatures exist eternally) in the west. With a pole set up in front of him, the shaman enters a trance and describes his soul's journey while people dance around him, men in one direction and women in another.

These eight short versions of the Yaruro myth show interesting variations (and structural similarities) within the central themes of creation, the descent of the culture hero, and the emergence of the people.

I At first there was nothing. Then Puana the Snake, who came first, created the world and everything in it, including the river courses, except the water. Itciai the Jaguar created the water. Kuma was the first person to people the land. Then the other people were created. Then came India Rosa from the east. The Guahibos were created last. That is the reason that they live in the forest.

Horses and cattle were given to the Yaruros. However, they were so large that the Yaruros were afraid to mount them. The "Racionales" were not afraid, and so the horses were given to them.

The sun travels in a canoe from east to west. At night it goes to Kuma's land. The stars are her children and they wander about at night. The moon, which is a sister to the sun, travels in a boat.

On the land of Kuma exists a large plant of each species. The plants which are cultivated by the Racionales were first given to the Yaruros. The Yaruros cut them down in such a way that the tops fell in the land of the Racionales. The roots remained in the land of the Yaruros, but the Racionales got the seed and that is why they have bananas, plantains, maize, tobacco, and the Yaruros have none of those things.

II Everything sprang from Kuma, and everything that the Yaruros do was established by her. She is dressed like a shaman, only her ornaments are of gold and much more beautiful.

With Kuma sprang Puana and Itciai; Hatchawa is her grandson and Puana made a bow and arrow for him. Puana taught Hatchawa to hunt and fish. When Hatchawa saw the people at the bottom of a hole and wished to bring them to the top Puana made him a rope and a hook.

Another figure that sprang with Kuma was Kiberoh. She carried fire in her breast and at Kuma's request gave it to the boy Hatchawa. But when the boy wanted to give it to the people Kuma refused and he cleverly threw live fish in the fire, spreading coals all about. The people seized the hot coals and ran away to start fires of their own. Everything was at first made and given to the boy and he passed it on to the people. Everybody sprang from Kuma, but she was not made pregnant in the ordinary way. It was not necessary.

III The first to appear was Kuma, the chief of all of us and the entire world. Itciai, Puana, and Kiberoh appeared with her. There was nothing then. Nothing had been created. Kuma was made pregnant. She wanted to be impregnated in the thumb but Puana told her that too much progeny would be produced that way. So she was made pregnant in the ordinary way. Hatchawa was born, grandchild (?) of Kuma, Puana, and Itciai. From then on the attention of the three was centered on the boy. Puana created the land; Itciai the water in the rivers. Hatchawa was very small, but soon grew to a very large size. Kuma and Puana took care of his education, though Puana took more care of him. Puana made a bow and arrow for him and told him to hunt and fish. Hatchawa found a hole in the ground one day and looked into it. He saw many people. He went back to his grandparents to ask them to get some of the people out. Kuma did not want to let the people come out, but Hatchawa insisted on it. Puana made a thin rope and hook and dropped it into the hole. The people came out, just as many men as women. Finally a pregnant woman tried to come out and she broke the thin rope in getting out. That is the reason there are few people.

The world was dark and cold. There was no fire. Puana had made the earth and everything on it, and Itciai had created the water. Hatchawa took a live jagupa (a fish) and threw it into the fire which was kept burning in the center of Kuma-land, a high circular pasture. The little fish struggled and knocked coals all about, and the people ran away in all directions with the coals. One part of these people were the Yaruros. Then Kuma wanted to give the horse to them, but the Pumeh (Yaruros) were afraid to mount it.

Of every plant in Kuma land there exists (or existed) a gigantic type, so big that an ax can't cut it. Of every animal there exists a gigantic representative.

IV India Rosa is the same as big Kuma. This Kuma lives in her city in the east. She is either the wife or sister of the sun. She is the younger sister of the other Kuma. She taught the women to make pottery and weave basketry in the same way as Puana taught the men. Itciai and the other Kuma look after everything.

V At first there was nothing. The snake, who came first, created the world and everything in it, including the water courses, but did not create the water itself. The jaguar, the brother of the snake, created the water. The people of India Rosa were the first to people the land. After them, the other people were created. India Rosa came from the east. The Guahibos were created last. That is the reason that they live in the bush.

Horses and cattle were given first to the Yaruros. However, they were so large that the Yaruros were afraid to mount them. The "Racionales" were not afraid, and so they were given the horse.

The sun travels in a boat from the east. It goes to a town at night. The stars are his children and they go out from the town at night. The moon, who is a sister of the sun, also travels in a boat.

VI A woman who came from the east went to live with the sun at his village in the west. She taught women how to do everything which women do. The sun taught the men. The sun and India Rosa are married, and probably were the first people from whom everyone has sprung. But the sun and India Rosa came out of the ground. They had children. Everything was dark at that time. The children dispersed in all directions. They became the different peoples of the world. Then everything was covered with water. Horses were given to the people but they were afraid and would not ride them. But a white man sick with smallpox rode the horse, and then the horse was given to his people. He asked the Yaruros to kill him and they did. Then his people killed the Yaruros.

VII India Rosa came first. She gave birth to a son and a daughter. The son impregnated his sister, who gave birth to all humanity. India Rosa went west, the daughter went east. The son is the sun. The moon is the daughter. The snake came afterwards, and the jaguar created the water.

VIII Kuma was first. God appeared. Had two children, brother and sister, and they married. There were no human beings at that time. One day Kuma said, "Let us have some people." So God went out to see about it. He found a man in a hole. He went back to Kuma, consulted with her, and went back to the man with a hook and a rope. A pregnant woman wanted to be the first to come out of the hole, but she was left to the last. Many people were brought out. The last to be brought out was the pregnant woman, and then the rope broke. The world was dark and cold. So God made a fire. A fish appeared and scattered it, so that each person could take a little of the fire. That is why all people have fire today. The people married among themselves. One of the woman descendants of India Rosa married a man of the new race and from them sprang the Yaruros. This was welcomed because the father of the girl said, "Here, a son-in-law will take care of me now!" Then the Yaruros lived. The shaman had a nephew and a son. The nephew fell in love with his own sister and married—he was changed into a jaguar and she into a snake (?). If it had not been for this there would not have been any snakes and jaguars. Human beings should not marry their own sisters. It was ordered by Kuma. Animals are different.

Then one man found a tree with all the fruits on it. He did not tell the others. A white man appeared on horseback. Said he would come back in eight days. He came back in a boat. Scattered seeds everywhere. Thus he changed the country. Before it was all open savanna, but now forests and agricultural products grew.

India Rosa taught the women. God taught the men. God wanted to give the horse to the Yaruros, but they were afraid to mount, so he gave it to the Racionales instead.

—Vincenzo Petrullo. "The Yaruros of the Capanaparo River, Venezuela." *U. S. Bureau of American Ethnology Bulletin 123 (Anthropological Papers, Number II)*. Washington, D.C.: Government Printing Office, 1939, pp. 238–241.

JIVARO

The Nuhiño or Earth Story
This highly complex and disparaging myth of the Jivaros of Ecuador tells of the generations of sacred powers who fought and mated with one another, producing creatures as often by one means as the other. Incest, unrequited love, patricide and matricide, the correction of one generation's errors by members of another—in tight and angry circles of sex and death, the myth unwinds gradually, showing not only the unhappy spirit of the Jivaros but also many of their central religious beliefs.

As the myth claims, the Jivaros are a warring and agricultural people. Once headhunters, they shrank the heads of their victims (like that of the first Jivaro, killed by the children of his wife and son) to obtain power against the much-feared ancestors who controlled crop growth. Without the heads (*tsantsa*), only women could raise the manioc plant, which they encouraged by squatting over the tubers as if giving birth to them.

As a result of seemingly endless battles between the divinities, Masata (war) himself is born and encourages the continuance of hostilities among the descendants of the first Jivaros. Even the sun and moon cannot rectify the situation, and creation continues in this unsatisfactory state.

IN THE BEGINNING there were two parents, Kumpara, the Creator, and Chingaso, his wife. They had a son, Etsa, the Sun. One day when Etsa was sleeping, Kumpara took a piece of mud and, placing it in his mouth, blew it on Etsa, with the result that it became a daughter, Nantu, the Moon.

Nantu was created in this fashion in order that Etsa might make her his wife, which he could not do were she a blood sister.

There was a bird, Auhu, the goatsucker, who was active only in the night-time. When the Moon appeared he became enamored of her and attempted to have an affair but his advances were not received by Nantu.

After a time Etsa likewise became enamored of Nantu, having a strong desire to have children. Although he paid ardent court to her, Nantu was coy and kept away from him. One day Etsa was painting his face with achiote to make himself attractive and, while he was doing so, Nantu took advantage of his preoccupation and disappeared by shooting up to the sky. Nantu, upon arriving at the sky, painted herself black with sua (witau) so that her body would become the night. She also painted her face, these being the markings on the surface of the Moon. Then Nantu followed a steep trail upward, climbing and climbing like a jaguar over the curving vault of the sky.

Auhu, seeing his loved one climbing thus above him and sensing that Nantu was escaping from Etsa, decided to try his luck again at courting. There was a vine hanging down from the sky and Auhu began to climb this in order to reach the object of his desire. Nantu, seeing him, cut the vine, which fell and became entangled in all the trees of the jungle where one may see it now. Auhu, foiled in his pursuit, fell with it, and once more sulked among his trees.

Now when Etsa discovered that Nantu had eluded him, he was very angry and immediately decided to go in pursuit. At first he knew no means of reaching her, but finally he caught two parrots, Awamasa, and two parakeets. On each wrist he fastened a parrot and on each knee a parakeet, saying to them: "Let us look for Nantu." The birds flew upward with him, carrying him to the sky, where he finally caught up with Nantu and a violent quarrel ensued. During the altercation Etsa became more and more angry and struck Nantu. When this happens the Sun eclipses the Moon [sic]. Nantu retaliated and struck Etsa; this is the Moon eclipsing the Sun. As a result of this exchange of blows, Nantu was subdued and began to cry, Etsa saying: "Now you see how much bigger and stronger I am than you and all you can do is weep." Now whenever the face of the Moon is red it is an indication that it is going to rain.

Following this quarrel, Nantu went off by herself to prove that she could produce a son unaided. She gathered some dirt and, blowing upon it, created a son, which she called Nuhi. Being lonely, she devoted her affection to this son. Auhu, seeing this, became jealous and, approaching stealthily, broke this son, modeled of clay, and Nuhi died, becoming the earth.

Nantu, lonely and now thoroughly subdued, received the advances of Etsa. They were married on the River Kanusa. Here a son was born to them, Unushi, the sloth, who was the first Jivaro. Being so old, he now moves very slowly. The waxing Moon indicates the period of pregnancy; it wanes as it gives birth. The mating of the Sun and the Moon takes place on earth when they have both descended from the sky. The earth was used as a place for Unushi and his descendants to live and also as a mating place for Etza and Nantu. Unushi was put into the forest, which was to be his home henceforth.

Nantu and Etsa then constructed a canoe of caoba wood and in it went out into the river where a second son was born. This was Apopa, the manatee. He was immediately placed in the water and told hereafter he was to live in the river and that whenever Unushi should encounter danger on the water he was to come to his assistance.

Following this, a third son was born to them in the mountains. This was Huangani, the peccary. He was born during a tempest to the accompaniment of rain and thunder, for which reason the peccaries always move about during storms, following the rain as the storm moves along; a fact of which the Jivaros take advantage in hunting.

Shortly after this, Etsa and Nantu were in an open space in the forest when a daughter was born. This was Nijamanche, the manioc plant. She was destined to be for all time the friend and intimate companion of the Jivaros.

Some time elapsed and no more children were born to Etsa and Nantu. Then it was that Chingaso gave them two eggs which they were told to place on a sand bar by the side of the river. This they did, but upon returning next day found that the two eggs had disappeared. While they were puzzling over this fact, Tingishapi, the cricket, came out of the ground and tried to speak to them. He was so small that they did not notice him, so to attract attention to himself he bit them on the feet. They picked him up and said: "Who are you?" The cricket replied: "I am Tingishapi. I am one of your family. I have come to tell you that Untujo, the egret, has flown away with the two eggs which you left here." Etsa immediately set out in pursuit of Untujo and finally caught up with him. Untujo, when caught, dropped one of the eggs, which fell and was broken. The other one Etsa recovered and returned to Nantu.

Remembering how they had almost missed seeing Tingishapi, Etsa instructed him not to move around during the daytime because then many people would be walking about and he would likely get stepped on. He was told that he should henceforth live in the houses of the Jivaros as a guardian. All of this transpired. However, in addition to the desire to guard the house, when night comes on he feels the desire to bite something so that he eats the clothes of the Jivaros.

The egg which had been recovered from Untujo was the color of the sun and, tending it carefully, they produced from it a woman, Mika. Then they brought Mika to the River Kanusa, where Unushi was sleeping, in order that Mika could become his wife.

They were married and then instructed by Etsa and Nantu as to what their respective duties should be as man and wife. Unushi was to do the clearing of the forest where their home was to be built and was to build the house in which they were to live, after being told the manner in which it was to be constructed. Mika was to attend to the planting and care of the manioc, to the preparation of food, and to general household duties. It developed, however, that Unushi was very lazy by nature, with the result that most of the disagreeable work was passed on to Mika, so that now the biggest share of Jivaro work is done by the women. After establishing their household, Unushi and Mika got into a canoe and started to go down the river. During the voyage, a son was born in the canoe. This was Ahimbi, the water serpent.

After the birth of Mika, Chingaso gave many eggs to Nantu from which were produced the birds and animals inhabiting the forests and mountains; these were to be the friends of the Jivaros and were to furnish them with food.

Now, however, Unushi and Mika were away from their home territory and they needed food. At this juncture two little birds flew to the canoe, calling to them to follow, so they left the canoe and went ashore. The two birds preceeded them, entering a hollow tree, which immediately was transformed into the chonta palm, laden with ripe fruit. Gathering the fruit, they cooked it and, after satisfying their hunger, they returned to the beach where they had left their canoe. There was a surging of waters and out of the river came Pangi, the anaconda. Crawling onto the gravel bar, he broke with his tail a large rock from which he fashioned a stone axe for them, showing them the method of its fabrication. With this, Ahimbi cut down a tree, Awamo (the cedro), and from it fashioned a canoe. He was of an adventurous disposition and wanted to shift for himself and see the world. Getting into his canoe, he left his parents and set out on a long trip.

Far down the river he met a white man, Apachi, who was traveling in an iron canoe. He showed Ahimbi iron and various mechanical contrivances, saying: "These are my things. You don't know them so I will show them to you." In order to show Ahimbi, Apachi constructed a large boat of iron, saying: "Now you know what these things are, but they are not for you. On the water you are to use canoes and balsas." Saying which, Apachi left. During a long period of time Ahimbi traveled and had many adventures, but finally decided to return to his parents.

On his way back, in the evening, he encountered Mika traveling alone. He asked her the whereabouts of Unushi. Mika replied that she did not know; she had not seen him for some time, because he had wandered off and become lost in the forest.

When night came on Ahimbi told his mother that he would like to sleep with her. This he did but overslept in the morning, so that when Etsa came at dawn he was still with Mika. Etsa was angry and awoke them, grasping them both by the hair, saying: "Why are you two together in this way?" Ahimbi replied: "We are doing nothing; it has been a long time since I have seen my mother. I am so pleased to be with her again that I merely wanted to be close to her." Not deceived by this tale, Etsa ordered them to leave immediately.

They went away together, after which several children were born to them as they wandered looking for a place to reestablish themselves, but all of the birds and animals who had previously fed them were so much offended by this unnatural union that they refused their help. When they wished to sleep in the cave of Yumbingi, the jaguar, their former friend drove them out and has been an enemy of man ever since.

Finally, Unushi learned what had happened and, much enraged, brooded upon the idea of taking revenge. When Nantu came down to visit her offspring, Unushi accused her of having consented with Etsa that Mika should go away with a man other than her husband and have children by him. Refusing to listen to her denial, and being much enraged, he fell upon her with his chonta lance and beat her violently, finally throwing her into a hole and covering her over with earth.

It so happened that the dove witnessed this episode and told Auhu what had happened. He also told him to put on fine beetle-wing ear ornaments and to paint his face bautifully with achiote; then to go to the river where he would find a large land snail. This Auhu did, and still following the instructions of the dove, made a trumpet of the snail shell. With this, he entered the hollow trunk of a fallen chonta palm where he blew upon the snail-shell trumpet. At this call, Nantu very suddenly burst out of the hole where she had been buried, passing through the hollow chonta palm, knocking Auhu violently out of it, and heading straight for the sky again. Auhu cried: "Come back! Come back!" in his most entreating tones, but Nantu was so anxious to return to her place in the sky that she did not even look back, let alone pause to thank Auhu for enabling her to escape. Thus once more, having had an opportunity to gain the favor of his loved one and again having had his hopes dashed to earth, Auhu resumed his melancholy condition. For this reason he sings only on moonlit nights his mournful cry, "Aishiru, Aishiru," meaning "Beloved."

When Nantu had made good her escape she told what had transpired. The sons of Mika and Ahimbi, hearing the tale, immediately sought out Unushi and cut off his head, making a tsantsa of it.

When Mika found out what had happened she beat her sons born of Ahimbi and killed them, saying that they had killed her husband. After this had taken place Ahimbi fought with Mika because she had killed his sons. They fought so violently that a great tempest was brought about. Huge black clouds came up, rolled along by a terrific wind; torrential rains descended with great fury; lightning flashed and terrific peals of thunder reechoed through the sky.

At the height of the hurricane there came a tremendous clap of thunder and out of the blackest cloud there flashed to earth a mighty bolt of lightning which struck the ground and at the spot there leaped up immediately a powerful Jivaro armed with lance and shield. This was Masata, the embodiment of war.

He viewed the fighting with great enthusiasm, enjoying it so much that when he saw signs of the struggle slackening, he encouraged both sides, going among the many children of Ahimbi, Unushi, and Mika, urging them to fight one another and assuring each faction that they were in the right. So successful was his propaganda thay they all separated into their various factions, this being the origin of the different Jivaro groups.

After this split had been completed Masata visited each group, secretly telling each that they were right and that those who possessed any manhood would go out and kill their enemies, and that he who killed the most would become powerful and would be a great Curaka. Some were partisans of Mika, some of Ahimbi, and some of Unushi. "Go out and avenge yourselves and you will become a strong Curaka," said Masata. This was the beginning of war.

When Etsa and Nantu looked down and saw the turmoil that had been created they were much displeased. They descended to earth and sought out

Ahimbi, accusing him of being responsible for all the trouble because of his conduct with Mika. Seizing him, they brought him to the Pongo Manseriche. Here Etsa took the trunk of a hollow chonta palm and thrust Ahimbi in it. Then Etsa, blowing upon the chonta tube after the fashion of a blowgun, turned it slowly while so doing. As he did so, Ahimbi slowly came forth from the other end in the form of Pangi, the boa. After he had emerged completely from the chonta log, Etsa bound him up and placed him under the waters of the Pongo Manseriche. The boiling, turbulent waters of this narrow gorge are brought about by Ahimbi's titanic efforts to free himself from his bonds.

After this punishment had befallen him Ahimbi desired that his sons should have peace, so he thrashed his tail and sprayed water into the air, forming the rainbow, as a sign to Etsa to be compassionate and release his bonds in order that he might restore peace among the warring factions. Masata, however, saw the rainbow and ingeniously placed clouds and rain in the way so that Ahimbi's signal would not be seen by Etsa, and thus bring about an end to the fighting. Whenever Ahimbi attempts his signal, he has always been thwarted thus far by Masata, who has obscured the rainbow with rain and mists.

Having successfully prevented this threat of peace, Masata once more started visiting each of the tribes, hurling out his slogan, "Make war! Make war!" Chingaso, however, feeling sorry for the plight of Ahimbi and desiring to see peace brought about, went down to the Pongo Manseriche in a canoe with the intention of releasing him. Ahimbi, however, thrashing about in his rage, did not recognize her. He overturned her canoe and ate her, thus ending his best opportunity for freedom.

Thus ends the Nuhiño of the Jivaros.

—M. M. Sterling. "The Nuhiño or Earth Story of the Jivaros," *U. S. Bureau of American Ethnology Bulletin 117 (Historical and Ethnographical Material of the Jivaros Indians)*. Washington, D.C.: Government Printing Office, 1938, pp. 124–129

MUNDURUCU

The People Climbed Out
Like many Indians of the Amazon Basin in Brazil, the Mundurucu have come to identify their creating culture hero with the Christian supreme god and thereby to elevate him to a position of equal prominence. In this earlier myth, however, Karusakaibo is still rather earthbound and immanent: with the help of an armadillo, he discovers people living in the womb of the earth and, like a midwife, begins to deliver them. Then the rope (symbolizing both the axis mundi and the umbilical cord) breaks, and half of the people remain in the earth as "ancestors." Thus the cycle of being emerging out of not-being at birth and eventually returning to it at death is established.

KARUSAKAIBO had made the world but had not created men. One day Daiiru, the armadillo, offended the creator and was forced to take refuge in a hole in the ground. Karusakaibo blew into the hole and stamped his foot on the earth. Daiiru was blown out of the hole by the rush of air. He reported that people were living in the earth. He and Karusakaibo made a cotton rope and lowered it into the hole. The people began to climb out. When half of them had emerged, the rope broke and half remained underground, where they still live. The sun passes through their country from west to east when it is night on the earth; the moon shines there when the earth has moonless nights.

—Donald Horton, "The Mundurucú." *U.S. Bureau of American Ethnology Bulletin 143 (Handbook of South American Indians) Vol. 3, The Tropical Forest Tribes.* Washington, D.C.: Government Printing Office, 1948, p. 281.

NINE

MYTHS OF AUSTRALIA AND THE PACIFIC

WULAMBA

The Origin of the Aborigines
While many Australian myths speak of an otiose sky deity, their main focus is on the great culture heroes of the beginning, the "Dreamtime." Typically, the Wulamba people of northeastern Arnhem Land on the northern tip of the continent recall the wondrous Djanggawul beings (Djanggawul and his two sisters), endlessly fertile and creative, who wandered over the earth creating plants, animals, and finally ancestors of the Aborigines. They arrived from Braglu, the island home of the dead for the *dua* moiety (the realm of not-being), with several sacred objects still used by the Wulamba: the *ngainmara* mat, symbolic of the womb, and the *rangga* poles, symbolic of the phallus. And in their wandering, in addition to creating, they ordered the land, removed other totemic beings, established moieties (among the Wulamba, everything belongs to either the *dua* or *jiridja* moiety), and created rituals. In all of these activities, the Djanggawul sisters took a most active role until, as is related in some parts of the long Djanggawul myth cycle, they left their sacred paraphernalia unguarded, and it was stolen by their brother and his companions. This presumption of sexual revolution is made in many Australian myths; here it is symbolized by the eventual shortening of the sisters' genitalia by their brother.

The great and easy fertility of the Djanggawul is celebrated by the entire people annually: women and children of the tribe wriggle under the mat in imitation of unborn babies, while the men dance around and poke it with their *rangga* poles; finally the women and children emerge, just as their ancestors did from the wombs of the Djanggawul sisters. In rites such as these, the Aborigines take unto themselves the roles of their ancestors, whose work they continue in ordering and maintaining the still sacred world.

I N THE BEGINNING there were land and sky, animals and birds, foliage and trees. There was sea, too, in the waters of which were fish and other creatures; and upon the land were beings of totemic origin. All these things were there, as they had always been; but man, as we know him today, was not among them.

Far out to sea, out of sight of the Arnhem Land mainland, was an island known as Bralgu (Bu'ralgu), the land of the Eternal Beings, which later became the home of the *dua* moiety dead. It lay to the south-east of Port Bradshaw, somewhere beyond Groote Eylandt.

It was here, at Bralgu, that the Djanggawul were living. They are said to have come from a big ceremony or meeting, in an unknown land far beyond the isle of Bralgu. On their arrival there they held another large ceremony, much larger than the contemporary *dua nara,* and used all their sacred objects. At that time they possessed a great many emblems, but only a few of these could be brought in the bark canoe to the Australian mainland.

They did not, however, spend very long at Bralgu, for it was only a "half-way" resting place on the journey they were attempting.

There were three of them: Djanggawul himself, his elder Sister, Bildjiwuraroiju, and his younger Sister, Miralaidj. With them, too, was another man, named Bralbral. The Two Sisters and their Brother, however, were nearly always known as the Djanggawul. Djanggawul himself had an elongated penis, and each of the Two Sisters had a long clitoris; these were so long that they dragged upon the ground as they walked. The penis of Djanggawul, *gurlga* or *dulparu* (ordinary name for penis) had a long foreskin *(dabin),* suggesting that it had not been circumcised; at various intervals along the penis were notches, or penis "rings" or "ridges," as on an ordinary penis towards the apex. These rings were called *bugalil,* a term also applied to the sacred invocations at present used among the north-eastern Arnhem Land peoples *(dua* moiety, *bugali,* or *jiritja* moiety, *bugalili).* The elder Sister's clitoris (the ordinary term being *gadin,* and the "inside" term *ngeribngerib)* was the longer, while the younger Sister's was almost snakelike in appearance.

At Bralgu, as they walked around with these, they left grooves in the ground from their dragging. And when the Djanggawul Brother had coitus with his Sisters, he lifted aside their clitorises, entering them in the usual way. He was able to have incestuous relations with his Sisters, because at that time there were no marriage rules, no moieties and no prohibition. Djanggawul had been having coitus with Bildjiwuraroiju for a long time; her breasts had grown large and "fallen down" with milk, and she had produced many children. Miralaidj, though, was quite young, having just passed puberty, and her breasts were rounded and firm. They lived at Bralgu for some little time, putting people there, and leaving "Dreamings" in the form of totemic origins, sacred emblems and body paintings. They also instituted their rituals and ceremonies. The Brother's penis and the Sisters' clitorises were sacred emblems, like *rangga* poles.

At last they made ready their bark canoe, and loaded it with "Dreamings," sacred drawings and emblems; the latter were kept in a conically-shaped *ngainmara* mat. When all this was ready they themselves, with their companion Bralbral, climbed into the canoe. Then they paddled out to sea, leaving the island of Bralgu far behind. For days and days they paddled, until they sighted the Arnhem Land mainland. At last they came to it, landing near Rose River. But they soon left this part of the country, and continued paddling along the coast until they reached Jelangbars, Port Bradshaw.

Near Gangudol Island, while still in their canoe, the Ancestral Beings saw some trees, in the branches of which were perched two *lindaridj* parakeets, drying themselves in the first rays of the sun. As they passed this island, the *djigai* morning pigeon was crying. "Maybe that bird is crying out on the land," said the Djanggawul, and so they sang about it. They saw, too, trepang on Bauwuling (or Bauwljans) Islands, and there were many *lindaridj* on Gagubam. A black cockatoo, immediately it caught sight of them, flew over to what are now the sacred sandhills near Ngadibaulwi (or Ngadibalji) rocks.

As the Djanggawul were nearing Port Bradshaw, and while they were still paddling, they could see the white foam from waves breaking around the sacred rock of Gulbinbol, just outside the entrance to the bay. As they looked they saw, too, myriads of small *lindaridj* parakeets flying over the mainland, the sun's rays catching the redness of their breast feathers. There was a constant roar of waves pounding on the beach. They paddled farther into the bay, coming to the Garingan rock, and saw the wide curving beach of Jelangbara. They sang with joy, and allowed the surf to take their canoe into the shallow water.

Then they dragged their canoe on to the beach and unloaded it, making this a sacred place. Jelangbara is the largest Djanggawul centre in north-eastern Arnhem Land and, today, the most important.

Here the Djanggawul Brother wished to shorten his Sisters' clitorises. But the elder Sister said, "No, wait till we reach Arnhem Bay. We can have a good rest, and put Dreamings there." So they walked around, still dragging the clitorises and elongated penis, leaving marks on the ground which may be seen to-day.

Leaving their canoe, the Djanggawul walked along the coast until they came to Ngadibalji, where they saw the *djawuldjanwul* mangrove bird. Here too the Djanggawul Brother left his hairbelt, but retained the parakeet-feathered waist-band and arm-bands he was wearing. The hairbelt is now a sandhill. On the sandhill, were track marks of the *damwmindjari (damburindari* or *waburunggu)* wild duck; these birds were eating the *murnji,* or wild peanut roots. On the opposite side was a large barren sandhill, on the surface of which were tracks of the *djanda* goanna, as well as of many birds. A *gamaru* tree with non-edible "apple"-like nuts was growing there, too. This tree is sacred; it is a *jirijiri* bullroarer tree, and to-day only those who are very old may look upon it. Here the Djanggawul paused and heard again the cry of the *ngadili (dangadilji* or *rirambung)* black cockatoo. Here too is the sacred waterhole, *milngur,* which the Djanggawul made by inserting the *mauwulan rangga* pole: a spring flows from it down to the beach. It is said that the four Beings entered this hole, and made their camp within.

Later, they walked farther along, and saw two *djanda* goanna resting on the peak of a sandhill. "Ah," said the Brother, "I am very surprised to see this goanna. I had better put it Dreaming *(wongar)* for this country." Bangguli is the goannas' "inside" sacred name. The goanna crawled up the smooth surface of the sandhill, dislodging the sand. It attempted to climb on to the sacred *djuda* pole (that is, tree) the Djanggawul had placed there, but could not do so, because the Djanngawul was still there. Today the *djuda* ironwood (or "black" bark) tree is still there, at Mauwulanggalngu, where it grew from the sacred *rangga*.

After leaving the sandhills the Djanggawul continued walking along. Near the beach at Gumararanggu (named from the *gamaru* tree there), still on the Port Bradshaw peninsula, they heard the noise made by the black malgu flying fox, and saw more sandhills and goannas, as well as *gunjan* beach worms.

Coming to Wabilinga Island, which was later to become a large Macassan settlement, they saw the Baijini folk who were working there. They were cooking trepang, where the tamarind trees stand to-day. The Djanggawul were much perturbed and said to the Baijini, "Baijini, you had better move from here to your own place; for this place must belong to us, and we are going to establish a sacred site." So some of the Baijini moved to the other side of the island, and some went to Dagu (vagina or vulva) on the mainland. But they left behind them on the island ashes from their fires, the crisscross elongated bars on which their trepang was left to dry, some huts, and a *djiru* trepang-stirring "spoon" or ladle. Djanggawul picked this up and looked at it. "Ah," he said, "this is a good colour. I shall have it for myself." The *djiru* was black, a colour that the Djanggawul now used for the first time, together with blackness from the charcoal in the ashes of the Baijini fires. In this way, the locality became partly *dua*, from the Djanggawul, and partly *jiritja*, from the Baijini.

Another *jiritja* moiety Ancestral Being, named Laintjung, was also present at this site. He exchanged gifts with the Djanggawul, and in return for some red parakeet feathered string gave them some black clan patterns, and opossum fur string. That is why, today, each moiety has something belonging to the other: the *jiritja* took from the *dua*, and vice versa. Laintjung was also given a red parakeet feathered *jiridbald* waist-band and some *judumiri* arm-bands. He possessed, too, a piece of cloth which he had obtained from the Baijini, but the Djanggawul refused to take any of this. The Djanggawul had apparently come prepared for this meeting with people of the *jiritja* moiety. They had half expected trouble from them when they requested the Baijini to move, and carried in readiness *gundmara* ("inside" name) fighting dilly bags.

Leaving Wabilinga Island behind them, the Djanggawul moved to Gagubam, where they heard the *djawuldjawul* mangrove bird calling out in the early morning. After this they heard "people and children" crying; and here spirit footprints of children may be seen on the rocks. These are the spirits who are as yet unborn, and remain in the uterus of the elder Sister, Bildjiwuraroiju. After leaving Gagubam the Djanggawul passed Bauwuling (or Bauwijara) where they saw *bauwaldja* catfish swimming after small fish and *bunabi* trepang slugs. And above Bauwuling, in the fresh water well on dry land, surrounded by mangroves and salt water, was *biabia* refuse from the trepang.

After spending some time in the Port Bradshaw country, establishing sacred sites, they decided to walk down the beach towards Caledon Bay; but there were so many totemic folk in those parts that they again got into their canoe and paddled down to Gambuga(wi) at Caldeon Bay, in territory of the Karlpu linguistic group. There they are said to have made a sacred place, and put special *djuda*. These were *rangga* emblems which, with others, they had carried from Bralgu in the *ngainmara* mat, and trees sprang up as they were pushed into the ground.

When they had done this they looked up, and saw a big dry weather cloud mirage, called *wulma*. It was coming from Buguwolumiri, in the country of the Djapu linguistic group, towards the "bottom" (or southern part) of Blue Mud Bay; so they travelled towards that place, and put more dreamings there. Their clitorises and penis were still dragging on the ground.

Then they saw another *wulma* towards the "top" of Blue Mud Bay, at Bugaliji, in Djarlwak linguistic group territory. They paddled around the coast to that place and left dreamings there. Then, abandoning their canoe, they went on foot through the bush until they came to Balimauwi; this is also in Djarlwak country, on the northern side of Rose River. They made a big camp, building a number of different "shades" of huts, which to-day are paperback trees; and there they also placed many dreamings.

Thus through the greater part of the country about Port Bradshaw, below Jelangbara almost to Rose River, all along the coast and even a little way inland, the Djanggawul left special drawings symbolically related to themselves and to totemic beings. They left, too, sacred *rangga* emblems, such as the *djuda,* the *djanda* (goanna) and *mauvulan* (associated with water springs), as well as sacred baskets. At all those places moreover, they established their cult, with the singing of songs and the ritual of the *dua* moiety *nara* ceremonies.

While at Balimauwi, they looked up into the north western sky and saw a great *wulma* hanging over Ngaluwi ("inside" name Waguralgu) at Arnhem Bay, in the territory of the Ngeimil and Dadawi linguistic groups. The Djanggawul eventually reached this place and made a camp, putting many dreamings there. They made a fish trap and caught many fish to eat. They also put the wild banana palm, and Djanggawul with his *mauwulan rangga* poked holes in the ground from which water flowed.

After a time they left Ngaluwi, walking along until they reached Gulugboi(wi), where they made a big "shade." They pushed their *djuda* into the ground, and trees sprang forth; and they put the *banggada* plants there.

At Daramur (or Darar'woi), inland from Arnhem Bay, the Djanggawul saw a *djanda* goanna in a fresh-water swamp that was covered with wild banana *dara* leaves; this was in Ngeimil territory.

Farther on a Mingu well, also in Ngeimil country, a *djanda* emerged from an open well which contained partially submerged banana foliage: new shoots had come up, completely covering the surface of the water.

Passing on to Djaddjananggu (also Ngeimil), they found a swamp where they saw *waragai* or *marabinj* fish; here too they saw lily roots and foliage, with flowers, and many ducks. Close by was the Maijulwi billabong where the *dadam* lily, with its round edible bulbs, was growing in great profusion. The Djanggawul Brother himself declared part of Maijulwi sacred, so that to-day only two tracks, one at each side, lead down to its banks; women may go down one of these only to get water, and must always return by the same road.

Continuing on, the Djanggawul reached Nganmaruwi, where they erected another large "shade." During all the time they had been on the Australian mainland, there is no mention of the Brother's having coitus with his Sisters: but while they were living here, he said to Bildjiwuraroiju, "I want to copulate with you, Sister."

But the elder Sister was shy. "Why?" she asked him.

"I want to put a few people in this place," the Brother replied.

So he lifted her clitoris and inserted his long penis. He did the same with Miralaidji. So they continued living there, and he copulated as a husband does with his wives.

After some time, Bildjiwuraroiju became pregnant, and her brother said to her, "Sister, may I have a look at you?"

"What for?" she asked.

"Because I want to put some people in this place.

"All right," she replied. She opened her legs a little, resting her clitoris on her left leg. The Brother sat before his Sister and placed his index finger into her vagina, up to the first joint. Then he pulled it away, and at the same time a baby boy came out. Bildjiwuraroiju was careful to open her legs only a little; if she had spread them out, children would have flowed from her, for she kept many people stored away in her uterus. These people (or children) in her uterus were like *rangga* emblems kept in the conical-shaped *ngainmara* mat, for the latter is a uterus symbol.

As the baby boy came out, the Brother stood listening to hear the sound of his cry. As soon as he heard this, he took hold of the child and put him on to the grass near by. Then he returned to his Sister, and saw a baby girl coming out. After she had cried, he lifted her gently and placed her under the *ngainmara* mat, which served to shelter her from the sun. The crying of a male child is *akai-'dugung,* a forceful "heavy" sound; while that of a girl is *akai njumulgunin,* a "small sound."

Then another male child issued from the elder Sister, and was put into the grass by the Brother. She continued giving birth to children of both sexes; when she had finished she closed her legs, and the Djanggawul Brother said to her:

"Sister, these little boys we will put in the grass, so that later, when they grow up, they will have whiskers; those whiskers are from the grass. We will always do that when we remove male children. And these little girls we have put under the *ngainmara* mat, hiding them there. That is because they must be smooth and soft and have no body hair, and because girls are really sacred. They must be kept under the *ngainmara,* just as the *rangga* emblems are kept. We will always do that when we remove female children."

The Djanggawul then left this place. The children they had produced grew up and married, and were the progenitors of the present Aborigines of those parts. From this time, too, the Two Sisters remained always pregnant, from having coitus with their Brother.

—Ronald M. Berndt. *Djanggawul: An Aboriginal Religious Cult of North Eastern Arnhem Land.* New York: Philosophical Library, 1953, pp. 24–28.

ARANDA

Myth of the Great Father
The very strong emphasis on masculine dominance in the social organization of the central Australian Aranda people is most evident in this myth: Karora, one of the great totemic ancestors, dreams and gives birth to animals and then (male) children through his navel and armpits. Presumably the protected nature of an armpit, its cupped shape, and the fact that it secretes sweat—structurally similar to a mouth, which produces saliva and words, and to a womb, which produces vaginal secretions and babies—qualify it as a source of divine masculine fertility.

The great Karora sleeps and dreams, waking only to find his new children and to inspire them with the stirring *raiankintja* call and dance, and then he sleeps again under the Australian earth for all time.

I N THE VERY BEGINNING everything was resting in perpetual darkness: night oppressed all the earth like an impenetrable thicket. The gurra ancestor—his name was Karora—was lying asleep in everlasting night, at the very bottom of the soak of Ilbalintja; as yet there was no water in it, but all was dry ground. Over him the soil was red with flowers and overgrown with many grasses; and a great tnatantja [ceremonial pole] was swaying above him. This tnatantja had sprung from the midst of the bed of purple flowers which grew over the soak of Ilbalintja. At its root rested the head of Karora himself: from thence it mounted up toward the sky as though it would strike the very vault of the heavens. It was a living creature, covered with a smooth skin like the skin of a man.

And Karora's head lay at the root of the great tnatantja: he had rested thus ever from the beginning.

And Karora was thinking, and wishes and desires flashed through his mind. Bandicoots began to come out from his navel and from his armpits. They burst through the sod above, and sprang into life.

And now dawn was beginning to break. From all quarters men saw a new light appearing: the sun itself began to rise at Ilbalintja, and flooded everything with its light. Then the gurra ancestor was minded to rise, now that the sun was mounting higher. He burst through the crust that had covered him: and the gaping hole that he left behind became the Ilbalintja Soak, filled with the sweet dark juice of the honeysuckle buds. The gurra ancestor rose, feeling hungry, since magical powers had gone out from his body.

As yet he feels dazed; slowly his eyelids begin to flutter; then he opens them a little. He gropes about in his dazed state; he feels a moving mass of bandicoots all around him. He is now standing more firmly on his feet. He thinks, he desires. In his great hunger he seizes two young bandicoots; he cooks them some little distance away, close to the spot where the sun is standing, in the white-hot soil heated by the sun; the sun's fingers alone provide him with fire and hot ashes.

His hunger satisfied, his thoughts turn towards a helpmate. But now evening is approaching over the earth; the sun hides his face with a veil of hair-string, covers his body with hair-string pendants, vanishes from the sight of men. And Karora falls asleep, stretching his arms out on both sides.

While he is asleep, something emerges from underneath his armpit in the shape of a bull-roarer [a carved piece of wood that when twirled in ceremonies produces a roaring noise]. It takes on human form, and grows in one night to a full-grown young man: this is his first-born son. At night Karora wakes up, because he feels that his arm is being oppressed with the weight of something heavy: he sees his first-born son lying at his side, his head resting on his father's shoulder.

Dawn breaks. Karora rises; he sounds the loud vibrating call known as raiankintja. The son is thereby stirred into life. He rises; he dances the ceremonial dance around the father who is sitting adorned with full ceremonial designs worked in blood and feather-down. The son totters and stumbles; he is still only half awake. The father puts his body and chest into a violent quiver; then the son places his hands upon him. The first ceremony has come to an end.

The son is now sent by his father to kill some more of the bandicoots which are playing peacefully about near by in the shade. The son brings them back to his father who cooks them in the sun-glowing soil as before, and shares the cooked meat with his son. Evening has come again, and soon both are sleep. Two more sons are born that night to the father, from out of his armpits; these he calls into life on the following morning by the raiankintja call as before.

This process is repeated for many days and nights. The sons do the hunting; and the father brings into life an increasing number of sons each night—as many as fifty on some nights. But the end cannot be delayed overlong; soon father and sons have succeeded in devouring all the bandicoots which had originally sprung from Karora's body. In their hunger the father sends his sons away on a three-days' hunt, to scour the great Ilbalintja Plain as far as Ininta and Ekallakuna. For hours they search patiently amongst the tall white grass, in the half-light of the almost limitless expanse of mulga-trees. But the vast mulga thicket is devoid of bandicoots, and they have to return.

It is the third day.

The sons are returning, hungry and tired, through the great stillness. Suddenly a sound comes to their ears, a sound like that of a whirling bull-roarer. They listen; they proceed to search for the man who may be swinging it. They search and search and search. They stab with their tjurunga sticks into all bandicoot nests and resting places. Suddenly something dark and hairy darts up and is gone. A shout goes up—"There goes a sandhill wallaby." They hurl their tjurunga sticks after it and break its leg. And then they hear the words of a song coming from the injured animal:

"I, Tjenterama, have now grown lame,

"Yes, lame; and the purple everlastings are clinging to me. I am a man as you are; I am not a bandicoot." With these words the lame Tjenterama limps away.

The astonished gurra brothers continue on their way home to their father. Soon they see him approaching. He leads them back to the soak. They sit on its edge in circles, one circle around the other, ever widening out like ripples in disturbed water. And then the great pmoara flood of sweet honey from the honeysuckle buds comes from the east and engulfs them; it swirls them back into the Ilbalintja Soak.

Here the aged Karora remained; but the sons were carried by the flood under the ground to a spot in the mulga thicket. Here they rejoined the great Tjenterama, whose leg they had unwittingly broken with their tjurunga sticks.

Today, at that new ceremonial ground the natives point out the rocks and stones which represent the undying bodies of the gurra brothers which lie on top of the round stone which is said to be the body of Tjenterama; and this Tjenterama whom they had injured, is now their new chief; and in all the present-day bandicoot ceremonies Tjenterama is represented as the great gurra chief of Ilbalintja. Karora, the natives say, remained behind at his original home: he is lying in eternal sleep at the bottom of the Ilbalintja Soak; and men and women who approach the soak to quench their thirst may do so only if they bear in their hands bunches of green inuruna boughs which they lay down on the edge of the soak. For then Karora is pleased with their coming and smiles in his sleep.

—T. G. H. Strehlow. *Aranda Traditions.* Melbourne: University of Melbourne Press, 1947, pp. 7–10.

KAKADU

Imberombera and Wuraka
Divine fertility is also the subject of this aboriginal myth, but, in contrast to the Aranda people, the Kakadus proclaim the creative power of the feminine side of the sacred. In each place she stops on her wanderings, Imberombera, the great mother, bears children and instructs them in language and culture. Meanwhile, her giant consort Wuraka, although equally fertile, seems fatigued by his potency and longs only to rest and join the sun in the east.

WURAKA came from the west, walking through the sea. His feet were on the bottom but he was so tall that his head was well above the surface of the water. He landed at a place called Allukaladi, between what are now known as Mts. Bidwell and Roe, both of which he made. His first sleeping place, after coming out on to land, was at Woralia. He then came on to Umurunguk and so to Adjerakuk and Aruwurkwain, at each of which he slept one night.

The woman, Imberombera, also walked through the sea and landed at which is now known as Malay Bay, the native name being Wungaran. She met Wuraka at Arakwurkwain. Imberombera said to him, "Where are you going?" He said, "I am going straight through the bush to the rising sun." The first language they spoke was Iwaidja, that is, the language of the people of Port Essington. Wuraka carried his penis, or *parla*, over his shoulder. He said to Imberombera, *ngainma parla nungeroboama*, my penis is too heavy; *ngainma wilalu jirongadda*, my camp is close by; *ngeinyimma ngoro breikul*, you go a long way.

At that time there were no black-fellows. Imberombera wanted Wuraka to come with her, but he was too tired and his penis was too heavy, so he sat down where he was, and a great rock, called by the natives Wuraka, and by the white men Tor Rock, arose to mark the spot. Imberombera had a huge stomach in which she carried many children, and on her head she wore a bamboo ring from which hung down numbers of dilly bags full of yams. She also carried a very large stick or *wairbi*.

At a place called Marpur, close to where she and Wuraka met, she left boy and girl spirit children and told them to speak Iwaidja. She also planted many yams there and said to the children whom she left behind, *mungatidda jam*, these are good to eat.

She went on to Muruni, leaving yams and spirit children, and told them also to speak Iwaidja. From Muruni she went on, by way of Kumara, to Areidjut, close to Mamul, on what is now called Cooper's Creek, which runs into the sea to the north of the mouth of the East Alligator River. At Mamul she left children, one boy being called Kominuuru, and told them to speak the Umoriu language. The only food supply she left here was Murarowa—a Cyprus bulb. She crossed the creek and went on to Yiralka but left no children there. This was close to the East Alligator River which she crossed and then came, in succession, to Jeri, Kumboyu, Munguruburaira and Uramaijino, where she opened up her dilly bags and scattered yams broadcast. She went on to Jaiyipali, where again she left food supplies. She searched around for a good camping place and, first of all, sat down in a water pool but the leeches came in numbers and fastened themselves on her, so she came out of the water and decided to camp on dry land, saying that she would go into the bush. Accordingly, she did so and camped at Inbinjairi. Here she threw the seeds of the bamboo, *Koulu*, in all directions and also left children, one of whom was a boy named Kalangeit Nuana.

As she travelled along, Imberombera sent out various spirit children to different parts of the country, telling them to speak different languages. She sent them to ten places, in each case instructing them as follows:—

Gnaruk ngeinyimma tjikaru, gnoro Koranger.
Watta ngeinyimma tjikaru, gnoro Kumboyu.
Kakadu ngeinyimma tjikaru, gnoro Munganillida.
Witji ngeinyimma tjikaru, gnoro Miortu.
Puneitja ngeinyimma tjikaru, gnoro Jaijipali.
Koarnbut ngeinyimma tjikaru, gnoro Kapalgo.
Ngornbur ngeinyimma tjikaru, gnoro Illari.
Umbugwalur ngeinyimma tjikaru, gnoro Owe.
Djowei ngeinyimma tjikaru, gnoro Nauillanja.
Geimbio ngeinyimma tjikaru, gnoro Waimbi.

The first word in each of these is the name of a language which the children were to speak; *ngeinyimma* means you or yours; *tjikaru* is talk or language; *gnoro* is go, and the last word is the name of the place to which she sent them.

Each of these places is regarded as the central camping ground of their respective tribes.

—B. Spencer. *The Native Tribes of the Northern Territories.* London: 1914, pp. 276–278.

YAMI

The Outbursters

When creation myths are retold and ritual reenactments performed, the time of the beginnings is recaptured; that is, the present, otherwise relative, time is understood as structurally similar to and grounded in absolute time. People participating in the ceremonies come to understand themselves in a "sacred" as well as a "profane" context, and they see themselves as doing now what the gods did then and do always. By these rituals, people come to understand the *formal* nature of their lives and to see how they fit an absolute pattern established at the beginning and perceivable within the most profound dimensions of themselves. This pattern may be as generalized as birth, initiation, marriage, old age, and death; in such cases where the experience is universal, all religions will ritualize the events in similar fashions. Or the pattern way be more specific and localized, having to do with a particular aspect of life in one culture.

Such a ritual is attached to this creation myth of the Yami, an Indonesian people living on the island of Batel-Tobago off the southeastern coast of Formosa. They repeat the myth of the sky and earth culture heroes, their discovery of metals, and their joint efforts in discovering the proper construction of boats, so that they might do these things now as the heroes did, as they should be done. And too, they perform the ritual so that they can feel themselves to be not just of the moment, but also part of an eternal and sacred process.

"GOOD is the island of Yami," said the god, looking down at the flat world, and dropped a big stone on the spot which is now the village of Ipaptok. The village is named that because there grows the bean-bearing plant called *paptok*, which the first man used for food.

The big stone fell upon Ipaptok, and out of it burst a man. He was hungry when he first came out and ate the *paptok*. Then he walked down to the sea.

He saw that a bamboo was growing by the sea, and as he watched, it split and out burst another man.

"Who are we?" said one. "We are man," said the other.

The son of the bamboo walked in one direction and found silver at a place named Kasavilugan. The son of the stone walked in another direction and found iron at a place named Imasapau. They returned to their house and beat out the hard iron and the soft silver.

One day the right knee-joint of the son of bamboo swelled and itched and a boy child burst out; from the left knee-joint came a girl child. The same thing happened to the son of stone: from his right knee burst out a boy child; from his left knee came a girl.

These children grew up and married. The daughter of the son of stone wed the son of the son of bamboo, and happy generations followed.

The people built themselves canoes. But the son of bamboo could not fell the heavy trees with his silver ax. "Hand me the iron," he said, "to cut the heavy tree." So the people learned that the silver ax was too soft for hewing wood, but because they loved the silver, they made themselves silver helmets. Today they wear the silver helmets adorned with beautiful silver leaf-shapes when they launch the canoes for the Flying-fish Festival and perform the fish-calling ceremony.

They built canoes and launched them with song. They were very beautiful, carved with trees and waves, and painted with black and white and red. The son of stone fixed ribs on the outside of his canoe; the son of bamboo put ribs on the inside of his. When the canoe of the son of bamboo was pushed into the sea, it broke. When the canoe of the son of stone entered the sea, it leaked. "That's bad," he said. Quickly he looked for something to plug the leaks and chose the fiber of the *kulau* tree. When the leaks were stopped, "Mended," he said. And the people use this fiber today to plug a leak.

Thus the people learned to make canoes and become fishermen. Every year during the season of flying-fish, they hold their Flying-fish Festival. At this time no one will offend the wonderful fish by spitting in the sea or throwing stones in the water. They fish at night by torchlight with torches in the end of each canoe. They perform the sacred fish-calling ceremony, and sing this song:

> From Ipaptok, the place of the outbursting of man,
> The first one descended to the plain of the sea.
> He performed the fish-calling rite;
> The torch was lighted: and the fish
> Were dazzled by the flames.

—Maria Leach. *The Beginning*. New York: Funk and Wagnalls, 1956, pp. 159–161. —Based on Arundel Del Re. *Creation Myths of the Formosan Natives*. Tokyo: 1951.

NEGRITOS

Dreaming People
The Negritos are Far Eastern pygmies, living in isolated areas of the Malay peninsula, who maintain themselves through primitive methods of food gathering, hunting, and fishing. Their creation myth envisages a chaotic, watery beginning brought to order by the dung-beetle, who formed land out of mud. The divine couple Pedn and Manoid then descended to earth and created children by a kind of mental generative formation: Manoid dreamed of a child, and from a tree (phallus) Pedn picked a fruit (seed) that turned into the very infant she requested.

AT FIRST only Pedn and Manoid his wife existed. The sun was already there, but not the earth. Then Tahobn, the dung-beetle, made the earth by pulling it out of the mud. The sun dried it and made it firm. When Pedn and Manoid saw the earth they descended to it. When the earth came into being trees grew out of it, but there were no animals or birds. Pedn and Manoid got two children in the following way. Manoid dreamt of a child and begged Pedn for one. Pedn went out to get some fruit and spread out a cloth for the fruit to fall on it, and, when the fruit fell, it became a child which began to scream. It was a boy. Manoid dreamt again, this time about a female child and begged her husband for it, so Pedn did as before and the fruit which fell into the cloth became a girl. The boy was Capai (identified. . . as the *kakuh*-bird) and the girl was called Pa'ig (identified . . . with *baul*, the tortoise). Both were *Cenoi-halek*. As there were no people, they married each other and had children. Two of these were Encogen and Kadjegn, both "grandchildren" of Ta Pedn. When Encogen came to a rock he heard the rushing of water. He shot an arrow into the rock so that water gushed forth. He became famous through this deed.

—Ivor N. Evans. *The Negritos of Malaya*. London: Cambridge University Press, 1937, pp. 159–160.

WEST CERAM

The Myth of Hainuwele

The wondrous generative power of the first beings is emphasized in this myth of Hainuwele, one of the three great goddesses of West Ceram in Eastern Indonesia. Like the vegetation from which she is born, Hainuwele ("Frond of the Cocopalm") produces life out of her own death; even her excrement is rich and valuable. Although the jealousy of men destroys her form, the life force that she embodied continues in new shapes as plants are born from buried parts of her corpse.

Enraged over the murder, her sister-goddess Satene (equally virginal, vegetal, and earth-born) forces people through a test of morality in which some are revealed to be the animals like which they have acted and others are confirmed as humans. The rite of passage also divides people and animals into appropriate social groups.

Having ordered the world in this fashion, Satene leaves for the land of the dead, further separating herself from all but those who can pass the most rigorous trials to reach her.

NINE FAMILIES of mankind came forth in the beginning from Mount Nunusaku, where the people had emerged from clusters of bananas. And these families stopped in West Ceram, at a place known as the "Nine Dance Grounds," which is in the jungle between Ahiolo and Varoloin.

Now there was a man among them whose name was Ameta, meaning "Dark," "Black," or "Night"; and neither was he married nor had he children. He went off, one day, hunting with his dog. And after a little, the dog smelt a wild pig, which it traced to a pond into which the animal took flight; but the dog remained on the shore. And the pig, swimming, grew tired and drowned, but the man, who had arrived meanwhile, retrieved it. And he found a coconut on its tusk, though at that time there were no cocopalms in the world.

Returning to his hut, Ameta placed the nut on a stand and covered it with a cloth bearing a snake design, then lay down to sleep. And in the night there appeared to him the figure of a man, who said: "The coconut that you placed upon the stand and covered with a cloth you must plant in the earth; otherwise it won't grow." So Ameta planted the coconut the next morning, and in three days the palm was tall. Again three days and it was bearing blossoms. He climbed the tree to cut the blossoms, from which he wished to prepare himself a drink, but as he cut he slashed his finger and the blood fell on a leaf. He returned home to bandage his finger and in three days came back to the palm to find that where the blood on the leaf had mingled with the sap of the cut blossom the face of someone had appeared. Three days later, the trunk of the person was there, and when he returned again in three days he found that a little girl had developed from his drop of blood. That night the same figure of a man appeared to him in dream. "Take your cloth with the snake design," he said, "wrap the girl of the cocoplam in the cloth carefully, and carry her home."

So the next morning Ameta went with his cloth to the cocopalm, climbed the tree, and carefully wrapped up the little girl. He descended cautiously, took her home, and named her Hainuwele. She grew quickly and in three days was a nubile maiden. But she was not like an ordinary person; for when she would answer the call of nature her excrement consisted of all sorts of valuable articles, such as Chinese dishes and gongs, so that her father became very rich.

And about that time there was to be celebrated in the place of the Nine Dance Grounds a great Maro Dance, which was to last nine full nights, and the nine families of mankind were to participate. Now when the people dance the Maro, the women sit in the center and from there reach betel nut to the men, who form, in dancing, a large ninefold spiral. Hainuwele stood in the center at this Maro festival, passing out betel nut to the men. And at dawn, when the performance ended, all went home to sleep.

The second night, the nine families of mankind assembled on the second ground; for when the Maro is celebrated it must be performed each night in a different place. And once again, it was Hainuwele who was placed in the center to reach betel nut to the dancers; but when they asked for it she gave them coral instead, which they all found very nice. The dancers and the others, too, then began pressing in to ask for betel and she gave them coral. And so the performance continued until dawn, when they all went home to sleep.

The next night the dance was resumed on a third ground, with Hainuwele again in the center; but this time she gave beautiful Chinese porcelain dishes, and everyone present received such a dish. The fourth night she gave bigger porcelain dishes and the fifth, great bush knives; the sixth, beautifully worked betel boxes of copper; the seventh, golden earrings; and the eighth, glorious gongs. The value of the articles increased, that way, from night to night, and the people thought this thing mysterious. They came together and discussed the matter.

They were all extremely jealous that Hainuwele could distribute such wealth and decided to kill her. The ninth night, therefore, when the girl was again placed in the center of the dance ground, to pass out betel nut, the men dug a deep hole in the area. In the innermost circle of the great ninefold spiral the men of the Lesiela family were dancing, and in the course of the slowly cycling movement of their spiral they pressed the maiden Hainuwele toward the hole and threw her in. A loud, three voiced Maro Song drowned out her cries. They covered her quickly with earth, and the dancers trampled this down firmly with their steps. They danced on till dawn, when the festival ended and the people returned to their huts.

But when the Maro festival ended and Hainuwele failed to return, her father knew that she had been killed. He took nine branches of a certain bushlike plant whose wood is used in the casting of oracles and with these reconstructed in his home the nine circles of the Maro Dancers. Then he knew that Hainuwele had been killed in the Dancing Ground. He took nine fibers of the cocopalm leaf and went with these to the dance place, stuck them one after the other into the earth, and with the ninth came to what had been the innermost circle. When he stuck the ninth fiber into the earth and drew it forth, on it were some of the hairs and blood of Hainuwele. He dug up the corpse and cut it into many pieces, which he buried in the whole area about the Dancing Ground—except for the two arms, which he carried to the maiden Satene: the second of the supreme Dema-virgins of West Ceram. At the time of the coming into being of mankind Satene had emered from an unripe banana, whereas the rest had come from ripe bananas; and she now was the ruler of them all. But the buried portions of Hainuwele, meanwhile, were already turning into things that up to that time had never existed anywhere on earth—above all, certain tuberous plants that have been the principal food of the people ever since.

Ameta cursed mankind and the maiden Satene was furious at the people for having killed. So she built on one of the dance grounds a great gate, consisting of a ninefold spiral, like the one formed by the men in the dance; and she stood on a great log inside this gate, holding in her two hands the two arms of Hainuwele. Then, summoning the people, she said to them: "Because you have killed, I refuse to live here any more: today I shall leave. And so now you must all try to come to me through this gate. Those who succeed will remain people, but to those who fail something else will happen."

They tried to come through the spiral gate, but not all succeeded, and everyone who failed was turned into either an animal or a spirit. That is how it came about that pigs, deer, birds, fish, and many spirits inhabit the earth. Before that time there had been only people. Those, however, who came through walked to Satene; some to the right of the log on which she was standing, others to the left; and as each passed she struck him with one of Hainuwele's arms. Those going left had to jump across five sticks of bamboo, those to the right, across nine, and from these two groups, respectively, were derived the tribes known as the Fivers and the Niners. Satene said to them: "I am departing today and you will see me no more on earth. Only when you die will you again see me. Yet even then you shall have to accomplish a very difficult journey before you attain me."

And with that, she disappeared from the earth. She now dwells on the mountain of the dead, in the southern part of West Ceram, and whoever desires to go to her must die. But the way to her mountain leads over eight other mountains. And ever since that day there have been not only men but spirits and animals on earth, while the tribes of men have been divided into the Fivers and the Niners.

—Adolf E. Jensen. "Die mythische Welt betrachtung der alten Pflanzer-Volker." *Eranos Jahrbuch 1949*. Zurich: Rhein-Verlag, 1950, pp. 34–38. —Quoted in Joseph Campbell. *The Masks of God: Primitive Mythology*. New York: Viking Press, 1959, pp. 173–176.

MELANESIA

Four Creation Myths
Stretching over 4,000 miles in the western Pacific, from New Guinea to Fiji, Melanesia encompasses the Solomon, New Hebrides, New Caledonia, and Admiralty Islands among many others. Although Melanesian cultures have been drastically and similarly altered by the rabid exploitation they suffered at the hands of colonizing Europeans (all too frequently abetted by Christian missionaries), they were originally quite diverse. They did share, however, a general lack of interest in radical cosmology, questioning the origin of their social groups and land but rarely dealing with the creation of the world as such, much less Being-Itself.

In the four creation myths outlined here, several common themes are sounded: emergence (here from a plant, not the womb of the earth), the competition of culture heroes who are brothers (often a mythic echo of tribal conquest and eventual merger where the god of the victor assumes a proper role over the god of the vanquished), and, where a high god is present at all, a sleeping deity who causes light and darkness and thus establishes the first ordering of chaos but who leaves the rest of creation to his more immanent and active son.

I The Papuan Keraki people of southwestern New Guinea say that the first people came out of a palm tree. Gainji was the Great Creator. He heard a babble of voices inside the palm and liberated the babblers in groups that spoke the same language. This explains the existence of different languages in the world.

II In the New Hebrides . . . the people tell about two Tagaros, twin culture heroes, one very wise, one foolish. Tagaro, the wise, created foods and useful artifacts for man; the other Tagaro created useless things and hindered or spoiled his brother's work to such an extent that he had to be tricked out of this world.

III The people of San Cristobal have Agunua, who made the sea and the land, caused storms, and created men and one woman. Agunua caused the rains to fall in order to quench his own thirst. He too had a brother companion to whom he gave a yam. He told the brother to plant it, and from this primeval yam grew all the banana and almond trees, coconuts, and other fruits. But one time the brother burnt up a mess of yams, thus causing some plants to be inedible forever.

IV In the Fiji Islands the people say that in the beginning there was no land—no land but the land of the gods. There was only the sea and the sea was everywhere. The sky which was over the sea touched nothing but the edge of the sea. There was no bright day, no night. A dim twilight lay upon the water.

The land of the gods was an island, as it is now. No one knows where it is for sure, but the old people say it floats in the sea on the edge of the world at the very point of sunrise. The people of Kandavu say they have seen it on the horizon lighted by the sun, but when they head their canoes toward it, it disappears before they can arrive.

Ndengei was the Great God of Fiji, the serpent-shaped creator, who made all things and taught the Fijians how to build canoes. He was chief of the *Kalou-Vu*, the "root-gods" of Fiji. They are called the root-gods because they were there first, the truly Fijian gods, rooted in Fiji before there was any Polynesian or European influence.

At night Ndengei went into a cave on the hill of Kauvandra to sleep. This is a hill in Great Fiji. When he closed his eyes it was dark over the islands and people called it "Night." If he turned over in his sleep, the people said "Earthquake." And when Ndengei opened his eyes again, it was day, and the people said "Work," and built their canoes.

Ndengei now pays no attention to the people, but because of his great hunger he accepts offerings of fruits of all kinds, vegetables, and pigs, and turtles. The people pray to him for good harvests.

His son Rokomautu created the land. He scooped it up out of the bottom of the ocean in great handfuls and piled it up in piles here and there. These are the Fiji Islands.

—Maria Leach. *The Beginning.* New York: Funk and Wagnalls, 1956, pp. 175–177. —Retold from and based on material in R. B. Dixon. *Oceanic Mythology*, in *The Mythology of All Races*, Vol. 9. Boston: 1916; L. Fison. *Tales from Old Fiji.* London: 1904; and "Melanesian Mythology" and "Kalou-Va" in the *Standard Dictionary of Folklore, Mythology and Legend.*

BANKS ISLANDS

The Myth of Qat
In this rewritten myth from the Banks Islands, north of the New Hebrides in Melanesia, Qat and his eleven brothers (one for each month of the year, equating these heroes' being with time itself) are born from a stone (a huge world seed). The vegetation metaphor is perpetuated when Qat formed men out of trees and inspirited them with his sacred drumming. Presumably people would have been as continuous in their generations as plants had Qat's stupid brother not bungled his imitation, buried the newly formed creatures, and thus brought about death. The duality of such culture heroes, their mixture of wisdom and stupidity, not only reflects the ambiguity of all sacred power, whose source is prior to distinctions of good and evil, but may also indicate social struggles wherein one group triumphed over another and their heroes did likewise.

The myth is particularly interesting for its depiction of the beginning as filled with unrelieved and homogeneous light, as much without internal distinction as endless darkness. Rather than having to create day, as is common in creation myths, Qat's problem concerns the establishment of night; having purchased it from neighbors or obtained it from the horizon (the limit of creation), he completes the world with darkness.

W HEN the Melanesian people in the Banks Islands see the shadow of a cloud moving swiftly over the face of the sea, they say "There flies Qat." Qat created men and pigs and food, they say, and if a pig runs into the house, they drive it out with the words "Qat says stay outside."

Qat himself was born on Vanna Lava (one of the Banks Islands), the very center of the world, and of what happened before that there is no tale.

Qat was born from the bursting of a stone. His mother was a great stone that split in two and Qat came forth and named himself. He had no father; but he had eleven brothers. They all lived together in the village of Alo Sepere. And there the mother, Qatgoro, can still be seen, the huge stone that gave birth to Qat.

Qat began to make things right away: men and pigs and plants and stones—or whatever he thought up.

He made mankind from the wood of the dracaena tree. He carved the arms and legs and torsos separately, and the heads and ears and eyes, and the fingers and toes, then fitted them all together, slowly and carefully. He made six figures and when they were finished he set about giving them life.

He stood the man-images up in a row and danced before them. After a while they moved a little—weakly, stiffly—but they moved. When Qat saw that, he began to beat upon his drum.

Soon the wonderful rhythmic magic of the drum filled the air. The figures began to move a little more, slowly and carefully at first, in time with each drum beat, then faster and faster, until they too were dancing the life dance of the drum. At last they were able to stand and walk and run by themselves.

Then Qat divided the six figures into men and women: three men and three women, so that each man had a wife, each woman had a husband.

Qat's brother, Marawa, came along while Qat was doing all this and watched. Marawa was the stupid one; he spoiled everything he tried to do. He thought he would like to create some people too.

So Marawa cut down a tree—another kind of tree, the *tavisoviso*—and from it carved six figures, as Qat had done. He set them up and danced before them and beat the drum to give the figures life, just as he had seen Qat do. But as soon as he saw them move, he dug a pit and buried them, and went away and left them.

In about a week he remembered them, and went and scraped the earth away. They were rotten. They stank, and Marawa had to leave them buried in the earth. This was the beginning of death in the world.

When Qat first made the pigs he made them to stand upright and walk on two legs. But his brothers all laughed. They pointed and laughed and said they looked just like men! So to save the pigs from ridicule, Qat shortened their fore-arms and fixed them to walk on all fours, as they do now.

Thus Qat made men and pigs. He made food plants, and canoes, and many other things. But he did not know how to make darkness. It was light in the world all the time, without dimness or dark or rest.

The eleven brothers did not like the world this way.

"Look here, Qat! It's too light," they said, or "There's nothing but light all the time, Qat!", or "Qat, can't you do something?"

Qat searched around and one day he heard that there was something called *night* over at Vava in the Torres Islands. So he tied up a pig and put it in his canoe and set sail across the water for Vava.

There he bought (in exchange for a pig) a piece of night (*qong*) from Qong, Night, who dwelt in that place. After that there were pigs in the Torres Islands, they say. Another story says Qat never went to the Torres Islands at all, but sailed out over the sea to the far edge of the sky, where Night himself touched him over the eyes and gave him black eyebrows and taught him sleep. Some say this can't be true because there are pigs in the Torres Islands and none in the sky.

At any rate, Qat returned to Vanna Lava bearing night and bringing also various birds and fowls to make a clamor when it was time for day.

Qat showed the brothers how to construct beds of coca fronds and spread them on the floor and how to lie down for rest.

The brothers looked out and saw the sun moving down the west.

"It is departing," they cried to Qat. "Will it come back?"

"What is happening is called *night*," Qat told them.

Then he let loose the night.

"What is spreading and covering the sky?" cried the brothers.

"This is night," said Qat. "Lie down and keep quiet."

The brothers lay down, and in the dark they felt strange and dreamy; their eyes grew heavy and closed.

"Are we dying?" said the brothers.

"This is sleep," said Qat.

Only the birds knew how long the night should last; so when the night had lasted as long as the night should last, the cock crowed and the birds began to call and answer.

Qat then took a piece of red obsidian for a knife and cut a hole in the night. The first light that showed through was red, and soon all the light the night had covered shone through once again. The brothers opened their eyes and started the work of the day.

This is the way mankind lives now: day—sleep—day.

—Maria Leach. *The Beginning*. New York: Funk and Wagnalls, 1956, pp. 178–181. —Rewritten from R. H. Codrington. *The Melanesians: Studies in Their Anthropology and Folklore*. Oxford: 1891, pp. 156–158.

MARSHALL ISLANDS

Long, Long, Long Ago
Spanning the western Pacific from the Marianas Islands some three thousand miles to the Gilberts, Micronesia has suffered greatly for the "strategic" value foreigners place on it. The Chamorro people of Guam, for instance, were decimated by the Jesuits and the Spanish soldiers who accompanied them to convert the people in 1688; twenty years later, only 3,500 of the original population of 100,000 remained.

The thirty-four atolls of the Marshall Islands have fared only somewhat better: a German protectorate from 1885 until 1914 when they were captured by the Japanese, they remained under Japanese control until they fell to the Americans in 1944 and were made a part of the U.S. Trust Territories of the Pacific in 1947. (The United States conducted nuclear bomb tests on some of the atolls in the Marshalls during the next twenty years.)

This creation myth was recounted by James Milne, a Marshallese, in the early 1950s. It depicts a two-part world, heavenly order and earthly chaos, and a great creator god Lowa, who made the islands by commanding them to appear. Four divine figures control the directions and the main powers in life: sun, wind, life, and death. Most interesting is the assignment given to two culture heroes to tattoo everything, thus determining function and rank and uniting the natural and social orders with the will of the gods. Appropriate behavior within these sacred orders is rewarded with eternal life and being; transgressors are weighted down by their crimes and fall into the ocean, the chaos of not-being.

LONG, LONG, LONG AGO there wasn't any land at all, only the ocean, but there was a god named Lowa who came down to an island (maybe this island was Ailinglaplap). This god made a command followed by a magical sound, *"Mmmmmm,"* and all of the islands were created. He went back to heaven and sent down four other men to this island. These four men each went in different directions, one to the east, one to the west, one to the south, and one to the north. [The Marshallese consider east the principal cardinal direction.] The man in the west was called Iroijdrilik; the man in the east, Lokumran, "the man who twists the daybreak"; the man in the south, Lorok, "the man of the south"; the man in the north, Lojibwineamen. Each of these men has duties to perform. Iroijdrilik is the king of all and it is his duty to see that all living things are produced, even plants and birds. The man in the south has the duty of looking after the winds. The man in the north takes care of all death; he kills everything by individual acts.

After these men were in their places, Lowa sent another man (name forgotten) down to arrange the islands. He put all the islands in a basket [not known how, or if they were in the water first] and, starting from the Carolines, put them into their present positions. Then he started placing all the Marshall Islands of the two chains into their proper order. As he came from Ailinglaplap to Jaluit, one island fell out of the basket. This island which fell was Namorik, and that is why it is out of line today. He just let it go and didn't bother to put Namorik back in order. He placed Jaluit, then Ebon, and then threw away the basket which became Kili (named after *Kilok*, a kind of strong working-basket plaited by men out of coconut leaflets). This ended the island-forming.

Next Lowa sent two men to Ailinglaplap again to tattoo everything in the world that had been created. All the individuals and animals were really off-spring of Lowa. These men were called Lanej and (name forgotten), they were to tattoo everything—the fish, the birds, all creatures, and men—all living things that walked or moved about. This is how each kind of animal got its characteristic markings, and also it started the rank-signifying tattoos for chiefs, commoners, and women.

Everybody in the world came to Ailinglaplap to be tattooed. From Bikini there came a canoe. There were no sails yet, but in those days there was a special part of each canoe called the "fish." This part of the canoe pushed it to Wotho, but there was a ghost on Wotho that speared the "fish" and killed it so that from then on they had to paddle the canoe to make it move. On their way paddling to Ailinglaplap, the people got so tired that no one wanted to bail. When they came to the south pass into the lagoon at a place called Buoj, as soon as they reached the edge of the reef, the canoe sank and the people had to swim, the birds had to fly, and all the others swam to shore except the rat who was a poor swimmer and almost drowned. As the rat was struggling, an octopus came up and said "Oh, my friend, I'll help you." The octupus put the rat on his head and took him ashore. Just before the rat jumped off he defecated on the octopus' head. Laughing, the rat called back to the octopus, "Ha, ha, I put something." The octopus heard him and felt his head and discovered the feces which he couldn't wipe off. The octopus was enraged, and swam back to shore, but since he could not walk up the beach, he couldn't catch the rat. From that day to the present, the octopus hates the rat. The rat finally got his tattooing, but he was the very last one and the soot dye was very weak; there was too much water. This is why the rat's tattoing is very bad and has a grey color, and why the rat always looks dirty. However, everyone else got a good tattoo.

Now everyone in the world had been tattooed, and the names of the fish and animals had been assigned to each. It was now up to Iroijdrilik to see that everything grows, is born and perpetuated. The man in the north, Lojibwineamen, is responsible for calling people to death when he wants to. After he calls them and they die, the people are always buried near the water on either side of the atoll, but more commonly near the lagoon side. After either three or six days, the soul arises out of the grave to go to Nako, an islet at Nadrikdrik, near Mille. Before the soul can enter this island it must cross a channel which is full of big fish. No one can escape this jump; the bad people, heavy with sin, can't make the leap and fall into the water for the fish to eat. The good jump across easily to the spirit place. (In order to get to the spirit land they must prepare for it; first, respect their mother; second, respect their father; third, be brave in battle; fourth, respect their chief; then there is no trouble in making the leap.) When the spirit island is reached, everlasting spirit food, the fat of the squirrel fish [*Myripristis*, sp.] is served so that no one will ever get hungry or thirsty, no matter how long he stays there. From the spirit island of Nako the person goes to where Lojibwineamen lives in the north.

—William H. Davenport. "Marshallese Folklore Types." *Journal of American Folklore*, 1953, *66*, 221–223. Philadelphia: American Folklore Society.

MAIANA ISLAND

Making Things

Southeast of the Marshall Islands, Maiana is a part of the Gilbert Islands, a British protectorate since 1892. Although there was considerable Christian missionary activity in these islands (Hiram Bingham even translated the Bible into Gilbertese in 1856), their creation myth is remarkably free of Western influence. In anything, it bears resemblance to Polynesian cosmologies of equal sophistication.

The Maiana myth envisages Na Arean as the source of all being and not-being. Passive in nothingness, he *is*. Finally he began to create and, in a kind of self-division, made water (chaos, non-being) with his left hand and land (order, being) with his right. Objectifying his creative thought, Na Arean gave birth ("conceived") to Na Arean the Younger and eventually sent him to inspect the creation. Because it was still chaotic in that it had no point of orientation (described here geographically, but a point equally well taken religiously), Na Arean plucked out a hollow tooth and with it created the navel, the center point of the world. With this absolute orientation, all other ordering could be done; Na Arean the younger then separated the sky and earth and light came through the great axis mundi of god's sacred tooth.

N A AREAN is pictured as a being who sat alone in space as "a cloud that floats in nothingness." He slept not, for there was no sleep; he hungered not, for as yet there was no hunger. So he remained for a great while, until a thought came into his mind. He said to himself, "I will make a thing." So he made water in his left hand, and dabbled it with his right until it was muddy; then he rolled the mud flat and sat upon it. As he said, a great swelling grew in his forehead, until on the third day it burst, and a little man sprang forth. "Thou art my thought," said Na Arean; "Thou art the picture of my thought (*taamnei-n an iango, ngkoe*). Thy name is Na Arean the Younger. Sit thou in my right eye or in my left eye, as thou wilt." So the little man sat sometimes in his father's right eye and sometimes in his left, and for a great while it was so. At last Na Arean the First-of-things called aloud, "Na Arean!" His son answered, "O?" He said, "Come forth from my eye. Go down and tread on the thing I have made. Where are the ends of it?" His father said again, "Where is the middle of it?" He answered, "I know not." So Na Arean the elder plucked a hollow tooth from his jaw and thrust it into the thing he had made, saying, "This is the navel!" Through the hollow tooth, Na Arean the Younger descended and found a Darkness and a Cleaving-together of the elements, which he proceeded to straighten out in the usual manner. When heaven stood on high, it was found that the light of the upper regions streamed through the hollow tooth of Na Arean the elder: thus, the sun came into being.

—A. Grimble. "Myths from the Gilbert Islands." *Folklore*, 1922, *33*, 106–107.

FOUR MAORI COSMOLOGIES

The Maori, Polynesian natives of New Zealand, were first visited by Europeans in 1642 when the Dutch navigator A. J. Tasman "discovered" the island. Captain Cook came there, too, in 1769, and by 1814 the first Christian missionary Samuel Marsden had arrived. Although the Maori received full possession of their land in exchange for surrender to the British in 1840 under the Treaty of Waitangi, the late 1840s and most of the 1860s were marked by warfare between them and the British.

All of this Western influence had relatively little effect on the basic tenets of Maori cosmology. Among the most profound in terms of the radicality of its questioning and the sophistication of its answers, Maori thought not only encompasses issues of being and not-being but also deals directly with the relation of spirit and matter.

The Maori envision a gradual evolution of Being-Itself, described as pure thought, first into not-being (the void, chaos, darkness) and then into being (sky and earth, order, light). Like the early Vedic thinkers, they argue that gods evolved with the specific forms of being; as personifications of great powers, they are still dependent on not-being. Being-Itself, on the other side of nothingness, is neither deified nor anthropomorphized.

Problems of description at this level of thinking are enormous. Because concepts all presume being and words are descriptive of things, a certain amount of awkwardness inevitably results when they are applied to the nothingness that preceded being and its forms.

A Genealogy
In this genealogical chant, the Maori adopt a vegetal metaphor and speak of sky and earth as the flowers of the roots of Being-Itself.

TE PU (The Root)
  Te More (The Taproot)
Te Weu (The Rootlet)
Te Aka (The Vine or Creeper)
Te Rea (The Growth)

Te Wao-nui (The Great Forest)
Te Kune (The Development)
Te Whe (The Sound)
Te Kore (The Nothing)
Te Po (The Night)

Rangi (Sky)   Papa (Earth)

—A. W. Reed. *Treasury of Maori Folklore.* Wellington, New Zealand: A. H. and A. W. Reed, 1963, pp. 19–20.

Po   The Maori are particularly adept at describing degrees and qualities of nothingness, stages in the evolution of not-being. In this chant, Po—the void, passive eons of nonexistence—succeed each other in subtle fashion.

T E PO-TE-KITEA, the unseen Po.
    Te Po-te-whaia, the unpossessed Po.
Te Po-te-wheau, the unpassing Po.
Te Po-tangotango, the Po of utter darkness.
Te Po-te-whawha, the untouched and untouchable Po.

—A. W. Reed. *Treasury of Maori Folklore*. Wellington, New Zealand: A. H. and A. W. Reed, 1963, p. 18.

The Creation   One of the grandest Maori chants reveals creation in abstract physical stages, evolving through the three periods of thought, night, and finally light. It is as dramatic and moving as any myth, not only because of its rich language and hypnotic rhythm, but also because its point of view is internal and participatory, not objective and reportorial.

There is no deity here, no fixing of a sacred process into one persona; nature itself is only a dependent part of the whole. Unknowable and inexplicable, Being-Itself evolves "from the conception" through thought, spirit and matter to the great climax, the "blaze of day from the sky."

F IRST PERIOD
    (*thought*)

From the conception the increase,
From the increase the thought,
From the thought the remembrance,
From the remembrance the consciousness,
From the consciousness the desire.

S ECOND PERIOD
    (*night*)

The world became fruitful;
It dwelt with the feeble glimmering;
It brought forth night:
The great night, the long night,
The lowest night, the loftiest night,

The thick night, to be felt,
The night to be touched,
The night not to be seen,
The night of death.

THIRD PERIOD
    (light)

From the nothing the begetting,
From the nothing the increase,
From the nothing the abundance,
The power of increasing
The living breath;
It dwelt with the empty space,
And produced the atmosphere which is above us,
The atmosphere which floats above the earth;
The great firmament above us dwelt with the early dawn,
And the moon sprung forth;
The atmosphere above us dwelt with the heat,
And thence proceeded the sun;
They were thrown up above,
As the chief eyes of Heaven:
Then the Heavens became light,
The early dawn, the early day,
The mid-day.
The blaze of day from the sky.

—Richard Taylor. *Te Ika a Maui.* London: Wertheim and Macintosh, 1855. —Quoted in A. W. Reed. *Treasury of Maori Folklore.* Wellington, New Zealand: A. H. and A. W. Reed, 1963, p. 19.

Heaven and Earth
Religious instruction took place in formal settings among the Maori. In *Whare Wananga* or sacred colleges, one could specialize either in "Upper Jaw" learning (the gods, origins, astronomy, time-keeping) or in "Lower Jaw" subjects (migrations, genealogies of the chiefs, the nature of taboos). Special restrictions were placed on the students, and these often included periods of seclusion, sexual abstinence, and specific food prohibitions. The chant form of much Maori theology lent itself not only to ritual use but also to easy memorization by students.

Maori creation myths did not stop with the more metaphysical issues of being and not-being but continued through the evolution of various forms of being to the creation of man. Like Hesiod's *Theogony,* these myths presume the primordial unity of sky and earth. Cramped between their parents, the natural powers—wind, forests, cultivated and uncultivated food plants, the oceans (fish and reptiles), and man—decided to rend apart sky and earth. While all struggled, only the gods of forests finally succeeded, and mankind was discovered hidden in the crevices of earth. Wind, the only child who had wanted sky and earth to remain together, went up with his father and attacked all the other children in revenge: the forests and oceans were both damaged by him; the foods hid in cowardly fashion close to their mother earth; and only man, still defiant, stood up to the wind and quelled his rage. In revenge for their cowardice, man then attacked all his earthly brothers and assumed control over them, using them and their offspring at his pleasure; only wind remained his perpetual enemy.

Seen as a dialectic of change and permanence, the myth ends in a tenuous draw. While the original stagnant unity of sky and earth has been destroyed, tension still is reflected in the hostility of wind (the advocate of permanence) and man (who wanted to kill his parents in the beginning). Eternal, but stagnant life has thus been transformed into the process of change, which incorporates both life and death.

M EN had but one pair of primitive ancestors; they sprang from the vast heaven that exists above us, and from earth which lies beneath us. According to the traditions of our race, Rangi and Papa, or Heaven and Earth, were the source from which, in the beginning, all things originated. Darkness then rested upon the heaven and upon the earth, and they still both clave together, for they had not yet been rent apart; and the children they had begotten were ever thinking amongst themselves what might be the difference between darkness and light; they knew that beings had multiplied and increased, and yet light had never broken upon them, but it ever continued dark. Hence these sayings are found in our ancient religious services: "There was darkness from the first division of time, unto the tenth, to the hundredth, to the thousandth," that is, for a vast space of time; and these divisions of times were considered as beings, and were each termed a Po; and on their account there was yet no world with its bright light, but darkness only for the beings which existed.

At last the beings who had been begotten by Heaven and Earth, worn out by the continued darkness, consulted amongst themselves, saying, "Let us now determine what we should do with Rangi and Papa, whether it would be better to slay them or to rend them apart." Then spoke Tu-matauenga, the fiercest of the children of Heaven and Earth, "It is well, let us slay them."

Then spoke Tane-mahuta, the father of forests and of all things that inhabit them, or that are constructed of trees, "Nay, not so. It is better to rend them apart, and to let the heaven stand far above us, and the earth lie beneath our feet. Let the sky become as a stranger to us, but the earth remain close to us as a nursing mother."

The brothers all consented to this proposal, with the exception of Tawhiri-ma-tea, the father of winds and storms, and he, fearing that his kingdom was about to be overthrown, grieved greatly at the thought of his parents being torn apart. Five of the brothers willingly consented to the separation of their parents, but one of them would not consent to it.

Hence, also, these sayings of old are found in our prayers, "Darkness, darkness, light, light, the seeking, the searching, in chaos, in chaos;" these signified the way in which the offspring of heaven and earth sought for some mode of dealing with their parents, so that human beings might increase and live.

So, also, these sayings of old time, "The multitude, the length," signified the multitude of the thoughts of the children of Heaven and Earth, and the length of time they considered whether they should slay their parents, that human beings might be called into existence; for it was in this manner that they talked and consulted amongst themselves.

But at length their plans having been agreed on, lo, Rongo-ma-tane, the god and father of the cultivated food of man, rises up, that he may rend apart the heavens and the earth; he struggles, but he rends them not apart. Lo, next, Tangaroa, the god and father of fish and reptiles, rises up, that he may rend apart the heavens and the earth; he also struggles, but he rends them not apart. Lo, next, Haumia-tikitiki, the god and father of the food of man which springs without cultivation, rises up and struggles, but ineffectually. Lo, then, Tu-matauenga, the god and father of fiery human beings, rises up and struggles, but he, too, fails. Then, at last, slowly uprises Tane-mahuta, the god and father, of forests, of birds, and of insects, and he struggles with his parents; in vain he strives to rend them apart with his hands and arms. Lo, he pauses; his head is now firmly planted on his mother, the earth, his feet he raises up and rests against his father the skies, he strains his back and limbs with mighty effort. Now are rent apart Rangi and Papa, and with cries and groans of woe they shriek aloud, "Wherefore slay you thus your parents? Why commit you so dreadful a crime as to slay us, as to rend your parents apart?" But Tane-mahuta pauses not, he regards not their shrieks and cries; far, far beneath him he presses down the earth; far, far above him he thrusts up the sky.

Hence these sayings of olden time, "It was the fierce thrusting of Tane which tore the heaven from the earth, so that they were rent apart, and darkness was made manifest, and so was the light."

No sooner was heaven rent from earth than the multitude of human beings were discovered whom they had begotten, and who had hitherto lain concealed between the bodies of Rangi and Papa.

Then, also, there arose in the breast of Tawhiri-ma-tea, the god and father of winds and storms, a fierce desire to wage war with his brothers, because they had rent apart their common parents. He from the first had refused to consent to his mother being torn from her lord and children; it was his brothers alone that wished for this separation, and desired that Papa-tu-a-nuku, or the Earth alone, should be left as a parent to them.

The god of hurricanes and storms dreads also that the world should become too fair and beautiful, so he rises, follows his father to the realms above, and hurries to the sheltered hollows in the boundless skies; there he hides and clings, and nestling in this place of rest he consults long with his parent, and as the vast Heaven listens to the suggestions of Tawhiri-ma-tea, thoughts and plans are formed in his breast, and Tawhiri-ma-tea also understands what he should do. Then by himself and the vast Heaven were begotten his numerous brood, and they rapidly increased and grew. Tawhiri-ma-tea despatches one of them to the westward, and one to the southward, and one to the eastward, and one to the northward; and he gives corresponding names to himself and to his progeny the mighty winds.

He next sends forth fierce squalls, whirlwinds, dense clouds, massy clouds, dark clouds, gloomy thick clouds, fiery clouds, clouds which precede hurricanes, clouds of fiery black, clouds reflecting glowing red light, clouds wildly drifting from all quarters and wildly bursting, clouds of thunder storms, and clouds hurriedly flying. In the midst of these Tawhiri-ma-tea himself sweeps wildly on. Alas! alas! then rages the fierce hurricane; and whilst Tane-mahuta and his gigantic forests still stand, unconscious and unsuspecting, the blast of the breath of the mouth of Tawhiri-ma-tea smites them, the gigantic trees are snapt off right in the middle; alas! alas! they are rent to atoms, dashed to the earth, with boughs and branches torn and scattered, and lying on the earth, trees and branches all alike left for the insect, for the grub, and for loathsome rottenness.

From the forests and their inhabitants Tawhiri-ma-tea next swoops down upon the seas, and lashes in his wrath the ocean. Ah! ah! waves steep as cliffs arise, whose summits are so lofty that to look from them would make the beholder giddy; these soon eddy in whirlpools, and Tangaroa, the god of the ocean, and father of all that dwell therein, flies affrighted through his seas; but before he fled, his children consulted together how they might secure their safety, for Tangaroa had begotten Punga, and he had begotten two children, Ika-tere, the father of fish, and Tu-te-wehi wehi, or Tu-te-wanawana, the father of reptiles.

When Tangaroa fled from safety to the ocean, then Tu-te-wehi wehi and Ika-tere, and their children, disputed together as to what they should do to escape from the storms, and Tu-te-wehi wehi and his party cried aloud, "Let us fly inland;" but Ika-tere and his party cried aloud, "Let us fly to the sea." Some would not obey one order, some would not obey the other, and they escaped in two parties: the party of Tu-te-wehi wehi, or the reptiles, hid themselves ashore; the party of Punga rushed to the sea. This is what, in our ancient religious services, is called the separation of Ta whiri-ma-tea. Hence these traditions have been handed down:— "Ika-tere, the father of things which inhabit the water, cried aloud to Tu-te-wehi wehi, 'Ho, ho, let us all escape to the sea.'

"But Tu-te-wehi wehi shouted in answer, 'Nay, nay, let us rather fly inland.'

"Then Ika-tere warned him saying, 'Fly inland, then; and the fate of you and your race will be, that when they catch you, before you are cooked, they will singe off your scales over a lighted wisp of dry fern.'

"But Tu-te-wehi wehi answered him, saying, 'Seek safety, then, in the sea; and the future fate of your race will be, that when they serve out little baskets of cooked vegetable food to each person, you will be laid upon the top of the food to give a relish to it.'

"Then without delay these two races of beings separated. The fish fled in confusion to the sea, the reptiles sought safety in the forests and scrubs."

Tangaroa, enraged at some of his children deserting him, and, being sheltered by the god of the forests on dry land, has ever since waged war on his brother Tane, who, in return, has waged war against him.

Hence, Tane supplies the offspring of his brother Tu-ma-tauenga with canoes, with spears and with fish-hooks made from his trees, and with nets woven from his fibrous plants, that they may destroy the offspring of Tangaroa; whilst Tangaroa, in return, swallows up the offspring of Tane, overwhelming canoes with the surges of his sea, swallowing up the lands, trees, and houses that are swept off by floods, and ever wastes away, with his lapping waves, the shores that confine him, that the giants of the forests may be washed down and swept out into his boundless ocean, that he may then swallow up the insects, the young birds and the various animals which inhabit them,—all which things are recorded in the prayers which were offered to these gods.

Tawhiri-ma-tea next rushed on to attack his brothers Rongo-ma-tane and Haumia-tikitiki, the gods and progenitors of cultivated and uncultivated food; but Papa, to save these for her other children, caught them up, and hid them in a place of safety; and so well were these children of hers concealed by their mother Earth, that Tawhiri-ma-tea sought for them in vain.

Tawhiri-ma-tea having thus vanquished all his other brothers, next rushed against Tu-matauenga, to try his strength against his; he exerted all his force against him, but he could neither shake him or prevail against him. What did Tu-matauenga care for his brother's wrath? He was the only one of the whole party of brothers who had planned the destruction of their parents, and had shown himself brave and fierce in war; his brothers had yielded at once before the tremendous assaults of Tawhiri-ma-tea and his progeny—Tane-mahuta and his offspring had been broken and torn in pieces—Tangaroa and his children had fled to the depths of the ocean or the recesses of the shore—Rongo-matane and Haumia-tikitiki had been hidden from him in the earth—but Tu-matauenga, or man, still stood erect and unshaken upon the breast of his mother Earth; and now at length the hearts of Heaven and of the god of storms became tranquil, and their passions were assuaged.

Tu-matauenga, or fierce man, having thus successfully resisted his brother, the god of hurricanes and storms, next took thought how he could turn upon his brothers and slay them, because they had not assisted him or fought bravely when Tawhiri-ma-tea had attacked them to avenge the separation of their parents, and because they had left him alone to show his prowess in the fight. As yet death had no power over man. It was not until the birth of the children of Taranga and of Makea-tu-tura, of Maui-taha, of Maui-rota, of Maui-pae, of Maui-waho, and of Maui-tikitiki-o-Taranga, the demi-god who tried to deceive Hine-nui-te-po, that death had power over men. If that goddess had not been deceived by Maui-tikitiki, men would not have died, but would in that case have lived forever, it was from his deceiving Hine-nui-te-po that death obtained power over mankind, and penetrated to every part of the earth.

Tu-matauenga continued to reflect upon the cowardly manner in which his brothers had acted, in leaving him to show his courage alone, and he first sought some means of injuring Tane-mahuta, because he had not come to aid him in his combat with Tawhiri-ma-tea, and partly because he was aware that Tane had had a numerous progeny, who were rapidly increasing, and might at last prove hostile to him, and injure him, so he began to collect leaves of the whanake tree, and twisted them into nooses, and when his work was ended, he went to the forest to put up his snares, and hung them up—ha! ha! the children of Tane fell before him, none of them could any longer fly or move in safety.

Then he next determined to take revenge on his brother Tangaroa, who had also deserted him in the combat; so he sought for his offspring, and found them leaping or swimming in the water; then he cut many leaves from the flax-plant, and netted nets with the flax, and dragged these, and hauled the children of Tangaroa ashore.

After that, he determined also to be revenged upon his brothers Rongo-ma-tane and Haumia-tikitiki; he soon found them by their peculiar leaves, and he scraped into shape a wooden hoe, and plaited a basket, and dug in the earth and pulled up all kinds of plants with edible roots, and the plants which had been dug up withered in the sun.

Thus Tu-matauenga devoured all his brothers, and consumed the whole of them, in revenge for their having deserted him and left him to fight alone against Tawhiri-ma-tea and Rangi.

When his brothers had all thus been overcome by Tu', he assumed several names, namely, Tu-kariri, Tu-ka-nguha, Tu-ka-taua, Tu-whake-ticke-tangata, Tu-mata-what-iti, and Tu-ma-tauenga; he assumed one name for each of his attributes displayed in the victories over his brothers. Four of his brothers were entirely deposed by him, and became his food; but one of them, Tawhiri-ma-tea, he could not vanquish or make common, by eating him for food, so he, the last born child of Heaven and Earth, was left as an enemy for man, and still, with a rage equal to that of man, this elder brother ever attacks him in storms and hurricanes, endeavouring to destroy him alike by sea and land.

—Sir George Grey. "The Children of Heaven and Earth." *Polynesian Mythology and Ancient Traditional History*. Auckland: H. Brett, 1885, pp. 1–8.

MAORI

The Myth of Io
In the middle of the nineteenth century, East Coast Maori priests, notably Te Matorohanga and Nepie Pohuhu, revealed a different creation myth which celebrated Io, "the hidden face." Io was described in *The Lore of the Whare Wananga* (in which the Maori council set forth their religious doctrines) as a part of esoteric theology, long known to the priests but hitherto unannounced to the public. While skeptics noted similarities between Io and the Christian god and suggested Io reflects assimilated Western doctrines more strongly than secret native traditions, others pointed out resemblances between this new Maori myth and older ones. Like other Maori creators, Io exists passively in chaos until he speaks, creates light and darkness (each within the other as well as opposed to the other—like the Taoist yin and yang), and separates heaven and earth out of the primeval waters. And like older Maori chants, this myth bears clear evidence of ritual application, its sacred words being equally efficacious in cosmic and human spheres.

1 Io dwelt within breathing-space of immensity.
  The Universe was in darkness, with water everywhere.
There was no glimmer of dawn, no clearness, no light.
And he began by saying these words,—
That He might cease remaining inactive:
  "Darkness, become a light-possessing darkness."
And at once light appeared.
(He) then repeated those self-same words in this manner,—
That He might cease remaining inactive;
"Light, become a darkness-possessing light."
And again an intense darkness supervened.
Then a third time He spake saying:
  "Let there be one darkness above,
  Let there be one darkness below (alternate).
  Let there be a darkness unto Tupua,
  Let there be a darkness unto Tawhito;
  It is a darkness overcome and dispelled.
  Let there be one light above,
  Let there be one light below (alternate).
  Let there be a light unto Tupua,
  Let there be a light unto Tawhito.
  A dominion of light,
  A bright light."
And now a great light prevailed.
(Io) then looked to the waters which compassed him about,
and spake a fourth time, saying:
  "Ye waters of Tai-kama, be ye separate.
  Heaven, be formed." Then the sky became suspended.
  "Bring-forth thou Tupua-horo-nuku."
And at once the moving earth lay stretched abroad.

2 Those words (of Io) became impressed on the minds of our ancestors, and
  by them were they transmitted down through the generations.
Our priests joyfully referred to them as being:
  "The ancient and original sayings.
  The ancient and original words.
  The ancient and original cosmological wisdom.
  Which caused growth from the void,
  The limitless space-filling void,
  As witness the tidal-waters,
  The evolved heaven,
  The birth-given evolved earth."

3 And now my friends, there are three very important applications of those original sayings, as used in our sacred rituals. The first occurs in the ritual for implanting a child within the barren womb. The next occurs in the ritual for enlightening both the mind and the body. The third and last occurs in the ritual on the solemn subjects of death, and of war, of baptism, of genealogical recitals, and such like important subjects, as the priests most particularly concerned themselves in.

The words by which Io fashioned the Universe—that is to say, by which it was implanted and caused to produce a world of light—the same words are used in the ritual for implanting a child in a barren womb. The words by which Io caused light to shine in the darkness are used in the rituals for cheering a gloomy and despondent heart, the feeble aged, the decrepit; for shedding light into secret places and matters, for inspiration in song-composing, and in many other affairs, affecting man to despair in times of adverse war. For all such the ritual to enlighten and cheer, includes the words (used by Io) to overcome and dispel darkness. Thirdly, there is the preparatory ritual which treats of successive formations within the universe, and the genealogical history of man himself.

—Hare Hongi (trans.). "A Maori Cosmology." *The Journal of the Polynesian Society,* 1907, *14* (63), 113–115. Wellington: Polynesian Society.

SAMOA

Tangaroa and the Rock

Some 2,500 miles northwest of New Zealand, Samoa comprises seventeen principal islands, only some of which are inhabited. Western Samoa, a U.N. Trust Territory under the control of New Zealand, became independent in 1962; American Samoa is administered by the U.S. Department of the Interior, and its Polynesian natives are considered American nationals.

In the Samoan creation myth, Tangaroa (a god of oceans and fishermen in many outer Polynesian regions, but here a primordial sky god) creates all things from a rock (the sacred seed of the world) that grows up where he stood. Typical of many Polynesian myths, the creation is first described in rather abstract terms: qualities of matter, the forms, are created before the contents, the things themselves. Once containing the potential of all things, the rock produces earth, sea, fresh water, sky, and all the necessary parts of man. Tangaroa ordered the world and organized people so that the various primary elements of nature could then join fruitfully to produce all the others. Finally creating objective manifestations of himself (beings evolving from the principle of being), Tangaroa made lesser gods to finish and rule over the earth.

THE GOD TANGAROA dwelt in the expanse. There was no sky, no country, no earth, no sea; he was alone, and went to and fro in the expanse; but, at the place where he stood, there grew up a rock. He was the creator of all things.

Tangaroa then said to the rock, "Be thou split up." Then were brought forth in succession a number of *papa* [rocks], each with its additional name, and the meanings of these additional names are 1: "To lie down," 2: "To run, or spread like creeping plants," 3: "Resembling a flat reef," 4: "Honeycomb," 5: "Soft volcanic mud or shale," 6: "To stand," 7: "A kind of branching coral" and his children.

Tangaroa spoke to the rock, and then struck it with his right hand; and it split open and brought forth, first the earth (the parent of all people in the world), and the sea. Then the sea covered To-run-or-spread; and To-lie-down said to To-run-or-spread, "Blessed are you in the possession of your sea"; but To-run-or-spread answered, "Don't bless me; the sea will soon reach you too." All the rocks in like manner called him blessed.

Then sprang up Fresh water; after which Tangaroa again addressed the rock, and the sky was produced; then Tui-te'e-langi or The-chief-to-prop-up-the-sky; then Ilu (Immensity) and Mamao (Space); then came Height.

Tangaroa again addressed the rock and Two-clouds (male) and Two-fresh-waters (female) came forth, and he appointed these two to the "race at the back of the sky." Then he spoke again and Aoa-lala (male) and Ngao-ngao-le-tai, or The-desolate-sea (female), were born; then came Man; then the Spirit, then the Heart; then the Will; then Thought.

That was the end of Tangaroa's creations, produced from the rock; but they were only floating about in the sea, and had no fixedness there. Tangaroa then made an ordinance to the rock as follows, and with the following results.

1. The Spirit, Heart, Will and Thought were to join together inside the man, which they did, and so converted him into an intelligent being. This man was then joined to Earth (female); and thus there was a couple—Fatu (the man) and 'Ele-ele (the woman).

2. Immensity and Space were ordered to unite with Height, up above the sky. They seem to have been regarded as the father and mother of Height, who was a boy. In the sky there was only a void, and nothing for the sight to rest upon.

3. Two-clouds and Two-fresh-waters were ordered to people the region of fresh water.

4. Aoa-lala and The-desolate-sea were ordered to go to the sea and people it.

5. The couple Fatu and 'Ele-ele were then ordered to people the left side, opposite the back of the sky.

6. Chief-to-prop-up-the-sky then by Tangaroa's orders propped up the heavens; but he was not able to hold them and they fell down again. Eventually he propped them up with the *masoa* and *teve* plants . . . and the sky remained up above, reaching to Immensity and Space.

Then Immensity and Space gave birth to Po (night) and Ao (day); and this couple was ordained by Tangaroa to produce the Eye-of-sky (the sun), after which Immensity and Space brought forth Le-langi, or the second heavens, and remained there and peopled the sky. Then Langi, the sky, brought forth in succession the third, fourth, fifth, sixth, seventh, eighth and ninth heavens; and each of these, as it came into being, was propped up by Chief-to-prop-up-the-sky, and was peopled by Immensity and Space.

After this Tangaroa-the-creator created Tangaroa-the-immovable, Tangaroa-the-omnipresent, Tangaroa-the-extender-of-lands (or peoples), Tangaroa-the-messenger, Tuli-the-bird, and Longonoa, Carrier of tidings.

Tangaroa-the-creator appointed Tangaroa-the-immovable to be the chief of the heavens. Tangaroa-the-messenger was appointed the ambassador of the heavens from the eighth down to the first. Night and day apparently dwelt in the original or first [lowest] heaven; and they had the following children or offspring: the dark cloudy heavens, the bright clear heavens, the stars, Manu'a, Samoa, the sun and the moon.

Night and day and their four children—the sun and the moon and Manu'a and Samoa—were summoned by Tangaroa-the-messenger to a general council to be held in "the council ground of tranquillity" in the ninth heaven, where dwelt Tangaroa-the-creator and Tangaroa-the-immovable; and at this council various decrees were issued. Among other things referred to in the legend, the two boys Manu'a and Samoa were sent down to be chiefs over the offspring of Fatu and 'Ele-ele. The sun and the moon were to go and follow night and day, the sun following when the day came, and the moon when the night came; there was to be one portion of the heavens in which they were to pass along; and in like manner the stars were to pass along. The narrator said that the sun and the moon were the shades of Tangaroa.

The legend then proceeds with a narrative of the creation of various islands; first were created the eastern groups—identified in a note as being Tahiti and the adjacent islands; then the Fijian group; then the Tongan group; and then the Samoan island of Savai'i. There is no actual reference to the creation of the Samoan island of Manu'a; but the island is referred to, evidently as actually existing, and was, apparently, the land which Tangaroa-the-messenger visited when on earth, and the earthly scene of his operations when creating the other islands, acting under the directions of Tangaroa-the-creator, who was up in the heavens. There is no explanation of the way in which these islands were created, except that Tangaroa-the-creator and Tangaroa-the-messenger caused them to spring up; but Tangaroa-the-creator came down from the heavens to tread them down and prepare them for people to dwell in.

Three couples, called in the two cases of the eastern islands and Fiji "the children" of Tangaroa, and in that of Tonga his "people," were then sent down by Tangaroa-the-creator from the heavens to possess the eastern islands, Fiji and Tonga respectively; reference is made to the fact that Fatu and 'Ele-ele and their children were already in Manu'a, and it is stated that two persons, named Valu'a and Ti'apa, then sent from Manu'a to Savai'i to people the latter, were children of Fatu and 'Ele-ele.

After this the two Tangaroas caused the Samoan islands of Upolu and Tutuila to spring up as resting-places for Tangaroa-the-messenger. In order to people these islands the *fue,* or peopling vine, was planted; and this brought forth a multitude of worms, which Tangaroa-the-creator shred into strips, and out of them created two couples, one to people the island of Upolu, and the other the island of Tutuila.

—R. W. Williamson. *Religious and Cosmic Beliefs of Central Polynesia.* Vol. 1. Cambridge, England: Cambridge University Press, 1933, pp. 50–53.

THREE TAHITIAN COSMOLOGIES

A part of the Society Islands almost two thousand miles east of Samoa, Tahiti was first settled by Polynesians c. the fourteenth century. It was visited by the English navigator Samual Wallis in 1767 and several times in the next decade by Captain James Cook. Missionaries arrived in the late 1700s, and by 1843 European influence had become so dominating that Queen Pomare was forced to submit to French control. On her death and the subsequent abdication of her son Pomare V, Tahiti became a French colony (1877). In 1946, after having supported the Free French in World War II, Tahitians were granted French citizenship.

Quite independent of Christian doctrine, the Tahitian creation myth exists in several different but related versions, three of which are included here.

Taaroa The first myth depicts Taaroa (the Tahitian equivalent of Samoa's Tangaroa) existing alone in the void; by command, he transformed himself into the universe and became "within . . . the germ . . . beneath." The visible world, and in particular Hawaii, seems to be his shell or outer covering. Thus Taaroa is immanent in all creation.

HE EXISTED, Taaroa was his name.
    In the immensity (space)
There was no earth, there was no sky.
There was no sea, there was no man.
Above, Taaroa calls.
Existing alone, he became the universe.
Taaroa is the origin, the rocks
Taaroa is the sands,
It is thus that he is named.
Taaroa is the light;
Taaroa is within;
Taaroa is the germ.
Taaroa is beneath;
Taaroa is firm;
Taaroa is wise.
He created the land of Hawaii,
Hawaii the great and sacred,
As a body or shell for Taaroa.

—E. S. Craighill Handy. *Polynesian Religion.* Bernice P. Bishop Museum Bulletin 34. Honolulu: Bishop Museum Press, 1927, p. 11.

Shells Within Shells

In the second Tahitian myth, the distinction between inner power and outer manifestation is drawn more clearly and evolves into a dichotomy of mind and body. Commencing in shells within shells, Taaroa tore them all apart to create the universe. Finally, the innermost shell, his own body, is used to make the world, and only his head (his mind) remains unmanifest, sacred to himself. The myth is clear in pointing out the structural similarity between macrocosm and microcosm: as Taaroa's body is to his mind, so the earth is to creatures and men and women are to each other.

FOR A LONG PERIOD Ta'aroa dwelt in his shell (crust). It was round like an egg and revolved in space in continuous darkness.

There was no sun, no moon, no land, no mountain, all was in a confluent state. There was no man, no beast, no fowl, no dog, no living thing, no sea, and no fresh water.

But at last Ta'aroa was filliping his shell, as he sat in close confinement, and it cracked, and broke open. Then he slipped out and stood upon the shell, and he cried out, "Who is above there? Who is below there?" No voice answered! "Who is in front there? Who is in back there?" No voice answered! Only the echo of his own voice resounded and nothing else.

Then Ta'aroa said, "O rock, crawl hither!" But there was no rock to crawl to him. And he said, "O sand, crawl hither!" But there was no sand to crawl to him. Then he got vexed because he was not obeyed.

So he overturned his shell and raised it up to form a dome for the sky and called it Rumia. And he became wearied and after a short period he slipped out of another shell that covered him, which he took for rock and for sand. But his anger was not yet appeased, so he took his spine for a mountain range, his ribs for mountain slopes, his vitals for broad floating clouds, his flare and his flesh for fatness of the earth, his arms and legs for strength for the earth; his finger nails and toe nails for scales and shells for the fishes; his feathers for trees, shrubs, and creepers, to clothe the earth; and his intestines for lobsters, shrimps, and eels for the rivers and the seas; and the blood of Ta'aroa got heated and drifted away for redness for the sky and for rainbows.

But Ta'aroa's head remained sacred to himself, and he still lived, the same head on an indestructible body. He was master of everything. There was expansion and there was growth.

Ta'aroa conjured forth gods, but it was much later that man was conjured, when Tu was with him.

As Ta'aroa had crusts, that is, shells, so has everything a shell.

The sky is a shell, that is, endless space in which the gods placed the sun, the moon, the Sporades, and the constellations of the gods.

The earth is a shell to the stones, the water, and plants that spring from it.

Man's shell is woman because it is by her that he comes into the world; and woman's shell is woman because she is born of woman.

One cannot enumerate the shells of all the things that this world produces.

—Teuira Henry. *Ancient Tahiti*. Bernice P. Bishop Museum Bulletin 48. Honolulu: Bishop Museum Press, 1928, pp. 339–340.

The Mitigator of Many Things

In many regards like the Maori myth of heaven and earth, the third Tahitian cosmology explains that Taaroa was known in four aspects as gods of the sky, foundation, earth, and underworld. With the help of his assistant Tu ("to stand," "to strike," a god of war), Taaroa conjured forth gods (powers) for every part of the universe, delivered Ti'i (the principle of masculinity) from mother earth and created Hina (the principle of femininity) to be his wife. The rest of the myth describes a struggle between forces of retribution and destruction on the one hand and preservation on the other, and it outlines the resultant nature of change that Hina manages to establish as a compromise.

TA'AROA (unique) was the great supreme being, who existed alone in a little world, in a shell like an egg, revolving in dark empty space for ages. At length, he burst forth from confinement, and finding himself quite alone he conjured forth the famous god Tu, who became his companion and artisan in the great work of creation. When the universe was completed, gods innumerable were conjured into existence to fill every region, and, last of all creatures, man was made to inhabit the earth, which was prepared for him.

Ta'aroa was known under four titles according to his attributes: Ta'aroa of the heaven, said to be ten in number; Ta'aroa the great foundation, in a rock in the centre of the earth, from which land grew; Ta'aroa of the surface of the earth; and Ta'aroa of the netherlands. . . .

The first man that was created was Ti'i, clothed in sand, whom Ta'aroa conjured from out of the earth, and then pronounced him perfect. Then was born a wife for Ti'i, Hina, to extricate and mitigate many things, a demi-goddess, whose parents were Te-fatu (the lord) and Fa'ahotu (be fruitful), and she had a face before and behind, and was full of goodness. Ti'i was malicious and had a white heron to bewitch and slay mankind.

After the creation, peace and harmony everywhere existed for a long time. But at last, discontentment arose and there was war among the gods in their different regions, and among men, so Ta'aroa and Tu uttered curses to punish them.

They cursed the stars, which made them blink; and they cursed the moon, which caused it to wane and go out. But Hina, the mitigator of many things, saved their lives since which the host of stars are ever bright, but keep on twinkling; and the moon always returns after it appears.

They cursed the sea, which caused low tide; but Hina preserved the sea, which produced high tide; and so these tides have followed each other ever since.

They cursed the rivers, which frightened away the waters, so that they hid beneath the soil; but Hina reproduced the shy waters, which formed springs, and so they continue thus to exist.

They cursed the trees, which caused their leaves to turn yellow and their fruit to go out of season; but Hina saved their lives, which caused new leaves ever to succeed the old and the fruit to return in their seasons. And so it would have been with people, they would have withered under the curse of the gods, while Hina would have saved their lives, had it not been that Ti'i conjured them to death.

Hina said, "Oh, Ti'i! do not persist in invoking man to death. When he suffers under the curse of the gods, I shall resuscitate him. Behold, my moon and glittering stars, my budding trees and my fruit that come in seasons, are they not more comely than thy dying men?"

But her husband was unyielding, and he replied, "My master, Ta'aroa, whose curse is death, loves to slay, and I shall conjure to death all whom I cause my white heron to enter." So, according to the Tahitians, the man and not the woman caused people to lose eternal life, and at length he fell and died beneath his own curse.

—Teuira Henry. "Tahitian Folklore." *Journal of the Polynesian Society,* 1901, *10* (37), 51–52. Wellington: Polynesian Society.

TUAMOTU ISLANDS

Cosmic Chant   East of the Society Islands and south of the Marquesas, the Tuamotu Islands or Low Archipelago comprise seventy-six atolls in a 1,000-mile chain. Annexed by France in 1881, they were originally "discovered" by the Spanish in 1606.

A cosmic chant from the Takaroa Atoll describes the source of life appearing first in Havaiki, a sacred land of the spirits or ancestors existing in the sky or to the west. Sleeping, this source remains passive in the evolution of the world from nothingness (the night) through various stages of pre-being.

L IFE appears in the world,
    Life springs up in Havaiki.
The Source-of-night sleeps below
    in the void of the world,
    in the taking form of the world,
    in the growth of the world,
    the life of the world,
    the leafing of the world,
    the unfolding of the world,
    the darkening of the world,
    the branching of the world,
    the bending down of the world.

—Kenneth Emory (trans.). "Cosmic Chant from the Takaroa Atoll of the Tuamotus." *Journal of the Polynesian Society,* 1920, *47* (5), 14.

TUAMOTU ISLANDS

The Dwelling Places of Kiho

Like the Maori myth of the primordial creator Io, this Tuamotuan cosmogony celebrates Kiho, the "source of sources." Dwelling before or outside creation in the void, Kiho first produced chaos (the dark-teeming waters) "through the potency of his eloquence"; that is, through the fertile power of his word. The connection between words and semen is clearly made here; the metaphors blur, but in their mixture, the unity of mental and physical creation is asserted.

Floating to the top of the chaotic waters, rich in potentiality, Kiho created the foundation of night (not-being) and light (being) and then, as he gradually turned over and stood up, the various realms of the heavens and earth. Finally he produced Atea-ragi (a masculine principle, like the sky god Rangi of the Maori myth) and Fakahotu-henua (a feminine principle, the fructifier-of-the-soil, akin to the Maori's Papa, but here connected more specifically with coral than with earth). And after ordering the sea, soil, and sand, Kiho embodied the inspirited Atea, his objective self, to rule the world. Lastly, Kiho left his sacred red girdle (the dawning horizon?) to Atea and retreated back beyond being and activity to the nothingness and passivity from which he came.

IT IS SAID that Kiho dwelt in the Void. It was said that Kiho dwelt beneath the foundations of Havaiki (in a place) which was called the Black-gleamless-realm-of-Havaiki.

Dwelling there below Kiho had no parents; he had no friend; he had no mate; there was none but him; he was not the root, he was the stability.

It was said that, at that time, Kiho conversed only with his Astral-double (Activating Self).

His musings were within himself; his acts were performed by his Activating-self.

That place wherein Kiho dwelt was said to be the Nonexistence-of-the-land; the name of that place was the Black-gleamless-realm-of-Havaiki.

It was there that Kiho dwelt; indeed, in that place he created all things whatsoever.

Hereafter (I give) the names of his dwelling places.

Kiho dwelt in his heaven at the nadir of the Night-realm,
Kiho dwelt in his heaven in the Black-gleamless-realm,
Kiho dwelt in his heaven in the Many-portioned-realm-of-night,
Kiho dwelt in his heaven in the Many-portioned-realm-of-night,
These places were situated within the Night-sphere,
Kiho dwelt below in Foundation-of-waters,
Kiho dwelt below in Foundation-unstable,
Kiho dwelt below in Foundation-thrust-upward.
Kiho dwelt below in Foundation-solidifying,
Kiho dwelt below in Foundation-quaking,

Kiho dwelt below in Foundation-extending,
Kiho dwelt below in Foundation-separated,
Kiho dwelt below in Foundation-(first)-appearing,
Kiho dwelt below in Foundation-tipping,
Kiho dwelt below in Foundation-moving-hither-and-thither,
Kiho dwelt below in Foundation-uprisen.

These rock-formations were situated in the Dark-teeming-waters; they were said to be the places wherein Kiho dwelt.

Kiho dwelt in the Zenith-of-the-heavens,
Kiho dwelt in the Narrow-borderlands-of-the-heavens,
Kiho dwelt in the Upper-regions-of-the-heavens,
Kiho dwelt in the Lower-regions-of-the-heavens,
Kiho dwelt in the Navel-of-the-heavens,
Kiho dwelt in the Planes-of-the-heavens,
Kiho dwelt in the Red-glow-of-the-heavens.

This is indeed that heaven which Kiho gave over to Atea.

It was also said that the Dark-teeming-waters were the first thing that Kiho evolved.

It was there that he dwelt in the house called Upholding-house-of-the-heavenly-regions.

THERE WERE THREE principal heaven-spheres (not-Earth-regions) created by Kiho; these were:
1. The Night-sphere-of-darkness of Kiho, or Region-of-the-spirit-world,
2. The Day-sphere-of-light of Atea, or Region-of-the-Earth-world,
3. The Sky-sphere of Tane, or Region-of-the-skies.

KIHO-THE-SOURCE, of whom I tell, is he who was said to be the god whose deeds are here recounted; and these are the deeds he performed up to the time of Atea.

Whilst Kiho was, the heavens were not;—there was no land, there was no man; there was no thing whatsoever.

Kiho-the-sleeper slumbered immemorially in the Void.

Kiho-the-precursor awoke.

Then Kiho glanced upward into the Black-gleamless-night, that is to say, the first beginning of all things whatsoever.

Thereupon Kiho glanced down at his dwelling-place within the Black-gleamless-night, and thus spake Kiho, "This is indeed the utterly black night of Havaiki."

Then Kiho mused of all (potential) things whatsoever; and he caused his thought to be evoked, and thereupon he spake to his Activating-self, saying, "May I be eloquent of my indwelling occult knowledge; may I be expressive of my outpouring eloquence, in order that all assembled beings shall give ear!"

Began to stir the inner-urge of the Dark-teeming-waters,
Began to stir the inner-urge of the land,

Began to stir the inner-urge of Havaiki.

(The night world lay in deep sleep beneath the Non-existence-of-the-land.)

It was the inner-urge stirring,

It was the inner-urge burgeoning,

It was the inner-urge sheath-wrapped,

It was the inner-urge reaching upward,

It was the inner-urge branching out above,

It was the inner-urge taking root below.

It was the inner-urge that would soon stand erect upon the Earth.

It was the inner-urge that would soon stand erect in Twilight-dark-Havaiki.

Non-existent was the upward urge of the land.

Non-existent was the stratification of the land,

Non-existent was the viscosity of the land,

Non-existent was the rigidity of the land,

Non-existent was the deployment of the land,

Non-existent was the multiplicity of the land,

Non-existent was the . . . of the land,

Non-existent was the divarication of the land,

Non-existent was the overhanging rim of the land,

Non-existent was the . . . of the land.

Foundation-darkness was sleeping beneath the Non-existence-of-the-land,

Foundation-light was sleeping beneath the Non-existence-of-the-land,

Foundation-fissured was sleeping beneath the Non-existence-of-the-land,

Foundation-thundering was sleeping beneath the Non-existence-of-the-land,

Columnar-support-of-land was sleeping beneath the Non-existence-of-the-land,

Sky foundation was sleeping beneath the Non-existence-of-the-land,

. . . was sleeping beneath the Non-existence-of-the-land,

Dark-concave-dome was sleeping beneath the Non-existence-of-the-land,

Gushing-murmur-of-waters was sleeping beneath the Non-existence-of-the-land,

Contiguous-support was sleeping beneath the Non-existence-of-the-land,

Standing-in-small segments were sleeping beneath the Non-existence-of-the-land,

Long-standing-scintillation was sleeping beneath the Non-existence-of-the-land,

Havaiki was sleeping beneath the Non-existence-of-the-land,

Peaha was sleeping beneath the Non-existence-of-the-land.

Fruitfulness was sleeping beneath the Non-existence-of-the-land,

Sky-expanse was sleeping beneath the Non-existence-of-the-land.

Intense-desire-speeding-to-the-night was sleeping beneath the Non-existence-of-the-land,

The-foundation-of-Kuporu was sleeping beneath the Non-existence-of-the-land,

The radiant-realm-of-Tane was sleeping beneath the Non-existence-of-the-land.

Then Kiho created the Primordial-waters through the potency of his outpouring eloquence.

And they commenced to evolve.

And they were evolved.

Now indeed Kiho spake to his Activating-self, saying, "Make thou violently to quake the rock-base of Havaiki that I become cognizant of all things,—that all things whatsoever be set apart in their rightful places!"

And at once Kiho made his eyes to glow with flame—and the darkness became light.

Now indeed his Activating-self caused the Rock-foundation of Havaiki to quake, and Kiho saw the position of all things where they were.

Then Kiho floated up upon the surface of the Primordial-waters,—it was his Activating-self who did so; he lay there floating upon his back.

Then Kiho created Foundation-of-the-night-world; it was a land-realm, it was below.

Then Kiho created Foundation-of-the-light-world; it was a sky-realm, it was above.

(These two realms were situated in the first plane.)

Now Kiho turned over upon his face in that place.

Then Kiho created Foundation-fissured; it was a land-realm, it was below.

Then Kiho created Foundation-thundering; it was a sky-realm, it was above.

(These two realms were situated in the second plane.)

Now Kiho raised himself up on an elbow in that place.

Then Kiho created Columnar-support-of-the-land; it was a land-realm, it was below.

Then Kiho created Sky-base; it was a sky-realm, it was above.

(These two realms were situated in the third plane.)

Now Kiho raised himself up on his hands and knees in that place.

Then Kiho created Matau-heti; it was a land-realm, it was below.

Then Kiho created Dark-concavity; it was a sky-realm, it was above.

(These two realms were situated in the fourth plane.)

Now Kiho arose to a stooping posture in that place.

Then Kiho created Gushing-murmur-of-waters; it was a land-realm, it was below.

Then Kiho created Contiguous-support; it was a sky-realm, it was above.

(These two realms were situated in the fifth plane.)

Now Kiho arose to a forward-leaning posture in that place.

Then Kiho created Standing-in-small-segments; it was a land-realm, it was above.

Then Kiho created Long-standing-scintillation; it was a sky-realm, it was above.

(These two realms were situated in the sixth plane.)

Now Kiho straightened up to a shortened posture in that place.

Then Kiho created Havaiki; it was a land-realm, it was below.

The Kiho created Peaha; it was a sky-realm, it was above.

(These two realms were situated in the seventh plane.)

Now Kiho straightened up to a fully extended posture in that place.

Then Kiho created Fructifier-of-the-soil; it was a land-realm, it was below.

Then Kiho created Sky-expanse; it was a sky-realm, it was above.

(These two realms were situated in the eighth plane of the Night-region-of-the-Spirit-world.)

This is what the sages told me concerning these last two realms, that is to say, Atea-ragi (Sky-expanse) and Fakahotu-henua (Fructifier-of-the-soil):

Sky-expanse was above,

Fructifier-of-the-soil was underneath.

Whence sprang the offspring of Sky-expanse!

Now Kiho set apart the sea in its place, and set apart the soil in its place, and set apart the white sand—leaving it in Havaiki; he then set apart the reddish earth for the mountains; he set apart the black sand for Vavau; then he took the foam of the waves and the viscous clay, and cast them down beneath his feet; then he trod upon them, saying, "You are indeed the origin of stratified rock foundations; may you rise, may you thrust upward, may you become firm!"

He then left the white sand along the rocky borders of the bedrock-foundation of Havaiki, and (when) all these deeds had been accomplished, he created the upper-heavens of Atea.

Then Kiho looked upon his Astral-self (Activating-self) who was lying stretched out below (him); then he took the red sand (earth) and shaped it together; next he exhaled upon it his vitalizing breath, and the sand became imbued with life, thereupon his Astral-self entered wholly into that red sand and immediately became transformed into a sentient being; this living creature was sleeping; then it awoke.

Now Kiho spake, saying, "Thou art Atea of the legion-of-the-gods to become as a firm foundation for Havaiki-the-above, as a sanctuary for the spirit-legions."

Atea then saw that the god was lying upon his face.

Then Kiho again spake thus to Atea:

"Thou art he who shall become far-famed through me,

Thou art he whom I shall inform with all esoteric arts and lore,

Thou shalt be the Expounder,

Thou art he whom I shall cause to beget progeny,

Thou art he whom I shall imbue with fertility that Havaiki teem with life.

Thou art he whom I shall avenge,

Thou art he whom I shall extol,

Thou art he whom I shall install in the Domed-firmament of Atea,
Thou shalt embark upon wars of reprisal,—
Thou shalt demean the prestige of my Prince,
Thou shalt impale my Prince upon thy spear;
Thou shalt be the instigator of disaster,
Thou shalt be the progenitor of fatherlands,
Thou shalt become the forefront of the Legion-of-the-gods that thou create the new Sky spheres;
Thou shalt evoke thy Activating-self,
Thou shalt make level the Sacred-heaven-of-Atea that my Prince may dwell therein, that he stand upright in his Sky-sphere;
Multitudes shall invoke him,—
See to it that thou troubles him not, and let the Spirit-legions be created;
Thou shalt rise upward,
Thou shalt soar upward,
Thou shalt inform infinite space,
Thou shalt become established in thy Heaven-sphere;
Thou art the Pillar of the Skies,
Thou art the Tie beam—
Verily thou art the Wall-plate of thy Heaven.
Thou art the First,
Thou art the Last,
Thou art the Above,
Thou art the Below—
Thou art the Completer!"

Then Kiho undid his girdle and gave it to Atea. The name of the girdle was "The-crimson-girdle-of-Atea."

It was said that Kiho knew not death; he turned his back upon Atea and disappeared (going) to the Black-gleamless-realm-of-Havaiki.

—Frank J. Stimson. *Tuamotuan Religion. Bernice P. Bishop Museum Bulletin 103.* Honolulu: Bishop Museum Press, 1933, pp. 12–19.

HAWAII

The Kumulipo (A Creation Chant)
At the northwest boundary of Polynesia, some 2,000 miles east of California, Hawaii was settled by Polynesians in c. 750 A.D. Although when Captain James Cook first visited the island in 1778 it was ruled by various warring native kings, Kamehameha I had won sole sovereignty by 1810. Seemingly at their height in this period of unification, Hawaiian culture and religion soon declined under the influence of the European and American traders whom Kamehameha I welcomed. Those who survived the new foreign diseases were nonetheless adversely affected by Western practices of trading for profit, warring with firearms, and drinking liquor. When the native religion crumbled along with the society, Kamehameha III (1825–

1842) invited Christian missionaries to preach Christianity. And Hawaii gradually came under United States influence as American commercial interests developed and flourished; Americans came to dominate Hawaiian politics, and eventually Hawaii became the 50th state in the American union.

More than any other Polynesian myth, the Hawaiian creation chant (the Kumulipo) celebrates the wondrous fertility of the seven stages of the primordial night. "Nothing but darkness that/Nothing but darkness this," the night is a chaos of potentiality and pre-being. Evolved from the primordial slime and divided into male and female principles, its stages give birth to staggering numbers of life forms: first simple sea creatures; then fish, insects, and birds, reptiles, mammals, and people. And finally, when all have evolved in this time of the past, the day breaks and the created world is established.

Most notable for its depiction of the sheer abundance and richness of creation, the Kumulipo presumes no single, supreme creator. Fertility itself and the desire to reproduce give birth to "all the myriad creatures."

I At the time when the earth became hot
At the time when the heavens turned about
At the time when the sun was darkened
To cause the moon to shine
The time of the rise of the Pleiades
The slime, this was the source of the earth
The source of the darkness that made darkness
The source of the night that made night
The intense darkness, the deep darkness
Darkenss of the sun, darkness of the night
  Nothing but night.
The night gave birth
Born was Kumulipo in the night, a male
Born was Po'ele in the night, a female
Born was the coral polyp, born was the coral, came forth
Born was the grub that digs and heaps up the earth, came forth
Born was his [child] an earthworm, came forth
Born was the starfish, his child the small starfish came forth
Born was the sea cucumber, his child the small sea cucumber came forth
Born was the sea urchin, the sea urchin [tribe]
Born was the short-spiked sea urchin, came forth
Born was the smooth sea urchin, his child the long-spiked came forth
Born was the ring-shaped sea urchin, his child the thin-spiked came forth
Born was the barnacle, his child the pearl oyster came forth
Born was the mother-of-pearl, his child the oyster came forth
Born was the mussel, his child the hermit crab came forth
Born was the big limpet, his child the small limpet came forth
Born was the cowry, his child the small cowry came forth
Born was the naka shellfish, the rock oyster his child came forth
Born was the drupa shellfish, his child the bitter white shellfish came forth

Born was the conch shell, his child the small conch shell came forth
Born was the nerita shellfish, the sand-burrowing shellfish his child came forth
Born was the fresh water shellfish, his child the small fresh water shellfish came
    forth
Born was man for the narrow stream, the woman for the broad stream
Born was the Ekaha moss living in the sea
Guarded by the Ekahakaha fern living on land
Darkness slips into light
Earth and water are the food of the plant
The god enters, man can not enter
Man for the narrow stream, woman for the broad stream
Born was the touch seagrass living in the sea
Guarded by the tough landgrass living on land . . .
Man for the narrow stream, woman for the broad stream
Born was the hairy seaweed living in the sea
Guarded by the hairy pandanus vine living on land
Darkness slips into light
Earth and water are the food of the plant
The god enters, man can not enter
The man with the water gourd, he is a god
Water that causes the withered vine to flourish
Causes the plant top to develop freely
Multiplying in the passing time
The long night slips along
Fruitful, very fruitful
Spreading here, spreading there
Spreading this way, spreading that wa,
Propping up earth, holding up the sky
The time passes, this night of Kumulipo
    Still it is night

II Born is a child to Po-wehiwehi
    Cradled in the arms of Po-uliuli [?]
A wrestler, a pusher, [?]
Dweller in the land of Poho-mi-luamea
The sacred scent from the gourd stem proclaims [itself]
The stench breaks forth in the time of infancy
He is doubtful and stands swelling
He crooks himself and straddles
The seven waters just float
Born is the child of the *bilu* fish and swims
The *bilu* fish rests with spreading tail-fin
A child of renown for Po-uliuli
A little one for Po-wehiwehi

Po-uliuli the male
Po-wehiwehi the female
Before is the I'a [fish], born the Nai'a [porpoise] in the sea there swimming
Born is the Mano [shark], born the Moano [goatfish] in the sea there swimming
Born is the Mau, born the Maumau in the sea there swimming
Born is the Nana, born the Mana fish in the sea there swimming
Born is the Nake, born the Make in the sea there swimming
Born is the Napa, born the Nala in the sea there swimming
Born is the Pala, born the Kala [sturgeon?] in the sea there swimming
Born is the Paka eel, born is the Papa [crab] in the sea there swimming
Born is the Kalakala, born the Huluhulu [sea slug] in the sea there swimming
Born is the Halahala, born the Palapala in the sea there swimming
Born is the Pe'a [octopus], born is the Lupe [sting ray] in the sea there swim-
    ming
Born is the Ao, born is the 'Awa [milkfish] in the sea there swimming
Born is the Aku [bonito], born the Ahi [albacore] in the sea there swimming
Born is the Opelu [mackerel], born the Akule fish in the sea there swimming
Born is the 'Ama'ama [mullet], born the 'Anae [adult mullet] in the sea there
    swimming
Man for the narrow stream, woman for the broad stream
Born is the 'A'awa fish living in the sea
Guarded by the 'Awa plant living on land

   Refrain

Man for the narrow stream, woman for the broad stream
Born is the Ulae [lizard fish] living in the sea
Guarded by the Mokae rush living on land

   Refrain

Man for the narrow stream, woman for the broad stream
Born is the Palaoa [walrus] living in the sea [?]
Guarded by the Aoa [sandalwood] living on land

   Refrain

The train of walruses passing by [?]
Milling about in the depths of the sea
The long lines of opule fish
The sea is thick with them
Crabs and hardshelled creatures
[They] go swallowing on the way
Rising and diving under swiftly and silently
Pimoe lurks behind the horizon
On the long waves, the crested waves
Innumerable the coral ridges
Low, heaped-up, jagged
The little ones seek the dark places

Very dark is the ocean and obscure
A sea of coral like the green heights of Paliuli
The land disappears into them
Covered by the darkness of night
  Still it is night

III A male this, the female that
A male born in the time of black darkness
The female born in the time of groping in the darkness
Overshadowed was the sea, overshadowed the land
Overshadowed the streams, overshadowed the mountains
Overshadowed the dimly brightening night
The rootstalk grew forming nine leaves
Upright it grew with dark leaves
The sprout that shot forth leaves of high chiefs
Born was Po'ele'ele the male
Lived with Pohaha a female
The rootstalk sprouted
  The taro stalk grew
Born was the Wood borer, a parent
Out came its child a flying thing, and flew
Born was the Caterpillar, the parent
Out came its child a Moth, and flew
Born was the Ant, the parent
Out came its child a Dragonfly, and flew
Born was the Grub, the parent
Out came its child the Grasshopper, and flew
Born was the Pinworm, the parent
Out came its child a Fly, and flew
Born was the egg [?], the parent
Out came its child a bird, and flew
Born was the Snipe, the parent
Out came its child a Plover, and flew
Born was the A'o bird, the parent
Out came its child an A'u bird, and flew
Born was the Turnstone, the parent
Out came its child a Fly-catcher, and flew
Born was the Mudhen, the parent
Out came its child an Apapane bird, and flew
Born was the Crow, the parent
Out came its child an Alawi bird, and flew
Born was the 'E'ea bird, the parent
Out came its child an Alaaiaha bird, and flew
Born was the Mamo honey-sucker, the parent
Out came its child an 'O'o bird, and flew

Born was the Rail, the parent
Out came its child a brown Albatross, and flew
Born was the Akikiki creeper, the parent
Out came its child an Ukihi bird, and flew
Born was the Curlew, the parent
Out came its child a Stilt, and flew
Born was the Frigate bird, the parent
Out came its child a Tropic bird, and flew
Born was the migrating gray-backed Tern, the parent
Out came its child a red-tailed Tropic-bird, and flew
Born was the Unana bird, the parent
Its offspring the Heron came out and flew
    Flew hither in flocks
    On the seashore in ranks
    Settled down and covered the beach
    Covered the land of Kane's-hidden-island
    Land birds were born
    Sea birds were born
Man born for the narrow stream, woman for the broad stream
Born was the Stingray, living in the sea
Guarded by the Stormy-petrel living on land . . .
    Refrain

This is the flying place of the bird Halulu
Of Kiwa'a, the bird that cries over the canoe house
Birds that fly in a flock shutting out the sun
The earth is covered with the fledgelings of the night breaking into dawn
The time when the dawning light spreads abroad
The young weak *'ape* plant rises
A tender plant with spreading leaves
A branching out of the nightborn
Nothing but darkness that
Nothing but darkness this
Darkness alone for Po'ele'ele
A time of dawn indeed for Pohaha
    Still it is night

IV Plant the *'abi'a* and cause it to propagate [?]
       The dusky black *'ape* plant
The sea creeps up to the land
Creeps backward, creeps forward
Producing the family of crawlers
Crawling behind, crawling in front
Advancing the front, settling down at the back
The front of my cherished one [?]

He is dark, splendid,
Popanopano is born as a male [?]
Popanopano, the male
Po-lalo-wehi, the female
Gave birth to those who produce eggs
Produce and multiply in the passing night
Here they are laid
Here they roll about
The children roll about, play in the sand
Child of the night of black darkness is born
   The night gives birth
The night gives birth to prolific ones
The night is swollen with plump creatures
The night gives birth to rough-backed turtles
The night produces horn-billed turtles
The night gives birth to dark-red turtles
The night is pregnant with the small lobster
The night gives birth to sluggish-moving geckos
Slippery is the night with sleek-skinned geckos
The night gives birth to clinging creatures
The night proclaims rough ones
The night gives birth to deliberate creatures
The night shrinks from the ineffective
The night gives birth to sharp-nosed creatures
Hollowed is the night for great fat ones
The night gives birth to mud dwellers
The night lingers for track leavers
Born is the male for the narrow stream, the female for the broad stream
Born is the turtle *[Honu]* living in the sea
Guarded by the *Maile* seedling *[Kuhonua]* living on land . . .

   Refrain

With a dancing motion they go creeping and crawling
The tail swinging its length
Sullenly, sullenly
They go poking about the dunghill
Filth is their food, they devour it
Eat and rest, eat and belch it up
Eating like common people
Distressful is their eating
They move about and become heated
Act as if exhausted
They stagger as they go
Go in the land of crawlers
The family of crawlers born in the night
   Still it is night

V The time arrives for Po-kanokano
    To increase the progeny of Po-lalo-uli
Dark is the skin of the new generation
Black is the skin of the beloved Po-lalo-uli
Who sleeps as a wife to the Night-digger
The beaked nose that digs the earth is erected
Let it dig at the land, increase it, heap it up
Walling it up at the back
Walling it up in front
The pig child is born
Lodges inland in the bush
Cultivates the water taro patches of Lo'iloa
Tenfold is the increase of the island
Tenfold the increase of the land
The land where the Night-digger dwelt
Long is the line of his ancestry
The ancient line of the pig of chief blood
The pig of highest rank born in the time
The time when the Night-digger lived
And slept with Po-lalo-uli
    The night gave birth
Born were the peaked-heads, they were clumsy ones
Born were the flat-heads, they were braggarts
Born were the angular-heads, they were esteemed
Born were the fair-haired, they were strangers
Born were the blonds, their skin was white
Born were those with retreating foreheads, they were bushy-haired
Born were the blunt-heads, their heads were round
Born were the dark-heads, they were dark
Born were the common class, they were unsettled
Born were the working class, they were workers
Born were the favorites, they were courted
Born were the slave class, and wild was their nature
Born were the cropped-haired, they were the picked men
Born were the song chanters, they were indolent [?]
Born were the big bellies, big eaters were they
Born were the timid ones, bashful were they
Born were the messengers, they were sent here and there
Born were the slothful, they were lazy
Born were the stingy, they were sour
Born were the puny, they were feeble ones
Born were the thickset, they were stalwart
Born were the broad-chested, broad was their badge in battle
Born were the family men, they were home lovers

Born were the mixed breeds, they had no fixed line of descent
Born were the lousy-headed, they were lice infested
Born were the war leaders, men followed after them
Born were the high chiefs, they were ruddy
Born were the stragglers, they were dispersed
Scattered here and there
The children of Lo'iloa multiplied
The virgin land sprang into bloom
The gourd of desire was loosened
With desire to extend the family line
To carry on the fruit of Oma's descendants,
The generations from the Night-digger
In that period of the past
   Still it is night

VI   Many new lines of chiefs spring up
      Cultivation arises, full of taboos
[They go about scratching at the wet lands
It sprouts, the first blades appear, the food is ready] [?]
Food grown by the water courses
Food grown by the sea
Plentiful and heaped up
The parent rats dwell in holes
The little rats huddle together
Those who mark the seasons
Little tolls from the land
Little tolls from the water courses
Trace of the nibblings of these brown-coated ones
With whiskers upstanding
They hide here and there
A rat in the upland, a rat by the sea
A rat running beside the wave
Born to the two, child of the Night-falling-away
Born to the two, child of the Night-creeping-away
The little child creeps as it moves
The little child moves with a spring
Pilfering at the rind
Rind of the 'ohi'a fruit, not a fruit of the upland
A tiny child born as the darkness falls away
A springing child born as the darkness creeps away
Child of the dark and child in the night now here
   Still it is night

VII   Fear falls upon me on the mountain top
      Fear of the passing night
Fear of the night approaching

Fear of the pregnant night
Fear of the breach of the law
Dread of the place of offering and the narrow trail
Dread of the food and the waste part remaining
Dread of the receding night
Awe of the night approaching
Awe of the dog child of the Night-creeping-away
A dog child of the Night-creeping-hither
A dark red dog, a brindled dog
A hairless dog of the hairless ones
A dog as an offering for the oven
Palatable is the sacrifice for supplication [?]
Pitiful in the cold without covering
Pitiful in the heat without a garment
He goes naked on the way to Malama
[Where] the night ends for the children [of night] [?]
From the growth and the parching [?]
From the cutting off and the quiet [?]
The driving Hula wind his companion
Younger brother of the naked ones, the 'Olohe
Out from the slime come rootlets
Out from the slime comes young growth
Out from the slime come branching leaves
Out from the slime comes outgrowth
Born in the time when men came from afar
   Still it is night

VIII

Well-formed is the child, well-formed now
Child in the time when men multiplied
Child in the time when men came from afar
Born were men by the hundreds
Born was man for the narrow stream
Born was woman for the broad stream
Born the night of the gods
Men stood together
Men slept together
They two slept together in the time long ago
Wave after wave of men moving in company
Ruddy the forehead of the god
Dark that of man
White-[bearded] the chin
Tranquil was the time when men multiplied
Calm like the time when men came from afar
It was called Calmness [La'ila'i] then
Born was La'ila'i a woman
Born was Ki'i a man

Born was Kane a god
Born was Kanaloa the hot-striking octopus
   It was day
The wombs gave birth [?]
Ocean-edge
The-damp-forest, latter of the two
The first chief of the dim past dwelling in cold uplands, their younger
The man of long life and hundreds upon hundreds of chiefs
Scoop out, scoop out,
Hollow out, hollow out, keep hollowing
Hollow out, hollow out, "the woman sat sideways"
La'ila'i, a woman in the time when men came from afar
La'ila'i, a woman in the time when men multipled
Lived as a woman of the time when men multiplied
Born was Groping-one [Hahapo'ele], a girl
Born was Dim-sighted [Ha-popo], a girl
Born was Beautiful [Maila] called Clothed-in-leaves [Lopala-pala]
Naked ['Olohe] was another name
[She] lived in the land of Lua [pit]
[At] that place called "pit of the 'Olohe"
Naked was man born in the day
Naked the woman born in the upland
[She] lived here with man [?]
Born was Creeping-ti-plant [La'i'olo] to man
Born was Expected-day [Kapopo], a female
Born was Midnight [Po'ele-i], born First-light [Po'ele-a]
Opening-wide [Wehi-loa] was their youngest
These were those who gave birth
The little ones, the older ones
Ever increasing in number
Man spread abroad, man was here now
   It was Day

—Martha Beckwith (trans. and ed.). *The Kumulipo: A Hawaiian Creation Chant*. Chicago: University of Chicago Press, 1951, pp. 58–60, 63–67, 71–73, 77–79, 82–84, 87–88, 92–93, 97–98.

ACKNOWLEDGMENTS

Acknowledgment is made to the following for permission to reprint copyrighted material:

George Allen and Unwin, Ltd., for extract from *The Nihongi*, translated by G. W. Aston.

The American Folklore Society for extracts from the following volumes in *Memoirs of the American Folklore Society: Mandan-Hidatsa Myths and Ceremonies*, by Martha Warren Beckwith (1938); *Myths and Tales of the Chiricahua Apache Indians XXXVII*, by Morris Edward Opler (1942); *Myths and Tales of the White Mountain Apache*, by Granville Goodwin (1939); *Myths and Legends of the Lipan Apache Indians*, by Morris Edward Opler (1940); *Myths and Tales of the Jicarilla Apache Indians*, by Morris Edward Opler (1938); and for "The Creation Myth and Acculturation in Acalan, Guatemala," by Morris Segal, in the *Journal of American Folklore* 56 (1943); "Marshallese Folklore Types," by William Davenport, in the *Journal of American Folklore* 66 (1953); "Chuckchee Tales," by Waldemar Bogoras, in the *Journal of American Folklore* 41 *(1928)*.

J. J. Augustin, Inc., for extract from *Dahomey*, Vol. 2, by Melville J. Herskovits.

Beacon Press for extracts from *The Gnostic Religion*, by Hans Jonas.

Bishop Museum Press for extracts from the *B. P. Bishop Museum Bulletin 103: Tuamotuan Religion*, by Frank J. Stimson (1933); *B. P. Bishop Museum Bulletin 34: Polynesian Religion*, by E. S. Craighill Handy (1927); *B. P. Bishop Museum Bulletin 48: Ancient Tahiti*, by Teuira Henry (1928).

George Braziller, Inc., for extract from *Alpha: Myths of Creation*, by Charles Long.

Cambridge University Press for extracts from *The Negritos of Malaya*, by Igor N. Evans; *Religious and Cosmic Beliefs of Central Polynesia*, by R. W. Williamson.

Columbia University Press for extracts from *Sources of Indian Tradition*, Vol. 1, edited by William Theodore DeBary *et al;* Sources of Chinese Tradition, Vol. 1, edited by William Theodore DeBary *et al.*

Thomas Y. Crowell Company for extracts from *The Beginning: Creation Myths Around the World*, by Maria Leach.

Dell Publishing Company for extracts from *African Myths and Tales*, edited by Susan Feldman.

J. M. Dent and Sons (Canada), Ltd., for extracts from *Hindu Scriptures*, translated by R. C. Zaehner.

E. P. Dutton and Company, Inc., for extracts from *Hindu Scriptures*, translated by R. C. Zaehner, an Everyman's Library Edition, published in the United States by E. P. Dutton and reprinted with their permission.

Heinemann Educational Books, Ltd., for extracts from *Myths and Legends of the Swahili*, by Jan Knappert.

Hodder and Stoughton, Ltd., for extracts from *Creation Myths of the Ancient Near East*, by S. G. F. Brandon.

Indiana University Press for extract from *Ovid's Metamorphosis*, translated by Rolphe Humphries.

International African Institute for extracts from *Conversations with Ogotemmeli*, by Marcel Griaule; "The Mande Creation Myth," in *Africa* 17, (April 1957).

Thomas Nelson and Sons, Ltd., for extracts from *The Holy Bible*, Revised Standard Version.

Oxford University Press for extracts from *Zurvan: A Zoroastrian Dilemma*, by R. C. Zaehner (1955), reprinted by permission of Oxford University Press; *The Thirteen Principal Upanishads*, translated by Robert Ernest Hume (1931), reprinted by permission of Oxford University Press.

Paragon Book Reprint Corp. for extract from *The Nihongi*, translated by W. G. Aston.

Penguin Books, Ltd., for extracts from *Lao Tzu: Tao Te Ching*, translated by D. C. Lau (Penguin Classics, 1963); *The Upanishads*, translated by Juan Mascaro (Penguin Classics, 1965); *Poems of Heaven and Hell from Ancient Mesopotamia*, translated by N. K. Sanders (Penguin Classics, 1971); *Hesiod and Theognis*, translated by Dorothy Wenger (Penguin Classics, 1973).

The Philosophical Library for extracts from *Djanggawul: An Aboriginal Religious Cult of North Eastern Arnhem Land*, by Ronald M. Berndt.

Princeton University Press for extracts from *African Folktales and Sculpture*, edited by Radin and Sweeney, copyright 1954, © 1964 by Princeton University Press, reprinted by permission of Princeton University Press; *Ancient Near Eastern Texts Relating to the Old Testament*, edited by James B. Pritchard, copyright © 1950, reprinted by permission of Princeton University Press.

A. H. and A. W. Reed, Ltd., for extracts from *Treasury of Maori Folklore*, by A. W. Reed.

Smithsonian Institution Press for extracts from "The Creation of the Earth (a Yuchi Story)," by John R. Swanton, in the section "Creek Stories," no. 90, of the *U.S. Bureau of American Ethnology Bulletin 88 (Myths and Tales of the Southeastern Indians)*, 1929, reprinted by permission of the Smithsonian Institution Press; "The Yaruros of the Capanaparo River, Venezuela," by V. Petrullo, in the *U.S. Bureau of Ethnology Bulletin 123 (Anthropoligical Papers, no. 11)*, 1939, reprinted by permission of the Smithsonian Institution Press; "The Nuhino or 'Earth Story' of the Jivaros," by M. W. Sterling, in the *U.S. Bureau of American Ethnology Bulletin 117 (Historical and Ethnographical Material of the Jivaros Indians)*, 1938, reprinted by permission of the Smithsonian Institution Press; "The Mundurucu," by D. Horton, in the *U.S. Bureau of American Ethnology Bulletin 143 (Handbook of South American Indians)*, Vol. 3. *The Tropical Forest Tribes*, 1948, reprinted by permission of the Smithsonian Institution Press.

T. G. H. Strehlow for extract from his *Aranda Traditions*, published by the Melbourne University Press.

University of California Press for extract from "Wyot Grammar and Texts," by Gladys A. Reichard, in the *University of California Publications in Archeology and Ethnology*, XXII, I, 1925.

University of Chicago Press for extracts from *The Babylonian Genesis* (1951), translated by Alexander Heidel; *The Kumulipo* (1951), translated by Martha Beckwith.

University of Oklahoma Press for extract from *Popol Vuh: The Sacred Book of the Ancient Quiche Maya*, translated by Adrian Recinos, copyright 1950 by the University of Oklahoma Press.

A. P. Watt, Ltd., for extracts from *The Greek Myths* by Robert Graves.

The Viking Press for extracts from *The Masks of God: Primitive Mythology,* by Joseph Campbell, copyright © 1959, 1969 by Joseph Campbell, all rights reserved, reprinted by permission of Viking Penguin, Inc.; *Book of the Hopi,* by Frank Waters, copyright © 1963 by Frank Waters, all rights reserved, reprinted by permission of Viking Penguin, Inc.; *The Incas: The Royal Commentaries of the Inca Garcilaso de la Vega 1539–1616,* edited by Alain Gheerbrant, copyright © 1961 by the Orion Press, Inc., all rights reserved, reprinted by permission of Viking Penguin, Inc.

INDEX